KU-943-899

Migration, Borders, and Borderlands

Migration, Borders, and Borderlands

Making National Identity in Southern African Communities

Edited by
Munyaradzi Mushonga, John Aerni-Flessner,
Chitja Twala and Grey Magaiza

LEXINGTON BOOKS
Lanham • Boulder • New York • London

Published by Lexington Books
An imprint of The Rowman & Littlefield Publishing Group, Inc.
4501 Forbes Boulevard, Suite 200, Lanham, Maryland 20706
www.rowman.com

86-90 Paul Street, London EC2A 4NE

British Library Cataloguing in Publication Information Available

Library of Congress Cataloging-in-Publication Data

Names: Mushonga, Munyaradzi, editor, author. | Aerni-Flessner, John, editor, author. | Twala, Chitja, editor, author. | Magaiza, Grey, editor, author.
Title: Migration, borders, and borderlands : making national identity in Southern African communities / edited by Munyaradzi Mushonga ; John Aerni-Flessner ; Chitja Twala and Grey Magaiza.
Description: Lanham : Lexington Books, [2024] | Includes bibliographical references and index.
Identifiers: LCCN 2023036525 (print) | LCCN 2023036526 (ebook) | ISBN 9781666942804 (cloth) | ISBN 9781666942811 (ebook)
Subjects: LCSH: Border crossing—Africa, Southern. | Borderlands—Africa, Southern. | Border security—Africa, Southern. | Smuggling—Africa, Southern. | Africa, Southern—Boundaries.
Classification: LCC DT1103 .M54 2024 (print) | LCC DT1103 (ebook) | DDC 320.120968—dc23
LC record available at https://lccn.loc.gov/2023036525
LC ebook record available at https://lccn.loc.gov/2023036526

Contents

Acknowledgments

This book has been, from the start, a team effort. The editorial team came together around the idea of working on a long-term project documenting the history of the Lesotho-South Africa border after a series of meetings in 2018. In 2020, the team applied for and received a generous grant from South Africa's National Institute for the Humanities and Social Sciences (NIHSS). Prior to the NIHSS grant funding, the team received earlier in 2020 "seed" money from the Office of the Dean of the Faculty of the Humanities at the University of the Free State (UFS) in Bloemfontein, South Africa.

Of course, the COVID-19 pandemic struck in the middle of these processes and disrupted the work of the team, as it did for many other things across southern Africa and the world. However, in the second half of 2021, the team was able to finally start its fieldwork, conducting oral interviews in both Lesotho and South Africa from Qwaqwa/Butha-Buthe in the north around to Matatiele/Qacha's Nek in the south. Funding from a Fulbright Fellowship allowed Dr. Aerni-Flessner to also participate in some of this research, as he was based in Bloemfontein from October 2021 to May 2022.

While the team was conducting its own research, it also started the process of soliciting contributors for this edited collection in February 2022. Focusing on obtaining contributions from scholars working on a wide variety of SADC countries, and cognizant of our desire to help capacitate a new generation of southern African academics, the editors also deliberately sought out people from smaller institutions in southern Africa, plus graduate and postgraduate scholars working on borders and borderlands issues. The result is a multidisciplinary work that is held together largely by these two principles. While grounded firmly in historical analysis, the collection has contributions from a range of academic disciplines and geographic focuses within SADC. While the chapters do not always directly speak to each other, though many do, we think the book holds together nicely as a compendium that neatly summarizes and highlights how borders in the SADC region hold striking similarities, despite their diversity of histories and contemporary governments. This is especially true for the most marginal within SADC, as contributions by the vast majority of authors show.

Because of this, we are grateful to all those who have helped us along the way in getting this book to the finish line. We have considerable debts within our own research, not least to the NIHSS, the Dean's Office in the Faculty of Humanities at UFS, Bloemfontein, and the Fulbright program. Additionally, we would like to thank Professor Heidi Hudson, former Dean of the Humanities Faculty at UFS, Bloemfontein, and all the staff and editors at Lexington Books for their help in bringing this project to fruition.

In South Africa, Munyaradzi would like to thank Dr. Stephanie Cawood, Director of the Centre for Gender and Africa Studies, UFS, for intellectual and logistical support and advice, including signing off on my many leave applications for fieldwork; Dr. Moorosi Leshoele for helping with the logistics of the UFS-AFDeL Think Tank Online Conference that was held in March 2022; graduate students from the Centre for Gender and Africa Studies at UFS and the History Department at UFS, who participated in the project as research assistants; UFS Finance Department for managing our finances and ensuring financial prudence; the Department of Cooperative Governance and Traditional Affairs (COGTA) in the Free State and Eastern Cape provinces for granting us access to their communities; Morena Gregory Lebenya and Mofumahali Doreen Moshoeshoe of Matatiele, and Morena Tshepang Kakudi of Telle Bridge in Sterkspruit for organizing informants in advance. Of course, we are thankful and grateful to all who created time to share their stories with us during the interview process. I would also like to thank my family for putting up with me working on this book project for all these years.

At Michigan State University, John would like to thank Residential College in the Arts and Humanities (RCAH) Dean Emeritus Steve Esquith for always supporting his research and fellowship applications, along with Dean Dylan Miner for continuing this support, especially on his sabbatical year to South Africa during a particularly trying year for the college. His colleagues and students in the RCAH have always been wonderfully supportive of this research as well, and their curiosity about the work has helped focus it in new and interesting ways. Andrew Midgley greatly assisted with the paperwork and accounting requirements for a sabbatical year in Bloemfontein, which was much appreciated. I am also grateful to Clement Masakure, Chitja Twala, and Pulane Xaba for facilitating my stay in Bloemfontein and welcoming me to the History Department at UFS. On behalf of the other editors, I also thank all the blind peer-reviewers for this volume, whose timely and helpful interventions have improved all the works individually and collectively. I also would like to thank my family for putting up with me working on this book and the border project in general for all these years.

Chitja would like to thank Dr. Clement Masakure, Academic Head of the History Department, for hosting Dr. Aerni-Flessner as a Fulbright Fellow in the Department. Thanks to Mohlomi Masooa and Mohau Soldaat for playing critical roles in conducting interviews for the purpose of this book. Lastly, many thanks to my family members for the support provided.

From the UFS Qwaqwa campus, Grey would like to thank the campus leadership, specifically Dr. Martin Mandew and Professor Pearl Sithole, for creating an enabling environment that allows emerging researchers to thrive. A further appreciation goes to Dr. Jared McDonald, who approved my research leave and also *enjoyed my tales* from the field. My biggest appreciation goes to our research informants, who not only sacrificed their time to share their knowledge and experiences of the border and borderlands but also welcomed us into their homes.

Introduction

Migration, Borders, and Borderlands in Southern Africa in Historical Perspective

Munyaradzi Mushonga, John Aerni-Flessner, Chitja Twala, and Grey Magaiza

Southern Africa, the region today joined into the Southern African Development Community (SADC), has long been marked by migration, and was a region where individuals and groups of people were on the move.[1] Precolonial trade networks long connected disparate groups in the interior of southern Africa with the wider Indian Ocean trading world, as evidenced by the finding of Indian Ocean trade goods at places like Great Zimbabwe.[2] Crops of foreign origin like *dagga* (*Cannabis*) and maize ended up as staple crops grown throughout the southern African region prior to the arrival of individuals from either India (where *Cannabis* originated) or the Americas (where maize originated).[3] These goods could only circulate on pre-existing networks of trade and diffusion. After the start of colonialism and the arrival of European settlers in southern Africa, processes of migration intensified, especially after the discovery of diamonds in Kimberley in the 1870s and gold on the Witwatersrand in the 1880s. Further mineral discoveries, including gold in what is now Zimbabwe and copper in contemporary Zambia and the Democratic Republic of the Congo (DRC), created new demand for migrant labor, causing more changes to the flows of labor in the region.

Mining and colonial taxation policies caused many southern Africans to migrate, and this included non-miners looking to make an economic livelihood from associated businesses catering to miners in the communities around mines. Still, labor migration remained but one source of movement in the region. Along with the mineral revolution came the codification of borders in southern Africa. Most of the literature on borders in Africa points to the Berlin Conference of 1884–1885 as laying the framework for the demarcation of many African boundaries, and the problems that have come about because of these colonial-era decisions.[4] This was true in southern Africa as well, with most boundaries set in the decades that followed the agreements reached in Europe. However, as the 1869 agreement to set the boundary between Lesotho and the various colonies that surrounded it shows, not all boundaries were set at or after the time of Berlin—though most border decisions, like this one, did not involve Africans at all. Still, the setting of boundaries represented the worst of structural colonial violence, and many of the current crises of migration, citizenship, identity, and belonging have their roots in the settlements derived from the Berlin framework (Figure 0.1).

However, the process of drawing borders is *always* violent and disruptive to individuals and groups that lived in areas near and far from the borders. This observation, of course, does not excuse the violence of the Berlin borders, but it does ask contemporary observers and scholars to consider that

Figure 0.1 Map of the Southern African Region. *Source*: Map created by Aharon deGrassi.

relations between territory, identity, and movement were fundamentally different in pre-colonial Africa. Assuming that borders could have been drawn that correlated cultural groups with political power is, as Mathys pointed out, deeply rooted in problematic Weberian ideas of space and identity, and the fundamental idea of a nation-state.[5] What the colonial boundaries did was to change ideas about belonging and overturn a greater fluidity that had been built into many systems of integration in southern Africa prior to the arrival of colonialism. The demarcation of hard borders forced groups to alter, or even create for the first time, categories of belonging that were more rigid, thus hardening ideas of ethnicity and group membership.

One of the main goals of this book is to interrogate how borders functioned in southern Africa during the twentieth century and into the contemporary period. We deliberately leave the definition of borders broad to encompass physical spaces where people have their passports checked, spaces where people cross what are defined as international boundaries without passing through official checkpoints, and even conceptions in peoples' minds that they think of as borders. Thus, for us, a border can be a place where people cross from one country, or one side of a line, to another; where identities are checked and verified; where heterogeneity and contradiction take place; where some people are fenced in while others are fenced out; that which signifies different things to different people at different times; a place of conflict and peace, illegality and legality; a definite marker of the political, defining friend and enemy, us and them; where there is diversity and singularity at the same time; a place of chaos and order; liberty and security; a place of power—power that serves some and punishes others; where there is de-individuation through regulated individuation; where people submit to security, inspection, and judgment; where a sense of interiority and exteriority is cultivated; a zone of surveillance, vigilance, and peripherality.[6]

Regional histories of the SADC area need to be more fully fleshed out, especially through an exploration of histories of those who have and continue to cross borders. In addition to the legacy of the Berlin Conference, this book also situates SADC borders in the context of the 1964 Organisation of Africa Unity (OAU) declaration that pledged all OAU member states to "respect the borders existing on their achievement of national independence."[7] While this statement was straightforward and, seemingly, without exceptions, that has not stopped border disputes from breaking out all across the continent in the intervening years.[8] The emergence of Eritrea in 1993 from a federation with Ethiopia and the independence of South Sudan in 2011 after a bitter war with the Khartoum government has shown that the OAU declaration on borders has been, at times, at a minimum malleable. As some of the chapters in this collection show, there have been competing border claims by states in the SADC region, as well as claims by individual communities that feel dispossessed and split by the national boundaries that came into existence in a reified form with independence.

Within SADC, as has also been true globally, it has often been easier for goods and capital to traverse national borders than it has been for individuals. The Southern African Customs Union (SACU) that today encompasses South Africa, Lesotho, Namibia, Botswana, and Eswatini is the world's oldest continuous customs union that facilitates the movement of goods through much of the region. The precursor to SACU was an agreement between the Cape Colony and the Orange Free State that dates to 1889, with Basutoland joining in 1891, Bechuanaland Protectorate in 1893, and Natal in 1889.[9] Other regional customs unions have linked states, including a deal between South Africa and Southern Rhodesia/Zimbabwe, and a labor deal between South Africa and Mozambique in the colonial period that paid a fee to the Lisbon government for every worker recruited to South Africa's mines.[10] The ease of trade and formal labor migration was in direct contrast to the difficulties that many Africans faced when they attempted to cross borders for purposes of their own choice, rather than for sanctioned forms of colonial exploitation like labor migration.[11] While it was difficult to cross these borders, many people still managed to get across frontiers from the nineteenth century to the present, but as many of the chapters in this collection note, these crossings were and are more difficult because of their illegality. Criminalization of border crossers has forced people to make difficult economic and personal decisions. SADC committed in 2005 to the free movement of people across boundaries, but this protocol has stalled as governments emphasize the securitization of borders over the free movement of people.[12] A report from the Institute for Security Studies notes that economic disparities and the "lack of political will" among SADC governments has hindered progress toward the free movement of people.[13]

Similarly, in 2018 the African Union (AU) declared its desire to create the African Continental Free Trade Area (AfCFTA) in an effort to open borders. This will, hopefully, redress the grievances many Africans have toward borders, that date to the colonial period. But this noble dream has not always matched the actions of governments. A closer look at the AfCFTA seems to suggest that there is greater preference for the movement of goods and services than people. The AU's Theme of the Year 2023 is *Acceleration of AfCFTA*. Its implementation plan notes: "As part of its mandate, the AfCFTA is to eliminate trade barriers and boost intra-Africa trade. In particular it is to advance trade in value-added production across all service sectors of the African Economy."[14] This promotion of trade and the dropping of trade barriers contrasts with member states' unwillingness to address visa-free entry and other policies that would allow for the free movement of people.[15] The goal of removing "restrictions on Africans' ability to travel, work and live within their own continent" through "Free Movement" is listed as one of the fifteen flagship projects of the AU's Agenda 2063, alongside the AfCFTA, but only the trade protocol gets its own "acceleration" year for implementation.[16]

Thus, in this book, we look to complicate narratives around borders, borderlands, and border crossing. By examining the historical roots of borders and crossers, we get a more nuanced view of the SADC region, a region that has been tied together now for a century and a half by "capital investment and labour migration, and railroads and roads, and close air links, and by politics both white settler and black nationalist."[17] In soliciting contributions, we deliberately emphasized excavating the stories of people impacted by these borders and borderlands. Some of the stories we hear are uplifting—of people triumphing in the struggle against bureaucratic procedures and processes designed to slow or prevent their crossing—but many are not. In these voices, however, we hear the possibilities of ways forward that are more humane and that might make it possible to one day surmount colonial legacies. These are the legacies of the Berlin borders, but they are also the borders perpetuated and defended by post-colonial governments. These post-colonial policies have upheld and, in some cases, made worse, the ways in which borders have disrupted and upended the lives of regional residents.

THE CENTRALITY OF BORDERLANDS

The SADC region is integrated in terms of trade, but still riven by a multiplicity of border regimes attempting to keep people in nation-states that, supposedly, correspond with their citizenship. Thus, there is an urgency to examine, as this book does, borders and borderlands and their impact on regional residents. Drawing on the idea of a "borderscape," the authors in this collection have taken a broad view of borders, borderlands, and who can claim to be a borderlands' resident, impacted by the long reach of borders. We draw a definition of "borderscape" from Brambilla who notes that the idea of studying borders means taking this type of broad lens to examine the "fluidity of nation-state borders and the complexity of the experiences of those who live in them and/or across them" in order to "define membership and exclusion."[18] Thus, borderlands are not marginal spaces at the edges of the nation-state, but are often, in fact, the central spaces where the nation-state is constituted, defined, and contested, even when these contestations are taking place far away from physical borders. As Nugent has argued, "the geographical margins have shaped states at least as much as the other way around."[19] This collection, however, goes further to argue that people can be on the "geographic margins" no matter where they reside or find themselves.

The idea of borders can live in the minds of people, shaping the economic, political, and social decisions they make.

This book actively takes the stance that southern Africans have agency around border matters, even in the face of what are quite frequently hostile border regimes attempting to control and contain them. Still, they persist. In crossing the borders. In undermining the idea of nation-states that have determined that certain border crossers are "illegal." And in undermining the raft of securitization measures that have branded them as "foreigners" who "like criminals, have become a target of state intervention, seemingly at the very moment that most governments have lost much of their capacity to secure their borders."[20] By recognizing and naming the agency that a wide variety of border crossers have historically had and continue to have, this collection excavates how SADC residents are "claiming and realizing citizenship—global, regional, national or otherwise . . . [to] negotiate away the boundaries of exclusion of which [they] are victim."[21] While these efforts are not always successful, and often come at quite a price to individuals and communities, these efforts remain central to truly understanding the political and economic dynamics of the SADC region.

The lives of borderlands residents and border crossers across SADC are often not easy. In fact, the lives of these individuals can be precarious and difficult.[22] Some of the border crossers are migrants and potential migrants, while others are simply looking to take advantage of short-term economic opportunities, medical care, or social needs when crossing borders.[23] In other cases, those impacted by borders are not crossing international borders, but crossing internal boundaries. These have taken the form of wartime boundaries, especially in the proxy conflicts encouraged by the South African apartheid regime and Ian Smith's Rhodesian regime. The fluid borders between rebel-held and government-held areas during civil conflicts like the Mozambican Civil War loom large, but so too do largely invisible borders set up by humanitarian organizations who control access to food and other necessities—qualifying or not for aid assistance can be seen as a "border" to crucial life-giving supplies. In these scenarios, some crossers are illegalized while others are encouraged.

Thus, the essays in this collection complicate our understandings of southern Africa in two interlocking and interdependent ways. First, they grapple, explicitly and implicitly, with the idea of internal or sub-national boundaries.[24] Sometimes these are physical and temporal boundaries within nation-states, and at other times, they are borders in the minds of regional residents or in the characterization accorded to them by rebel groups, wartime combatants, and non-governmental organizations. Second, they take seriously the spatial turn in African historical studies that looks at what Achille Mbembe has called the "*imaginaries* and autochthonous practices of space."[25] Rather than redrawing maps, as Luyia communities in Kenya were doing in an effort to remake colonial spaces, SADC borderlands residents are redrawing circulation networks and border practices through their movements in the face of similar bureaucratic intransigence.[26] Through these processes, we see SADC residents remaking border policy and practice out of necessity, but reflecting profound personal, group, and structural ingenuity. These efforts challenge the hegemonic power of governments to not only demarcate and control boundary lines but also more broadly reshape the national communities on all sides of borders.

BORDERMAKING, SMUGGLING, AND POLICY IN THE LIVES OF RESIDENTS

The essays in this collection elucidate many themes, but the issue of smuggling is recurrent and common across many national contexts in the SADC region. The authors who take up the issue of smuggling do so from the frame that Gallien and Weigand suggest, whereby smuggling is studied "at the centre of a field of study, not casting it at the margins, merely as a policy implication or a bogeyman."[27] Tshabalala (chapter 3), in examining the smuggling of passports across the Zimbabwe-South Africa border to get border stamps through illicit processes, and Muguti (chapter 5), in looking at the ways that Tonga residents on both the Zambian and Zimbabwean sides of the Zambezi River continue to move people and goods back and forth, both complicate our understandings of smuggling for commodities and communities that find themselves near borders. Similarly, Simões Henrique (chapter 8) and Mushonga and Cawood (chapter 10) both examine the ways that people and goods for commercial purposes are smuggled across the Mozambique-South Africa and Lesotho-South Africa borders, respectively. All of these chapters adroitly note that borders are, indeed, "no longer understood as material, static, homogenous, and binary," but rather are a "social product . . . where multiple actors are engaged in the process of creating meaning and symbolism."[28] Twala and Magaiza (chapter 12), by examining the nature of those who "work" at the informal border crossings between Lesotho and South Africa, exemplify the fact that while "policing [borders] is intended to stamp out smuggling, the very act of cementing a border ironically renders contraband more attractive."[29]

But smuggling is not the only result of the process of bordermaking. While colonially defined boundaries still demarcate the frontiers of nation-states throughout the SADC region, the meanings that local communities and post-independence governments have made from these lines on a map have differed wildly. They have also, at times, not been accepted by these same governments. Panzer (chapter 1) explores this dynamic by narrating the 1960s diplomatic spate between Julius Nyerere's Tanzania and Hastings Kamuzu Banda's Malawi over where the border between their two states should be defined in Lake Nyasa/Malawi. Nyachega (chapter 4) narrates how border communities in Zimbabwe during the liberation struggle deliberately used and re-claimed borders by smuggling people, including top commanders in the liberation struggle like Robert Mugabe and Edgar Tekere, across them. Similarly, Aerni-Flessner (chapter 2) examines the ways that Lesotho's continued claim to the so-called Conquered Territory in South Africa shaped the ways in which people could and could not cross borders through government policies that encouraged some crossers (tourists) while discouraging and criminalizing others (herders), a process which discriminated against the Basotho who most frequently used the borderlands for economic purposes. Finally, Siluonde (chapter 9) uses characters in two Zambian novels to explore the ways in which people who had gone into exile continued to, in some ways, still mentally reside in their former national spaces rather than the country in which they were physically present.

REFUGEES AND INFORMAL TRADE

Three of the most vulnerable populations in the context of borders and borderlands are migrants, refugees, and informal traders. All of these groups are, unfortunately, well represented in the population of border crossers in the SADC region and this volume examines them in a variety of contexts.[30] As Dobler writes, borders defined by international recognition are "containers of sovereignty" and, thus, of great value to governments, especially those in southern Africa looking for legitimacy after years of colonial rule and postcolonial conflict fueled by the apartheid regime and the global Cold War of the late twentieth century that led to more violence in the region.[31] This emphasis on bordering, as well as the large number of refugees that historical and contemporary conflicts have created, means that refugee policy has loomed large. Guardião (chapter 6) examines these dynamics for Angolan refugees attempting to settle in the Congo during the fight against colonial rule. While not formally refugees, the liberation fighters transiting through Zimbabwe's Eastern Highlands (Nyachega, chapter 4) fall under this type of analysis as well. Siluonde's work on South Africans in exile in Zambia (chapter 9) explores similar themes of home/away and what it means to leave the country where you feel you belong. Musoni (chapter 11) further explores this dynamic with women from Zimbabwe trying to cross the border into South Africa. While not formal refugees, they are certainly seeking a refuge, at least economically, as Zimbabwe has lurched from political crisis to economic implosion in the twenty-first century.

The women Musoni meets in his research along the border are also often involved in cross-border trade. They would prefer *not* to be smuggling goods (see section above on smuggling), but find their options often limited to this option only. Moyo argues that SADC has done a good job of facilitating legal cross-border trade, but that the ways the block has done this have foreclosed opportunities for those without access to large-scale capital and, hence, has made life considerably more difficult for informal cross-border traders.[32] Many of the chapters in this volume, such as the one by Simões Henrique (chapter 8) on informal traders from Xai-Xai in Mozambique and Tshabalala (chapter 3) on passports that are smuggled across the border without their owners being present, elucidate interesting cases that complicate our understanding of these processes. Formal trade links, and the relation between trade and migration between Angola and Namibia and between Mozambique and South Africa, are further explored by Udelsmann Rodrigues (chapter 7).

GENDER AND BORDER CROSSING

One particularly important component of border crossing in the SADC region that this volume explores is the nature of gendered crossings of borders, and how gender plays into the informal economies and ecosystems around borders. To state it clearly: In many cases, women face more danger than men when crossing borders in SADC, as they do around the world.[33] While none of the chapters explicitly address the issue of trafficking, they do seek to explore and explain the perils that women, especially, face crossing borders in SADC. Twala and Magaiza (chapter 12) examine the ways that individuals who informally work at illicit crossing points between Lesotho and South Africa see their jobs as both precarious and professional, and how that impacts their relations with those crossing. Mushonga and Cawood (chapter 10) look at the same crossing points, but through the explicit lens of gender to elucidate the ways that women face higher degrees of danger when crossing the border, including gruesome and traumatic gender-based violence. Simões Henrique (chapter 8) also describes the ways that informal trade is gendered, as well as being structured by nationality, across the Mozambique-South Africa border. Finally, Musoni (chapter 11) explores gendered dynamics of crossing along the Zimbabwe-South Africa border. These chapters, when read together, are a damning indictment of both border policy and the ways that governments have failed to set up structures to support women in the informal economies that allow many to eke out a living across SADC.

African borders are often not welcoming to women, as a majority of female crossers must contend with the significant challenges of limited employment opportunities and low wages, along with cultural and social factors that leave them as second-class citizens in many cases. This is in addition to facing and/or dealing with gender-based violence. These challenges are magnified at the borders by the fact that many African women have limited access to legal documentation and financial resources, which tends to push them to cross borders outside legal crossing points, thus exposing them to more dangers within this liminal space.

Taken as a whole, thus, the volume brings together a wide range of perspectives from borderlands across the SADC region, providing a much-needed synthesis of the experiences of borderlands residents. With xenophobia on the rise in South Africa and other regional states, especially in the wake of the economic devastation caused by COVID-19 lockdowns and border closures, the volume historicizes and re-assesses the relationship between the often-rural borderlands areas and the urban areas of southern Africa, bringing them into conversation and showing, again, the "centrality of the margins."[34] By having disparate chapters in one volume, we, hopefully, have shown not just how the SADC region is integrated in ways that move beyond the well-trod literature on regional labor migration, but also opened new avenues for inquiry in the realm of "borderscapes," or how the idea of borders and bordering extends well beyond the physical frontiers of nation-states and formal border mechanisms and policies. In SADC, as with many regions in the world, the history of borderlands and borderlands' residents impacts heavily on the present and future of border crossing, national belonging, identity, and economic futures. Individuals, communities, and states themselves in SADC are constantly being made and remade, imagined and re-imagined by migration, movement, and the willingness of large numbers of citizens to flaunt border requirements, often at great risk to themselves. With the act of creating borders and bordering being one fundamentally rooted in inclusion/exclusion and violence, borders will continue to be contested in the SADC region for many years to come. It is our hope that government officials will take seriously the stories here and strive to set policies for crossing borders that emphasize human rights and center economic justice, rather than focusing solely on short-term security, trade, or national interests that tend to militate against humane border policy.

NOTES

1. Today, SADC consists of Angola, Botswana, Comoros, Democratic Republic of the Congo, Eswatini, Lesotho, Madagascar, Malawi, Mauritius, Mozambique,

Namibia, Seychelles, South Africa, United Republic of Tanzania, Zambia, and Zimbabwe.

2. Shadreck Chirikure, "Land and Sea Links: 1500 Years of Connectivity Between Southern Africa and Indian Ocean Rim Regions, AD 700 to 1700," *African Archaeological Review* 31 (2014): 705–724; Innocent Pikirayi, "The Demise of Great Zimbabwe, AD 1420–1550: An Environmental Re-Appraisal," in *Cities in the World: 1500–2000: V. 3* ed., Adrian Green (London: Routledge, 2006).

3. Chris Duvall, *The African Roots of Marijuana* (Durham: Duke University Press, 2019); James McCann, "Maize and Grace: History, Corn, and Africa's New Landscapes, 1500–1999," *Comparative Studies in Society and History* 43, no. 2 (2001): 246–272.

4. John Reader, *Africa: A Biography of the Continent,* (London: Penguin, 1977); Adekeye Adebajo, *The Curse of Berlin: Africa after the Cold War* (London: Hurst, 2010).

5. Gillian Mathys, "Questioning Territories and Identities in the Precolonial (Nineteenth Century) Lake Kivu Region," *Africa* 91, no. 3 (2021): 493.

6. Matthew Longo, "From Sovereignty to Imperium: Borders, Frontiers and the Specter of Neo-Imperialism," *Geopolitics* 22, no. 4 (2017): 757–771; Matthew Longo, *The Politics of Borders: Sovereignty, Security, and the Citizen after 9/11* (Cambridge: Cambridge University Press, 2017); Mark Salter, "At the Threshold of Security: A Theory of International Borders" in *Global Surveillance and Policing* eds., Elia Zurek and Mark Salter (London: Willan, 2013); Daromir Rudnycki, "Technologies of Servitude: Governmentality and Indonesian Transnational Labor Migration," *Anthropological Quarterly* 77, no. 3 (2004): 407–434.

7. "Border Disputes Among African States," *Resolutions Adopted by the First Ordinary Session of the Assembly of Heads of State and Government Held in Cairo, UAR, from 17 to 21 July 1964.* https://au.int/sites/default/files/decisions/9514–1964_ahg_res_1–24_i_e.pdf, accessed 11 May 2023.

8. Patience Munge Sone, "Interstate Border Disputes in Africa: Their Resolution and Implications for Human Rights and Peace," *African Security Review* 26, no. 3 (2017): 325–339; Gbenga Oduntan, *International Law and Boundary Disputes in Africa* (Oxford: Routledge, 2015).

9. Sean Maliehe, "A Historical Context of Lesotho's Integration into the 1910 Customs Union Agreement, 1870–1910s," *Southern Journal for Contemporary History* 46, no. 2 (2021): 24–47.

10. Alois Mlambo, "Settler Colonialism and Trade in the Periphery: Customs Relations between Southern Rhodesia and South Africa," *African Economic History* 47, no. 1 (2019): 92–115; Allen Isaacman and Barbara Isaacman, *Mozambique's Samora Machel* (Auckland Park: Jacana, 2020), 39.

11. Enid Guene, *Copper, Borders and Nation-Building: The Katanganese Factor in Zambian Political and Economic History* (Leiden: African Studies Centre, 2017); Jonathan Crush, Alan Jeeves, David Yudelman, *A History of Black Migrancy to the Gold Mines* (Boulder: Westview Press, 1992); Harvey Chidoba Banda, "Migration, Economy and Politics: Unprecedented Increase in Informal Labour Migration from Northern Malawi to South Africa in the 1990s," *African Renaissance* 15, no. 4

(2018): 53–74; Eddy Tshidiso Maloka, *Basotho and the Mines: A Social History of Labour Migrancy in Lesotho and South Africa, c. 1890–1940* (Dakar: CODESRIA, 2004).

12. Christopher Changwe Nshimbi and Lorenzo Fioramonti, "The Will to Integrate: South Africa's Response to Regional Migration from the SADC Region," *African Development Review* 26, no. S1 (2014): 52–63.

13. Ottilia Anna Maunganidze and Julian Formica, *Freedom of Movement in Southern Africa: A SADC (Pipe)Dream?* (Pretoria: Institute for Security Studies, 2018). https://issafrica.s3.amazonaws.com/site/uploads/sar-17.pdf accessed 12 May 2023.

14. More information can be found on the Africa Union's website:https://au.int/en/theme/2023/acceleration-of-afcfta-implementation, accessed 11 May 2023.

15. Alan Hirsh, "The African Union's Free Movement of Persons Protocol: Why has it Faltered and how can its Objectives be Achieved?" *South African Journal of International Affairs* 28, no. 4 (2021): 497–517.

16. The AU Agenda 2063 Flagship Projects can be found here: https://au.int/en/agenda2063/flagship-projects, accessed on 11 May 2023.

17. Alois Mlambo and Neil Parsons, *A History of Southern Africa* (London: Macmillan, 2019), xi.

18. Chiara Brambilla, "Exploring the Critical Potential of the Borderscapes Concept," *Geopolitics* 20, no. 1 (2015): 19.

19. Paul Nugent, *Boundaries, Communities and State-Making in West Africa: The Centrality of the Margins* (Cambridge: Cambridge University Press, 2019), 524.

20. Mary Bosworth, "Border Control and the Limits of the Sovereign State," *Social & Legal Studies* 17, no. 2 (2008): 200.

21. Francis B. Nyamnjoh, *Insiders and Outsiders: Citizenship and Xenophobia in Contemporary Southern Africa* (London: Zed Books, 2006), 25.

22. Melissa Kelly, 'Malilimala Moletsane, and Jan K. Coetzee. "Experiencing Boundaries: Basotho Migrant Perspectives on the Lesotho-South Africa Border," *Qualitative Sociology Review* 13, no. 1 (2017): 92–110.

23. Jonathan Crush and David A. McDonald, "Transnationalism, African Immigration, and New Migrant Spaces in South Africa: An Introduction," *Canadian Journal of African Studies* 34, no. 1 (2013): 1–19.

24. Maano Ramutsindela, "Placing Subnational Borders in Border Studies," *South African Geographical Journal* 101, no. 3 (2019): 349–356.

25. Achille Mbembe, "At the Edge of the World: Boundaries, Territoriality, and Sovereignty in Africa," *Public Culture* 12, no. 1 (2000): 262.

26. Julie MacArthur, *Cartography and the Political Imagination: Mapping Community in Colonial Kenya* (Athens: Ohio University Press, 2016).

27. Max Gallien and Florian Weigand, "Studying Smuggling," in *The Routledge Handbook of Smuggling*, eds., Max Gallien and Florian Weigand (London: Routledge, 2021), 1.

28. Sergio Peña, "Borderlands, Frontiers, and Borders: Changing Meanings and the Intersection with Smuggling Practices," in *The Routledge Handbook of Smuggling*, eds., Max Gallien and Florian Weigand (London: Routledge, 2021), 107–108.

29. Paul Nugent, "Making Borders, Closing Frontiers and Identifying Smuggling," in *The Routledge Handbook of Smuggling,* eds., Max Gallien and Florian Weigand (London: Routledge, 2021), 95.

30. Chitja Twala, "An Analysis of Attempts by the United Nations High Commission for Refugees (UNHCR) in Solving Immigrants and Refugees Problem in the SADC Region: A Case of South Africa," *Journal of Human Ecology* 44, no. 1 (2013): 65–73.

31. Gregor Dobler, "The Green, the Grey and the Blue: A Typology of Cross Border Trade in Africa," *Journal of Modern African Studies* 54, no. 1 (2016): 148.

32. Inocent Moyo, "The Vacuity of Informal Cross-Border Trade Facilitation Strategies in the SADC Region," *Political Geography* 101 (2023). https://doi.org/10.1016/j.polgeo.2022.102816

33. Sharon Pickering, *Women, Borders, and Violence: Current Issues in Asylum, Forced Migration, and Trafficking* (New York: Springer, 2010).

34. Nugent, *Boundaries, Communities, and State Making.*

BIBLIOGRAPHY

Adebajo, Adekeye. *The Curse of Berlin: Africa after the Cold War.* London: Hurst, 2010.

Banda, Harvey Chidoba. "Migration, Economy and Politics: Unprecedented Increase in Informal Labour Migration from Northern Malawi to South Africa in the 1990s." *African Renaissance* 15, no. 4 (2018): 53–74.

Bosworth, Mary. "Border Control and the Limits of the Sovereign State." *Social & Legal Studies* 17, no. 2 (2008): 199–215.

Brambilla, Chiara. "Exploring the Critical Potential of the Borderscapes Concept." *Geopolitics* 20, no. 1 (2015): 14–34.

Chirikure, Shadreck. "Land and Sea Links: 1500 Years of Connectivity Between Southern Africa and Indian Ocean Rim Regions, AD 700 to 1700." *African Archaeological Review* 31 (2014): 705–724.

Crush, Jonathan, Alan Jeeves, and David Yudelman. *A History of Black Migrancy to the Gold Mines.* Boulder: Westview Press, 1992.

Crush, Jonathan, and David A. McDonald. "Transnationalism, African Immigration, and New Migrant Spaces in South Africa: An Introduction." *Canadian Journal of African Studies* 34, no. 1 (2013): 1–19.

Dobler, Gregor. "The Green, the Grey and the Blue: A Typology of Cross Border Trade in Africa." *Journal of Modern African Studies* 54, no. 1 (2016): 145–169.

Duvall, Chris. *The African Roots of Marijuana.* Durham: Duke University Press, 2019.

Gallien, Max, and Florian Weigand. "Studying Smuggling." In *The Routledge Handbook of Smuggling,* edited by Max Gallien and Florian Weigand, 1–15. London: Routledge, 2021.

Guene, Enid. *Copper, Borders and Nation-Building: The Katanganese Factor in Zambian Political and Economic History.* Leiden: African Studies Centre, 2017.

Hirsh, Alan. "The African Union's Free Movement of Persons Protocol: Why has it Faltered and How can its Objectives be Achieved?" *South African Journal of International Affairs* 28, no. 4 (2021): 497–517.

Isaacman, Allen, and Barbara Isaacman. *Mozambique's Samora Machel.* Auckland Park: Jacana, 2020.

Kelly, Melissa, 'Malilimala Moletsane, and Jan K. Coetzee. "Experiencing Boundaries: Basotho Migrant Perspectives on the Lesotho-South Africa Border." *Qualitative Sociology Review* 13, no. 1 (2017): 92–110.

Longo, Matthew. "From Sovereignty to Imperium: Borders, Frontiers and the Specter of Neo-Imperialism." *Geopolitics* 22, no. 4 (2017): 757–771.

Longo, Matthew. *The Politics of Borders: Sovereignty, Security, and the Citizen After 9/11.* Cambridge: Cambridge University Press, 2017.

MacArthur, Julie. *Cartography and the Political Imagination: Mapping Community in Colonial Kenya.* Athens: Ohio University Press, 2016.

Maliehe, Sean. "A Historical Context of Lesotho's Integration into the 1910 Customs Union Agreement, 1870–1910s." *Southern Journal for Contemporary History* 46, no. 2 (2021): 24–47.

Maloka, Eddy Tshidiso. *Basotho and the Mines: A Social History of Labour Migrancy in Lesotho and South Africa, c. 1890–1940.* Dakar: CODESRIA, 2004.

Mathys, Gillian. "Questioning Territories and Identities in the Precolonial (Nineteenth Century) Lake Kivu Region." *Africa* 91, no. 3 (2021): 493–515.

Maunganidze, Ottilia Anna, and Julian Formica. *Freedom of Movement in Southern Africa: A SADC (Pipe)Dream?* Pretoria: Institute for Security Studies, 2018.

Mbembe, Achille. "At the Edge of the World: Boundaries, Territoriality, and Sovereignty in Africa." *Public Culture* 12, no. 1 (2000): 259–284.

McCann, James. "Maize and Grace: History, Corn, and Africa's New Landscapes, 1500–1999." *Comparative Studies in Society and History* 43, no. 2 (2001): 246–272.

Mlambo, Alois. "Settler Colonialism and Trade in the Periphery: Customs Relations Between Southern Rhodesia and South Africa." *African Economic History* 47, no. 1 (2019): 92–115.

Mlambo, Alois, and Neil Parsons. *A History of Southern Africa.* London: Macmillan, 2019.

Moyo, Inocent. "The Vacuity of Informal Cross-Border Trade Facilitation Strategies in the SADC Region." *Political Geography* 101 (2023). https://doi.org/10.1016/j.polgeo.2022.102816

Nshimbi, Christopher Changwe, and Lorenzo Fioramonti. "The Will to Integrate: South Africa's Response to Regional Migration from the SADC Region." *African Development Review* 26, no. S1 (2014): 52–63.

Nugent, Paul. *Boundaries, Communities and State-Making in West Africa: The Centrality of the Margins.* Cambridge: Cambridge University Press, 2019.

Nugent, Paul. "Making Borders, Closing Frontiers and Identifying Smuggling." In *The Routledge Handbook of Smuggling,* edited by Max Gallien and Florian Weigand, 95–106. London: Routledge, 2021.

Nyamnjoh, Francis B. *Insiders and Outsiders: Citizenship and Xenophobia in Contemporary Southern Africa.* London: Zed Books, 2006.

Oduntan, Gbenga. *International Law and Boundary Disputes in Africa.* Oxford: Routledge, 2015.

Peña, Sergio. "Borderlands, Frontiers, and Borders: Changing Meanings and the Intersection with Smuggling Practices." In *The Routledge Handbook of Smuggling,* edited by Max Gallien and Florian Weigand, 107–117. London: Routledge, 2021.

Pickering, Sharon. *Women, Borders, and Violence: Current Issues in Asylum, Forced Migration, and Trafficking.* New York: Springer, 2010.

Pikirayi, Innocent. "The Demise of Great Zimbabwe, AD 1420–1550: An Environmental Reappraisal." In *Cities in the World, 1500–2000: V. 3*, edited by Adrian Green. London: Routledge, 2006.

Ramutsindela, Maano. "Placing Subnational Borders in Border Studies." *South African Geographical Journal* 101, no. 3 (2019): 349–356.

Reader, John. *Africa: A Biography of the Continent.* London: Penguin, 1977.

Rudnycki, Daromir. "Technologies of Servitude: Governmentality and Indonesian Transnational Labor Migration." *Anthropological Quarterly* 77, no. 3 (2004): 407–434.

Salter, Mark. "At the Threshold of Security: A Theory of International Borders." In *Global Surveillance and Policing*, edited by Elia Zurek and Mark Salter, 36–50. London: Willan, 2013.

Sone, Patience Munge. "Interstate Border Disputes in Africa: Their Resolution and Implications for Human Rights and Peace." *African Security Review* 26, no. 3 (2017): 325–339.

Twala, Chitja. "An Analysis of Attempts by the United Nations High Commission for Refugees (UNHCR) in Solving Immigrants and Refugees Problem in the SADC Region: A Case of South Africa." *Journal of Human Ecology* 44, no. 1 (2013): 65–73.

Part I

BORDERMAKING, SMUGGLING, AND CONTEMPORARY RESONANCES

Chapter 1

"Putting Gunboats on the Lake"

Frelimo's Guerrilla War and Malawi's Border Dispute with Tanzania in the 1960s

Michael G. Panzer

A quick search of southern Africa using the online application "Google Earth Pro" reveals vivid yellow lines that demarcate the polygon contours of the borders between African nations. However, zooming in a little closer over the adjacent border of Malawi and Tanzania reveals something different. A conspicuous red line emerges, indicating a contested border along the eastern shore (the Tanzanian side) of Lake Malawi/Nyasa.[1] Upon independence, most African states maintained the same borders as their previous colonial demarcations. New national borders were maintained, often with minimal disagreement between neighbors, as a matter of *uti possidetis juris*, convenience, and OAU resolutions. The lake border dispute between Malawi and Tanzania involving Lake Nyasa/Malawi first emerged in official discourse in 1964, but three years later in 1967, the issue became particularly divisive.[2] As of the completion of this chapter in early 2023, the lake border dispute remains a significant point of contention between both states.

In September 1964, three years before the tensions about the lake border grew especially vitriolic, the Mozambique Liberation Front (Frelimo) began its war against Portugal in the effort to liberate Mozambique from Portuguese colonial rule. To achieve military objectives, the movement of Frelimo guerrillas from bases in Tanzania into Mozambique often involved clandestine violations of Malawi's sovereign territory, something that the first president of Malawi, Dr. Hastings Kamuzu Banda, was loath to permit. Importantly, small, landlocked Malawi relied extensively on rail and road networks through Portuguese-held Mozambique to sustain its fledgling national economy.[3] Any overt sign of sympathy from Banda or his government for Frelimo's liberation war might have imperiled Malawi's relations with Portugal and jeopardized the vital economic links to the east African coastline. Further complicating the issue of Frelimo's transitory presence in Malawi was Banda's accommodationist approach to white minority regimes in southern Africa. Banda differed from the majority of first-generation African leaders in the region who generally despised lingering colonialism and white political entrenchment in South Africa, the Portuguese colonies of Mozambique and Angola, and Southern Rhodesia. Conversely, the first president of Tanzania, Julius Nyerere, was an ardent supporter of Frelimo and believed that support for the armed struggle against the Portuguese and white minority regimes in southern Africa was the primary means to liberate the region. The specific problem for Banda, however, was the location and size of Lake Malawi/Nyasa, which offered Frelimo ample opportunities to ferry their guerrillas from bases in neighboring Tanzania through Malawian territory and into Mozambique. Thus, Lake Nyasa/Malawi was an important conduit for the movement of Frelimo guerrillas and a potential diplomatic and economic flashpoint for Banda and his regime if Malawi did not prevent the guerrillas from using the lake and its shoreline as a route to infiltrate Mozambique.

In 1967, nearly three years into the liberation war in Mozambique, Frelimo guerrillas who crossed into Malawi without permission further expanded their war effort to a third front in Mozambique's northwestern Tete Province. This move by Frelimo against the Portuguese threatened Portugal's nascent Cahora Bassa Dam project on the Zambezi River.[4] As an independent nation, Malawi's sovereign territory offered a bit of cover (without permission) for Frelimo guerrillas to hide and regroup from the onslaught of Portuguese military counter-attacks. It was in mid-1967, as Frelimo's war expanded into Tete, that the diplomatic tension between Nyerere and Banda over the lake border dramatically escalated. Speeches by Nyerere and Banda in May and June 1967, respectively, brought the issue of the eastern lakeshore border into the discourse of national and regional politics. The disparate political views of both men regarding the exact border and sovereign jurisdiction of the lake were informed by their differing international, regional, and domestic political agendas, and their public spat significantly influenced public opinion on the issue.

Relying on archival sources, speeches, and newspaper coverage of the dispute, this chapter argues that the presence of Frelimo guerrillas who routinely traversed the sovereign territory of Malawi from bases in Tanzania to infiltrate Mozambique greatly exacerbated the debate over the lake border between the two nations, a conflict which reached its apogee in September 1968. Newspaper sources offer a rich fount of political and public discourse involving the lake dispute between the two governments. In particular, the Tanzanian *Nationalist* newspaper and the *Malawi News*, both of which were unapologetic state news/propaganda organs, contain important insights into the official positions, personal disputes, name-calling, and social discourse around the lake border dispute. Even with pro-government bias clear in both newspapers, reading against the grain nevertheless allows for a nuanced analysis of how the lake border dispute played out over a finite period of months, weeks, and sometimes days, especially during the height of tension in September 1968.[5] Although this chapter explores the history of how Nyerere and Banda differed in their stance toward Frelimo's use of the lake for their guerrilla activities, it also provides historical insights into how the Lake Malawi/Nyasa border dispute that emerged in the 1960s still informs the challenges associated with locating, legally defining, and accepting sovereign jurisdiction over an exact and legally enforceable lake border between these two African nations to this day.[6]

There is growing scholarly interest in the intersections between liberation politics and borderland and frontier histories in Africa. This chapter is situated within this emergent historiographical canon that focuses on spatial and temporal histories of southern African liberation movements in the 1960s. The edited volume *Transnational Histories of Southern Africa's Liberation Movements* stands out for its wide array of chapters dedicated to cross-border and international collaborations between African states, liberation movements, and foreign actors, all of whom contributed to the historical-political evolution of southern Africa during the 1960s and 1970s.[7] Historical analyses of Tanzania during the 1960s and early 1970s are replete with numerous works dedicated to state-development, high-politics, and the presidency of Julius Nyerere.[8] Although scholarly attention on Tanzania during this era is abundant, fewer studies on the politics in Malawi during the 1960s and 1970s exist, but two exemplary historiographical contributions include Power's *Political Culture and Nationalism in Malawi: Building Kwacha* and McCraken's *A History of Malawi: 1859–1966*. These two books, in particular, offer nuanced analyses of the political history of Malawi, the ascendency of the Malawi Congress Party, and they trace the policies of Malawi's first president, Dr. Hastings Kamuzu Banda. However, all of these works on Tanzania and Malawi in the 1960s devote little attention to the history of this lake border dispute, and especially, Frelimo's role in the events.

This chapter was also written in context of other border histories from elsewhere in Africa. Notable among them are Nugent's *Boundaries, Communities and State-Making in West Africa*; Weitzberg's *We Do Not Have Borders: Greater Somalia and the Predicaments of Belonging in Kenya*; the edited volume *The Borderlands of South Sudan: Authority and Identity in Contemporary and Historical Perspectives*; and, Aerni-Flessner and Twala's article "Bargaining with Land: Borders, Bantustans, and Sovereignty in 1970s and 1980s Southern Africa."[9] Although only a fraction of the recent scholarly production on the subject, these books and articles collectively demonstrate the recent vibrancy and interest in historical borderlands' research in Africa.

When independence was achieved in Tanzania in 1961 and Malawi in 1964, neighboring Mozambique remained a Portuguese colony until 1975.

When the anticolonial war started between Frelimo and the Portuguese military in September 1964, significant disparities in ideological and local geopolitical national strategies arose between Banda and Nyerere, and Frelimo was one of the most significant of these. The movement of Frelimo guerrillas from Tanzania across and around the shorelines of Lake Nyasa/Malawi was a primary cause of the diplomatic and political tension between two of southern Africa's most formidable leaders in 1967 and 1968. Frelimo's military strategy, which required the use of rear-bases in Tanzania, as well as flanking maneuvers and retreats through Malawi, was a source of significant frustration for Banda. The antagonism between Banda and Nyerere over Frelimo's activities also led Banda to provocatively assert that, not only was the entirety of the northern lake a part of Malawi's sovereign domain, but that the territory beyond the eastern shoreline *into* Tanzania was, as well.

COLONIAL CARTOGRAPHY AND THE ORIGINS OF THE DISPUTE OVER LAKE MALAWI/NYASA

The origin of the lake border dispute between Tanzania and Malawi can be traced to the borderlands' disagreements of European colonizers in Africa in the late nineteenth century. During the so-called scramble for Africa, the territorial claims of European colonizers often relied upon microgeographic features and other topographical contours as boundary markers to delineate the borders between colonies. African colonial borders, however, were largely determined by officials on the ground after the debates among European representatives at the Berlin Conference (1884–1885). Colonial authorities also typically neglected pre-existing African political and cultural boundaries in their boundary-making schemes.[10] For example, the location of the Ruvuma River provided a convenient riparian border for colonizers to delineate the border between German East Africa (Tanganyika, today Tanzania) and Portuguese East Africa (Mozambique). However, when the Germans and Portuguese agreed to use the river as the political boundary between Tanganyika and Mozambique, they also separated communities of Yao and Makonde from kin groups on either side of the border, regardless of how, for centuries, Africans had traversed this river for trade with the east coast and interactions with kith and kin.

A few years after the Berlin Conference, the Heligoland Treaty of 1890 between Germany and the United Kingdom (UK) determined a more exact border between Tanganyika and Nyasaland (Malawi), that drew the border as the eastern shoreline of the lake.[11] As the third largest lake on the African continent, Lake Malawi/Nyasa was situated between colonial German East Africa (Tanganyika) and British-held Nyasaland. After the Allied victory in World War I (1914–1918), the UK acquired Tanganyika as a League of

Nations "mandate," but the eastern lakeshore border nevertheless remained intact. In essence, there was no need to move the border elsewhere since the British controlled both adjacent territories. In the wake of the Treaty of Versailles, then, the matter of the lake border seemed of little political or economic consequence to British colonial officials. Ostensibly, the eastern shoreline border between two British colonies meant that the majority of the lake, especially in the north and west, was designated to Nyasaland, as had been true under previous German colonial rule.

In 1953, with the amalgamation of the Rhodesias and Nyasaland into the Central African Federation (CAF), the lake border along the eastern littoral remained unchanged. The CAF, which lasted from 1953 to 1963, was designed to maintain white minority control over Nyasaland (Malawi), Northern Rhodesia (Zambia), and Rhodesia (Zimbabwe). This political arrangement also recognized the eastern shoreline as the border for much of the period because neighboring Tanganyika was still under British control until late 1961. A smaller section of the lake, in the southeast, abutted Mozambique and was earlier allocated to Portugal in the 1954 Anglo-Portuguese Treaty.[12] Importantly, throughout the sequential German, British, and CAF colonial eras, British colonial officials in Tanganyika recognized that "not a part of the Lake lies within the boundaries of Tanganyika," which would later give Malawi a basis to claim the lake border was, indeed, set on the eastern shoreline.[13] While this official, colonial, border of Malawi on the eastern shoreline was largely recognized as the border, with Tanzania's independence in December 1961, Nyerere and his TANU government began to make the case to Tanzanian citizens that colonial border determinations were problematic carry-overs that needed to be reevaluated and reconsidered in the new, post-colonial national context. Further, at independence, the Tanzanians who lived along the eastern shoreline of Lake Nyasa/Malawi were then legally recognized as *citizens* of Tanzania and not Malawi. At the same time, the CAF was still in existence in December 1961 and held tacit dominion over Nyasaland, which, two years earlier in 1959, had experienced significant internal political turmoil that greatly contributed to the CAF's demise in 1963. Nyerere, who faced several early challenges to his own domestic consolidation of power under TANU, sidelined the lake boundary issue in the first six years of his presidency, focusing instead on more pressing international and domestic matters.

With the independence of Malawi almost three years later than Tanzania, on July 6, 1964, the lake border along the eastern shore remained unchanged since cartographic evidence from the colonial era seemed to affirm this boundary in the mind of Malawi's President Banda. As mentioned earlier, there had been a 1954 agreement between the Portuguese and the UK government that allocated a smaller section of the lake to the Portuguese, since Mozambique's Niassa Province abutted the southeastern lakeshore. That portion of the lake remained in the possession of the Portuguese even after Malawi's independence in July 1964. Banda wanted to preserve the entirety of the northern lake to the eastern littoral of Tanzania, as had been true from the colonial era. This was something Nyerere fundamentally disagreed with since Tanzanian citizens who lived along the eastern lakeshore and who had depended on the lake for decades for fishing and freshwater, would ostensibly be trespassing on Malawian territory if they simply stepped foot into the lake. In sum, from the colonial era until the independence of Malawi in July 1964, the eastern lakeshore was widely considered the official border between Tanzania and Malawi. However, and quite problematically, there were other maps from the colonial era that illustrated the boundary between Tanzania and Malawi as being situated in the *center* of the lake.[14] The lack of historical-cartographic exactitude in regard to the lake border was undoubtedly a major problem as the border dispute manifested in 1967 (Figure 1.1).

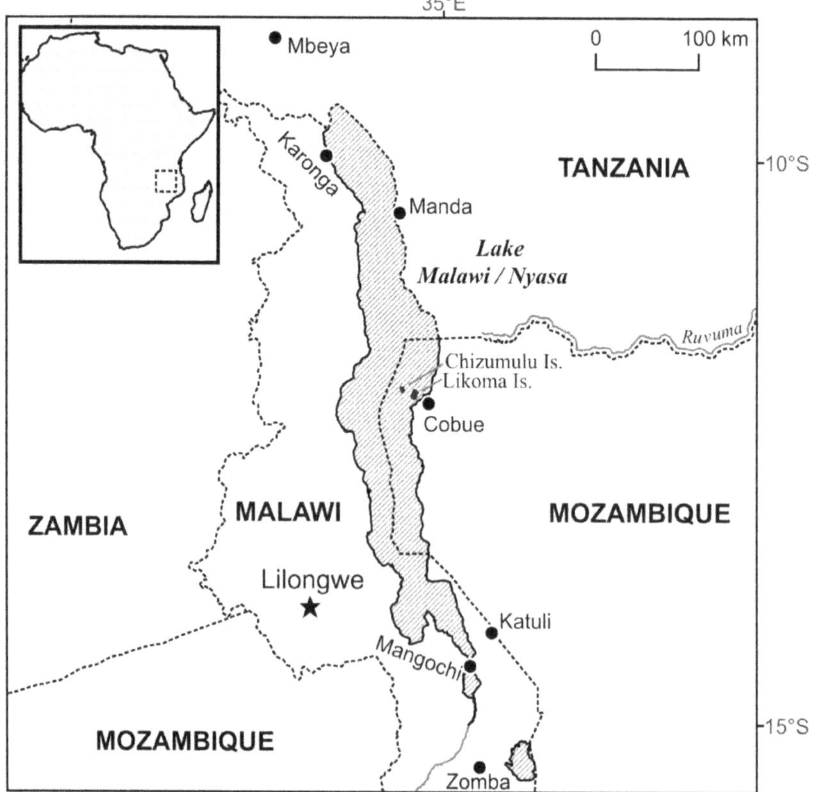

Figure 1.1 Northern Region of Lake Malawi/Nyasa. *Source*: Map created by Aharon deGrassi.

MAKING WAVES: FRELIMO, MOZAMBICAN REFUGEES, AND THE BATTLEFRONT OF LAKE NYASA/MALAWI

From the start of the liberation war in Mozambique on September 25, 1964, the lake border became an increasingly problematic political space between Malawi and Tanzania. Frelimo's military strategy to defeat the Portuguese involved the occasional use of the lake and its eastern shoreline to send guerrillas from Tanzania into Mozambique. The most contentious issue regarding the border was Nyerere's and Banda's disagreement over providing aid and sovereign territorial "safety" to southern African liberation movements, such as Frelimo, that fought against white minority rule and/or lingering Portuguese colonialism. The infiltration of Frelimo guerrillas from Tanzania into Mozambique, and their general disregard for Malawian sovereignty to achieve this objective, drew the ire of Banda, whose domestic economic and political agenda were paramount to securing Malawi and its borders.

Tense diplomatic relations and personal animus between Nyerere and Banda over the lake border was one of numerous political and philosophical disagreements that arose between the two men and their respective governments during the 1960s. Faced with several overlapping economic, political, and geographic challenges for his small landlocked country, President Banda deviated from Nyerere in his treatment and views of southern African liberation movements. From Banda's perspective, overt support for regional liberation efforts, and specifically for Frelimo's liberation war in Mozambique, were likely to anger the Portuguese, thus potentially rendering Malawi's ill-defended and ill-defined borders vulnerable to military threats. Additionally, Malawi's reliance on rail lines for the import/export of goods that extended across colonial Mozambique to the ports of Beira and, later, Nacala meant that Malawi needed to maintain good relations with the Portuguese. Malawian tobacco and other crops, key foreign currency earners, also utilized those same rail lines. What was clear to Banda in mid-1964 was that any support for Frelimo might result in a Portuguese invasion of Malawi and/or the severing of vital rail lines that linked Malawi to the east African coast.[15]

In June 1962, Frelimo elected its leaders in Dar es Salaam, Tanganyika, with the full knowledge and support of Nyerere and other members of his TANU government. Nyerere was a staunch supporter of southern African liberation, and his support for Frelimo, in particular, was a part of his pan-African vision and international agenda to end Portuguese colonial rule and white minority governments in Africa. Despite the euphoric sense of Pan-Africanism and continental liberation that marked the era of African independence in the 1960s, by 1967 Nyerere raised the border issue around Lake Malawi/Nyasa because of its strategic military value to Frelimo. With the war in Mozambique looming and Malawi newly independent, Banda's domestic political and economic concerns factored heavily into his views of Frelimo and the increasingly problematic eastern border of the lake.[16] In general, Banda was sympathetic to working with and accommodating colonial and white minority rule in southern Africa because his regime and the economic solvency of Malawi depended on it, even if he may have personally sympathized with the nationalist sentiments of southern Africa's liberation movements. After all, Banda was a dedicated and devoted Malawian nationalist and politician who famously rejected Nyasaland's continued membership in the CAF.

Frelimo began its guerrilla war in Mozambique on September 25, 1964, with an attack on a Portuguese outpost in Chai, a northern Mozambican town in Cabo Delgado Province. With settlement camps in Tanzania from where they could recruit Mozambican refugees as guerrillas and its headquarters located in Dar es Salaam, Frelimo had a powerful ally in Nyerere and his TANU government. For the duration of the war, Frelimo guerrillas infiltrated northern Mozambique to fight the Portuguese military from base camps inside Tanzania. For the first three years of the liberation war (1964–1967), Frelimo mostly engaged with the Portuguese in skirmishes and hit-and-run battles in rural parts of northern Mozambique. After an attack, Frelimo guerrillas often retreated for cover in the "bush," into local Mozambican villages, or escaped back across the border into Tanzania, which curtailed but did not prevent Portugal's ability to pursue them.

Although northern Mozambique was remote with major areas woefully un(der)developed throughout most of the colonial era, Portuguese military leaders did their best to fortify, surveil, and patrol the provinces of Cabo Delgado and Niassa, as well as the Ruvuma River border with Tanzania against Frelimo guerrillas.[17] In order to avoid detection, Frelimo guerrillas relied on local intelligence gained from Mozambican and Tanzanian sympathizers and sought to expand their war into other regions of Mozambique. Of particular concern to the Portuguese was the distinct possibility that Frelimo would use Lake Nyasa/Malawi and even Malawi itself as a conduit of infiltration from their rear bases in Tanzania. Portuguese military patrols along the southeastern lake shore were meant to prevent this possibility. In a Frelimo war "Communique," the liberation front revealed that local Africans were also part of the intelligence gathering on Portuguese military movements on and along Lake Malawi/Nyasa. The "Communique" stated:

> On the 5 January 1965 a nationalist, inhabitant of a village near Nyasa Lake, came and told our militants that a boat loaded with Portuguese soldiers was patrolling the lake. Our Freedom fighters went to the landing place and

camouflaged themselves with the vegetation. When the Portuguese soldiers landed, they were machine-gunned. 15 died, and several were wounded.[18]

The "Communique" did not reveal if any Frelimo guerrillas were wounded or killed, nor the exact location of the attack, but it was clear that Portuguese patrol boats and soldiers charged with defending Lake Malawi/Nyasa from guerrilla infiltration were susceptible to Frelimo raids. Three months later, in late March, Frelimo guerrillas struck again. This time, they "attacked with machine-gun fire a small boat travelling [*sic*] along the dge [*sic*] of Lake Nyasa, from Maniamba to Cobue. The boat was carrying Portuguese soldiers and the administrator of the circunscricao [*sic*] of Maniamba. As a result of the attack several Portuguese soldiers were killed and others wounded; however, we do not know their number."[19] Clearly, if the opportunity presented itself, Frelimo's war strategy included attacking the Portuguese on Lake Nyasa/Malawi.

From the start of the war, a steady stream of Mozambicans also fled across the border into Malawi, Tanzania, and Zambia.[20] Since the southern half of Malawi forms a geographic wedge between Mozambique's Tete and Niassa Provinces, the country was situated between war zones and many Mozambicans who fled the war as refugees sought the relative safety of neighboring Malawi. On May 22, 1965, the president of Frelimo, Dr. Eduardo Mondlane, had a conversation with a British official about the refugee situation in Malawi. According to the British official, "Mondlane was . . . full of praise for the Malwians [*sic*], although they were in a more delicate position vis-a-vis the Portuguese. They were co-operating far more with Frelimo and never questioned the movement of refugees. He said that he knew there were over 2,500 Mozambican refugees in Malawi."[21] Interestingly, Mondlane had expressed to the same British official that his, and Frelimo's, "relations with Banda were good, and that he was giving them as much cooperation as he could afford to without inviting Portuguese retaliation. They understood perfectly well that [Banda] could not actively support the FRELIMO freedom fighters, and were satisfied that his 'open door' policy for Mozambican refugees was as far as he could afford to go."[22] Although Mondlane's rosy description of Frelimo's relationship with Banda could have been a necessary act of diplomacy for the liberation front, it was not long before Frelimo's omnipresence in Malawi became a potential problem for Banda and a significant cause of the lake border dispute between Banda and Nyerere.

One of the most significant issues that arose pertaining to Mozambican refugees came only a few weeks after Mondlane's kind remarks about Banda. To highlight how Frelimo's cross-border actions undermined Malawian territorial sovereignty to the growing irritation of Banda, in July 1965, an estimated 3,000 Mozambicans who lived along the southeastern shore of Lake Malawi/Nyasa were unable to flee north to Tanzania to escape the fighting. Instead, they fled by fisherman's boats to Malawi's Likoma and Chizumulu Islands in the middle of the lake.[23] The flight of these Mozambican refugees to the Malawian islands was the result of numerous Portuguese "incendaries [*sic*] [that] were dropped by two aircraft to ignite the forest with the hope of thereby driving out FRELIMO 'Freedom fighters'" from neighboring Niassa province.[24] This concentrated and vulnerable population of Mozambican refugees who fled potentially offered Frelimo the chance to recruit guerrillas and, as such, the Portuguese countered this possibility with immediate food and medical aid to the refugees on the Malawian islands.[25] Frelimo's guerrilla activities on the periphery of the lake also prompted the Portuguese to inform Malawian authorities of their desire to search Lake Malawi/Nyasa for Frelimo guerrillas using "four gunboats equipped with radar and at least one Oerlikon type gun" from Mozambique's "shoreline on the Lake from Metangula in the south to at least as far as the Tanzanian border in the north."[26] Concerned that this rapid influx of Mozambican refugees would complicate his precarious relations with the Portuguese, Banda expressed how he was "worried about overcrowding" but had "no current intention of removing any refugees from Likoma to the mainland" of Malawi.[27] This potential humanitarian crisis would have burdened the local Malawian population and overstretched the meager resources of the Malawian state to ameliorate the refugees' plight. Moreover, the overcrowding of refugees on the islands might lead Mozambicans, instead, to leave the islands for the Malawian mainland, or push them into the arms of Frelimo cadres who infiltrated the region to recruit guerrillas.

Despite the presence of thousands of Mozambican refugees on Likoma and Chizumulu Islands and the possibility of their resettlement in Mozambique or Malawi, Malawian authorities on the islands with knowledge of the situation nevertheless expressed doubts that the refugees would actively seek to join Frelimo since "about two-thirds of them have relatives on Likoma and are thus being absorbed into the community there."[28] The Portuguese were not so convinced. When news of the Mozambican refugees on the island reached Portuguese authorities, they immediately suspected that Frelimo would actively recruit among them, since guerrillas often took advantage of the lake and the adjacent Ruvuma River when crossing into Mozambique.[29] British officials in Zomba with knowledge of the refugee situation on Likoma Island, in particular, were confident that to deter Frelimo from infiltrating and recruiting among this marooned Mozambican population, the Malawian "police will presumably investigate" the possibility of Frelimo activities on the island.[30] To sustain and facilitate positive diplomatic relations between the Portuguese and Malawians, officials in the British Commonwealth Relations Office (CRO) took it upon themselves to forward news of these refugees and their presence on the larger Likoma Island to Portuguese authorities in Lisbon and Lourenço Marques (Maputo).[31] It is unclear to what extent Frelimo managed to actively recruit from among the refugees ensconced on either island, but British and Malawian concerns about this possibility led them both to alert Portuguese authorities in the region, who began increased military patrols of Lake Malawi/Nyasa to deter Frelimo (Figure 1.2).

THE LAKE MALAWI/NYASA SHOWDOWN BETWEEN BANDA AND NYERERE

As the war in Mozambique escalated to include areas along and around Lake Nyasa/Malawi in 1967, the Mozambican refugee presence in Malawi's hinterland was viewed by Banda as potentially destabilizing to both rural communities in the south of the country and to the national economy. To shore-up

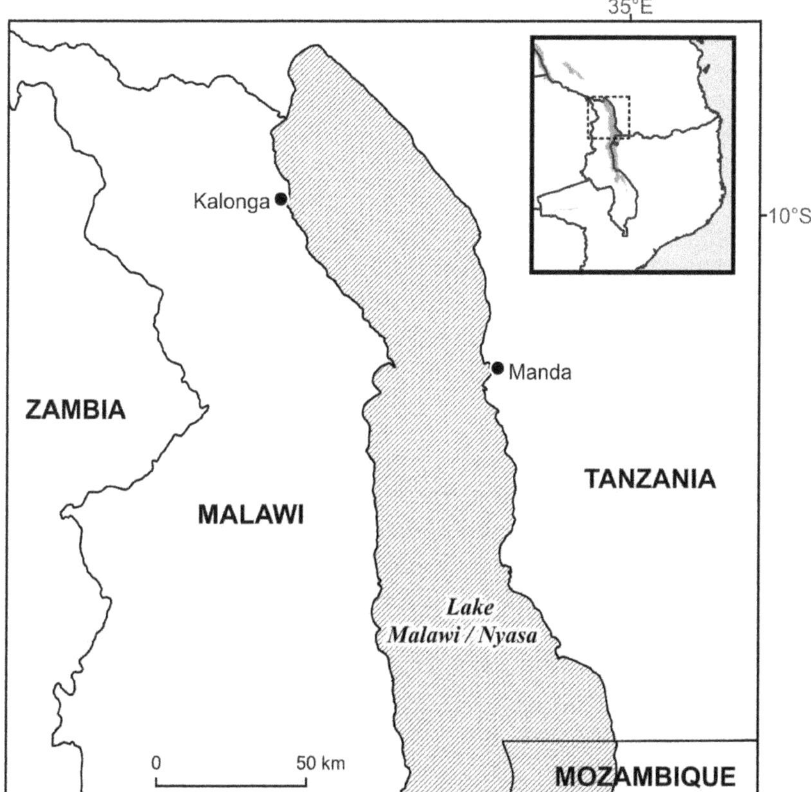

Figure 1.2 Lake Nyasa/Malawi. *Source*: Map created by Aharon deGrassi.

Malawi's diplomatic and economic relationship with the Portuguese, Banda sent ministerial representatives for a state visit to Lisbon in March 1967, which was followed, in turn, by a visit from Portuguese Foreign Minister Dr. Franco Nogueira to Malawi in late July and early August of the same year.[32] These diplomatic interactions between Malawian officials and the Portuguese government highlighted Banda's delicate position vis-à-vis an entrenched colonial power across Malawi's extensive southern and eastern border. In reference to Banda's views on apartheid South Africa and colonial Portugal, an editorial in the *Malawi News* emphasized how "if [Malawi] take[s] a pragmatic attitude to these two countries our economy will not only remain unharmed but might even blossom. . . . Let other people criticise us. They only make us even more determined in our plans, when they criticise us."[33] The high-profile talks between Nogueira and Malawian ministers John D. Msonthi and John Tembo lasted for nearly a week and were by all accounts "very successful. [Msonthi] thanks the Portuguese for their hospitality."[34] Msonthi debriefed the Malawian Parliament in early April about the trip to Lisbon and reflected on how "they were treated in Lisbon with utmost courtesy" and that "their talks with the officials there were very successful—the talks were aimed at the use of Ports of Nacala and Beira."[35]

A few weeks earlier, in March 1967, Frelimo's war against the Portuguese had expanded into Tete Province and Portugal clearly looked to solidify their political and economic bond with Banda as part of their strategy to defeat Frelimo. It was clear to William Farnworth, a reporter for the *Daily Telegraph*, that the diplomatic exchanges and high-profile meetings between Portugal and Malawi were "an unusual anomaly on this bewildering continent—a dedicated colonialist and an ardent African nationalist patting each other on the back." But the most significant issue beyond the pleasantries and promises of cultivating economic ties between Malawi and Portugal was the omnipresent "problem of the infiltrating 'freedom fighters' from Tanzania . . . because both countries have hard-to-police borders with Tanzania and the northern tip of Lake Malawi. . . . At present, the threat is there to both Malawi and Mozambique, and both countries have been unofficially acting in concord to contain it."[36] Nearly a year later, in April 1968, after establishing warmer ties with the Portuguese, Banda had clearly solidified his opposition to allowing Frelimo's clandestine operations through Malawian sovereign territory. He issued stern warnings to Frelimo, whose guerrillas continually used Malawian territory, to leave his country at once or face armed eviction at the hands of the Malawian military and police.

Another source for Banda's ongoing antipathy for Tanzania and Nyerere's support of Frelimo was the lingering fallout from his own government's internal crisis shortly after independence, when several political rivals challenged him on numerous ideological and personal fronts. When these significant disagreements between Banda and members of his cabinet surfaced shortly after independence, several Malawian ministers fled to Tanzania in the early fall of 1964 and began to plot against Banda. Among them was Banda rival and Malawian nationalist Henry Chipembere who, after a failed rebellion against Banda in February 1965, fled into exile first in Tanzania and then later to Canada and the United States before returning to Tanzania.[37] In March 1965, Malawian citizens and security forces in the Malawian town of Chitipa, a short distance from the Tanzanian border, thwarted an attack by Yatuta Chisiza, another former Malawian minister, who also fled to Tanzania and was opposed to Banda. In the attack, "Chisiza sent armed men into the country. Two of these men were hacked to death by villagers . . . with axes and hoes while a third man was shot by Security Forces."[38] By early May 1967, Banda's northern and lake border regions were on high alert as Banda anticipated other attacks from exiled Malawian political dissidents in Tanzania, Zambia, or both. "Let them come: We are ready for them," Banda boasted in a nationwide broadcast. "From now on, look out. Watch everyone from Tanzania or Zambia or anywhere else since" if they seemed suspicious and "any resisted arrest, you know what to do with him. You have your axes, hoes, spears, bows and arrows, if you haven't got a gun."[39] With tensions between Malawi and Tanzania clearly escalating by May 1967, the lake border issue became a major flashpoint of tension between Banda and Nyerere, just at the same time that Frelimo extended their war into Tete Province.

At the apogee of the lake border dispute in September 1968, and while still living in exile in Tanzania, Malawian dissident Henry Chipembere gave a rousing speech to a group of exiled Malawians and Tanzanian officials in Dar es Salaam's famous Arnautoglu Hall. Chipembere beseeched the audience to remember that "Dr. Banda's regime is a passing phase" and his "expansionist" claims about the lake border reflected the obvious influence of white minority regimes' over Banda.[40] For his part, Nyerere had allowed these high-profile exiled Malawian ministers like Chipembere, Yatuta Chisiza, and Kanyama Chiume to, at least initially, remain in Tanzania, which was a source of consternation for Banda who alleged that Nyerere was purposefully harboring these dissidents who were intent on toppling his regime.[41] According to Banda, Nyerere had a chance to make amends over these issues "as long as [Nyerere] ws [*sic*] willing to expel the rebels, Chiume and his gang. If he finds it impossible to expel Chiume and the rest of them, then he must not allow them his hospitality for subversion against us."[42] Moreover, Banda and Nyerere rarely saw eye-to-eye on issues involving interpretations and strategies of southern African liberation, particularly in regard to Frelimo's armed insurgency against the Portuguese in Mozambique.[43] It is not surprising, then, that Banda came to detest Frelimo's routine violations of Malawian territorial sovereignty. Nyerere's support for Frelimo and his all-encompassing domestic agenda based on a socialist model of development and self-reliance also made the issue of the lake border a focal point in his national political rallies in the wake of the Arusha Declaration.[44] In June 1967, six months after the adoption of the policies articulated in the Arusha Declaration, Banda challenged Nyerere in a provocative speech to the Malawian Parliament. Banda called out Nyerere for not allowing people on the eastern shore near the Songwe River to cross over the lake if they so chose, as well as for harboring and abetting Banda's enemies who fled Malawi in 1964. Although both Nyerere and Banda's public statements were meant to express their national policies to supportive audiences, as Frelimo's war in Mozambique intensified in Tete Province in 1967, the tensions over the lake border dramatically escalated in September 1968.

If Banda wanted to close Malawi to the trespasses of Frelimo guerrillas in order to keep the Portuguese mollified, as well as to bolster domestic support for his regime, he needed to make a convincing, sovereign claim to the eastern lakeshore. However, Banda's territorial claims went well beyond the eastern lakeshore. On September 9, 1968, Banda gave a speech to a group of supporters in Chitipa in northwest Malawi. In the address, Banda provocatively exclaimed, "That is my land over there . . . Tukuyu, Njombe, and Songea, all of them must be given back. . . . What was stolen from us by the colonial regime must be given back to us now." Nyerere's assertion that the lake be divided evenly in two was also resoundingly rejected by Banda, who subsequently added that "anyone talking that kind of language is looking for trouble, we are not going to surrender a single inch of the lake. . . . The people across there must surrender all that land near the lake and give it to me."[45] Banda's assertion that the physical territory east of the shoreline itself into Tanzania was also a part of his expansive vision for a "greater Malawi policy" was a shocking claim to the Tanzanian citizens/residents of those shoreline communities.[46] Tukuyu, Njombe, and Songea had long been part of Tanzania, and the people who lived there held Tanzanian citizenship. Banda's claims appeared to be an imperialistic shift in Malawi's foreign policy that provoked ordinary Tanzanians to express their outrage in the media and to their government representatives.

In the wake of Banda's Chitipa speech, the editorials and headline stories in the Tanzanian media castigated Banda in ways that questioned his mental health and capacity to lead Malawi. Framing Banda's assertion that the entirety of the lake and parts of sovereign Tanzanian soil were Malawian territory as the "hallucinations of a day-dreamer," Tanzania's *Nationalist* newspaper stressed that the audacity of "Banda's outbursts" was clearly motivated by more nefarious forces. "We are not dealing with the Malawian learned doctor," a *Nationalist* editorial claimed, but rather, "We are dealing with the forces of the Lisbon-Pretoria-Salisbury axis which have found in the person of Dr. Banda an unashamed spokesman."[47] Tanzanian authorities and journalists believed that Banda's territorial claims were a way to signal his accommodationist leanings toward the white regimes, but others in the Tanzanian media went further arguing, instead, that Banda's mental capacity was clearly in question. The *Nationalist* cover story on September 13, 1968 was especially blunt in this regard, provocatively stating "Banda is Insane" in large type.[48]

The outrage expressed by citizens in the Tanzanian media was also vitriolic. An anonymous letter writer to the *Standard* contended that "people living on the east side of the lake have every right to use and claim part of it. But Dr. Banda is never consistent. He allows the Portuguese, who continually terrorize the people of Likoma and Chizumulu Islands with their gunboats, to own a third of Lake Malawi."[49] A few days later, another Tanzanian contributor to the *Standard*, expressed with gendered nationalistic bravado:

> If they belong to [Banda], let him take them and we will be ready to meet him. He shamelessly claims that any person saying that Lake Nyasa (which he calls Lake Malawi) also belongs to Tanzania is seeking trouble. What trouble can this imperialist stooge and his fellow men stand? . . . We will never surrender even a grain of sand to him. We share the lake and there is no question about it. If he causes trouble along the border, we are not going to waste the energies of our troops to make him shut his big mouth. We will send our women to teach him a lesson.[50]

A Tanzanian from Njombe, one of the places claimed by Banda, Emmanuel F. Sanga, made specific reference to an oral history passed down in his family to refute Banda. Sanga was especially direct about his feelings regarding Banda's expansionist comments when he said, "I, as a native of Njombe District, have never had any contact whatsoever with Malawi. My great-grandfather who was living in Njombe District never explained to my grandfather, who is still living today, that Malawi chiefs of the past ever attempted to invade Njombe District . . . It is time that Dr. Banda realised that he has antagonised Tanzania in the extreme."[51] For Sanga, the border dispute could not escape the reality of his family's recollections, passed down orally over generations, that never witnessed a dispute over the land or the boundary on either side of the lake.

Undeterred by the pushback in the Tanzania media to his expansionist claims, Banda doubled down by personally calling out Nyerere. Speaking to nearly 1,500 delegates at the closing session of the Malawi Congress Party conference in late September 1968, a steadfast Banda stated, perhaps with some sarcasm since Nyerere did not hold a doctorate: "Dr. Nyerere should be the last person to squeal and squeak. He began it. He provoked me last year by claiming part of our lake. Did he expect me to remain silent? What does he think I am—a jellyfish like himself. . . . I am no jellyfish. In my back there is a bone. If Dr. Nyerere provokes me, he must expect me to take up the challenge."[52] In a similar speech in late September, this time in the western lakeshore town of Karonga in northern Malawi, Banda reiterated his position in regard to his expansive claims into Tanzanian territory, again antagonizing Nyerere: "If Tanzania is one nation, and Africa one Africa; if Africa is so much one; if he (Nyerere) believes Africa is so much one, why does he not agree to make adjustments to the boundary?"[53]

In the midst of this vitriolic back-and-forth, Tanzanians across the nation answered TANU's call and took to streets in rural communities, towns, and cities on September 25, 1968 to protest against Banda and to show solidarity for both Nyerere and Frelimo's war effort. The nationwide rally was organized by the National Union of Tanganyika Workers (NUTA) and boosted that nearly "10,000 condemn Banda."[54] The NUTA rally in Dar es Salaam drew a crowd, estimated at 6,000, who heard a fiery speech from Rashidi Kawawa, the second-vice president of Tanzania, who denounced Banda and, even more provocatively, allowed Malawian exiles and anti-Banda politicians Henry Chipembere and Kanyama Chiume to join the rally.[55] At the NUTA rally in Arusha, one placard stated quite dramatically, if not ironically: "Drown Banda in Lake Malawi."[56] The anti-Banda protests in Tanzania dovetailed with support marches in favor of Frelimo, which, at that moment, was commemorating four years of fighting in Mozambique.

Throughout October 1968, eleven editorials appeared in the *Nationalist* and six in the more mainstream paper the *Standard*, all of which questioned Banda's sanity, motivations, and expansionist agenda. On November 9, 1968, the *Standard* carried a nearly full-page article entitled, "Background to the Lake Squabble." The article sought to explain Banda's motivations, the historical contexts, and how internal political crises in Malawi were to blame for his behavior and statements on the lake border and adjacent Tanzanian territory. This article also directly quoted the dictator of Portugal, Antonio Salazar, who, the article claimed, supposedly tried to entice Banda to support Portugal in its war against Frelimo by offering up part of northern Mozambique to Malawi. While it was unlikely that Portugal would carve out a section of their colony as an olive branch to Banda, it was more likely that Portuguese military concerns about the ongoing war with Frelimo motivated Salazar to approach Banda. Salazar is quoted as having said to Banda that part of Mozambique might be offered up: "On condition that you promise us to do all in your powers to stop Frelimo freedom fighters from coming into the rest of Mozambique from your part of it."[57] If nothing else, Portuguese concerns about Frelimo's continued use of Lake Malawi/Nyasa as a conduit into Mozambique clearly confirmed that Banda was firmly opposed to Frelimo's uninvited presence in Malawi. Like many editorials and stories in Tanzanian newspapers at the time of the lake border dispute, this article is remarkable both for what it states openly and accurately, but also for what it silences and omits about the issue. For example, the article was written by an unnamed "Correspondent" for the *Standard*, who attempted to explain Banda's behavior as an act of colonial duplicity.

> This at least explains Banda's recent expansionist outbursts to some parts of Tanzania, especially the lake at its adjacent areas for he knows to get the "promised land" of Northern Mozambique—which he should in practice now start to negotiate with Dr. Mondlane rather than Lisbon—he had to get a sort of a springboard like Songea, Njombe and Tukuyu. . . . All of these facts help to explain the motives behind Banda's madness.[58]

The article does not mention how or if Mondlane would be willing to even negotiate this possibility with Banda, but given Mondlane's, and Frelimo's, dependence on Tanzania as a rear-base for their guerrilla operations, it is highly unlikely that Mondlane would be in a position to negotiate or even consider this a possibility with Banda. Despite the raw emotion expressed in the views of Tanzanian media about Banda's mental health, it was unlikely that Banda was truly "insane." Rather, although his expansionist claims into Tanzania were certainly provocative, it is more likely that he was motivated by other factors to make such a statement in the first place. First, he was angry at Nyerere for harboring his political rivals and for his unequivocal support for Frelimo's exploitation of Malawi's sovereign territory. Secondly, he wanted to demonstrate to the Portuguese, with whom he needed friendly relations for economic reasons, that he and his country were being victimized by Frelimo guerrillas' frequent border violations.

The diplomatic row between Banda and Nyerere also deeply concerned British officials who were genuinely concerned that the tension was not just posturing but could lead to broader regional instability and possibly war. In a "Secret" memorandum, a British official in the Foreign and Commonwealth Office (FCO) reported to Sir Lesley Monson, the British High Commissioner in Zambia, that the diplomatic row between Nyerere and Banda had reached a breaking point. On September 16, 1968, Banda had told the press "that he was putting patrol vessels on Lake Malawi" and reportedly claimed "that Britain was supplying three gun boats" to shore up Malawi's territorial claim to the eastern shoreline that abuts Tanzania.[59] Banda's "statement was interpreted by the press to mean that Britain was supplying three gun-boats" but, in fact, the British official who reported on this situation to Monson, clarified:

> In point of fact the first steamer, as we know from secret sources, was supplied by Portugal. It is reputed to be worked by Portuguese engineers although it is under the general control of the Malawi Young Pioneers. It is armed with a 20 mm cannon and two machine guns. The remaining two boats are indeed coming from Britain but they are standard fibre-glass [*sic*] 30-foot launches which anyone can buy. They are not specifically adapted to carry arms and they are not being bought with British aid.[60]

Either way, it put British officials in a tricky position to navigate, since they wanted to preserve friendly ties with both Banda *and* Nyerere.

Further adding to the tension, about a month after the lake border imbroglio, in October 1968, Malawian authorities received news that a significant number of Frelimo guerrillas were secretly encamped near Fort Johnston (now Mangochi) in southern Malawi: a city situated along the Shire River that links Lake Nyasa/Malawi with the smaller Lake Malombe. Upon learning that the guerrillas were overtly using Malawian territory in violation of Banda's policies, and in the midst of the lake border dispute, he threatened "to eject 200 armed Frelimo guerrillas" by force if they did not leave by October 19.[61] Banda's threat apparently worked, but the fate of the guerrillas once they crossed into Mozambique was unknown, since "there was no question of the Portuguese security forces ambushing Frelimo guerrillas as they crossed the frontier." Yet, ironically, "there was no evidence to suggest" the British believed "there is collusion [between Banda and the Malawian military] with the Portuguese security forces."[62]

Three days later, Banda met with Portuguese officials in Mozambique's Tete Province to discuss the situation and other matters pertaining to Frelimo's (c)overt activities in Malawi.[63] The day before Banda met with the Portuguese, word reached the British High Commissioner in Dar es Salaam "that the Frelimo Central Committee was prepared to regard Frelimo militants in Malawi as deserters who should be forced back in to [*sic*] Mozambique."[64] This curious response on the part of the Frelimo Central Committee likely allowed the liberation front to save face, especially in regard to their guerrillas' obvious presence in Malawi without official permission in the midst of the lake border dispute. Two months later, in December 1968, a report on the incident at Fort Johnston noted that a Frelimo "base commander" had been given orders to execute those guerrillas near the town of Katuli in Malawi, because Frelimo commanders believed those guerrillas to be in the act of defection to the Portuguese.[65] By December, the "present whereabouts" of the 200 unfortunate guerrillas who were accused of defection and forced over the border into Mozambique were still "not known" to British or Malawian officials.[66] Banda's threat to forcibly remove these guerrillas signaled to the Portuguese that no Frelimo rear bases would be tolerated in Malawi, but it was also evidence that Malawian authorities, including Banda, were limited in their ability to consistently prevent overt violations of their national territory by a neighboring liberation movement, regardless of the motivations of its members.

By early 1969, the issue of the lake border seemed to abate somewhat between Banda and Nyerere, but the circumstances for Frelimo had also changed. On February 3, 1969, Frelimo President Eduardo Mondlane was assassinated in Dar es Salaam by a parcel bomb. Although Frelimo's war effort continued in Mozambique, the organization was thrown into political disarray for a short period. Despite Mondlane's assassination, Frelimo guerrillas and their commanders continued to fight in Mozambique and gradually took more control over the northern provinces of Niassa, Cabo Delgado, and Tete during 1969. As Portuguese military setbacks mounted in the north, Frelimo expanded many of its camps, "bush schools," and other operations into Mozambique from Tanzania and Zambia. From Frelimo's military point of view, Malawi and the lake began to matter less as a conduit for guerrillas in their overall military strategy. This did not mean that Frelimo completely ceased to rely on the lake, but overt cross-border violations via the lake became less frequent. When Portuguese military officers launched a coup in Lisbon on April 25, 1974, against Salazar's replacement, Marcello Caetano, the end of Portugal's empire was near. A little over a year later, on June 25, 1975, Mozambique became independent, and Frelimo took control of Mozambique and pivoted toward a Marxist-Leninist doctrine under former Frelimo military commander turned president: Samora Machel.

Despite these political developments, the lake border dispute between Malawi and Tanzania has remained a source of ongoing tension between both countries. Unwilling to risk war over the issue, Nyerere, who remained in power until 1985, had more pressing domestic and economic issues to contend with from the 1970s and the rise of neoliberalism in the 1980s. Banda, who remained in power until 1994, believed that the lake border remained the eastern shoreline, but his inflammatory rhetoric about Songea, Njombe, and Tukuyu as being part of Malawi slipped from official discourse and therefore also out of Tanzanian newspapers. During the 1980s, a significant number of Mozambicans, once again, fled into Malawi to escape the violence of the Mozambique National Resistance (RENAMO) insurgency, as well as Frelimo's retribution on communities believed to support this South Africa/Rhodesian-backed anti-Frelimo militia. As Englund has convincingly argued, the ebb and flow of Mozambican refugees across the Malawian border fluctuated according to the course of the Mozambican civil war in the 1980s.[67] During that time, most Mozambican refugees depended on cross-border ethnic and family connections in Malawi for survival.

CONCLUSION

Starting in the mid-to-late 1960s, the Lake Malawi/Nyasa border between Malawi and Tanzania became a flashpoint of tension between the two independent African governments. The movements of Frelimo guerrillas on and around the lake were the primary source of the feud that emerged between Banda and Nyerere from 1967 to 1968 and the feud reflected their respective views on the liberation war in Mozambique. Tensions between the two countries reached a crescendo in September 1968. For a short period, it appeared that Malawi and Tanzania might go to war at some point over the issue, but that did not happen.[68] Malawian President Hastings Kamuzu Banda's threat to "put gunboats on the lake" to preserve Malawi's control over the majority of the lake was also widely chastised and berated in the Tanzanian press and society. These discursive provocations raised the specter of potential armed conflict between Malawi and Tanzania and highlighted how fluid, mostly indefensible borders could be exploited by an armed liberation movement that sought to free Mozambique from Portuguese colonial rule. In an era that is usually defined by referring to African independence and collaborative acts of Pan-Africanism, the lake/littoral border dispute between Malawi and Tanzania was the result of Frelimo's war efforts to send guerrillas into Mozambique to fight the Portuguese. Frelimo's presence in Malawi threatened the tenuous political stability and the territorial sovereignty of that country and brought the issue of the lake border to a dramatic apex in September 1968.

The dispute over the border of Lake Nyasa/Malawi remains, to this day, unresolved. Although the politics of liberation, nation-state formation, and regional Pan-Africanism related to the struggle against colonialism and white-minority rule are now history, contemporary disputes over the lake border between the two nations center on tourism, contracts for oil and gas exploration, and fishing rights.[69] The possibility that the decades-old dispute might reach the International Court of Justice (ICJ) at The Hague to determine an outcome remains a strong possibility. Ideally and perhaps optimistically, however, the matter may yet be settled among African politicians and policymakers from both countries, instead of by third-party international mediation. As legal scholar Gbenga Oduntan has argued: "The development of viable political, diplomatic and legal mechanisms and institutions in which African scholars, jurists, technocrats, leaders and elders of repute participate as the main engines of decision making in resolving African boundary disputes is imperative for the future" of the continent.[70]

As of April 2023, the official moniker of the lake remains disputed on various online and physical maps that refer to it as either "Lake Malawi" or "Lake Nyasa." Little has changed in this debate, and the eastern lakeshore border remains a source of animus. The Tanzanian Tourist Board still advertises the lake on its website as "Lake Nyasa": a deliberate strategy to avoid officially referring to it as "Lake Malawi," which might, in turn, give Malawi further grounds upon which to claim the lake as its own.[71] However, on Malawi's "Official Tourism Website," the lake is consistently referred to as "Lake Malawi." Nowhere on the Malawi tourism website does it refer to the lake as "Lake Nyasa."[72] The semantics matter: the name of the lake itself remains a powerful, discursive strategy in the ongoing territorial and legal dispute between both African states.

NOTES

1. To remain objectively neutral in the ongoing border dispute and to avoid any possible unintended consequences that might bias one side in a potential resolution of the lake dispute between Malawi and Tanzania, I have opted to alternate the name of the lake as "Lake Malawi/Nyasa" and "Lake Nyasa/Malawi" throughout this chapter. Where grammatically appropriate, I will simply refer to it as "the lake." Additionally, I would like to thank the librarians at Marist College and Yale University for helping me to locate and access vital microfilms for this chapter.

2. James Mayall, "The Malawi-Tanzania Border Dispute," *The Journal of Modern African Studies* 11, no. 4 (1973): 620; Mi Yung Yoon, "Colonialism and Border Disputes in Africa: The Case of the Malawi-Tanzania Dispute over Lake Malawi/Nyasa," *The Journal of Territorial and Maritime Studies* 1, no. 1 (2014): 75–89. Coincidentally, in the same month that Malawi attained independence (July 1964), the Organization of African Unity (OAU) met in Cairo and stipulated that colonial-era borders should be preserved to avoid internecine conflicts from occurring between newly independent African nations. See, https://au.int/sites/default/files/decisions/9514–1964_ahg_res_1–24_i_e.pdf, 16–17.

3. Mayall's article on the lake border dispute does include analyses of several key issues that informed the tension between Malawi and Tanzania, including some cursory analysis of how Frelimo's role was a contributing factor in the dispute. Other works with some mention of Frelimo's role in the dispute from the time period under study include Ian Brownlie. "A Provisional View of the Dispute Concerning Sovereignty on Lake Malawi/Nyasa," *The Eastern Africa Law Review* 1, no. 3 (1968): 258–73; Aleck H. Che-Mponda, "The Malawi-Tanzania Border and Territorial Dispute, 1968: A Case Study of Boundary and Territorial Imperatives in the New Africa" (PhD diss., Howard University, 1972).

4. Renato Matusse, *Frente de Tete: No context da Luta de Libertação Nacional e da África Austral* (Maputo: Indicus, Lda, 2016), 127–143; Allen F. Isaacman and Barbara S. Isaacman, *Dams, Displacement, and the Delusion of Development: Cahora Bassa and Its Legacies in Mozambique, 1965–2007* (Athens: Ohio University Press, 2013), 57–58, 89–94.

5. With page constraints in mind, in addition to selecting primary archival and secondary sources, I prioritized particular newspaper articles, headlines, and

editorials as sources for this chapter. A more complete historiographical sketch of works related to this topic follows below.

6. Growing scholarly interest in African borders, boundaries, migration, and frontiers sheds light on how these spaces inform the histories of African societies and nation-states and, at times, necessarily complicate contemporary legal and Western-centric orthodoxies related to sovereignty, political power, and nation-states. See Gbenga Oduntan, *International Law and Boundary Disputes in Africa* (New York: Routledge, 2015); Paul Nugent, *Boundaries, Communities and State-Making in West Africa: The Centrality of the Margins* (New York: Cambridge University Press, 2019); Chris Mahony, et al., "NZ Human Rights Working Paper 21: Where Politics Borders Law: the Malawi-Tanzania Boundary Dispute," New Zealand Centre for Human Rights Law, Policy and Practice, Africa Working Paper Series, (2014), accessed 15 August 2022 https://www.legal-tools.org/doc/f78000/pdf/; Francis Musoni, *Border Jumping and Migration Control in Southern Africa* (Bloomington: Indiana University Press, 2020). There is also a specific network of scholars who belong to the "African Borderlands Research Network," including this author, who focus extensively on this burgeoning field of research in Africa. See, https://www.aborne.net/

7. Jocelyn Alexander, Joann McGregor, and Blessing Miles-Tendi, eds., *Transnational Histories of Southern Africa's Liberation Movements* (New York: Routledge, 2021).

8. For examples on Tanzania, see Paul Bjerk, *Building a Peaceful Nation: Julius Nyerere and the Establishment of Sovereignty in Tanzania, 1960–1964* (Rochester: University of Rochester Press, 2015); James R. Brennan, *Taifa: Making Nation and Race in Urban Tanzania* (Athens: Ohio University Press, 2012); Emma Hunter, *Political Thought and the Public Sphere in Tanzania: Freedom, Democracy and Citizenship in the Era of Decolonization* (New York: Cambridge University Press, 2015); Cranford Pratt, *The Critical Phase in Tanzania 1945–1968: Nyerere and the Emergence of a Socialist Strategy* (New York: Cambridge University Press, 1976); George Roberts, *Revolutionary State-Making in Dar es Salaam: African Liberation and the Global Cold War, 1961–1974* (New York: Cambridge University Press, 2022); Leander Schneider, *Government and Development: Peasants and Politicians in Postcolonial Tanzania* (Bloomington: Indiana University Press, 2014); Joanna T. Tague, *Displaced Mozambicans in Postcolonial Tanzania: Refugee Power, Mobility, Education, and Rural Development* (New York: Routledge, 2019).

9. Nugent, *Boundaries*; Keren Weitzberg, *We Do Not Have Borders: Greater Somalia and the Predicaments of Belonging in Kenya* (Athens: Ohio University Press, 2017); Christopher Vaughan, Marieke Schomerus, and Lotje de Vries, eds., *The Borderlands of South Sudan: Authority and Identity in Contemporary and Historical Perspectives* (New York: Palgrave Macmillan, 2013); John Aerni-Flessner and Chitja Twala, "Bargaining with Land: Borders, Bantustans, and Sovereignty in 1970s and 1980s Southern Africa," *Journal of Southern African Studies* 47, no. 6 (2021): 993–1009.

10. Oduntan, *International Law*, 21; A.I. Asiwaju ed., *Partitioned Africans: Ethnic Relations across Africa's International Boundaries, 1884–1984* (New York: St. Martin's Press, 1985).

11. Mayall, "The Malawi-Tanzania Border Dispute," 612–614. The Heligoland Treaty of 1890 can be found in English. https://ghdi.ghi-dc.org/sub_document.cfm?document_id=782 (accessed 13 August 2022). The specific reference to the Lake Malawi/Nyasa border is found in Article 1, Section 2.

12. The Anglo-Portuguese Treaty of 1954 reflected the UK's ongoing influence over the affairs of colonial Nyasaland in the early years of the Central African Federation. According to the U.S. State Department, "International Boundary Study: Number 112, August 13, 1971 (Malawi-Mozambique Boundary)", 5: "An Anglo-Portuguese agreement of November 18, 1954, made various changes in the alignment of the Mozambique-Nyasaland boundary, which resulted in a net territorial gain of 2,496 square miles of land and water surface for the Portuguese overseas province. In Lake Nyasa the boundary was shifted from the eastern shore to overseas province. In Lake Nyasa, the boundary was shifted from the eastern shore to the median line annexing 2,471 square miles of water surface to Mozambique, and an additional water area of 23 square miles was included in the entity by re-demarcating the line westward in Lake Chiuta. Approximately two square miles of land also was given to Mozambique in the vicinity of Nsanje. Nyasaland received about eight square miles of Portuguese territory in the Angonia area of the Tete District of Mozambique." accessed 15 August 2022 http://library.law.fsu.edu/Digital-Collections/LimitsinSeas/pdf/ibs112.pdf

13. Tanganyika Legislative Council. *Official Report* (Dar es Salaam), 15 December 1959.

14. A quick Google Image search of historical maps of Lake Malawi/Nyasa and the surrounding region should suffice to prove the point.

15. Robert D'A Henderson, "Relations of Neighbourliness—Malawi and Portugal, 1964–74," *The Journal of Modern African Studies* 15, no. 3 (1977), 426–28.

16. Ibid, 440–43.

17. John P. Cann, *Brown Waters of Africa: Portuguese Riverine Warfare 1961–1974* (West Midlands: Helion and Company, 2013); John P. Cann, *Counterinsurgency in Africa: The Portuguese Way of War, 1961–1974* (West Midlands: Helion and Company, 2012).

18. The National Archives of the United Kingdom (hereafter TNA), DO 213/101 "Mozambique Liberation Movements in Tanzania," C.R.O. Telegram No. 12, 23 January 1965, point 2. Taken from *Mozambique Revolution*, no. 14, January 1965, Communique #8.

19. TNA, DO 213/102 "Mozambique Liberation Movements in Tanzania," Unclassified, No. 8.73, "Frelimo Activities," Nyasa Province, excerpted from Frelimo "Communique no. 18," 30 April 1965.

20. Michael G. Panzer, "Building a Revolutionary Constituency: Mozambican Refugees and the Development of the FRELIMO Proto-State, 1964–1968," *Social Dynamics: A Journal of African Studies* 39, no. 1 (2013): 5–23.

21. TNA, DO 213/102 "Note of conversation with Dr. Mondlane, President of FRELIMO, on 22 May 1965, arising out of problems of FRELIMO Refugees."

22. Ibid., Letter from P.G.P.D Fullerton to J.S. Renwick, Esq., Zomba, 26 May 1965.

23. TNA, DO 183/845, Refugees in Malawi, Telegram no. 643 to C.R.O, 31 July 1965, 2.

24. TNA, DO 183/845, Likoma Island, Letter from R. Bloom to Murray McMullen, Esq., Malawi and Zambia Department, C.R.O., 28 August 1965, point 5.

25. Ibid., point 6.

26. Ibid., point 4.

27. TNA, DO 183/845, Refugees in Malawi, Telegram no. 643 to C.R.O, 31 July 1965, 2.

28. Ibid.

29. Ibid.

30. Ibid.

31. Ibid, 3.

32. "Two Malawi Ministers in Lisbon for talks," *Malawi News*, 17 March 1967.

33. "We do what we say," *Malawi News*, 17 March 1967, 2.

34. "Msonthi back from Portugal," *Malawi News*, 24 March 1967. Msonthi was Malawi's Minister of Transport and Communications and John Tembo was the Minister of Finance.

35. "Lisbon received us with courtesy-Msonthi," *Malawi News*, 4 April 1967.

36. TNA, FCO 9/362 Malawi Political Affairs with Portugal, William Farnworth, "Dr. Salazar's Black African Friend," *Daily Telegraph*, 1 August 1967.

37. Power, *Political Culture and Nationalism*, 188–198; McCracken, *A History of Malawi,* 429–445. Chipembere was also involved in a failed cross-lake raid of Malawi from Tanzania in early May 1967. It is unknown to what extent, if any, Tanzanian officials may have been involved.

38. "Kamuzu Reveals Rebels' Plans," *Malawi News*, 25 April 1967, 2. Chisiza later attempted and failed another infiltration of Malawi in October 1967 from Tanzania.

39. Ibid.

40. *Standard*, "Don't Blame Us All, Pleads Chipembere," 19 September 1968, 1.

41. TNA, DO 208/1 STATEMENTS MESSAGES AND SPEECHES BY DR BANDA OF MALAWI, "Dr. Banda's Press Conference on Thursday, 21 April 1966, at Zomba, 10 a.m., point 5.

42. Ibid. The speech was given to an audience of supporters and journalists in April 1966 in Domasi, Malawi.

43. "Malawi claims part of Tanzania," *Standard*, 10 September 1964, 1.

44. While visiting south-central Tanzania as part of his post-Arusha Declaration campaign to rally support throughout the country for his socialist project, Nyerere visited the Tanzanian town of Iringa in late May 1967. There he gave a speech to a group of secondary students with the intention of highlighting the responsibilities of Tanzanian youth to the developing nation, but he also made an assertive statement about his interpretation of the lake border.

45. "Banda claims big part of Tanzania," *Nationalist*, 10 September 1968, 1.

46. TNA, FCO 29/293, "Secret," 7a, Telegram number: 1857 to Foreign and Commonwealth Office, 7 November 1968.

47. "Banda again," *Nationalist*, Editorial, 11 September 1968, 4.

48. "Banda is Insane," *Nationalist*, 13 September 1968, 1.

49. "Let us watch Dr. Banda," *Standard,* Readers' Forum, 12 September 1968, 4.

50. Mpfungie Kessy, "Dr. Banda" *Standard*, 18 September 1968, 4.

51. "No, Dr. Banda," *Standard*, Readers' Forum, 20 September 1968, 4.

52. "Banda raves on about Dar 'Provocation'," *Standard*, Cover Story, 22 September 1968.

53. "Kamuzu Slashes Nyerere," *Malawi News*, 24 September 1968

54. "10,000 condemn Banda," *Standard*, Cover Story, 27 September 1968.

55. Ibid.

56. Ibid.

57. "Background to the Lake Squabble," *Standard*, 9 November 1968, 4. This condition was assuming that Portugal actually carried through with its part of the bargain to cede part of Mozambique to Malawi. Extant documentation on this situation hinted at that possibility.

58. Ibid. Unlike the sarcastic use of "Dr. Nyerere" by Banda in certain speeches, the leader of Frelimo Eduardo Chivambo Mondlane held a doctorate, hence the "correspondent's" use of "Dr. Mondlane."

59. TNA, FCO 29 210, Malawi and Tanzania Border Dispute, Secret letter from E.H.M. Counsell to Sir Leslie Monson, 21 October 1968, "Problem," 1. In this case, the "press" was the Malawi News, which was a pro-Banda organ that served a dual role as a source of domestic and international news, as well as a purveyor of Malawian state propaganda.

60. Ibid., Letter from E.H.M. Counsell to Lesley Monson, "Argument" 5, 3. 3.

61. TNA, FCO 29/293 "Possible action by Malawi army against Frelimo guerrillas in Malawi," "Background," point 4, file 10.

62. TNA, FCO 29/293 "Possible action by Malawi army against Frelimo guerrillas in Malawi," W. Peters to Central African Department, FCO, Point 5, "Submission," file 7.

63. Ibid.

64. Ibid.

65. TNA, FCO 29/293 "Extract J.I.C. Report December 1968, Letter "C," "African Nationalist Parties / Frente de Libertacao de Mocambique," [*sic*], point 16.

66. TNA, FCO 29/293 Telegram no. 1934, 12.

67. Harri Englund, *From War to Peace on the Mozambique-Malawi Borderland* (Edinburgh: Edinburgh University Press, 2001).

68. Indeed, although the prospect of war between Tanzania and Malawi was unlikely, hostilities continued into the 1970s. In his 1972 dissertation on the subject, Tanzanian scholar Aleck Che-Mponda argued that war remained a distinct possibility in March 1971 when, according to Tanzanian witnesses he interviewed, Malawian gunboats landed on the eastern shoreline at Manda. Che-Mponda said, "Malawi apparently was not bluffing when it threatened Tanzania with a military confrontation." It was unclear if this was just an isolated incident or part of strategic posturing along the eastern lakeshore. Tanzania did not respond militarily to the incident. Che-Mponda, "Malawi-Tanzania Border," 194–196.

69. Tiyanjana Maluwa, "Oil Under Troubled Waters? Some Legal Aspects of the Boundary Dispute between Malawi and Tanzania over Lake Malawi," *Michigan Journal of International Law* 37, no. 3 (2016): 395–96. See also, Yoon, "Colonialism and Border Disputes," 85–89.

70. Oduntan, *International Law and Boundary Disputes*, 3. Oduntan also explains the more recent history of the dispute in the same volume on pages 159 and 206–217.

71. https://www.tanzaniatourism.go.tz/en/destination/lake-nyasa (accessed 15 June 2022).

72. https://www.visitmalawi.mw/ (accessed 15 June 2022).

BIBLIOGRAPHY

Aerni-Flessner, John, and Chitja Twala. "Bargaining with Land: Borders, Bantustans, and Sovereignty in 1970s and 1980s Southern Africa." *Journal of Southern African Studies* 47, no. 6 (2021): 993–1009.

Alexander, Jocelyn, Joann McGregor, and Blessing Miles-Tendi, eds. *Transnational Histories of Southern Africa's Liberation Movements*. New York: Routledge, 2021.

Asiwaju, A.I., ed. *Partitioned Africans: Ethnic Relations across Africa's International Boundaries, 1884–1984*. New York: St. Martin's Press, 1985.

Bjerk, Paul. *Building a Peaceful Nation: Julius Nyerere and the Establishment of Sovereignty in Tanzania, 1960–1964*. Rochester: University of Rochester Press, 2015.

Brennan, James R. *Taifa: Making Nation and Race in Urban Tanzania*. Athens: Ohio University Press, 2012.

Brownlie, Ian. "A Provisional View of the Dispute Concerning Sovereignty on Lake Malawi/Nyasa." *The Eastern Africa Law Review* 1, no. 3 (1968): 258–73.

Cann, John P. *Brown Waters of Africa: Portuguese Riverine Warfare 1961–1974*. West Midlands: Helion and Company, 2013.

———. *Counterinsurgency in Africa: The Portuguese Way of War, 1961–1974*. West Midlands: Helion and Company, 2012.

Che-Mponda, Aleck H. "The Malawi-Tanzania Border and Territorial Dispute, 1968: A Case Study of Boundary and Territorial Imperatives in the New Africa." PhD diss., Howard University, 1972.

Englund, Harri. *From War to Peace on the Mozambique-Malawi Borderland*. Edinburgh: Edinburgh University Press, 2001.

Henderson, Robert D'A. "Relations of Neighbourliness—Malawi and Portugal, 1964–74." *The Journal of Modern African Studies* 15, no. 3 (1977): 425–455.

Hunter, Emma. *Political Thought and the Public Sphere in Tanzania: Freedom, Democracy and Citizenship in the Era of Decolonization*. New York: Cambridge University Press, 2015.

Isaacman, Allen F., and Barbara S. Isaacman. *Dams, Displacement, and the Delusion of Development: Cahora Bassa and Its Legacies in Mozambique, 1965–2007*. Athens: Ohio University Press, 2013.

JSTOR, ALUKA Project, Struggles for Freedom: Southern Africa https://www.jstor.org.marist.idm.oclc.org/site/struggles-for-freedom/southern-africa/

Mahony, Chris, Hannah Clark, Meghan Bolwell, Tom Simcock, Richard Potter, and Jia Meng, "NZ Human Rights Working Paper 21: Where Politics Borders Law: the Malawi Tanzania Boundary Dispute," New Zealand Centre for Human Rights Law, Policy and Practice, Africa Working Paper Series, 2014. https://www.legal-tools.org/doc/f78000/pdf/

Maluwa, Tiyanjana. "Oil Under Troubled Waters?: Some Legal Aspects of the Boundary Dispute Between Malawi and Tanzania Over Lake Malawi." *Michigan Journal of International Law* 37, no. 3 (2016): 351–419.

Matusse, Renato. *Frente de Tete: No contexto de Luta de Libertação Nacional e da África Austral*. Maputo: Indicus, Lda., 2016.

Mayall, James. "The Malawi-Tanzania Border Dispute." *The Journal of Modern African Studies* 11, no. 4 (1973): 611–628.

McCracken, John. *A History of Malawi: 1859–1966*. Suffolk: James Currey, 2012.

Nugent, Paul. *Boundaries, Communities and State-Making in West Africa: The Centrality of the Margins*. New York: Cambridge University Press, 2019.

Oduntan, Gbenga. *International Law and Boundary Disputes in Africa*. London: Routledge, 2015.

Organization of African Unity, Resolutions Adopted by the First Ordinary Session of the Assembly of Heads of State and Government Held in Cairo, UAR, from 17 to 21 July 1964 https://au.int/sites/default/files/decisions/9514–1964_ahg_res_1–24_i_e.pdf

Panzer, Michael G. "Building a Revolutionary Constituency: Mozambican Refugees and the Development of the FRELIMO Proto-State, 1964–1968." *Social Dynamics: A Journal of African Studies* 39, no. 1 (2013): 5–23.

Phiri, S.H. "National Integration, Rural Development and Frontier Communities: The Case of the Chewa and the Ngoni Astride Zambian Boundaries with Malawi and Mozambique." In *Partitioned Africans: Ethnic Relations across Africa's International Boundaries, 1884–1984*, edited by A.I. Asiwaju, 105–125. New York: St. Martin's Press, 1985.

Power, Joey. *Political Culture and Nationalism in Malawi: Building Kwacha*. Rochester: University of Rochester Press, 2010.

Pratt, Cranford. *The Critical Phase in Tanzania 1945–1968: Nyerere and the Emergence of a Socialist Strategy*. New York: Cambridge University Press, 1976.

Roberts, George. *Revolutionary State-Making in Dar es Salaam: African Liberation and the Global Cold War, 1961–1974*. New York: Cambridge University Press, 2022.

Schneider, Leander. *Government and Development: Peasants and Politicians in Postcolonial Tanzania*. Bloomington: Indiana University Press, 2014.

Tague, Joanna T. *Displaced Mozambicans in Postcolonial Tanzania: Refugee Power, Mobility, Education, and Rural Development*. New York: Routledge, 2019.

Tanganyika Legislative Council. *Official Report* (Dar es Salaam), 15 December 1959.

United States State Department, *International Boundary Study: Number 112*, August 13, 1971 (Malawi-Mozambique Boundary).

Vaughan, Christopher, Marieke Schomerus, and Lotje de Vries, eds. *The Borderlands of South Sudan: Authority and Identity in Contemporary and Historical Perspectives.* New York: Palgrave Macmillan, 2013.

Weitzberg, Keren. *We Do Not Have Borders: Greater Somalia and the Predicaments of Belonging in Kenya.* Athens: Ohio University Press, 2017.

Yoon, Mi Yung. "Colonialism and Border Disputes in Africa: The Case of the Malawi-Tanzania Dispute over Lake Malawi/Nyasa." *The Journal of Territorial and Maritime Studies* 1, no. 1 (2014): 75–89.

Chapter 2

Permitless Crossing and Tourism

Constructing Border Regimes in the Drakensberg Mountains, 1950s–Present

John Aerni-Flessner

For as long as borders have been demarcated and policed, people have found ways to get across them.[1] In the SADC region, borders are noted for being "porous" in many cases, even when there were strict security, pass, and permit regimes, such as under the South African apartheid government. Geography can render such extreme state measures difficult to enforce, but perhaps even more importantly, the needs and desires of individuals to get across have also meant that people were willing to take great risks, at times, to move across boundaries. Government officials and their surveillance regimes are, usually, aware of these extra-legal movements and so have to decide what their reactions to such crossings will be.

Along the Lesotho-South Africa border, especially in the Drakensberg Mountains, both governments have long worried about people crossing the borders. Not all people who cross, however, have equally worried the governments. Prior to 1963, there were no formal border posts at the official crossing points between the two countries, though a pass was usually required for the African residents from either side to legally cross the border. Starting in the 1950s, though, the South African government in particular became more concerned about Basotho crossing the border and the ease with which the crossings seemed to happen.[2] This came about because the apartheid regime was attempting to consolidate its policy toward African communities and was facing stiffening resistance from groups like the African National Congress (ANC), Pan-Africanist Congress (PAC), the Non-European Unity Movement (NEUM), and protest movements that turned violent in areas along the Lesotho border like Witsieshoek/Qwaqwa (1949–1950) and Pondoland (1959–1961).

The increased concern around border crossers and border crossing led officials on both sides to increasingly desire to categorize and classify border crossers in an attempt to define categories of legality and illegality. This had the dual purpose of attempting to keep out those deemed "illegitimate" and to make it easier for those who were crossing "legally" to do so. Desired border crossers included individuals who had the proper permits to export cattle, sheep, wool, and mohair from Lesotho to South Africa, contractors coming into Lesotho to work on the development projects that the Basutoland government was increasingly funding from the 1950s, and tourists as part of the plan to bring in more revenue to the territory.[3] The two governments attempted to keep out permitless crossers who were coming to shop in South Africa and/or smuggle goods into or out of Lesotho. What the attempted surveillance of the border and the increasing emphasis on permits, passports, and paperwork did, however, was to criminalize the everyday lives of poorer borderlands residents, especially those attempting to make a living by farming, pastoralism, and informal migrant labor in the harsh climates of the Lesotho mountains. These processes, falling into the category of increased "governmentality," were, and remain, attractive to officials because they can then, at least theoretically, better surveil and control border crossers. The supposed need for stricter procedures also gives justification to beef up the state bureaucracy that gives those same officials their power over those passing through as well as residents of the border zones.

By privileging border crossers who could access legal paperwork, the governments of both South Africa and Lesotho have sided with the tourists, businesspeople, and formally employed, while increasingly criminalizing the survival strategies of small-scale Basotho businesspeople and traders, and mountain community residents in general, who often lack access to the services, opportunities, and legal paperwork of their counterparts in other parts of Lesotho. This has made life consistently harder for poor Basotho residents in mountain borderlands. It has also had the effect of increasing the power of border officials, which helps explain how and why the contemporary border regime evolved in a region long known for its labor migration.

MOUNTAIN PASSES, GOVERNMENT POLICIES, AND SMUGGLING REGIMES IN THE 1950S AND 1960S

Almost from the creation of the Lesotho/South Africa border in the mid-nineteenth century when Basutoland was annexed as a British colony, the focus of the Maseru administration was on monitoring and controlling the border.[4] In particular, the administration focused on regulating the ways in which Basotho and their animals could and could not cross the line. Stock theft loomed large in these administrative discussions, even though the scale of theft did not always match the emphasis placed on it by border farmers, Basotho chiefs, and various colonial officials. The presence of some theft, and of the narrative of theft being an omnipresent threat, forced officials to take note of what was happening along the border, especially in those areas like the Drakensberg Mountains that largely lacked an official administrative presence.[5] Many of these areas, even today, still lack that presence because the harsh climate and lack of permanent human settlements keep these areas largely free from human presence, especially in the winter.

The emphasis on attempting to control routes through the mountains, thus, began in the nineteenth century and continued into the twentieth and twenty-first. This was especially true as an increasing human population in Lesotho put more pressure on the land. Animal owners looked for more summer grazing in the mountains, and by the late nineteenth century, settlements in the river valleys of the Senqu (Orange) and its tributaries began in earnest. The most common routes over the mountains were well known to the local herders, who utilized them to get their animals up and down from the highlands, and for trade. The most commonly used pass in the northern Drakensberg was the Namahali Pass that connected the Mokhotlong District with Witsieshoek/Qwaqwa in the far eastern Orange Free State (OFS). This pass was proclaimed an official border post from 1917, and the Basutoland Mounted Police (BMP) staffed a small station that was initially placed at the top of the pass. Quickly, however, the station was moved down into OFS territory because of the harsh winds at the top of the pass, showing how policing the border was a collaborative affair for both colonial governments.

A pass, like the Namahali, was not just one route to the top. In 1979, South African officials interviewed a Mr. Grey, a man of European descent who had long operated a store in the Qwaqwa area that did most of its business trading for wool and mohair from Lesotho farmers. These farmers brought sheep and Angora goats down the passes or had them shorn in Lesotho and brought the produce down to his store for transportation onward to the main markets in Port Elizabeth. Mr. Grey reported that at some point in the 1930s, he had been engaged by the OFS government to blow up between eight and twelve of the smaller passes in the Khoptjoane area (nearby to the official Namahali Pass), claiming that they were "used for cattle rustling." These alternative routes could also be used by Basotho farmers looking to evade paying the wool and mohair duty that was collected by the police post at Namahali when they brought their animals or wool and mohair through. Closing them, thus, forced more animal owners to document and pay taxes on their produce. It also allowed the police on both sides to better surveil who was coming down the mountains, as they had fewer passes to monitor.[6]

Writing a history of the nearby (Royal) Natal National Park, Carruthers claimed that the proclamation of the park in 1916 and the use of the mountains by European climbers and their African cooks/guides did not interrupt or disrupt "economic activities over the mountains between Basutoland, the Orange Free State, and Natal."[7] While it is true that none of the more commonly used passes were directly within the boundaries of the park, the grazing areas on the Lesotho side extended into park land on top of the escarpment. Further, the herders who used that grazing often came down the Namahali or other smaller passes just to the north of the park to sell animals and their wool and mohair. So, the closing of areas below the escarpment and the increased official presence due to park staffing certainly impacted the herders by changing the routes and grazing areas that they used. A secondary goal of the national park was the better control and policing of mountain crossings, especially between Lesotho and the Native Reserves that abutted the park on its south side in Natal. Having park staff monitoring the area served the purpose of limiting the unrestricted movement of Africans, a constant colonial concern.

The strategy of focusing on the borders as a way of controlling the rural Basotho populace, that was largely outside the gaze of the colonial authorities thanks to the system of "Parallel Rule" that had grown up in colonial Basutoland, can be seen in the organization of the BMP.[8] The system of parallel rule had developed because it was cheaper to rely on the chiefs to administer large swathes of the rural territory and because the British had been unable to fully break the power of the chieftaincy, despite a series of administrative reforms stretching from the 1930s to the 1950s that disrupted the chiefly hierarchy.[9] One of the main responsibilities of the police through the colonial era was the staffing of a series of small posts along Lesotho's borders. In 1950, for instance, with the population of the territory climbing over half a million, there were only 16 European and 347 African members of the BMP for the entire territory.[10] Of those, 74 African troopers and 3 non-commissioned officers—or almost 25 percent of the force—were stationed at 35 small border posts, mainly enforcing laws relating to "customs, the collection of revenue, the import and export of cereals and livestock, the export of wool and the issue and checking of passes for Africans to leave the Territory."[11] With an average of about two officers at each of these isolated posts, the vast majority of which still had no radio communication, the officers had to stay at the top of Drakensberg passes and could not perform other police duties. They were, in short, less police officers and more glorified border guards tasked primarily with collecting taxes and monitoring and controlling who could and could not leave the territory via isolated mountain passes.

Through the early 1950s, the BMP closed a number of these posts. Responding to local complaints of increased stock theft in the mountainous interior, the BMP constructed more posts there and moved its officers away from the small, lightly trafficked mountain pass border posts. By 1952, the number of staffed border posts had dropped from 35 to 28. The main concern of police administrators, as well as the rest of the administration, was that the police at these posts were "unable to patrol the Border."[12] This re-orientation of the BMP from glorified border tax collectors to more proactive police came in the wake of increased complaints not only from Basotho chiefs and herders in the mountains of Lesotho about more stock theft but also from South African authorities about the rise of smuggling.[13] Also factoring into this changed focus were the 1949–1950 Witsieshoek Uprising that caused an exodus of Basotho and Batlokoa from Witsieshoek across the border into Lesotho and the start of formalized apartheid in South Africa from 1948 that put increased pressure on the Basutoland authorities to crack down on the movement of Basotho across the South African border.[14]

During this time, the constant assumption that undergirded changes in policy and policing was that Basotho herders from Lesotho on the mountain passes were transgressive and/or undesirable in some way. For example, the District Commissioner (DC) for the Mokhotlong District wrote in October 1950 about the mountain passes. This letter was written while protests were underway in Qwaqwa against the proposed culling of Basotho cattle under the apartheid regime's "Betterment" schemes, but before the open violence at the protest meeting at Namoha in November 1950 led to Basotho protestors fleeing into Lesotho. The DC proposed blocking most smaller Drakensberg passes from Mokhotlong down to Qwaqwa to ensure that all trade went through the officially recognized border posts and said that this should be done "with dannert wire or . . . blowing up the passes."[15] To so casually propose permanently blocking the mountain passes, on which the local residents depended for trade and, in many cases, for getting food that was unavailable in Lesotho's high mountains, suggests that the colonial administration was either not aware of the struggles facing many of the mountain herders and their communities, or was so enamored with instituting a regime of control that they were willing to sacrifice the livelihoods and potentially the lives of mountain dwellers.[16] It does accord, however, with colonial administrators seeing border crossers of similar ethnic groups as a threat to their administration and suggests that the idea of "governmentality" or increasing bureaucratic state power, was driving many of these administrative policy changes.[17]

In a similar vein, further south in the Drakensberg, the DC of Qacha's Nek wrote in 1951 complaining about how the border fence was being continually cut in his district. Rather than proposing blockading the passes like his Mokhotlong colleague, however, he identified the problem as tax evasion. Basotho herders would drive their flocks down over the passes to stores owned by traders of European descent in South Africa to sell their wool and mohair, thereby evading the Basutoland tax that was supposed to be paid at the border posts. He called for the police and chiefs, in conjunction with South African authorities, to "go and squat at all the Trading Stores on our borders" and arrest Basotho from Lesotho who appeared at the stores without a paid tax receipt. Again, the solution was more government intervention to better monitor and control the lives of borderlands residents.

Ruminating on the border, the DC noted that the "border fence is no more than a boundary. It is not an effective border." As with the other officials, the DC in Qacha's saw the tax evasion of the Basotho herders as the source of problems around the border. However, with either a colonial paternalism or a dose of realism, he also noted that South African traders were the "real source of trouble" as they were marketing to the Basotho a higher price than Lesotho stores could, because they did not have to pay the wool and mohair levy. They also saved on transport by being nearer to coastal markets.[18] Still, the net impact for residents of the mountains was a draconian border regime that criminalized their efforts to fully partake in the capitalist system by getting the best price available for their agricultural and pastoral produce, and produced even more government surveillance during the implementation of apartheid.

South African officials, too, concurred with the DC of Qacha's Nek that South African storeowners were part of the problem, but they were only too happy to pass the blame primarily onto the herders themselves who were crossing. This was heightened by the start of formal apartheid after 1948 and officials' increased worries about an influx of Africans from the British High Commission Territories (HCT).[19] South African officials, in particular, worried most about Lesotho due to the number of people crossing the border regularly. Apartheid authorities also increasingly desired to make all African populations more legible to the official bureaucracy, through things like stricter pass laws. After decades of haphazard, piecemeal fence repairs and continued protests from farmers in Griqualand East, Barkly East, the Transkei, and other border districts, the governments of Basutoland and South Africa agreed in the late 1950s to fully reconstruct the border fence that ran along the Drakensberg escarpment on Lesotho's southern border. Despite some hesitancy on the part of officials, like the Chief Magistrate of the Transkeian Territories who wrote in October 1956 that he feared the fence would be "cut and damage[ed] as fast as it is being erected," the project to reconstruct and rebuild over sixty miles of fencing commenced in early 1957.[20] This followed a conference on stock theft in Matatiele (Griqualand East District) in October 1954 where representatives from the OFS, Cape Province, and Natal all declared that stock theft was "inextricably bound up" with control of the border and, in particular, the fence.

Controlling mountain residents coming across for trade, shopping, or theft was a priority for all these officials. Not all border crossers, however, received the same scrutiny, and some individuals wanted exemptions from the increasingly onerous restrictions that were placed on borders and crossers from the 1950s onward. It was only in 1963, following South Africa's departure from the Commonwealth in 1961, that official border posts were even instituted between South Africa and Lesotho. Almost as soon as the posts were declared and opened on June 1, 1963, there were people asking for exemptions to be able to cross more easily, more conveniently, and with concessions from officials.

Those who were looked upon favorably by South African officials tended to be of European descent, but even beyond this obvious caveat, they also tended to look favorably upon those, regardless of background, who were formally employed. Taking the Qacha's Nek border crossing as an exemplar shows how this played out. The architects of the new Tebellong Hospital, located in a rural part of Lesotho's Qacha's Nek District across the *Senqu* River applied for relief from what they called the short hours of the border saying that with a 4:00 p.m. closing time, they did not have time to "cross the border, do the work, and get back before the post closes." They went on to note that "access across the border is a courtesy that has been traditionally offered at all hours of the day and night, for travelers cannot reasonably be expected to spend the night in the snow waiting for the gate to open" and they wanted to be able to cross with "advance telephonic advice."[21] In a similar vein, the Native Recruiting Company that supplied Basotho mineworkers to the Witwatersrand mines also petitioned South African authorities on behalf of Mr. Peterson, their representative stationed in Qacha's Nek, for permission to cross outside the official hours. Company officials in Johannesburg noted that Peterson's sons went to school in Matatiele and that the 4:00 p.m. border closure made it impossible to pick them up and return them home some days. They also noted, thinking it might help their cause, that Peterson "has assisted the Security Branch on occasion in regard to matters at Qacha's Nek."[22]

In both cases, the supplicants were primarily professionals of European descent, but employed Basotho were also petitioning the South African authorities. While they were not asking for permission to cross outside of the normal hours, they did receive some concessions at the border from the South African Secretary for Bantu Administration and Development. In February of 1964, that office gave permission that Basotho from Lesotho "employed in the Republic may be allowed to visit Basutoland on short leave and return with reference books only. No passport necessary."[23] While it was not clear just how successful the European-descendant applicants were at getting special border permissions, the fact that they were confident enough of some amount of success to send the petitions suggests that they were likely to be successful at gaining relief. But in all these examples, those with formal employment had some expectation of being able to bypass border regulations. This contrasts sharply with the treatment of the Basotho herders and small-scale traders who were also attempting to come across the border in these decades. These individuals were treated as would-be criminals—tax evaders or thieves—and colonial Basutoland and South Africa were both much more interested in regulating, making visible their movements, and potentially criminalizing their behaviors than they were in the passage back and forth of those with formal jobs.

TOURISM, NATURE CONSERVATION, AND THE CONSTRUCTION OF "ILLEGALITY," 1970S–1990S

The construction of the mountain border as a space hostile to subsistence farmers and small-scale wool and mohair traders continued into the 1970s and beyond, but as a focus on tourism expanded in both the Republic of South Africa and in now-independent Lesotho, a new category of desired border crosser—the tourist—arose. One of Lesotho's first strategies to break free from dependency on the South African economy and migrant labor was, a bit ironically, an attempt to lure South African tourists to the country. Thus, in 1970, the Holiday Inn hotel and casino opened not far from Kingsway, the main street, in Maseru, and in 1979 the Hilton Hotel and casino opened on a hill overlooking the central business district and government offices. These hotels were successful at getting South Africans across the border as long as relations between the two countries were stable, as they were through most of the 1970s, but when Lesotho's support for the ANC and South Africa's support for the Lesotho guerilla group, the Lesotho Liberation Army (LLA), started a proxy war in the years following 1979, these hotels became less popular. There was also more competition from Sol Kerzner's Sun Hotels, which built similar resorts in the "independent" Bantustans at this time.[24] On the South African side, the tourism potential of the Drakensberg region was certainly recognized by private enterprise, as well as by the South African government, but apartheid ideology meant that this tourism would be only for white South Africans and overseas visitors through the 1970s and 1980s.[25]

However, by the late 1970s, the Lesotho government was looking to expand the country's tourism sector and was increasingly looking to the mountains to attract visitors, especially from overseas. Thus, in 1977 the Lesotho government commissioned, with Swiss government funding, a study of conservation in the mountains, asking the consultants to find and suggest suitable plans for developing national parks. In these plans, however, Basotho who lived in and used these mountains for subsistence were seen as a hindrance to progress, continuing the administrative disdain that marked colonial border controls toward residents of mountain communities.[26] The Swiss study authors noted that they were looking for "extensive tracts of uninhabited land remaining close to its original state prior to the advent of man" in which to set up a National Park, and that these lands could only be found along the Drakensberg escarpment.[27] While these lands in Lesotho were technically uninhabited in that they did not contain houses and villages, they were an integral part of the seasonal grazing system long practiced by Basotho herders and given sanction by the chiefs in mountain communities.[28] The report ended up recommending the creation of a National Park along most of the Lesotho Drakensberg escarpment, from Mont-aux-Sources in the north above Qwaqwa to the already existent Sehlabathebe National Park in the south bordering Natal.

The design of the park as a Nature Reserve with its goal of attracting tourists would adversely impact the Basotho subsistence herders who used the land in the summer and those looking to drive sheep, goats, or cattle across the park and down the Drakensberg passes into South Africa. The study authors understood this and so the report called for the "strict application of controls, already available, under the Land Husbandry Act of 1969" to control access to the escarpment lands.[29] The report's authors clearly did not consult with local communities about this plan, as they go on to say that "vegetation burning and the cutting of shrubs could not be permitted" though "some grazing of domestic stock could continue at least for an experimental period . . . [and that] the cooperation of local chiefs would of course be necessary."[30] This proposal would have decimated the vast majority of the local economic activity in Basotho mountain communities, and made it hard for people to even survive. Mountain communities relied on seasonal grazing for their animals—lower down in the river valleys in the winter and higher up along the escarpment in the summer—and relied on the local cutting and collection of shrubs as fuel for cooking year-round.[31]

Thus, the study points to the ways that planners saw the poorer residents of the mountain districts as an impediment to the goals of tourism and conservation and aligns with the increased surveillance that colonial administrators had earlier proposed for those living in these areas. The successful implementation of this plan would have entailed setting up measures to surveil and control local populations—increased governmentality—constructing these residents as illegitimate trespassers who had to be denied access to the border regions in the name of greater national priorities. In the end, the park never came to fruition, not only because of the disruptions that it would have taken to make it happen, but also because the budget for parks was extremely limited, as seen by the fact that the one National Park, Sehlabathebe, had almost no funding for this entire period. However, the report still importantly shows that the

Lesotho government's view of mountain residents and mountain communities had not changed appreciably from views held by the colonial administration.

The official drive to disallow Basotho borderlands residents from crossing the border heightened in the 1980s as the fight against apartheid intensified and the proxy war between Lesotho and South Africa continued. Despite the poor relations at the highest levels of government, 1981 saw the two governments form the Inter-Governmental Liaison Committee (IGLC) that was supposed to meet periodically to work on and resolve border issues that could be solved below the ministerial level. The IGLC met for the first time in June 1981 in Maseru and conservation in the Drakensberg mountains was one of the topics for discussion. South African officials, in particular, were concerned about setting up a conservation region in the mountains because they were concerned about animal and foot traffic at eighteen "entry points," referring to border crossings at informal and non-monitored passes that Basotho used to come down into South Africa. South African officials did note, however, that most of these passes, other than at Sani Top where the only road crossing the Drakensberg was located, and at Bushman's Nek near Sehlabathebe Park, were only occasionally used.[32]

The 1982 meeting of the committee was much more focused on these passes and the people crossing the border there. Officials on both sides saw the residents of mountain communities as threats to the supposedly "pristine" nature of the mountains, and as potential security threats. In the time since the 1981 meeting, a Joint Planning Team had investigated the crossing points between Natal and Lesotho. This group recommended that the countries only have two official crossing points—Sani and Bushman's Nek—in an effort to crack down on "illegal" border crossing at the other, less-heavily traveled passes. The team hoped that "people will be discouraged from using unofficial passes by persuasion and tighter control measures."[33]

Those "people" as a category were assumed to be local Basotho residents, and the plan to use tighter controls on them was in stark contrast to the desire of the same committee to better facilitate access to these same mountain regions for tourists from the South African side. While "recreational travelers" would still be required to have travel and identity documents on them, the committee expressed interest in allowing "bona fide recreational traffic to have free access to all passes, official and non-official."[34] This striking contrast between the access that mountain community residents would not have and the access that "bona fide" tourists would have is the culmination of the ways in which the governments had conceived of and constructed the border in the preceding decades. It also showed how monied interests played into calculations around the border.

The IGLC resolved to have joint patrols of officials from the Lesotho police, the South African police, and representatives of Natal Parks and the

Directorate of Forestry. Even though South Africa was very worried at this time about ANC infiltration from Lesotho, it was the Lesotho officials who expressed the most concern about illegal border crossings in the Drakensberg.[35] They claimed that "multifarious illegalities [are] perpetrated across these points. These included the smuggling of guns and ammunition, dagga and even stolen animals."[36] Thus, Basotho mountain dwellers were again smeared as tax-dodging smugglers who were often thieves, while South African hikers and mountaineers were a desired group that should have priority of access to the mountains. But the drive for increased governmentality through border control in the mountain areas brought together officials from both sides of the border. In this case, it was happening despite lines drawn by the apartheid system and a proxy war taking place between the two governments. Despite all this, representatives from both governments agreed on more surveillance of mountain communities and their residents.

The meeting at which these views were aired took place in November 1982. Relations between the two governments hit a new low the next month when South African security forces launched their biggest raid ever across the border into Maseru, a raid that killed forty-two people, split between ANC refugees and ordinary Basotho unwittingly caught up in the raid.[37] This slowed any cooperative progress that the two governments had been making and led to the Lesotho government retaliating against South African border crossers, including tourists. In mid-1983, Lesotho authorities detained some hikers in the mid-Drakensberg region around Cathedral Peak, leading the South African Mountaineering Club to issue a warning to its members to "avoid areas in Lesotho where unrest has escalated" including the northern Drakensberg around Qwaqwa and the Cathedral Peak area.[38] Harassment of South African tourists by Lesotho security personnel continued sporadically as inter-governmental relations remained at a low ebb. In late July 1984, four South African climbers in the southern Drakensberg around Bushman's Nek reported that they were shot at by Lesotho security forces while hiking near the border with the Sehlabathebe National Park.[39] Lesotho officials were capable, therefore, of weaponizing their increased governmentality against tourists, but they only did so when geopolitical relations were at a low ebb between the two countries.

However, the lucrative potential of cross-border tourism was too great for Lesotho officials to ignore over the long-term, and relations shifted again by the mid-1980s. In January 1986, a military coup replaced the unelected and increasingly unpopular government of Prime Minister Leabua Jonathan with military rule under Lt. Gen. Metsing Lekhanya. Officials in Pretoria supported the coup.[40] Not surprisingly, the Lekhanya regime was open to working more closely with South Africa, even if the power dynamics shifted to favor the apartheid regime. For Basotho in the mountains, though, this détente at the highest levels meant more surveillance and further suspicion of their motives for border crossing. This was evident at the IGLC meeting held in Cape Town in September 1987. Discussing the proposed conservation area in the Drakensberg, a Lesotho representative highlighted the fact that there were local communities living in and near the area that was to be declared a nature reserve. He stated that these communities needed to be "informed about and convinced of the importance of proper range management in the catchment area."[41] These communities were not to be consulted, but rather "convinced of" the need for this program—one-way communication in an already-decided process—that saw residents of these communities yet again as potential impediments to conservation rather than partners. Having officials be more concerned with notification than consultation is a long-standing feature of development work in Lesotho.[42] The rhetoric of the IGLC suggests that Lesotho officials were still seeing residents of mountain communities in a similar way.

This dim view of mountain community residents and the two-tiered system that prioritized tourists over residents remained constant through the end of the decade. During a detailed discussion at the 1989 meeting about tourism and conservation, the two governments talked about setting up a special system so that tourists could "travel anywhere within the mountain protected areas, on either side of the international boundary" for a small fee, revenues from which would be divided between the two countries. This preferential access for tourists would not be available for local residents, who were referred to in the discussion as "transit traffic."[43] Those attempting to make a living traveling between the two countries for trade or shopping were viewed as problematic and a bureaucratic hassle, while those bringing money to the area as tourists were classified as desired, with efforts made to reduce bureaucratic hassles for them.

CONTEMPORARY BORDER CROSSING IN THE DRAKENSBERG

Despite the return of democratic rule to Lesotho in 1993 and the first free elections open to all in South Africa in 1994, the dynamics of tourism and border policy changed very little in the Drakensberg region. The same suspicions that marked democratic leaders in Lesotho (1965–1970), unelected despots (1970–1986), and military leaders (1986–1993) were retained after the return of multi-party democracy. There was still a strong sense that bureaucrats in Maseru were not working in the interest of mountain communities and, thus, government officials "are hated by the people in the [mountains]" because "they don't like to see people [in the mountains] make money" from the natural resources there.[44]

For mountain community residents in the contemporary period, most say that the border is still a source of stress as they attempt to navigate it, especially with the recent stringent regulations around COVID-19. On the eve of the COVID pandemic during the 2019–2020 December/January festive season, over half a million Basotho from Lesotho legally crossed South Africa's borders in both directions. This was the second highest total from any country in southern Africa, just behind Zimbabwe, a country with a population seven times larger than Lesotho.[45]

Still, despite the high volume of legal crossing, the amount of illegal crossing is very high as well. This is especially true in the Drakensberg Mountain region, where the need for passports keeps some people from crossing. A woman who spoke Xhosa in the villages outside Matatiele reported that she "would like to visit" Lesotho but that she doesn't "have a passport" or family across the border and so it is just too much hassle to cross.[46] Those who cross in the Qacha's Nek—Matatiele area often do so illegally via a spot about 500 meters from the official border post, informally known as the *paqama* spot. *Paqama* is a Sesotho word meaning "to lie or crawl on the stomach" and refers to those who go under a fence this way.[47] The border fence at the paqama spot is long-gone, but the name remains. A taxi driver on the Lesotho side of the border who went by the name Cobra said that the COVID-19 restrictions had forced many to use the paqama spot. When queried about whether the crossers he ferried to the border had passports, Cobra replied: "They actually have their passports. . . . It's just that crossing at the border requires you to have 300 rand [for the Covid test]."[48] His business as a taxi operator had been booming in the months since the COVID restrictions went into effect, making between five and nine trips a day between Qacha's Nek town and the unofficial crossing spot. This meant that Cobra was making a lot of money and he noted that "if there was no longer *paqama* [illegal crossing] all of us [taxi drivers] would be broke to death."[49]

While the COVID-19 regulations were certainly in the interest of public health, they most directly impacted the residents of the mountain districts where crossings are fewer and further between. The other nearby smaller official border posts like Ramatšeliso's Gate and Ongeluksnek were still closed in October 2021 when the research team conducted interviews. This, combined with the closure of the Tele Bridge crossing in Quthing District, meant that every formal border post in the two southern districts was closed, save the one at Qacha's Nek. This forced residents who wanted to cross legally into a long and expensive journey to Qacha's Nek. That crossing, however, was only open from 8:00 a.m. to 4:00 p.m., Monday through Friday. The next-nearest post that was open was over 200 kilometers and a four-hour journey by road away, near Mohale's Hoek. Thus, the regulations, while not specifically designed as such, continued the lack of concern that earlier governments had shown for mountain residents who needed to cross the border.

The one difference that the COVID regulations had with earlier efforts to police the border was that they impacted tourism and local border traffic equally. Of course, most tourists to the region were wealthy enough that the requirement to take a COVID test, the cost for which varied from 1,300 rand at one point in the pandemic to as low as 300 rand by mid-2022, did not send them across illegal crossing points. The limited border hours and need for the test did limit the number of tourists who could cross. A tourist operator from Matatiele who regularly took clients across the Drakensberg into southern Lesotho noted that the border officials had to rigorously enforce the measures, which hurt his business. He also claimed that strict enforcement "opened the door for criminal elements" like stock thieves and dagga smugglers, thus perpetuating illegal crossings and forcing more governmentality—surveillance and red-tape through increased paperwork for legal border crossers.[50]

The belief that the border had gotten harder to cross in recent years was echoed by a number of the people interviewed in the mountain borderlands. A woman who was originally from Lesotho but whose parents had brought her to live near Matatiele forty-two years ago noted that "it doesn't sit well with me . . . [that] I live so close to the border but it's still difficult to get to the other side" to see friends and family. She went on to complain more specifically about the conduct of Lesotho officials at the border. She said that all of her children have passports, but officials will "ask for more documents from Home Affairs" than just the passports and therefore she often "ends up paying those boys [at the *paqama* spot] to help me to get across [illegally]."[51] She contrasted this with the time around the year 2000 as she noted that crossing was easier in that time period because area residents could get a permit allowing them to "stay for six months [in South Africa] without any problems with the passport."[52]

The woman's assertion in Matatiele that crossing had become harder was echoed on the Lesotho side by a fifty-nine-year-old man from a border community. He noted that the border had become more militarized of late, especially on the South African side, with soldiers patrolling regularly. He noted that border crossing during apartheid was "much more difficult" than "compared to [the first years] after apartheid." However, in recent years, it had become much harder again because of the presence of soldiers near the border that forced people to "avoid being arrested" by "walking along very dangerous terrain, such that in the recent past we heard of people who died there as a result."[53] Thus, the recent turn to the securitization of the border had made it more dangerous for those who wanted to cross the border for non-nefarious reasons, suggesting that there was a moment in the first years after the fall of apartheid that the surveillance of borderlands residents had dropped, but that the logic of governmentality had returned again to increase the surveillance regime. The crossers he was describing were those simply attempting to see family or shop in South Africa, but they were being forced into more dangerous crossings. This was emblematic of border crossing by the second and third decades of the twenty-first century and, unfortunately, continued the trend of the Lesotho and South African governments seeing crossings by residents of mountain communities in the Drakensberg as problematic.[54] They viewed these crossings as a "problem" to be solved rather than national policy flaws, emanating from Maseru and Pretoria, stemming from foolhardy and ultimately futile attempts to police a border that residents will continue to cross to access family, services, and employment.

CONCLUSION

It is too early to tell what the long-term changes from the COVID-19 pandemic will be along the border and whether it will end the bifurcated treatment that local residents and tourists get at the Lesotho-South Africa border. However, it is likely, given the long history of increased governmentality and the deliberate construction of two categories of border crossers, that when these extraordinary regulations are finally ended, border officials and those in charge of policy will revert to encouraging one group (tourists) and attempting more regulation of the rest (local residents and subsistence border crossers). Given the statements from border residents in the contemporary period, it is highly unlikely that any future policies will be any more successful at stopping those who want and need to cross from doing so.

Economic hardship, family connections, and differences in rules and regulations between Lesotho and South Africa all encourage people to cross whether they can access the proper paperwork, medical tests, or an official border crossing point. Thus, policy should be cognizant of the fact that crossings will continue and work to make it safer and easier to transit legally for the majority of residents who do want to follow the procedures. As the fifty-nine-year-old man from Lesotho said of those in his mountain community: "We are struggling . . . government must look into this matter of the borders, of coming and going" because border crossing is going to continue and making a more rational policy will "be to [the] advantage of people who live down there [in South Africa]; it will be a benefit to us [in Lesotho]."[55]

NOTES

1. Funding for this research came from the National Institute for the Humanities and Social Sciences (NIHSS), the University of the Free State (UFS) Humanities

Interdisciplinary Research Project from the Dean's Office, and from a Fulbright Fellowship.

2. Basotho is the plural form of the residents of Lesotho. The singular is Mosotho. While the territory was officially called Basutoland during the colonial period (1868–1966), I will refer to it as Lesotho throughout, as that is what residents called the land. References to Basutoland will only be direct references to the colonial regime. Similarly, while "South Africa" was officially the Union of South Africa until 1961, and the Republic of South Africa after that date, I will refer simply to South Africa in most cases. All interviews conducted for this chapter have been anonymized.

3. There is relatively little written about the history of tourism in the Drakensberg in the context of the border. What has been written has tended to focus on the South African side, and in particular on the history of the South African National Parks nearby. Jonathan Linde and Stefan Grab "Regional Contrasts in Mountain Tourism Development in the Drakensberg, South Africa," *Mountain Research and Development* 28, no. 1 (2008): 65–71; Jane Carruthers, "The Royal Natal National Park, KwaZulu-Natal: Mountaineering, Tourism, and Nature Conservation in South Africa's First National Park c. 1896 to c. 1947," *Environment and History* 19, no. 4 (2013): 459–486; Cobus Rademeyer and W. van Zyl, "Golden Jubilee for Golden Gate—A Concise History of Golden Gate Highlands National Park, 1963 to 2013," *Mediterranean Journal of Social Sciences* 5, no. 27 (2014): 1169–1177. A study that looks at the politics of park construction and local subsistence livelihoods, in a similar manner to this chapter, does so for the Basotho communities around what was then the Qwaqwa National Park, now part of Golden Gate National Park: Rachel Slater, "Between a Rock and a Hard Place: Contested Livelihoods in Qwaqwa National Park, South Africa," *The Geographic Journal* 168, no. 2 (2002): 116–129.

4. When Basutoland was annexed, there was no such entity as "South Africa," which only emerged in 1909 as the Union of South Africa. For ease of comprehension, this chapter will refer to "South Africa" to describe the Cape Colony, Orange Free State, and Natal for the pre-1909 period, unless referencing a specific government. The Union of South Africa became the Republic of South Africa in 1961. Basutoland officially became Lesotho in 1966.

5. John Aerni-Flessner, Chitja Twala, Munyaradzi Mushonga, and Grey Magaiza "A Transnational History of Stock Theft on the Lesotho-South Africa Border, Nineteenth Century to 1994," *South African Historical Journal* 73, no. 4 (2021): 903–926.

6. This attempted surveillance through bordering is common in African history. For another southern African example, see Francis Musoni, *Border Jumping and Migration Control in Southern Africa* (Bloomington: Indiana University Press, 2020). For an example from the Horn of Africa, see Karen Weitzberg, *We Do Not Have Borders: Greater Somalia and the Predicaments of Belonging in Kenya* (Athens: Ohio University Press, 2017).

7. Carruthers, "Royal Natal National Park," 473.

8. L.B.B.J. Machobane, *Government and Change in Lesotho, 1800–1966: A Study of Political Institutions* (London: Macmillan, 1990).

9. Colin Murray and Peter Sanders, *Medicine Murder in Colonial Lesotho: The Anatomy of a Moral Crisis* (Edinburgh University Press, 2005).

10. *Basutoland 1956 Population Census, 8th April 1956* (Maseru: Basutoland Government, 1958).

11. Lesotho National Archives, Maseru (hereafter LNA), 2494/2 Basutoland Mounted Police Annual Report 1950.

12. LNA 2494/6 Basutoland Mounted Police Annual Report 1952.

13. Aerni-Flessner, et al., "Stock Theft," 919–921.

14. Leo Barnard, Jan-Ad Stemmet, Stephen Semela, "The Battle of Namoha, Qwaqwa (1950): An Oral History Perspective," *Southern Journal for Contemporary History* 30, no. 3 (2005): 183–198; Balam Nyeko, "Resistance to Colonial Rule and the Emergence of Anti-Colonial Movements," in *Essays on Aspects of the Political Economy of Lesotho 1500–2000,* eds. Neville Pule and Motlatsi Thabane (Roma, Lesotho: Institute of Southern African Studies, 2002).

15. LNA 394 IV and V: Border Fences District Commissioner Mokhotlong to Government Secretary Maseru, 4 October 1950.

16. Into the 1950s, there were very few stores in the Mokhotlong District, and they were concentrated in the center of the district around the government reserve as well as around mission stations. James Colman, *Sani Pass: Revealing Its Secrets* (Pietermaritzburg: Otterley Press, 2016).

17. For similar changes in the Kenyan context, see Julie MacArthur, *Cartography and the Political Imagination: Mapping Community in Colonial Kenya* (Athens: Ohio University Press, 2016).

18. All quotations from LNA 394 IV and V: Border Fences Letter District Commissioner Qacha's Nek to Government Secretary, Maseru, 7 February 1951.

19. Basutoland, Bechuanaland Protectorate, and Swaziland were often referred to as the High Commission Territories (HCT), as the ultimate executive authority in all three was the British High Commissioner in South Africa.

20. Western Cape Archive and Record Service, CMT 3/1337 25/A/1 Basutoland Border Fence 1932–1963 Chief Magistrate Umtata to Secretary for Native Affairs, Pretoria, 8 October 1956.

21. South African National Archives, Pretoria (hereafter SANA P) BAO 4077 C166/3/1888 Passport Controls—Borderposts, Letter Frolich, Kass and Watkins, Durban to Minister of Bantu Admin and Development, 19 June 1963

22. SANA P BAO 4077 C166/3/1888 Passport Controls—Borderposts, Native Recruiting Corporation, Johannesburg to H.H.L. Smuts, Deputy Secretary of Bantu Admin and Development, 29 October 1963.

23. SANA P BAO 4077 C166/3/1888 Passport Controls—Borderposts, Telegram Secretary for Bantu Admin and Development to Passport Control Officer, Matatiele, February 1964.

24. For a good summary of these years, see: Jonathan Crush and Paul Wellings, "The South African Pleasure Periphery, 1966–1983," *Journal of Modern African Studies* 21, no. 4 (1983): 673–698.

25. Melanie Duval and Benjamin Smith, "Rock Art Tourism in the uKhahlamba/ Drakensberg World Heritage Site: Obstacles to the Development of Sustainable

Tourism," *Journal of Sustainable Tourism* 21, no. 1 (2013): 134–153; R.O. Pearse, *Barrier of Spears: Drama of the Drakensberg* (Cape Town: H. Timmins, 1973).

26. This phenomenon was, of course, not confined to Lesotho and was in fact a feature of park development in many countries. For South Africa, see Jacob Dlamini, *Safari Nation: A Social History of the Kruger National Park* (Athens: Ohio University Press, 2020). For an example from the USA, see Daniel S. Pierce, *Great Smokies: From Natural Habitat to National Park* (Knoxville: University of Tennessee Press, 2015).

27. Donald N. McVean, *Nature Conservation in Lesotho: Report on Current Progress and Forward Planning* (Morges, Switzerland: International Union for the Conservation of Nature, 1977), 6.

28. Colin Hoag, "The Ovicaprine Mystique: Livestock Commodification in Postindustrial Lesotho," *American Anthropologist* 120, no. 4 (2018): 725–737.

29. McVean, *Nature Conservation*, 25.

30. McVean, *Nature Conservation*, 27.

31. Colin Hoag, *The Fluvial Imagination: On Lesotho's Water-Export Economy* (Berkeley: University of California Press, 2022), 39–45. Mpho 'M'atsepo Nthunya, *Singing Away the Hunger: The Autobiography of an African Woman* (Bloomington: Indiana University Press, 1997).

32. SANA P DCD 2904 7/2/5/2/18 RSA/Lesotho Liaison Committee 1981–85, Minutes of Inter-Governmental Liaison Committee Meeting, Maseru, 11 June 1981.

33. SANA P DCD 2904 7/2/5/2/18 RSA/Lesotho Liaison Committee 1981–85, Minutes of Inter-Governmental Liaison Committee Meeting, Maseru, 17 Nov. 1982.

34. SANA P DCD 2904 7/2/5/2/18 RSA/Lesotho Liaison Committee 1981–85, Minutes of Inter-Governmental Liaison Committee Meeting, Maseru, 17 November 1982.

35. This is likely because most ANC infiltration came either via the lowland areas in the Maseru and Mafeteng areas, or the Lesotho/Transkei border regions near Quthing and Qacha's Nek. See, for instance, Hugh Macmillan, *Chris Hani* (Athens: Ohio University Press, 2021); Janet Smith and Beauregard Tromp, *Hani: A Life Too Short* (Johannesburg: Jonathan Ball Publishers, 2010).

36. SANA P DCD 2904 7/2/5/2/18 RSA/Lesotho Liaison Committee 1981–85, Minutes of Inter-Governmental Liaison Committee Meeting, Maseru, 17 November 1982.

37. Phyllis Naidoo, *Le Rona Re Batho: An Account of the 1982 Maseru Massacre* (Verulam: P. Naidoo, 1992).

38. Mohokare Trust Archives, Ladybrand, South Africa (hereafter MTA), Lesotho Newspaper Clippings, Oct.-Dec. 1983, "A Warning for Mountaineers," *The Friend* (Bloemfontein), 5 October 1983.

39. MTA, Lesotho Newspaper Clippings, July-Sept 1984, "Climbers Shot at in Lesotho Mountains," *Star* (Johannesburg), 1 August 1984.

40. Robert Edgar "The Lesotho Coup of 1986," *South African Review* 4 (1988): 373–382.

41. SANA P, DCD 2904 7/2/5/2/18 Lesotho Liaison Committee 1985–1992, 8th RSA/Lesotho Intergovernmental Liaison Committee Minutes, Cape Town, 21 September 1987.

42. For detailed histories of this official view, see James Ferguson, *The Anti-Politics Machine: "Development", Depoliticization, and Bureaucratic Power in Lesotho* (Cambridge: Cambridge University Press, 1990); John Aerni-Flessner, *Dreams for Lesotho: Independence, Foreign Assistance, and Development* (Notre Dame: Notre Dame University Press, 2018).

43. LNA MT 1/C/CUS/Intergov/II/2/I Intergovernmental/Liaison Committee, Minutes of the Kingdom of Lesotho/RSA 10th Intergovernmental Liaison Committee Held at Golden Gate, 15 November 1989.

44. Interview DA, Ladybrand, South Africa. Interview conducted by John Aerni-Flessner, 28 October 2021.

45. Aaron Motsoaledi: "Border Management Authority Bill and Home Affairs capacity during festive season." Media Briefing: 11 February 2020. https://www.gov.za/speeches/minister-aaron-motsoaledi-border-management-authority-bill-and-home-affairs-capacity-during, accessed 20 June 2022.

46. Interview focus group with three participants, informant MM1, Nkululekong—Skete, Matatiele, South Africa. Interview conducted by Grey Magaiza and Tokoloho Lephoto, 22 October 2021.

47. See the chapter by Twala and Magaiza as well as the one by Mushonga and Cawood in this volume for a more robust discussion of *paqama*.

48. Interview with Cobra, Taxi Driver, Paqama Spot, Qacha's Nek, Lesotho. Interview conducted by Grey Magaiza and Tokoloho Lephoto, 23 October 2021.

49. Interview with Cobra, 23 October 2022.

50. Interview Tourist Operator, Matatiele, South Africa. Interview conducted by John Aerni-Flessner, Tokoloho Lephoto, and Mamollo Sebolao, 21 October 2021.

51. Interview DM, Nkululekong, Matatiele, South Africa. Interview conducted by Grey Magaiza and Tokoloho Lephoto, 22 October 2022.

52. Interview DM, Nkululekong, 22 October 2022.

53. Interview fifty-nine-year-old man, Makhalong, Qacha's Nek, Lesotho. Interview conducted by Maneo Ralebitso, 15 November 2021.

54. Büscher notes that conservation processes, such as the creation of the Maloti-Drakensberg Transfrontier Park along much of the border discussed in this chapter, have tended to elide dissenting views in the same way to foreclose alternative realities in the name of consensus politics. He attributes this to neoliberalism at work. Bram Büscher, *Transforming the Frontier: Peace Parks and the Politics of Neoliberal Conservation in Southern Africa* (Durham: Duke University Press, 2013): xiii.

55. Interview fifty-nine-year-old man, Makhalong, Lesotho, 15 November 2021.

BIBLIOGRAPHY

Aerni-Flessner, John. *Dreams for Lesotho: Independence, Foreign Assistance, and Development.* Notre Dame: Notre Dame University Press, 2018.

Aerni-Flessner, John, Chitja Twala, Munyaradzi Mushonga, and Grey Magaiza. "A Transnational History of Stock Theft on the Lesotho-South Africa Border, Nineteenth Century to 1994." *South African Historical Journal* 73, no. 4 (2021): 903–926.

Barnard, Leo, Jan-Ad Stemmet, and Stephen Semela. "The Battle of Namoha, Qwaqwa (1950): An Oral History Perspective." *Southern Journal for Contemporary History* 30, no. 3 (2005): 183–198.

Basutoland 1956 Population Census, 8th April 1956. Maseru: Basutoland Government, 1958.

Büscher, Bram. *Transforming the Frontier: Peace Parks and the Politics of Neoliberal Conservation in Southern Africa*. Durham: Duke University Press, 2013.

Carruthers, Jane. "The Royal Natal National Park, KwaZulu-Natal: Mountaineering, Tourism, and Nature Conservation in South Africa's First National Park c. 1896 to c. 1947." *Environment and History* 19, no. 4 (2013): 459–486.

Colman, James. *Sani Pass: Revealing Its Secrets*. Pietermaritzburg: Otterley Press, 2016.

Crush, Jonathan, and Paul Wellings. "The South African Pleasure Periphery, 1966–1983." *Journal of Modern African Studies* 21, no. 4 (1983): 673–698.

Dlamini, Jacob. *Safari Nation: A Social History of the Kruger National Park*. Athens: Ohio University Press, 2020.

Duval, Melanie, and Benjamin Smith. "Rock Art Tourism in the uKhahlamba/Drakensberg World Heritage Site: Obstacles to the Development of Sustainable Tourism." *Journal of Sustainable Tourism* 21, no. 1 (2013): 134–153.

Edgar, Robert. "The Lesotho Coup of 1986." *South African Review* 4 (1988): 373–382.

Ferguson, James. *The Anti-Politics Machine: "Development", Depoliticization, and Bureaucratic Power in Lesotho*. Cambridge: Cambridge University Press, 1990.

Grab, Stefan, and Jonathan Linde. "Regional Contrasts in Mountain Tourism Development in the Drakensberg, South Africa." *Mountain Research and Development* 28, no. 1 (2008): 65–71.

Hoag, Colin. *The Fluvial Imagination: On Lesotho's Water-Export Economy*. Berkeley: University of California Press, 2022.

Hoag, Colin. "The Ovicaprine Mystique: Livestock Commodification in Postindustrial Lesotho." *American Anthropologist* 120, no. 4 (2018): 725–737.

MacArthur, Julie. *Cartography and the Political Imagination: Mapping Community in Colonial Kenya*. Athens: Ohio University Press, 2016.

Machobane, L.B.B.J. *Government and Change in Lesotho, 1800–1966: A Study of Political Institutions*. London: Macmillan, 1990.

Macmillan, Hugh. *Chris Hani*. Athens: Ohio University Press, 2021.

McVean, Donald N. *Nature Conservation in Lesotho: Report on Current Progress and Forward Planning*. Morges: International Union for the Conservation of Nature, 1977.

Motsoaledi, Aaron. "Border Management Authority Bill and Home Affairs capacity during festive season." Media Briefing, 11 February 2020. https://www.gov.za/speeches/minister-aaron-motsoaledi-border-management-authority-bill-and-home-affairs-capacity-during accessed 20 June 2022.

Murray, Colin, and Peter Sanders. *Medicine Murder in Colonial Lesotho: The Anatomy of a Moral Crisis*. Edinburgh: Edinburgh University Press, 2005.

Musoni, Francis. *Border Jumping and Migration Control in Southern Africa*. Bloomington: Indiana University Press, 2020.

Naidoo, Phyllis. *Le Rona Re Batho: An Account of the 1982 Maseru Massacre*. Verulam: P. Naidoo, 1992.

Nthunya, Mpho 'M'atsepo. *Singing Away the Hunger: The Autobiography of an African Woman*. Bloomington: Indiana University Press, 1997.

Nyeko, Balam. "Resistance to Colonial Rule and the Emergence of Anti-Colonial Movements." In *Essays on Aspects of the Political Economy of Lesotho 1500–2000* edited by Neville Pule and Motlatsi Thabane, 131–152. Roma: Institute of Southern African Studies, 2002.

Pearse, R.O. *Barrier of Spears: Drama of the Drakensberg*. Cape Town: H. Timmins, 1973.

Pierce, Daniel S. *Great Smokies: From Natural Habitat to National Park*. Knoxville: University of Tennessee Press, 2015.

Rademeyer, Cobus, and W. van Zyl. "Golden Jubilee for Golden Gate—A Concise History of Golden Gate Highlands National Park, 1963 to 2013." *Mediterranean Journal of Social Sciences* 5, no. 27 (2014): 1169–1177.

Smith, Janet, and Beauregard Tromp. *Hani: A Life Too Short*. Johannesburg: Jonathan Ball Publishers, 2010.

Slater, Rachel. "Between a Rock and a Hard Place: Contested Livelihoods in Qwaqwa National Park, South Africa." *The Geographical Journal* 168, no. 2 (2002): 116–129.

Weitzberg, Karen. *We Do Not Have Borders: Greater Somalia and the Predicaments of Belonging in Kenya*. Athens: Ohio University Press, 2017.

Chapter 3

Posted Passports and Fake Stamps

Documented Mobility, Invisibility, and the Informal Enforcement of South Africa's Border with Zimbabwe

Xolani Tshabalala

On August 14, 2019,[1] South Africa's new head of the domestic branch of the State Security Agency (SSA), Mahlodi Muofhe, again sought to make a direct connection between the country's so-called porous borders, undocumented migrants, and threats to domestic security.[2] Although he is not the first senior government figure to stoke a public fire that has seen hundreds of foreigners—often called "illegal aliens"—murdered and thousands more displaced across the country in recent years, he is one of several public figures that turn a blind eye to the fact that a significant number of "illegalized" migrants arrive and exit South Africa with valid entry visas.[3] The understanding that this chapter adopts toward illegalization is one coined by Bauder to refer to the role state institutions play to make people illegal.[4] Such an understanding is helpful in exploring illegalization as a process that often gets concealed by such terms as "unauthorized," "clandestine," "undocumented," "irregular," and *denied* (emphasis my own) migration. In line with Consoli's more recent qualification of this notion, this chapter also approaches illegalization as the ability to reside, travel, and work in a country other than one's own both by lacking the necessary authorization and through the mobilization of resources and capacities available at a personal (social capital, relations to transporters, etc) as well as contextual (ability to manipulate border enforcement systems, etc.) level.[5]

Such illegalization is therefore not a uniquely South African phenomenon. Available figures show how important visas have become as a mode of entry for illegalized migrants around the world.[6] What is of interest in the South

African case are the specific characteristics of this illegalization, and the patterns, structures, and relationships migration builds upon and shapes. At Beitbridge, a key port of entry along South Africa's northern border with Zimbabwe, illegalization sometimes appears to take on an invisible form, by which holders of international travel documents, such as passports with legitimate visa stamps, enlist the services of third parties, such as individual cross-border transport operators, regular bus drivers, and local fixers, to take passports across the border and to get them stamped on their behalf. Lacking adequate financial resources or time to extend the duration of their stay under the most accessible ninety-day visa, many Zimbabweans turn to the services of third parties who cajole immigration officers at the border to extend visa stamps on unaccompanied passports for a fee.

This phenomenon of "posted passports" inverts the lens often associated with undocumented travel. In this case, documents get to travel without their holders. Holder-less (or "posted") passports distort further the state's ability to enforce its territorial borders by decoupling the movement of people from that of the documents that identify them and register their movement. Thus, a significant portion of cross-border mobility can proceed in this invisible manner, while in the public imaginary, the media, and in political corridors, Beitbridge remains a key point for South Africa's "containment development."[7] This ideology and approach of the state toward defending its northern border against a specific group of migrants has seen the establishment of the Border Management Authority (BMA) in July 2020, with the mandate to execute "frontline border law enforcement."[8] With both Beitbridge and strict border enforcement in focus, it is pertinent to explore how so many unskilled and semi-skilled Zimbabwean travelers cross this border to stay and work in South Africa routinely beyond their ninety-day visa allocation.

This chapter uses the twin ideas of illegalization and invisibility around border enforcement to connect to broader discussions on the discretionary prerogatives, or the magic of the state[9] and its ability to see its subjects, and ultimately, from an everyday southern African perspective, to discuss the sites where people's agency encounters South African state power in the area of border enforcement.[10] It traces how cross-border travelers seeking longer stays in South Africa creatively use the ninety-day free visa for Zimbabweans and its rules to subvert border enforcement procedures. Colin Hoag has already discussed how migrants can manipulate the discretion of South Africa's immigration enforcement procedures to their ends.[11] To advance that argument, this discussion takes the example of the Beitbridge border to suggest that the manipulation of enforcement procedures, what Hoag calls the "magic of the populace," represents a strategy of invisibility that is rooted in an "acknowledged" mismatch between human mobility and attempts to manage it.[12] Available enforcement mechanisms deny and push back against the sheer magnitude of Zimbabwean travelers seeking to enter South Africa, resulting in various forms of their circulation, filtering, and rejection at the border.[13] These processes often push travelers into illegal statuses of a different kind, what this chapter advances as their illegalization. In response, travelers become creative in employing strategies of invisibility to navigate this illegalization.

The literature on borders and migration acknowledges the importance of restrictive visa policies, and their enforcement, for the illegalization of human mobility, as well as the importance of visas as a mode of illegalized migration.[14] Few scholars, however, have discussed the techniques and practices of subversion that manipulate documents and visas to both aid and counter modes of illegalization in recent southern African mobility studies.[15] Of note is how posted passports work on the logic of a symbolic fake visa, represented by a stamp issued on a passport whose holder is absent. This manipulation of both documents and their associated border enforcement techniques, this chapter argues, helps to move migrants in and out of legal status as much as keeps them in a loop of illegalization. While attempting to navigate a restrictive regime of border enforcement through strategies of invisibility, the logic of the fake stamp or visa equally demonstrates how such invisibility achieves short-term mobility gains, while keeping migrants trapped in an ongoing cycle of vulnerability and precarity.[16] The invisibility symbolized by posted passports and fake stamps has implications for our understanding of how borders function and exposes the border as a site where migrant labor precarity in a regional neoliberal regime of migration governance is uncovered.

This chapter is based on ethnographic fieldwork I conducted while I accompanied cross-border private transporters, locally known as *omalayitsha* (plural: transporters) between South Africa and Zimbabwe between 2014 and 2017 on a staggered basis. The longest uninterrupted observation period lasted four months. Participant observation and extensive conversations were conducted with five transporters, their clients, and with local fixers. Participant observation was carried out at loading and embarkment points in South Africa, along the different routes transporters use between South Africa and Zimbabwe, as well as on their delivery errands in southwestern Zimbabwe. The limitations and ethical dilemmas associated with accessing these practices and the population groups meant that only some of these observations and notes could be used. Observation was complemented by interviews with migrants who had posted their passports across the border, using the services of transporters.

THE PROMISE OF MAKING IT ACROSS THE BORDER: ILLEGALIZATION, INVISIBILITY AND THE MAKING OF SOUTH AFRICA'S BORDER ENFORCEMENT REGIME

In 2015, during the course of the fieldwork that informs this discussion, Thembelihle[17]—a young Zimbabwean woman who at the time worked in the hospitality industry in South Africa without a required permit, needed the visitors' visa on her passport extended by a few more months.[18] By utilizing a network of people that connected her to a trusted *umalayitsha* (singular), she was eventually able to post her passport to Beitbridge, the port of entry on the border with Zimbabwe, where it got stamped out of South Africa and then back in soon after. This way she was able to reside longer in South Africa legally, preserve her undocumented job, and retain a measure of control over her somewhat precarious existence in the country. In some ways, Thembelihle was lucky that her passport returned to her with the requisite official stamps. There are occasions when passports sent to the border in this way get lost. In other cases, however, they may not be processed at all, although unscrupulous *omalayitsha* and immigration officers at Beitbridge may connive to issue such passports with fake stamps.

Posted passports are one avenue some Zimbabwean migrants use to contend with the South African migration regime that robustly restricts their movement into the country.[19] In order to preserve available opportunities for precarious, often undocumented, work within the country's mining, agriculture, hospitality, domestic, and informal sectors, migrants without long-term work permits must regularly travel to the country's border posts, such as Beitbridge, to negotiate more residence days on their passports.[20] Without adequate financial resources or time to do this, many Zimbabweans who seek such extensions turn to the services of *omalayitsha* and other third parties who promise to do this on their behalf.

The phenomenon of posting passports as narrated above directs attention at two issues of importance for this discussion. The first relates to the restrictions placed on unskilled and semi-skilled Zimbabweans seeking entry into South Africa. The other is the daily volumes of people that cross the border, particularly at Beitbridge, on foot, bicycles, and motor vehicles of different kinds. While increased volumes[21] of border crossings can easily be tied to what scholars[22] have termed Zimbabwe's exodus, which was triggered by that country's economic and political decline from around the year 2000, restrictions along the border have more to do with overzealous border enforcement practices where state capacity is historically lacking and contested, and where local moral orders of non-state violence and banditry contribute to the border enforcement space.[23]

Migrants who share Thembelihle's predicament have the option to not use documents to cross the border, but instead to cross on foot away from the border post. However, as several scholars highlight, crossing the border this way is significantly more dangerous (see also Musoni's chapter in this volume for more on this).[24] Maxim Bolt has previously observed that travelers seek to avoid the violence and danger that attends the Beitbridge cross-border space by staying visible to the authorities.[25] In such declarations of dependence on the enforcement apparatus of the state for relative protection, migrants accept the illegalization that this submission engenders and prefer to navigate it instead through manipulation.[26]

In the case of Thembelihle, after she entrusted her passport with Msholozi, one of *omalayitsha* I followed extensively, she could only wait until it returned from across the border.[27] Once in possession of several such passports, however, Msholozi could either take them across as they were, or loan them out to undocumented migrants wishing to use his transport. Msholozi may otherwise have been compelled to hide such passports, only revealing them to carefully selected state officials for stamping, but he instead often called his trusted border enforcement officers while on the road to alert them to what designs he had for his bundle of passports.

Focusing on how *omalayitsha* and other middleman handle and get posted passports stamped at the border uncovers crucial but largely invisible ways in which cross-border actors use "sly civility" as a strategy of false compliance.[28] In this way, posted passport handlers use "vernacular forms of legal knowledge in which the passport is embedded."[29] Such forms of invisibility re-inscribe undocumented mobility into the border enforcement matrix, while creatively manipulating it for elementary, albeit short-lived, cross-border mobility. The phenomenon of posted passports emerges as a site where both undocumented and documented mobility and residence get entangled, while also simultaneously submitting to an invisibility that partly defines the Beitbridge borderscape.[30]

Machinations that tie Thembelihle, Msholozi, and associated state officials largely succeed because this form of mobility is rejected by the mobility governance regime that presides over the Beitbridge border. The manipulation of documents and the infrastructure that sometimes misreads human mobility persists not because manipulation is unknown, but because it is made invisible by a broader mobility governance regime of restriction. Manipulation is an outcome that Nshimbi has articulated well at the level of southern African regional mobility governance.[31] Illegalization and the invisibility that emerge from the phenomenon of posted passports highlight a disconnect between the neoliberal pull for cheap migrant labor and the securitization of the border enforced by states, on one hand, and the unenforced regional framework for governing mobility that is nonetheless overridden by a *de facto* system of regional labor migration governance that favors relatively rich economies such as South Africa.

POINT-OF-ENTRY VISA STAMPS AND THE POLITICS OF INVISIBILITY

Recent history presents a checkered past for a Zimbabwean passport entering South Africa in a regional regime of unfree migration governance. Despite progress in economic integration, the southern African region remains the only region within Africa to reject the idea of the free movement of persons within the regional economic community (REC).[32] Without a formalized migration governance framework in a region of significant informal cross-border mobility, South Africa, as the regional economic powerhouse and attractive destination for migrants, dominates a contradictory, asymmetrical, and increasingly securitized approach to migration governance.[33] Such an approach sees migrants as a threat while furnishing avenues for their exploitation as cheap labor as a matter of historical routine (see also chapters by Mushonga and Cawood, Twala and Magaiza, and Aerni-Flessner in this volume).

Meanwhile, post-independence Zimbabwe already had a strong pattern of cross-border mobility into South Africa owing to civil instability caused by state repression in the southwestern parts of the country.[34] It was, nonetheless, the revitalization of trade union politics in the late 1990s that ushered in a new era of "national dissent" that simultaneously highlighted the continued repressive elements in the regime of former president Mugabe at a time of accelerated neoliberalism that also saw the structural adjustment of the country's economy.[35] The resulting political authoritarianism and shrinking economic opportunities ushered in a prolonged crisis that has become such a characteristic feature of present-day Zimbabwe.[36]

It was within this accelerated decline of the country's political and economic situation that the number of people seeking to travel outside Zimbabwe increased significantly starting in the late 1990s and continuing into the early 2000s and beyond. The visa conditions tied to entry into South Africa and Britain, two of the most popular destinations at the time, quickly drew the spotlight to the passport as a site for various strategies of bypassing such travel conditions and possible eventual illegalization. For those travelers who could not furnish the requisite supporting information regarding their intentions to travel to and reside in prospective host countries, a common solution was often to manufacture proof of ability to visit, in lieu of an extended stay, in the form of borrowed cash or forged bank statements, improvised host addresses, next-of-kin, or even accommodation. The passport, especially in some instances where a travel visa was eventually granted, came to play the extended role of validating these half-truths.

The obfuscation did not end when the passport holder successfully acquired the first travel permissions. In the case of South Africa, the only case this chapter examines, these pretences required that the visit be officially "completed" by acquiring subsequent stamps that reflected that the traveler had crossed back into Zimbabwe before expiry of the permitted visa days. In many cases, this could and continues to be done by asking transporters to take the passports back through the border gates, where intermediaries persuade immigration officials to stamp them out of the country even in the absence of the rightful passport holders. Such forms of manipulation have progressively become entrenched at Beitbridge in the twenty-first century.

While such manipulation can appear liberative for individuals, the invisibility of cross-border mobility that it engenders further removes the ubiquity of this form of movement from official view. In southern Africa as elsewhere, a regime that pays a blind eye to the realities of regional mobility succeeds in "illegalizing" a significant proportion of migrants.[37] The enlightened ignorance regarding the mobility that Thembelihle and others who use the posted passport system embody contributes to the "machine of illegalization" that is discernible not just in southern Africa but also globally.[38]

Illegalization at the global level often manifests itself as a "paper curtain" of visa requirements that fail to reduce volumes of entry as much as it constrains mobility.[39] In South Africa, the claim that South Africa's immigration policy is ad-hoc and reactionary fails to appreciate the fact that, at a border enforcement level, an unresponsive policy has historically been both undisruptive and accommodative for cross-border mobility.[40]

In any case, when significantly more Zimbabwean travelers started crossing the border to South Africa in the mid-2000s, for instance, collaborative efforts between the two countries saw travel conditions, in the form of supporting documents, become progressively relaxed. This was partly in response to an increasing proportion of travelers who found such travel conditions too stringent and cumbersome to comply with and were therefore traveling clandestinely. Proof of financial self-sufficiency as a requisite for acquiring a travel visa, for instance, was scrapped in 2005.[41] This partial easing of the requirements of cross-border travel encouraged more people to seek passports, applying even greater pressure on the issuing offices.

By the second half of 2006, the Zimbabwean immigration department's passport issuing offices could no longer cope with the number of lodged applications, whether for new passports or for the renewal of old ones. The pressure became so great that the paper used to make passports itself started to run out, a trend that has periodically returned. In 2006, for example, Zimbabwean passport offices were not able to replenish it in sufficient quantities.[42]

Some travelers greeted such developments with cynicism. At around nineteen months, the waiting period for a regular passport, assuming the application had been accepted, was a lengthy inconvenience. Many migrants thus simply traveled without their own passport, routinely choosing to borrow passports from *omalayitsha* to get across the border.

Such practices are everyday manifestations of the failures of governance and the consequent southern African mobility that ushers Zimbabwean migrants into South Africa. Upon arrival, undocumented travelers sometimes choose to avoid arrest by claiming political asylum,[43] while others go underground.[44] A further segment of travelers illegitimately obtain authentic South African identity documents. As a way of further simplifying the conditions for documented cross-border travel, the South African Department of Home Affairs (DHA) introduced, by the end of 2009, a free ninety-day travel visa for Zimbabwean travelers, usable within a twelve-month window. Still, many Zimbabweans traveling into South Africa via Beitbridge often get two-week visas with no explanations given for why they have not received the full ninety days. In response, many take the fourteen days, but instead of returning to the border themselves, they post their passports back to Zimbabwe through *omalayitsha*. Officials on both sides of the border know about these practices, which has had the effect of making the exercise both more invisible and economically lucrative for those involved in passport stamping.

It would appear, therefore, that the relationship between the passport and mobility during Zimbabwe's last twenty years has been loosely structured around, on one hand, manipulating the strict regime of cross-border enforcement and, on the other hand, border enforcement that in South Africa is at the same time both strict and porous. The manipulation of the ninety-day visa scheme, therefore, does not render the passport irrelevant to cross-border travel. Rather, it increases its importance. The passport, in so far as it complicates the distinction between documented and undocumented travel, can be seen as the vehicle through which travelers reshape the enforcement of South Africa's border with Zimbabwe in an informal way. When I asked Msholozi if his own passport was part of the batch he intended to present to South African border officials, he responded, assuredly, that "my face is my passport." The possibility of posting passports relies on embedded relations of invisibility and proximity between migrants, transporters, and state border officials. Posted passports and the bureaucratic systems that produce and enable their possibility define the landscape of invisibility that governs migration crossings between South Africa and Zimbabwe.

With the advent of the ninety-day visitors' visa in 2009, as well as the possibility to get work permits if migrants could prove employment status, a renewed importance was attached to the passport. After 2009, however, other policy shifts also came to regulate movement in and out of South Africa. For instance, a previous moratorium on the arrest of undocumented Zimbabweans living and working in South Africa was lifted in 2011. This was after the year 2010, during which several Zimbabwean consulates in South Africa started to issue passports for their nationals. In general, the pressure on the application and waiting times for Zimbabwean passports was, thus, eased, but at the same time robust arrests of undocumented migrants resumed.[45] However, while this signalled a desire by state authorities to recouple regulative processes to movement patterns—thus aligning documents back to their stated purpose—not all Zimbabweans living in South Africa applied for or received work permits; that is, they did not become fully visible to the state.

Nevertheless, by granting thousands of permits to Zimbabweans working in South Africa, the so-called Zimbabweans' Dispensation Project (ZDP) brought an estimated 250,000 people out of the shadows and into the realm of documented migrant.[46] This represents one of the most comprehensive attempts in recent times to create an avenue for Zimbabweans traveling to, living in, or working in South Africa, to be visible to state bureaucracies,[47] and be amenable to their control.[48] Nevertheless, some of those who participated in this project, as well as others who did not, have failed to fulfill all or some of the conditions set for documented travel. The critical difference has been that while those with jobs did get work permits with possibilities for multiple entry, those who did not now fall within only the ninety-day visitor's visa category. Thus, they have been left with little other choices than to continue to find creative strategies, what some have called "forced fraud," to evade or bypass the demands for and compliance with immigration and border enforcement.[49]

It is in this context that South African border enforcement presides over a tough migration governance regime that, however, can be manipulated in equal measures. The possibility of employment and trade immediately across the border tends to import the logic of managing employed and trading migrants to border management, which is mainly structured along totalistic lines, and sometimes in paternalistic ways.[50] A pertinent question therefore also relates not just to the incentive for keeping undocumented cross-border mobility invisible, and therefore profitable, but also to the extent to which this burgeoning border economy is part of broader migration governance across the South Africa-Zimbabwe border.

A SLAP IN THE FACE: FAKE STAMPS AND THE LIMITS OF INVISIBILITY

Practices that revolve around posted passports, because they rely on pretense and invisibility, resist official acceptance. Even if they appear creative and lend themselves to forms of resistance, they struggle to transform themselves into state-legitimized forms of cross-border mobility. As such, posted passports are doomed to remain clandestine, facilitating the kind of mobility that works in the service of illegalization. The disadvantages of posted passports are illustrated no better than by the frequency with which they attract fake stamps.

Mnyamana, another one of the many migrants who post passports through Msholozi's services, once ventured inside the South African immigration offices of the Beitbridge border to present his passport for a routine entry.[51] The immigration officer on duty informed Mnyamana that his passport had an "overstay," meaning that he had previously overstayed his visa-allocated days in South Africa. Astonished, Mnyamana tried to argue, in vain, that he had never breached immigration requirements. After spending a few hours in detention, he was escorted back to Zimbabwe, with a five-year ban on entering South Africa freshly stamped on his passport.

Whereas posted passports sometimes get genuine and verifiable entry and exit stamps, when transporters and state officials conspire to withhold these, operators can instead get passports validated only with fake stamps. Fake stamps are neither registered in the digitized immigration databases in which every South African border official is supposed to log entries and departures from the country, nor can they be traced to the actual officers who issued them. When posted passports arrive at the border, part of the fee *omalayitsha* pocket is given to chosen immigration officials, who then issue stamps on the presented passports and return them to private transporters. Fake stamps in passports mean that this line of communication and trust has been breached at some point.

This breach means that apart from the financial motive, other relationships drive the stamping of bunches of passports whose holders are miles away from the visa queue. *Omalayitsha* rely on certain officials, who work at certain times, and are willing to risk their jobs by issuing visa stamps for a fee. It goes without saying that migrants who post passports wish for nothing other than for their prized documents to return to their possession with newly valid permission to stay in South Africa. Nevertheless, officials who issue fake stamps on posted passports often cover the part of the stamp that will give them away, should there be official suspicion of the passports. If such suspicion were to be aroused, an investigation can, for instance, match the stamp to the official who used it in a specific office and given time. Officials who issue fake stamps will usually take care to cover the number that reflects the stamp prints on a passport (see figure 3.1). When a passport receives a fake stamp, *omalayitsha* would say that the owner of that passport has been given "a slap in the face," or *bamtshaye ngempama*.

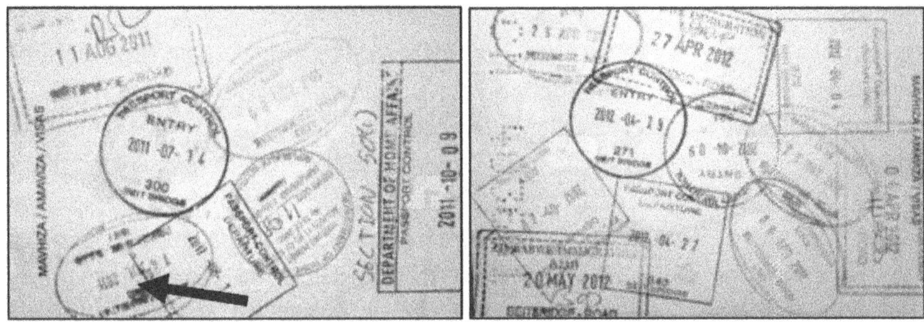

Figure 3.1 The Two Images Above Show Ordinary Immigration Stamp Imprints on a Passport for Entry and Exit at the Beitbridge Border. The image on the left includes a fake stamp on the bottom center. *Source*: Photograph by author.

A slap in the face offers a good opportunity to problematize interactions and relations between "street-level" or front-desk border officials, *omalayitsha,* and other intermediaries, and the holders of posted passports. Msholozi was keen to point out that *omalayitsha* who allow fake stamps on the passports of their clients are unscrupulous and smear hard-working transporters who insist on genuine stamps, like him. He felt that genuine *omalayitsha* "fight" for their clients, and they treat them with respect and care, and should never take people's money only to ruin their documents and newly "legalized" status. For that reason, he often kept posted passports in the body of his car until he could find the right immigration official to stamp them for him.

This attitude comes with the risk of misplacing the passports, increasing the potential for getting caught with holder-less passports should he be searched by security officials, or straining his relationships with anxious passport owners. Nevertheless, Msholozi preferred to accept these risks rather than jeopardize his business by being "deceptive," a catch-all category that included accepting actual fake stamps. He presented himself as an honest mediator in an inherently compromised system.

Fake stamps, the so-called slap in the face, underline the contested nature of immigration enforcement practices, relationships, and allegiances, and the place of make-believe in immigration enforcement. At the level of border crossings, faking compliance manipulates visa rules, while at the same time embracing local and conflicting moral border-crossing norms that undermine those same rules. Internal contestations around the manipulation of visa stamps uncover the layering of unpredictable alliances that characterize practices of invisibility around the border. Nevertheless, these internal contestations also represent pathways of fragmentary resistance that reflect how individual actors across the border enforcement spectrum encounter immigration and border enforcement at an everyday level. The pretense around faking and issuing visa stamps shows how mobility governance in the region is sometimes dictated by the means, methods, and practices that convert mobility control into mechanisms that allow for its illegalization.

Illegalization, therefore, creates avenues for forms of fraud that see the entanglement of state officials, middlemen, and migrants working together in a quasi-clandestine manner to manufacture border crossings, creating legality out of illegality.[52] Nevertheless, part of the hotbed of pretense that characterizes illegalization at Beitbridge stems from a migration governance regime that does not champion the "free movement of people" in a manner similar to that of the European Union (EU) and, to some degree, the Economic Community of West African States (ECOWAS) and the Common Market for East African States (COMESA) migration corridors do. Instead, border enforcement in southern Africa appears imbued with closure rather than facilitation, where border systems appear suspicious of people rather than facilitating their mobility.

This observation compels the proposition that border enforcement procedures can elicit a contrary reaction from those who interact with them. They can limit, rather than accelerate, complicate rather than ease, mobility. In southern Africa, they speak a language of colonization, subjugation, and domination. Their enforcement often reflects a legacy of negative surveillance and policing. In effect, they are also a source of anxiety and angst for regular border crossers. Such apprehension manifests itself in the ways migrants experience bureaucratic discretion, the outcomes of which seldom favor the poor.[53] Migrant suspicion is well-founded, because manipulation and strict enforcement eventually lead to encounters that illegalize migrants, and often punish their mobility as well.

For instance, a "slap in the face" worsens the problems that already attend a posted passport. The next time such a passport passes through the border, usually with its rightful owner accompanying it, the system will pick up the fact that the owner has previously engaged in a transgression. The overstay will persist in official records, the penalties will increase, and the money paid to fix the passport would have been in vain. In short, the holder, likely already a precarious migrant, will slide further into their precarity.

A "slap in the face" also introduces another dimension to the limitations of invisibility. In a general context of make-believe around visa stamps, those who are caught violating the laws around posted passports cannot plead innocence. Rastaman, a Zimbabwean national who has traveled repeatedly to South Africa by means of *omalayitsha*, sometimes without documents, explained how he understood the acceptability of the phenomenon of posted passports. After saying he often sent his passport to be stamped out of South Africa whenever his visa expired while he remained in South Africa, he went on to detail his experience of living without a residence visa and crossing the border without a passport.

> The danger is ever-present, my friend, it's always there. But, only in the law. . . . But then, one must learn to evade the law. They most likely will arrest you when they catch you, but until such a time arrives, it means you can thrive. Even when I cross the border, if I manage to avoid questions about my passport, then there is no story. If they should find a way to put me in a corner regarding the status or whereabouts of my passport, then that means I have been caught.[54]

Rastaman also justified the logic of invisibility in the following way:

> Of course, people break the law. We *must* break the law! But the law puts us in a position where we are left little choice but to break it. Is that wrong? If you don't give a person a passport (*or a permit*), don't expect that person to sit around and do nothing until you feel like it (*honouring the requirements for documented travel*). People will always find a way to travel (*even if it means evading legal requirements*). But *omalayitsha* are better placed to deal with the law on our behalf. They understand the border.[55]

It is such invisibility that perpetuates relationships that form around the manipulation of the ninety-day visa, and pushes migrants into illegalization. On one hand, it is not just migrants, but also state officials, local fixers, and other third parties that are drawn toward this collective illegalization. Certainly, for migrants who are unable to acquire the necessary documentation for travel and work in South Africa, practices of invisibility remain an important option. However, because no one takes any responsibility for such practices in the face of direct official denial, and especially because even migrants approach invisibility as less hazardous than undocumented travel itself, posted passports retain some viability for all involved. As an element of the magic of the state, however, the "slap in the face" dramatizes the precarity of this option, whereby the fake stamp fails to afford any real escape from the gaze of the state and from productive migrant labor, even if it stands as an alibi for the stalled life, broken mobility promises, and entrenched precarity that characterize the lives of many migrants.

ILLEGALIZATION AND MOBILITY GOVERNANCE BETWEEN SOUTH AFRICA AND ZIMBABWE

Those involved in cross-border transportation are primarily driven by financial gain. However, the transport also relates to sly civility, and poses important questions about the nature of migration governance in the region. Some scholars have discussed the disconnect between the wish to bring southern African regional mobility within a free movement protocol in the same way that underpins mobility in both east and west Africa, as well as in the EU regions, and the historically conditioned segregative mobility governance regime currently defining the region.[56] If southern African goods, money, and information travel relatively freely, why is it so difficult for people to move in a similar way? In the region, this question has broader governance resonance.

The possibility for mobility to involve various middlemen is testimony to the structural challenges that shape regional mobility governance in general. When asked to reflect on his middleman position in facilitating posted passports, Msholozi threw the question back at me. "What do you think?" he asked, before offering a meandering answer. He pointed out that it was not his making that people needed the help of transporters like him to resolve their passport and visa stamp difficulties. When challenged that he was himself not reluctant to receive the money his customers were offering, and that in fact he had a lot of leeway to charge them what he wished, he disclosed a tapestry of networked individuals who inevitably each take a bit of the money that he charges migrants, money that drives the phenomenon of invisibility itself.

Invisibility is a strategy of the weak, but it is present across Beitbridge largely because it challenges cross-border mobility that is curtailed rather than encouraged.[57] The decline of Zimbabwe's economy is of course a factor regarding how the resulting increase in border crossings is presently managed. But there is historical precedent to how South Africa responds to migrants seeking refuge and economic shelter at its doors. Nshimbi,[58] Pophiwa,[59] and Moyo,[60] agree that there is a contradiction between how SADC wishes to regulate regional mobility, and how rich states like South Africa slow-walk toward those agreements. We have, therefore, the willingness to liberate mobility at the regional policy level, but that goodwill must deal with resistance from elements in South Africa that benefit from the illegalization of mobility.

The borderscape in which Thembelihle, Msholozi, Mnyamana, and South African state officials and capital operate can be explained in both Marxist and neoliberal frames, and in how the interplay between the two fashion a contradictory mobility regime between South Africa and Zimbabwe, with which everyday mobility must live.[61] On one hand, Marxists accept that poor Zimbabweans follow the route of labor migration as a matter of historical dispossession, as cheap labor, seeking better opportunities across the border. On the other hand, in opposition to a Marxist view, a neoliberal justification for border crossings at Beitbridge suggests that people get caught up in a system that views them as simple, exploitable labor.

Omalayitsha and their place in the cross-border mobility space therefore furnish a governance perspective on posted passports and the kind of mobility they create. Just like other middlemen, *omalayitsha* operate in relationships of illegalization in which they often position themselves as invisible figures who redistribute state resources to those without access in ways that nevertheless work through an invisibility logic. It is this identity and role of *omalayitsha* that further imbues the practices of invisibility with the primary element of "illegalization." Some approaches to this handling of posted passports have drawn attention to mobility as a domain where different forms of opportunism "grease the engines of international migration."[62] The phenomenon of posted passports thus directs analysis to a part of the cross-border mobility that makes up this broader international migration borderscape.

Omalayitsha like Msholozi are proof that a difficult southern African mobility borderscape forces people to pay a premium on posted passports and is worth discussing regarding regional mobility governance. The remaining challenge, and one which demands regional eyes, is how to fashion regional migration governance mechanisms in the service of regular migrants who daily appear at the border, both trying to cross legally and in the company of *omalayitsha*.

CONCLUSION

Scholars have previously demonstrated how, by following the lives of documents and by paying attention to the bureaucratic practices and processes they travel through, it is possible to catch a glimpse of some of the complex and changing meanings that documents take on.[63] This chapter proposes that the illegalization of a section of Zimbabweans compels us to think not just about the strategies migrants use to challenge their own precarious states but also the place of illegalization in southern African border studies.

Documents obviously play a big role in border enforcement, but how they move and get handled plays an even greater role for the understanding of mobility, where the rules are set up to discourage the poor. In tracing the practices that place posted passports at the center of strategies of invisibility, this discussion joins other voices that have exposed a disequilibrium regarding the southern African mobility governance regime. The chapter looked at invisibility as a weapon of the weak but conceded that there is little that invisibility avails for legitimation with the state. While some scholars suggest that movement is capable of constructing its own pathways beyond those imposed from above by states, the consequences the analysis of such pathways have for the understandings of illegalization need further debate.[64]

The phenomenon of posted passports suggests an ongoing entanglement of enforcement procedures and their discretionary, negotiated, and sometimes manipulative implementation by border officials. Such entanglement, or contestation, comes about from and generates conditions of subversion that this chapter has approached as practices of both illegalization and invisibility. The ways in which such "practices of contestation by the governed play a role in the transformation of regimes of government" suggest, at least at Beitbridge, that illegalization and its manipulation through strategies of invisibility produce an illusion of mobility that benefits the state, private capital, and regular migrant laborers in their own different, and often contradictory ways.[65]

This chapter proposes that in contexts like Beitbridge, where formal regulations on movement exist in a contradictory entanglement with the reality of movement to the degree that even state actors see through the pretense, migrants do not need to act unilaterally to appropriate such restrictions. They can do so, however, in collusion with other actors, including facilitators and state employees themselves. Therefore, the manipulation of South Africa's ninety-day visa regime at Beitbridge needs to be understood not so much as an escape from state-led enforcement processes. The very fact that the passport establishes grounds for cross-border movement and various strategies of its own manipulation suggests that clandestine movement is a direct property of governance of movement through which such enforcement exists.

NOTES

1. This chapter is made possible with the financial assistance of Kungligavetenskapsakademien and REMESO, Linköping University.

2. Prince Mangosuthu Buthelezi, the first Home Affairs minister in post-apartheid South Africa, is remembered for his explicitly anti-immigrant policies. After him, many others have followed suit, including Zulu King Goodwill Zwelithini, and current president Cyril Ramaphosa; "Porous borders biggest threat to domestic security in SA: new spy boss," *TimesLive,* 14 August 2019. https://www.timeslive.co.za/news/south-africa/2019-08-14-porous-borders-biggest-threat-to-domestic-security-in-sa-new-spy-boss/

3. Harald Bauder, "Why We Should Use the Term Illegalized Migrant," RCIS Research Brief No. 2013/1, Toronto: Ryerson Center for Immigration & Settlement, 1–7; Stephan Scheel, "'The Secret is to Look Good on Paper': Appropriating Mobility within and against a Machine of Illegalization," in *The Borders of Europe: Autonomy of Migration, Tactics of Bordering*, ed. Nicholas De Genova (Durham: Duke University Press, 2017), 37–62.

4. Bauder, "Illegalized Migrant."

5. Liala Consoli, Claudine Burton-Jeangros, and Yves Jackson, "Transitioning out of Illegalization: Cross-border Mobility Experiences," *Frontiers in Human Dynamics.* 4:915940 (2022): 1–18.

6. See, for instance, Scheel, "Look Good on Paper," 37; Peter Andreas, *Border Games, Policing the US-Mexico Divide* (New York: Cornell University Press, 2000), 100; Nando Sigona and Vanessa Hughes, *No Way Out, No Way In: Irregular Migrant Children and Families in the UK* (Oxford: ESRC Centre on Migration, Policy and Society, 2012), 6; International Organization for Migration, *World Migration Report 2010. The Future of Migration: Building Capacities for Change* (Geneva: IOM, 2010), 29. https://publications.iom.int/system/files/pdf/wmr_2010_english.pdf (Accessed 28 February 2023).

7. Understood in line with Landau's exposition, containment development has the twin goals of coercive control and furnishing potential mobility destinations as unwelcoming, thus encouraging migrants to stay at "home." See Loren Landau, "A Chronotope of Containment Development: Europe's Migrant Crisis and Africa's Reterritorialisation," *Antipode* 51, no. 1 (2019): 169–186.

8. https://bma.gov.za/about-us/

9. Michael Taussig, *The Magic of the State* (London: Routledge, 2013).

10. James Scott, *Seeing like a State: How Certain Schemes to Improve the Human Condition have Failed* (New Haven & London: Yale University Press, 1999).

11. Colin Hoag, "The Magic of the Populace: An Ethnography of Illegibility in the South African Immigration Bureaucracy," *PoLAR* 33, no. 2 (2010): 6–25.

12. Christopher Nshimbi has explored how the migration governance regime in southern Africa proceeds along a formalized unofficial regional legislative governance framework that runs parallel to a non-multilateral system of regional labor migration governance that is tailored to the needs of rich countries like South Africa, "(Ir)relevant Doctrines and African Realities: Neoliberal and Marxist Influences on Labour Migration Governance in Southern Africa," *Third World Quarterly* 43, no. 7 (2022): 1728.

13. Thomas Nail, *Theory of the Border* (New York: Oxford University Press, 2016).

14. See, for instance, Nicholas De Genova, *The Borders of Europe: Autonomy of Migration, Tactics of Bordering* (Durham: Duke University Press, 2017); Scheel, "Look Good on Paper"; Consoli, "Transitioning out of Illegalization."

15. Hoag, "Magic of the Populace"; Xolani Tshabalala, "Hyenas of the Limpopo: The Social Politics of Undocumented Movement across South Africa's Border with Zimbabwe" (PhD Diss., Linköping University, 2017).

16. Standing coined the term "precariat" to refer to a class of people that face economic insecurity, move in and out of jobs, and lead a life that has little meaning for them. Schierup engages in a robust discussion on how precarity is largely driven by poverty, inequality, and unemployment, problems that are a particular property of the migrant labor system and have historical roots in the southern African case. Guy Standing, *The Precariat: The New Dangerous Class* (London: Bloomsbury, 2011); Carl-Ulrick Schierup, "Under the Rainbow: Migration, Precarity, and People Power in Post-Apartheid South Africa." *Critical Sociology* 42, no. 7–8 (2016): 1051–1068.

17. All names in the chapter have been changed.

18. I met Thembelihle at a popular loading spot for private transporters in Johannesburg during routine participant observation in February 2015. After explaining my

presence there, she agreed to share her documentation needs, and we kept in touch for a while afterward.

19. Darshan Vigneswaran, *Free Movement and the Movement's Forgotten Freedoms: South African Representations of Undocumented Migrants,* RSC Working Paper 41 (Oxford: Refugee Studies Centre, 2007).

20. Shireen Hassim, Tawana Kupe, and Eric Warby, *Go Home or Die Here: Violence, Xenophobia, and the Reinvention of Difference in South Africa* (Johannesburg: Wits University Press, 2008).

21. Estimates place daily crossings at about 25,000 persons. See Ray Ndlovu, "Upgrade of One of Africa's Busiest Border Points to Cause Delays," *Bloomberg*, 2 May 2021.

22. Jonathan Crush, and Daniel Tevera, "Exiting Zimbabwe," in *Zimbabwe's Exodus: Crisis, Migration, Survival*, eds., Jonathan Crush and Daniel Tevera (Cape Town: SAMP, 2010).

23. For a nuanced discussion on local moral orders that may include non-state forms of violence, see, for instance, Maxim Bolt, "Waged Entrepreneurs: Policed Informality: Work, the Regulation of Space and the Economy of the Zimbabwe-South Africa Border." *Africa*, 82, no. 1 (2012): 111–130; Karl von Holdt, "Institutionalisation, Strike Violence and Local Moral Orders," *Transformation* 72/73 (2010): 127–151.

24. Inocent Moyo, "On Borders and the Liminality of Undocumented Zimbabwean Migrants in South Africa," *Journal of Immigrant and Refugee Studies* 18, no. 1 (2020): 60–74; Inocent Moyo and German Mafindo Moyo, "Sustaining Family Ties Across the Border: Unaccompanied Child Migration Across the Botswana-Zimbabwe and South Africa-Zimbabwe Borders," in *Borders, Sociocultural Encounters and Contestations: Southern African Experiences in Global View*, eds. Christopher Nshimbi, Inocent Moyo, and Jussi Laine (London: Routledge, 2021); Inocent Moyo and Jussi Laine, "Precarity of Borders and Migration Regimes in the Southern African Region," in *Intra-Africa Migrations: Reimaging Borders and Migration Management*, eds. Christopher Nshimbi, Inocent Moyo, and Jussi Laine (London: Routledge, 2021).

25. Bolt, "Waged Entrepreneurs."

26. James Ferguson, "Declarations of Dependence: Labour, Personhood, and Welfare in Southern Africa," *Journal of the Royal Anthropological Institute* 19, no. 2 (2013): 223–242.

27. I first met Msholozi in Johannesburg March 2014, at the beginning of the fieldwork that informs this study, through a research respondent in the same study. Msholozi would eventually become one of the main transporters that I conducted participant observations with up to the end of the study in 2017.

28. Homi Bhabha, *The Location of Culture* (New York: Routledge, 1994); Peter Nyers, "Migrant Citizenships and Autonomous Mobilities," *Migration, Mobility and Displacement*, 1, no. 1 (2015): 29.

29. Heath Cabot, "The Governance of Things: Documenting Limbo in the Greek Asylum Process," *PoLAR*, 35, no. 1 (2012): 20.

30. Chiara Brambilla, "Exploring the Critical Potential of the Borderscapes Concept," *Geopolitics* 20, no. 1 (2014): 14–34.

31. Nshimbi, “(Ir)relevant doctrines.”

32. Christopher Nshimbi and Lorenzo Fioramonti, “The Will to Integrate: South Africa’s Responses to Regional Migration from the SADC Region,” *African Development Review* 26, no. S1 (2014): 52–63.

33. Nshimbi, ”(Ir)relevant doctrines,” 1737; Khangelani Moyo and Franzisca Zanker, “Political Contestations Within South African Migration Governance,” Deutsche Stiftung Friedensforschung, 2020.

34. Zimbabwe attained majority rule from the white settler government in 1980. For an extended discussion on political disturbances in Southwest Zimbabwe, see Lena Reim, "‘Gukurahundi Continues’: Violence, Memory, and Mthwakazi Activism in Zimbabwe," *African Affairs* 122, no. 486 (2023): 95–117.

35. Brian Raftopoulos, “Trade Unions, Labour, and Politics in Zimbabwe since the Late 1990s,” in *The Oxford Handbook of Zimbabwean Politics*, eds. Miles Tendi, JoAnn McGregor, and Jocelyn Alexander (Oxford: Oxford University Press, 2020), 1–25.

36. Joe Sutcliffe, “Shinga Mushandi, Shinga! Qina Msebenzi, Qina! (Workers be Resolute! Fight On!). The Labour Movement in Zimbabwe 1980–2012,” *Journal of Politics and International Studies* 8 (2012): 1–42.

37. De Genova, *Borders of Europe,* Introduction.

38. Scheel, “Look Good on Paper.”

39. Sandra Lavanex and Emek Uçarer, “The External Dimension of Europeanization: The Case of Immigration Policies,” *Cooperation and Conflict* 39, no. 4 (2004): 417–443.

40. Aurelia Segatti and Loren Landau, *Contemporary Migration to South Africa: A Regional Development Issue* (Washington: The International Bank for Reconstruction and Development/The World Bank, 2011); Vusilizwe Thebe, “‘Two Steps Forward, One Step Back’: Zimbabwean Migration and South Africa’s Regularising Programme (the ZDP),” *Journal of International Migration and Integration* 18, no. 2(2017): 613–622.

41. “Zim, SA Travel Visas ‘To Be Scrapped,’” *Mail and Guardian*, 13 October 2005. https://mg.co.za/article/2005-10-13-zim-sa-travel-visas-to-be-scrapped.

42. ‘Zim Runs Out of Passport Ink’. *News24,* 12 December 2006. http://www.news24.com/Africa/Zimbabwe/Zim-runs-out-of-passport-ink-20061212.

43. Roni Amit, *Queue Here for Corruption: Measuring Irregularities in South Africa’s Asylum System* (Pretoria & Johannesburg: LHR and ACMS, 2015).

44. Vigneswaran, *Free Movement.*

45. Darshan Vigneswaran, Tesfalam Araia, Colin Hoag, and Xolani Tshabalala, ”Criminality or Monopoly: Informal Immigration Enforcement in South Africa,” *Journal of Southern African Studies* 36, no. 2 (2010): 465–481.

46. Sintha Chiumia and Anim van Wyk, “FACTSHEET: The New Special Dispensation Permit & What it Means for Zimbabweans in SA,” *Africa Check*, 26 September 2014. https://africacheck.org/factsheets/what-does-the-new-special-dispensation-permit-mean-for-zimbabweans-in-sa/.

47. James Scott, *Domination and the Arts of Resistance: Hidden Transcripts*. New Haven: Yale University Press, 1990.

48. Cabot, "Governance of Things."

49. Alexis Spire, *Accueillir ou reconduire: Enquete sur les guitchets de l'immigration* (Paris: Raisons d'Agir Éditions, 2009).

50. Maxim Bolt, "Making Workers Real: Regulatory Spotlights and Documentary Stepping-Stones on a South African Border Farm," *HAU, Journal of Ethnographic Theory* 7, no. 3 (2013): 305–324.

51. Mnyamana had been traveling with Msholozi on a South Africa-bound trip that I was observing in February 2015, around the time that I met Thembelihle. Msholozi later informed me that Mnyamana had eventually made it into South Africa after a week, on a borrowed passport, after which I arranged to meet him in Johannesburg.

52. Spire, *Accueillir ou reconduire.*

53. Veena Das, "Signature of the State: The Paradox of Illegibility." In *Anthropology at the Margins of the State*, eds. Veena Das and Deborah Poole (Santa Fe: SAR Press, 2004).

54. Interview with Rastaman, October 2014, Bulawayo, Zimbabwe.

55. Interview with Rastaman, October 2014, Bulawayo, Zimbabwe.

56. Nshimbi, "(Ir)relevant doctrines."

57. Scott, *Arts of Resistance.*

58. Nshimbi, "(Ir)relevant doctrines,"

59. Nedson Pophiwa, "Cashing in on Mobility: Cross-Border Shopping and the Political Economy of the Zimbabwe–South Africa Borderland," in *Migration, Cross-Border Trade and Development in Africa*, eds. Christopher Nshimbi, and Inocent Moyo Cham: Palgrave Macmillan, 2017.

60. Inocent Moyo, "COVID-19, Dissensus and de facto Transformation at the South Africa-Zimbabwe Border at Beitbridge," *Journal of Borderlands Studies* 37, no. 4 (2022): 781–804.

61. Brambilla, "Borderscapes Concept."

62. Ruben Hernandez-Leon, *The Migration Industry in the Mexico-US Migratory System* (UCLA: California Center for Population Research, 2005); Thomas Gammeltoft-Hansen and Ninna Nyberg Sorensen, *The Migration Industry and the Commercialization of International Migration* (London: Routledge, 2013).

63. Don Brenneis, "Reforming Promise," in *Documents: Artifacts of Modern Knowledge*, ed. Annelise Riles (Ann Arbor: University of Michigan Press, 2006); Cabot, "Governance of Things."

64. Nestor Rodriguez, "The Battle for the Border: Notes on Autonomous Migration, Transnational Communities, and the State," *Social Justice* 23, no. 3 (1996): 21–37; Dimitris Papadopoulos, and Vassilis Tsianos, "After Citizenship: Autonomy of Migration, Organisational Ontology and Mobile Commons," *Citizenship Studies* 17, no. 2 (2012): 178–196; Nyers, "Migrant Citizenships"; Kim Rygiel, "Governing Border Zones of Mobility Through E-borders: The Politics of Embodied Mobility," in *The Contested Politics of Mobility: Border Zones and Irregularity*, ed. Vicki Squire (London: Routledge, 2011).

65. Scheel, "Look Good on Paper," 50.

BIBLIOGRAPHY

Ahearn, Laura. “Language and Agency.” *Annual Review of Anthropology* 30 (2001): 109–137.

Amit, Roni. *Queue Here for Corruption: Measuring Irregularities in South Africa's Asylum System*. Pretoria & Johannesburg: LHR and ACMS, 2015.

Andreas, Peter. *Border Games, Policing the US-Mexico Divide*. New York: Cornell University Press, 2000.

Bauder, Harald. *Why We Should Use the Term Illegalized Migrant*. RCIS Research Brief No. 2013/1. Toronto: Ryerson Centre for Immigration and Settlement, 2013.

Bhabha, Homi. *The Location of Culture*. New York: Routledge, 1994.

Bolt, Maxim. “Making Workers Real: Regulatory Spotlights and Documentary Stepping-Stones on a South African Border Farm.” *HAU, Journal of Ethnographic Theory* 7, no. 3 (2017): 305–324.

Bolt, Maxim. “Waged Entrepreneurs: Policed Informality: Work, the Regulation of Space and the Economy of the Zimbabwe-South Africa Border.” *Africa* 82, no. 1 (2012): 111–130.

Brambilla, Chiara. “Exploring the Critical Potential of the Borderscapes Concept.” *Geopolitics*, 20, no. 1 (2014): 14–34.

Brenneis, Don. “Reforming Promise.” In *Documents: Artifacts of Modern Knowledge*, edited by Annelise Riles, 41–70. Ann Arbor: University of Michigan Press, 2006.

Cabot, Heath. “The Governance of Things: Documenting Limbo in the Greek Asylum Process.” *PoLAR*, 35, no. 1 (2012): 11–29.

Consoli, Liala, Claudine Burton-Jeangros, and Yves Jackson. “Transitioning Out of Illegalization: Cross-Border Mobility Experiences.” *Frontiers in Human Dynamics*. 4, no. 915940 (2022): 1–18.

Crush, Jonathan, and Daniel Tevera. “Exiting Zimbabwe.” In *Zimbabwe's Exodus: Crisis, Migration, Survival*, edited by Jonathan Crush and Daniel Tevera, 1–51. Cape Town: SAMP, 2010.

Chiumia, Sintha, and Anim van Wyk. “FACTSHEET: The New Special Dispensation Permit and What it Means for Zimbabweans in SA.” *Africa Check*. 26 September 2014. https://africacheck.org/factsheets/what-does-the-new-special-dispensation-permit-mean-for-zimbabweans-in-sa/.

Das, Veena. “The Signature of the State: The Paradox of Illegibility.” In V. Das & D. Poole (Eds.), *Anthropology in the Margins of the State*, edited by Veena Das and Deborah Poole, 225–252. Santa Fe: SAR Press, 2004.

De Genova, Nicholas. *The Borders of Europe: Autonomy of Migration, Tactics of Bordering*. Durham: Duke University Press, 2017.

Ferguson, James. “Declarations of Dependence: Labour, Personhood, and Welfare in Southern Africa.” *Journal of the Royal Anthropological Institute* 19, no. 2 (2013): 223–242.

Gammeltoft-Hansen, Thomas, and Ninna Nyberg Sorensen. *The Migration Industry and the Commercialization of International Migration*. London: Routledge, 2013.

Hassim, Shireen, Tawana Kupe, and Eric Warby. *Go Home or Die Here: Violence, Xenophobia, and the Reinvention of Difference in South Africa*. Johannesburg: Wits University Press, 2008.

Hernandez-Leon, Ruben. *The Migration Industry in the Mexico-US Migratory System*. UCLA: California Center for Population Research, 2005. Available online at https://escholarship.org/uc/item/3hg44330.

Hoag, Colin. "The Magic of the Populace: An Ethnography of Illegibility in the South African Immigration Bureaucracy." *PoLAR*, 33, no. 2 (2010): 6–25.

International Organization for Migration. *World Migration Report 2010. The Future of Migration: Building Capacities for Change*. Geneva: IOM, 2010.

Landau, Loren. "A Chronotope of Containment Development: Europe's Migrant Crisis and Africa's Reterritorialisation." *Antipode*, 51, no. 1 (2019): 169–186.

Lavanex, Sandra, and Emek Uçarer. "The External Dimension of Europeanization: The Case of Immigration Policies." *Cooperation and Conflict* 39, no. 4 (2004): 417–443.

Moyo, Inocent. "COVID-19, Dissensus and de facto Transformation at the South Africa–Zimbabwe Border at Beitbridge." *Journal of Borderlands Studies* 37, no. 4 (2022): 781–804.

Moyo, Inocent. "On Borders and the Liminality of Undocumented Zimbabwean Migrants in South Africa." *Journal of Immigrant and Refugee Studies* 18, no. 1 (2020): 60–74.

Moyo, Inocent, and German Mafindo Moyo. (2021). "Sustaining Family Ties Across the Border: Unaccompanied Child Migration Across the Botswana-Zimbabwe and South Africa-Zimbabwe Borders." In *Borders, Sociocultural Encounters and Contestations: Southern African Experiences in Global View*, edited by Christopher Nshimbi, Inocent Moyo, and Jussi Laine. London: Routledge, 2021.

Moyo, Inocent, and Jussi Laine. "Precarity of Borders and Migration Regimes in the Southern African Region." In *Intra-Africa Migrations: Reimaging Borders and Migration Management*, edited by Inocent Moyo, Jussi Laine, and Christopher Nshimbi. London: Routledge, 2021.

Moyo, Khangelani, and Franzisca Zanker. "Political Contestations Within South African Migration Governance." Deutsche Stiftung Friedensforschung, 2020.

Nail, Thomas. *Theory of the Border*. New York: Oxford University Press, 2016.

Nshimbi, Christopher. "(Ir)relevant Doctrines and African Realities: Neoliberal and Marxist Influences on Labour Migration Governance in Southern Africa." *Third World Quarterly* 43, no. 7 (2022): 1724–1743.

Nshimbi, Christopher, and Lorenzo Fioramonti. "The Will to Integrate: South Africa's Responses to Regional Migration from the SADC Region." *African Development Review,* 26, no. S1 (2014): 52–63.

Nyers, Peter. "Migrant Citizenships and Autonomous Mobilities." *Migration, Mobility and Displacement* 1, no. 1 (2015): 23–39.

Papadopoulos, Dimitris, and Vassilis Tsianos. "After Citizenship: Autonomy of Migration, Organisational Ontology and Mobile Commons." *Citizenship Studies* 17, no. 2 (2012): 178–196.

Pophiwa, Nedson. "Cashing in on Mobility: Cross-Border Shopping and the Political Economy of the Zimbabwe–South Africa Borderland." In *Migration, Cross-Border Trade and Development in Africa: Exploring the Role of Non-State Actors in the SADC Region*, edited by Christopher Nshimbi and Inocent Moyo, 151–190. Cham: Palgrave Macmillan, 2017.

Raftopoulos, Brian. "Trade Unions, Labour, and Politics in Zimbabwe since the Late 1990s." In *The Oxford Handbook of Zimbabwean Politics*, edited by Miles Tendi, JoAnn McGregor, and Jocelyn Alexander, 1–25. Oxford: Oxford University Press, 2020.

Reim, Lena. "'Gukurahundi Continues': Violence, Memory, and Mthwakazi Activism in Zimbabwe." *African Affairs* 122, no. 486 (2023): 95–117.

Riles, Annelise. *Documents: Artifacts of Modern Knowledge*. Michigan: University of Michigan Press, 2006.

Rodriguez, Nestor. "The Battle for the Border: Notes on Autonomous Migration, Transnational Communities, and the State." *Social Justice* 23, no. 3 (1996): 21–37.

Rygiel, Kim. "Governing Border Zones of Mobility Through E-borders: The Politics of Embodied Mobility." In *The Contested Politics of Mobility: Border Zones and Irregularity*, edited by Vicki Squire, 1–26. London: Routledge, 2011.

Scheel, Stephan. "'The Secret is to Look Good on Paper': Appropriating Mobility within and against a Machine of Illegalization." In *The Borders of Europe: Autonomy of Migration, Tactics of Bordering*, edited by Nicholas De Genova, 37–62. Durham: Duke University Press, 2017.

Schierup, Carl-Ulrick. "Under the Rainbow: Migration, Precarity, and People Power in Post-Apartheid South Africa." *Critical Sociology* 42, no. 7–8 (2016): 1051–1068.

Scott, James. *Seeing like a State: How Certain Schemes to Improve the Human Condition have Failed.* New Haven: Yale University Press, 1999.

Scott, James. *Domination and the Arts of Resistance: Hidden Transcripts.* New Haven: Yale University Press, 1990.

Segatti, Aurelia, and Loren Landau. *Contemporary Migration to South Africa: A Regional Development Issue*. Washington: The International Bank for Reconstruction and Development/The World Bank, 2011.

Sigona, Nando, and Vanessa Hughes. *No Way Out, No Way In: Irregular Migrant Children and Families in the UK.* Oxford: ESRC Centre on Migration, Policy and Society, 2012.

Spire, Alexis. *Accueillir ou reconduire: Enquete sur les guitchets de l'immigration.* Paris: Raisons d'Agir Éditions, 2008.

Standing, Guy. *The Precariat: The New Dangerous Class.* London: Bloomsbury, 2011.

Sutcliffe, Joe. "Shinga Mushandi, Shinga! Qina Msebenzi, Qina! (Workers be Resolute! Fight On!) The Labour Movement in Zimbabwe 1980–2012." *Journal of Politics and International Studies* 8 (2012): 1–42.

Taussig, Michael. *The Magic of the State*. London: Routledge, 2013.

Thebe, Vusilizwe. "'Two Steps Forward, One Step Back': Zimbabwean Migration and South Africa's Regularising Programme (the ZDP)." *Journal of International Migration and Integration* 18, no. 2 (2017): 613–622.

Tshabalala, Xolani. “Hyenas of the Limpopo: The Social Politics of Undocumented Movement across South Africa’s Border with Zimbabwe.” PhD Diss., Linköping University, 2017.

Vigneswaran, Darshan. *Free Movement and the Movement’s Forgotten Freedoms: South African Representations of Undocumented Migrants.* RSC Working Paper 41. Oxford: Refugee Studies Centre, 2007.

Vigneswaran, Darshan, Tesfalam Araia, Colin Hoag, and Xolani Tshabalala. “Criminality or Monopoly: Informal Immigration Enforcement in South Africa.” *Journal of Southern African Studies* 36, no. 2 (2010): 465–481.

von Holdt, Karl. “Institutionalisation, Strike Violence and Local Moral Orders.” *Transformation* 72/73 (2010): 127–151.

Chapter 4

Contested Borderscapes, Border Farms, and Guided Travels in Zimbabwe's Struggle for Self-Rule, 1960–1970s

Nicholas Nyachega

This chapter focuses on how the Nyafaru Farm and Tangwena people in Zimbabwe's Eastern Highlands used their border locations to fight for self-determination against Rhodesian oppression. Conceiving Nyafaru and the Tangwena area as a borderscape, this chapter underscores how local, national, and transnational ideas of and approaches toward self-determination transformed these regions into contested landscapes. The chapter contributes to and builds on a body of literature covering border/scape studies, borderlands, and Southern African liberation war scholarship. While there is a rich body of scholarship on the Zimbabwe liberation war,[1] there is an unexplored story of how farms and borderland villages became contested spaces and centers for the recruitment of guerrilla fighters and nationalist leaders, and for the prosecution of the war. The spatial and cultural dimension, including the role of farms and community-owned development cooperatives such as Nyafaru, has not been a central part of Zimbabwe's liberation war historiographies.

Since the 1980s, successive generations of scholars have illuminated various aspects of the Zimbabwean liberation war. It is apparent that most of the pioneering writings about this war largely focused on battles, biographies of generals, and autobiographies of soldiers.[2] As Bhebe and Ranger point out, other major studies coming out from the 1980s to the early 2000s explored the impact of the war on Zimbabwean peasantries, African women's war experiences, ideology, religion, and the need for healing after the war.[3]

Among the works that stand out is an anthropological study on the Tangwena people by Donald Moore, which illuminates the politics of land and racialized dispossession in colonial Zimbabwe, showing how they shaped land struggles in Tangwena territory.[4] Moore provides a critical genealogy of modes of power, subjection, and territory in the Tangwena borderlands, not only foregrounding notions of power but also extending the analytical gaze to the "spatiality of power relations and politics of positioning." For the Tangwena people, their politics of positioning included physically evading Rhodesian atrocities by crossing over to the Mozambican side of the border, as well as using formal avenues such as colonial courts and the international community to challenge the Rhodesian government's racialized and violent land displacements. Furthermore, in *Peasant Consciousness*, Terrence Ranger reveals the wartime interactions between the Tangwena spirit mediums and the peasantry.[5] Citing interviews conducted by anthropologist Anna Weinrich (also known as Sister Mary Aquina), he noted that spirit mediums directed the lives of the Tangwena people, and the members of Nyafaru Farm also respected and listened to a medium and executed its orders.[6] As soon as Nyafaru was reorganized under completely African leadership, the whole way of life became much more focused on traditional values than had ever been the case at Cold Comfort Farm, where Europeans dominated and actively shared in the lives of the youth.[7]

Following borderscape scholars, Elena Dell'Agnese and Anne-Laure Amilhat Szary, this chapter conceptualizes borderscapes as areas re/shaped by transnational flows of goods, cultures, and ideas that transcend national territories.[8] It argues that political and social ideas of self-liberation shared at Nyafaru and the entire Tangwena area transcended national territories, but they were so much grounded in the local ideas of sovereignty (*kuzvitonga*) and control of their *nyika* (the land, its boundaries, and people). Yet, the Tangwena and Nyafaru people's struggle for self-rule reveals the limits of colonial state sovereignty and the utility of state borders and patrols, as the local always challenged the state, consistently invoking discourses of indigenous sovereignty, and demonstrating the knowledge of their local boundaries in ways that contradicted the Rhodesian and Portuguese versions of boundaries, state territory, and state land. Thus, as border/scape scholar Arjan Harbers argues, the notion of borderscapes reveals the distortions imposed by the limits of sovereignty on the physical management and ownership of the land.[9]

The chapter argues that different historical contexts, shaped by the repressive Rhodesian government's brutal and racialized forced removals and "counterinsurgency" measures against Africans' fight for self-rule in the 1970s, have influenced how the Nyafaru and Tangwena people experienced and responded to colonial oppression and contributed to the prosecution of the liberation war. For instance, because of Nyafaru's proximity to Mozambique, wartime recruits came through Nyafaru. Consequently, the Rhodesian Security Forces (RSF) singled out the Nyafaru Farm as a serious threat in the eastern border area. By 1975, the Rhodesians were seriously concerned about the activities of freedom fighters, particularly in the northeastern border region, including the Tangwena, Honde Valley, and Nyamaropa areas. As reported in the *Rhodesia Herald* of February 1975, the Rhodesian government worried that "terrorists are waging war indiscriminately throughout the north-east border areas of Rhodesia."[10]

Indeed, it was Nyafaru's proximity to Mozambique and the Tangwena borderlands' "difficult" terrain that worried the Rhodesia government and its security forces. The RSF heavily patrolled this region during the liberation war, yet their patrols were not always successful. The porous nature of the border region due to its rough terrain made it difficult for the RSF to monitor and restrict the mobilities of those who desired self-determination. Since the delimitation of the Anglo-Portuguese boundary (now Zimbabwe-Mozambique) in 1891, African villagers as well as Portuguese and British colonial officials have exploited the opportunities that porous state borders provide. For the British colonial officials, the nature of the boundary often escalated governance problems as colonial officials from both the British and Portuguese "fought" about administrative issues including collecting tax from and double-taxing Africans.[11] Indeed, during the 1970s, Nyafaru Farm and the Tangwena borderlands became frontiers for self-determination for African villagers and other white collaborators such as Guy Clutton-Brock.

METHODOLOGICAL NOTE

This chapter combines archival sources and oral histories. Most of the archival research was done at the National Archives of Zimbabwe (NAZ) and Nyanga Museum between 2016 and 2022. During different fieldworks between 2015 and 2022, I co-created oral histories with men and women from the Nyafaru, Magadzire, and Tsatse areas of Nyanga. These areas are under Chief Tangwena's traditional jurisdiction. The words of the Tangwena elders enabled me to understand the role of Nyafaru Farm and the Tangwena people in the liberation war, including Mugabe's and Tekere's recruitment to Nyafaru and their guided journey across the Southern Rhodesia-Mozambique border.

I identified the individuals who shared their knowledge with me based on my prior knowledge of them and their social-political statuses in the area.[12] Growing up in Honde Valley's Chavhanga area, a walking distance from the Nyafaru area, my grandparents and elders shared different versions of liberation war stories, and that of Mugabe escaping through a window at Nyafaru. As I grew older, I knew some of these people and interacted with them informally at the dip tank meetings, and general work meetings at school. When I started doing research on Nyafaru and the Tangwena people in June 2015, Sa (Mister) Muomba became my interlocutor. As a local leader and resident, SaMuomba's presence and introductions to interviewees put many locals at ease. His wife, Amai (Mother) Muomba, then a nurse at Nyafaru Clinic, welcomed me into their home.

Two of my initial group interviews were conducted at Nyafaru Clinic with one group of men and another of women led by SaMuomba and Amai Muomba in 2015. In addition, I visited Nyafaru in 2016, 2019, 2021, and 2022. Several other interviews were conducted in Nyanga, Honde Valley in 2022. My analysis of the interviews and archival sources has, thus, occurred over a long period, allowing for a re-engagement with and revisions of my earlier questions and conclusions.

THE BIRTH OF NYAFARU FARM

In 1961, a group of African nationalists (J. Mutasa, S. Tsungo, and S. Muranda), and "white nationalists" or collaborators (G. Clutton-Brock, R. Ibot, S. Grahamme, and others) formed Nyafaru Development Community, which they later decided to turn into a farm known as Nyafaru/o.[13] As Cephas Muropa, one of the collaborators at Nyafaru recalled, Nyafaru was formed after its sister farms, Cold Comfort and St. Faith were closed by the Rhodesian government as subversive organizations under the Law-and-Order Maintenance Act of 1960.[14] When these two farms were banned, some of their members including Guy Clutton-Brock, left to start a new community farm at Nyafaru in 1961, in the Tangwena area. Upon its foundation, Nyafaru's several objectives included, "to develop, through all activities, a spirit of friendship and co-operation between people and a tradition of disciplined life and work for the common good" and "to educate people politically, socially, spiritually and economically, so as to improve the social conditions of mankind."[15]

The agricultural, educational, and health works carried out at Nyafaru's plots, secondary school, and clinic bear testimony to its members' commitment to the welfare of the people living at Nyafaru and the entire Tangwena area. Throughout the 1960s and 1970s, Nyafaru Farm became not only a model for the development and welfare of Africans living in this area but a frontier of self-determination. For instance, following the forced removals of the Tangwena people from their Gairezi homelands, most of the displaced children were accommodated at Nyafaru Farm. Consequently, the Nyafaru leaders issued a newsletter denouncing the horrible acts of the Rhodesian government, calling it a "rebel regime" in November 1969. The *Newsletter* called out the Rhodesian government, stating that:

> The main event of this year has been a crescendo of attacks on the Tangwena by the rebel regime. Rekayi and the people of the tribe are our immediate

neighbors. Their land adjoins Nyafaru; their children attend the school; their troubles are our troubles. Rekayi, the Chief, is a determined man.[16]

The late 1960s and early 1970s transformed the geopolitics at Nyafaru and the Tangwena borderlands. The colonial conditions, socio-economic and political, imposed by a brutal Rhodesian "rebel regime" pushed the associates of Nyafaru Farm and the Tangwena people to escalate their anti-colonial operations. As SaMuomba, who was the first political commissar of the Zimbabwe African National Union (ZANU) at Nyafaru Farm, remembered:

At Nyafaru, we began the work of politicizing the *povo* (civilians) and recruited many freedom fighters who used this border area as a transit zone to Mozambique in the late 1960s and 1970s. Some of our prominent recruits were Robert Mugabe and Edgar Tekere, who arrived at the farm in April 1975. By the time of their arrival, we had been forcibly moved by the Hanmer brothers from the Gairezi ranch, our ancestral homeland. Some of our people were living in the mountains and our children were here at Nyafaru. Our removal had begun in 1963, and since that time, we were fighting the colonial regime. It was a bitter struggle. In 1966, the Rhodesian regime served us with a notice and gave us the option to leave Gairezi for Gokwe, but Chief Rekayi Tangwena refused. We protested. My mother's breast was mauled by a Rhodesian police dog at the Inyanga District office while protesting. She later passed away because of the injuries. We turned Nyafaru into a fortress, a school for political education, and our home. Our advantage was that we are in the border region. When the Rhodesians burned our homes and food, we crossed the border to the Gonakudzingwa area. While many people crossed to Mozambique, others stayed at Nyafaru Farm caring for the displaced children. Because some of our members at Nyafaru were white, Mr. Kirbo, Mr. Ibot, Mr. Grahamme, and Mr. Clutton-Brock, very few Rhodesians suspected our work in coordinating the fight. Disguised as a farming community, we farmed ideas of the struggle, educated our people, and recruited many to fight.[17]

By SaMuomba's account, Nyafaru Farm was a fortress, a home, and a place for education, where ideas of the liberation of Africans were "farmed" and where the recruitment of fighters took place. It was at Nyafaru Farm that Robert Mugabe and Edgar Tekere's guided journey to Mozambique was organized in 1975. So important was Tekere and Mugabe's guided journey to Mozambique via Nyafaru that it shaped what was to become the post-colonial Zimbabwean nation.[18] Although Mugabe and Tekere journeyed together across highly patrolled and contested Tangwena borderscapes, sharing "guerilla snuff," and the "long comradely walks," the two disagreed in principle to the point that they even stayed in different tents at Gonakudzingwa.[19] Post-independence, Tekere became the harshest critic of Mugabe and formed his own opposition party, the Zimbabwe Unity Movement (ZUM), in 1989.

He fervently regarded ZUM as an antidote to the increasing corruption and human rights abuses under the Mugabe regime.[20]

NYAFARU AS A CONTESTED BORDERSCAPE

Before what has been known as the 1960s "Tangwena Land Struggle," the colonial state put in place legislations that sought to displace Africans from their homelands and to define the roles of African chiefs in lands that became known as Native Lands or Tribal Trust Lands. Rhodesia's racialized colonial displacements of the indigenous people from their ancestral lands inspired various African communities, such as the Tangwena, to organize local and transnational responses.[21]

The implementation of colonial laws such as the Land Apportionment Act of 1930 alongside settler violence combined to enable the Rhodesia colonial government to exercise "spatial discipline"—the control of land, territory, and its people. Colonial laws segregated land ownership, leading to most indigenous African homelands being turned into Crown Lands, while the lands Europeans did not desire to settle on would become Native Reserves and Tribal Trust Lands. The 1930 Act, and later the Land Tenure Act of 1969, "which became the white man's 'Magna Carta,' was to the Africans the basic law of insulting segregation, deprivation, and indignity as well as an instrument for maintaining the master-servant relationship."[22]

Through such colonial laws, the Tangwena homelands in the Gairezi area were purchased for 8,400 pounds in 1944 by a private Gairesi (distorted colonial version of Gairezi) Ranch owned by William and Charles Hanmer.[23] The two Hanmer brothers, upon their acquisition of the Gairezi lands from the Anglo-French Matabeleland company, had initially agreed to work without interfering with the Tangwena who had been providing labor to the French company.[24] But the Hanmers' attitude changed when they decided to erect a fence that marked the boundaries of the Ranch land and the Tangwena homelands. While demarcating European and African Land, the new fence boundaries reduced the Tangwena people to squatters and enabled European farmers to secure African labor supply. In addition to the boundaries, new laws including the Native Land Husbandry Act (NLHA) of 1951 imposed restrictions on African agricultural practices, disrupting local land-based livelihoods (Figure 4.1).

Throughout the 1960s and 1970s, Chief Rekayi Tangwena, the leader of the Tangwena people who lived on both sides of the colonial border, was accused by the Rhodesian government of trespassing and illegally residing in European Land in the Gairezi area. But the Tangwena people, led by Chief Tangwena, resisted the payment of native rent, and crossed the colonial

Figure 4.1 The Fence Boundary of the Gairezi Ranch That Caused Conflicts with the Tangwena People. *Source*: NAZ, MS 325.33, Guy Clutton-Brock, G. Nyafaru:1962–1971.

border, causing different kinds of "administrative problems" for the colonial state. As often admitted by the Native Commissioner of Inyanga during the early colonial period, colonial officials worried about the possibility of Africans' exodus to adjoining Mozambican territories.[25]

The conflict between the Tangwena people and the white farmers escalated in July 1966, when Chief Tangwena and his people were served with an eviction notice to move from their ancestral lands. The then-Minister of Lands, Phillip Van Heerden, visited Chief Tangwena and offered him Gokwe as an alternative resettlement place. But the chief refused and rejected the offer. The Eviction Notice of 1966, written by Gairesi Ranch owner William Hanmer, stated:

African Rekany (distorted name of Rekayi),

> I understand that you're living in the Tsatse Kraal area, on Gairesi Ranch. You have never worked for me to my knowledge, and I never gave you leave to settle on this property. I, therefore, give you notice to leave the property by 12th October 1966, with your dependents and personal property. When Mr. Dunn, the enumerator, came around in August 1965 to take a census of the population . . . you apparently were not there . . . you have come into the Tsatse Kraal area on my property since 1965, and therefore it must be assumed that you have come in since illegally, hence this short notice to quit the property by 12th October 1966.[26]

With his people living on both sides of the Rhodesia-Mozambique border, Chief Tangwena resisted a possible eviction. He stated that:

> I was offered land at Gokwe for my people. . . . I declined this . . . go to a place where I would be called a "dog" by another Chief. . . . .I don't like any fight—I want to keep on land from following ancestral chiefs Sakara, Nyamadodzo, Chiwaura, Kubina, Tsatse, Gwindo, Dzeka, Mudima, and Kenya. . . . for me to leave this area, my heart will be very sore—that even might cause my death . . . when I complain, I want the Government to listen. . . . I don't want any fighting. . . . I want bread, not stones. . . . I have a very big family, where can I put it? . . . I won't leave this land.[27]

As a local Tangwena elder, SaIbwe remembered:

> The hot issue then was that the Tangwena people refused to be evicted from their land. The whites did not want Tangwena to rule, and they wanted to remove him and resettle him in Gokwe. We also refused, together with Tangwena, and said we cannot leave our ancestral land. Rekayi said if Smith's people wanted him to go to Gokwe, they must move him and the Tangwena soil, its mountains, and rivers to Gokwe.[28]

The above narratives reveal three main issues. First, while the colonial state used its power over property rights, land ownership, and labor exploitation to evict the Tangwena people, the state's action shows the limits of il/legality. The legal boundaries of the so-called European land and African areas (Native Reserves) were not clearly marked. The chief thus used this as an opportunity to contest the boundaries which colonial officials attempted to codify in the court proceedings of 1967.[29] Secondly, Chief Tangwena, knowing the history of his Gairezi homelands, invoked idioms of indigenous sovereignty, arguing that removal from his ancestral lands would cause his death. Thirdly, if the Chief accepted being moved to Gokwe, he feared having conflicts with chiefs he would find there. He used the image of a dog to show his rejection of subjecthood under another chief. He preferred to be a sovereign chief on his ancestral lands to being a subject of another chief.

With the help of the Rhodesian government and media outlets, the Hanmer brothers and the colonial state framed Tangwena as an unlawful resident and criminal—a "troublesome," "defiant," and "self-styled" African chief. Despite Chief Tangwena's refusal, he was, on June 2, 1967, convicted in the Inyanga Magistrate's Court, for contravening section 42 (1) of the Land Apportionment Act (Chapter 257). It was alleged that he wrongfully and illegally occupied land on the Gairezi Ranch in a European area. "The chief was sentenced to a fine of 30 pounds or, in default of payment, three months' imprisonment with hard labor, of which 20 pounds or, two months' imprisonment with hard labor were suspended until the 31st of July 1967 on condition that he ceased to occupy the land in question by the date."[30] However, Chief Tangwena appealed to the Rhodesian Appellate Division against his conviction, and the Division upheld his appeal. It was argued that Chief Rekayi

Tangwena had been wrongly accused on the previous occasion in June 1967. Thus, his conviction and sentence were set aside, and a total fine of 30 pounds was refunded to the chief.[31] Despite Tangwena's sentence being set aside, the Rhodesian government did not stop their violent removals in the Tangwena homelands, as shown in figure 4.2.

The major impact of the violent colonial displacements was the rapid growth of localized resistance in the Tangwena area, a growth that resonated with the mass nationalist movements. The affected people eventually supported nationalist activities in the 1970s, especially through the work of the Nyafaru Farm community. As local elders revealed, these communities considered the start of the war of liberation in the Tangwena area to be prior to the arrival of guerrilla fighters and nationalist leaders in the region. SaMuomba, revealed that:

> The land struggle and displacement infuriated the Tangwena people and prepared them for the war. Our war began in the 1960s. And later, the nationalist joined us. From them, we got political ideas and legal representations in courts to challenge the colonial government. When people resisted eviction in 1967, they were arrested and brutalized, and their children and livestock were taken. I lost my mother when she was bitten by the white men's dogs on the march to Inyanga in 1969. This made me realize how bad the Rhodesians were. I became very determined to fight for freedom with tears on my face! My mother was

Figure 4.2 "Tangwena land issue. When tribesmen disobeyed a court order to demolish their 20 huts on the disputed land, the Ministry of Internal Affairs sent a land rover to knock the huts down." *Source*: NAZ, MS 325/33 Guy Clutton-Brock, G. Nyafaru:1962-1971.

> gone because of the whites. This broke my spirit for a while, but as a political commissar, I had an obligation to fight. When Mugabe and Tekere came in 1975, we were forward with the struggle.[32]

Similarly, SaIbwe recalled:

> Following the court petitions, our chief was arrested, and our homes were destroyed during the night using bulldozers and fire. We assembled in the morning and marched to demand the return of our chief, but we did not find him. Women left their children at Nyafaru Farm, where the Headmaster, Mr. Matewa, took care of the children. Women marched naked demanding the return of their chief and that they were never going to move away from their homes. The war began much earlier here than in other areas of the country.[33]

These testimonies reveal the centrality of *nyika* (land) to the local struggles of the Tangwena people. For them, being forcibly removed from their ancestral land was a "war." In addition, family loss caused by Rhodesian brutality obligated individuals like SaMuomba to fight the Rhodesian regime. It is also interesting to note that the narratives show that the relationship between nationalists and peasants was not always a leaders-follower one. At Nyafaru, local leaders and mediums spiritually led and advised nationalists, as the following sections show. The Tangwena people were more engaged in localized resistance movements that also resonated with nationalist ideas of winning back ancestral lands from colonizers.

"BRING US TWO RAMS OF SHEEP": MUGABE'S AND TEKERE'S GUIDED JOURNEY VIA NYAFARU

Farms owned by Africans and whites who supported the liberation struggle in Rhodesia played a critical role in guiding nationalist leaders, as well as in the recruitment of guerrilla fighters and the prosecution of the war. In this context, Nyafaru Farm played a crucial role in the recruitment of freedom fighters, with people such as Maurice Nyagumbo, John Mutasa, and Abraham Nyagumbo using it to cross the Rhodesia-Mozambique border.[34] Coordination between supportive white farmers and African nationalists, who disguised politics with farming activities, provided recruitment opportunities at Nyafaru Farm, making it difficult for Rhodesians to detect. Through the work of Cephas Muropa, Basil Nyabadza, and the managers of Nyafaru Farm, including Moven Mahachi and Guy Clutton-Brock, the entire Tangwena area was transformed into a contested landscape—a hive of nationalist activities, but also a landscape of colonial violence.

At Nyafaru Farm and in the entire Tangwena area, indigenous ideas of self-rule and ownership of *nyika* (land) inspired individuals and their families to fight against colonial domination. At the same time, the colonial state, and pro-government white farmers like William and Charles Hanmer imposed various control mechanisms on Africans, including redefining boundaries as well as forced removals. As such, these areas were turned into contested zones of conflict between the colonial state and the local Tangwena people. These borderlands became frontiers of conflict, as well as centers of nationalist movements and the recruitment of freedom fighters. It is from Nyafaru that Moven Mahachi and Cephas Muropa, then in Salisbury (now Harare), deceived the colonial state in a telephone call when organizing the escape of Mugabe and Tekere from Salisbury. As SaMuomba remembered, they used a "farming language" saying they would "bring two rams of sheep to Nyafaru"—referring to Mugabe and Tekere.[35]

Nyafaru Farm was used as one of the many staging points to help Mugabe and Tekere escape out of the country into Mozambique. Mugabe and Tekere were guided by the Nyafaru Farm people and Chief Tangwena from Salisbury to Chimoio, Mozambique. The two nationalists required the leadership and spiritual guidance of Chief Tangwena, who by the 1970s had become well-known for his supernatural powers and resistance to colonial violence and expectations. As an elder, SaChazanawako, who lived with the Tangwena people during the war, recalled:

> Mugabe and Tekere came in 1975 to Gonakudzingwa. They were with Matimbura, Nyakurita, and Muomba, who knew Tangwena's home on the Mozambican side of the border. This man (Chief Tangwena) was mysterious. He got his powers from Nyamutsaka who lived in the Sagambe area. Mugabe knew about Tangwena's powers. He came to get purified by Tangwena. He stayed with him *kuMundawenyemba* (the peas field). Because they needed to be purified before going to meet Samora, Mugabe was not allowed to live among the *povo* (civilians). They lived in separate tents at the margins of the field in a forest. They would not appear in public, the rituals needed them to be pure and away from the *povo*. Only a few people, like Nyakurita who supplied them with *bute* (snuff) and newspapers they bought him from Nyanga, had access to these two.[36]

SaChazanawako reveals a spiritual dimension of Mugabe and Tekere's relationship with the Tangwena people during their journey to Mozambique. Chief Tangwena's supernatural power, as well as his socio-political position in this border region and his relationship with Samora Machel, were also important reasons why Mugabe and Tekere would be guided by him to cross the border to Mozambique. He added, "Tangwena had contact with Samora because he assisted the Liberation Front of Mozambique [Frente de Libertação de Moçambique, FRELIMO] fighters in previous years. No one except for Tangwena, whose family originally came from the Barwe in Mozambique, could help Mugabe."[37]

The guided journey of the two nationalists to Nyafaru Farm was proposed soon after Herbert Chitepo's assassination on March 18, 1975 in Zambia. Following the assassination and the imprisonment of ZANU leaders, including Ndabaningi Sithole, ZANU's Central Committee decided to meet and review the situation. The members secretly convened at Mushandirapamwe Hotel.[38] According to Henry Moyana, the meeting was conducted in Crispen Mandizvidza's room, and members present were Simon Vengai Muzenda, Maurice Nyagumbo, Moton Malianga, Edison Sithole, Edgar Tekere, and Robert Mugabe.[39] Here, the members agreed to send Robert Mugabe, who was the party's Secretary General (SG), to Mozambique to "lead the struggle." Mugabe was to be accompanied by the most senior party member, Edgar Tekere, who had just come out of a decade-long incarceration.[40]

After the Mushandirapamwe Hotel meeting, Mugabe and Tekere were to be guided across Rhodesia's northeastern borderlands. The RSF had already transformed the region into a war zone by deploying brutal counterinsurgency measures, including torturing suspected freedom fighters, burning homes, and destroying the Tangwena people's property. "Mugabe and Tekere's recruiters were mostly Nyafaru Farm members, including the Clutton-Brock family, Didymus Mutasa, Moven Mahachi, Chief Rekayi Tangwena."[41] As SaMuomba stated, Mugabe and Tekere were guided from Salisbury via Nyafaru, a route set up with the help of Sister Mary Aquina, a German-born Catholic nun, as well as John Deary and Cephas Muropa. The route was via Murehwa, then Mutoko, through Tanda Tribal Trust Lands (TTTL) in Inyanga North, through Nyafaru Farm, and finally into Mozambique's Villa Catandica, from where they proceeded to Chimoio.[42]

Per the narratives of SaMuomba, Amai Muomba, and SaIbwe, Mugabe, and Tekere arrived during the night, sometime in early April 1975. Amai Muomba said "others had gone for weaving since we had orders from Salisbury. Mr. Mahachi had ordered me to prepare for our guests during the night. It was on 3 or 4, April 1975. I can't quite remember."[43] However, they had not stayed long when the RSF arrived. SaMuomba recalled:

> They came with comrade Mahachi. I was at Nyafaru as one of the cooperators. Mugabe was guided, with the help of Roman Catholic sisters, to Ruwa Wayside Properties where they stayed together with comrade Tekere. Another Roman Catholic, John Deary, helped us, through Cephas Muropa. We used some codes somehow, saying we were to collect two rams of sheep, and we all knew that this referred to the two men. Mahachi rushed there in his little Renault 12 car, collected the two, and brought them to Nyafaru. Early in the morning, Mahachi woke me up together with Phineas Hazangwi, who was my assistant, and we went to the dining room where we were introduced to

Mugabe and Tekere as nationalists who wanted to cross into Mozambique. When they were reported missing in Salisbury, the RSF suspected that they might have gone through Nyafaru Farm. They sent policemen in five Land rovers to Nyafaru, and my wife rang a warning bell. When the RSF arrived, they asked if we heard any news about Tekere's and Mugabe's whereabouts. We said that we last heard they were in prison, and they left, after a short search.[44]

The coordination between Nyafaru, the ex-Cold Comfort members like Cephas Muropa as well as the Roman Catholics based in Salisbury made it possible to guide Mugabe and Tekere from Salisbury to a crossing of the then-highly patrolled Rhodesia-Mozambique border. While the role of farms in Zimbabwe's liberation movements is a largely ignored aspect of the war's historiographies, farms were crucial not only to the movement of freedom fighters but also to the prosecution of the war.

"ARE YOU GOING TO UNIVERSITY OR WAR?" NYAFARU'S ENCOUNTERS AND ESCAPE PLANS

When Mugabe and Tekere arrived at Nyafaru Farm, Mugabe brought a lot of books with him, and that did not impress Chief Tangwena, who immediately questioned him. As recalled by SaMuomba:

> The chief was not happy to see Mugabe so attached to his bookcase. Immediately, the Chief, with a faded smile, asked Mugabe "are you going to University or war?" Mugabe did not seem happy about the question. The Chief immediately asked for a private talk, and I was later called. Chief Rekayi order me to pick up Mugabe's bookcase and asked me to keep it safe for the next years. The only safe place I could keep it was the *kuwira* (an underground tunnel). Keen to read, I opened the bookcase after they left, and saw Machiavelli's *The Prince*. I read it. I kept the books until I returned them to Sabina Mugabe in 1979. Mugabe had promised a big reward if I would keep the books safely. He only returned to Nyafaru in 1981, to thank our community, with a lot of bodyguards. I never talked to him again.[45]

SaMuomba's words reveal the different approaches to war and liberation that local leaders and nationalists had. It seemed that Mugabe was an intellectual rather than an organic revolutionary or local freedom fighter like Tangwena was. Despite these differences, there was a shared goal of self-rule. It is this goal that motivated individuals like Muomba to keep Mugabe's books and assist Mugabe and Tekere in crossing the border to Mozambique (Figure 4.3).

Figure 4.3 SaMuomba and SaIbwe Showing the Author the Window through Which Mugabe Escaped the RSF Hunt-down at Nyafaru. They fled to the Chiri forest where Chief Tangwena and his people were living after being evicted from their ancestral land. *Source*: Photograph by author, July 2016.

At Nyafaru Farm, Mugabe and Tekere were involved in a guided escape from the attempted RSF dragnet. The escape was made possible by Amai Muomba, who was the "eye of the farm." She stated:

> While others had gone to continue weaving at the hall, I saw cars passing right here where we are (we were at Nyafaru clinic) and then rang a bell. I was given a task to be the eye of the farm and any moment I rang the bell people realized that something was unusual. When I rang the bell, they looked outside and noticed the cars. Mugabe escaped through the window, while Tekere used the door, and together, they joined the Tangwena people who were living in the Chiri mountain.[46]

After the escape, Rekayi Tangwena, thus, guided Mugabe and Tekere across the border into Mozambique. In the forests, a Tangwena spirit-medium advised them on how they would cross to Mozambique under the leadership of Chief Tangwena. As Chief Tangwena recalled:

> *Masvikiro* (spirit mediums) came to us in the bush hideout and said to me "you Rekayi, carry these people and go with them. If they stay here, including Tekere, it's hell for us all." I escorted them up to 5.00 AM. We stayed there in the bush. . . . From there *Masvikiro* said to me "if you stay with these people here, they will die." I tried to argue, and I was answered, "no, no, Rekayi, go with them."[47]

Tangwena took heed. He crossed to Mozambique and opened contacts with FRELIMO officials. He informed FRELIMO's leadership that Mugabe and Tekere had come on war businesses.[48] "Langton Tangwena (Rekayi's younger brother), together with Muomba, were responsible for leading the nationalists and other guerrilla recruits from Nyafaru across the Jora River into Mozambique where they were received by Rekayi's first wife, Amai Erija. This powerful woman, the medium of the Tangwena people, stayed with Mugabe and Tekere, and another elderly man called Tagadza, who later became Mugabe's best friend."[49] SaMuomba, however, returned to report to Moven Mahachi about the journey and to continue with his political teachings and recruitment at Nyafaru Farm.

NYAFARU FARM DECLARED A NO-GO AREA, 1976–1980

The recruitment and guerrilla infiltration into Rhodesia compelled the RSF to respond. The RSF's counterinsurgency measures are documented elsewhere.[50] Part of the measures to curb self-determination movements ("guerrilla activities" in the eyes of colonial media and officials) in the Eastern Highlands, for instance, included the closure of Nyafaru Farm. Nyafaru Farm was declared a no-go area in 1976 because its members were now suspected of aiding the guerrillas by sheltering them and helping them to cross to and from Mozambique.[51] It was closed also because the Rhodesians did not want the locals to get politicized by Clutton-Brock, Mahachi, Mutasa, Muomba, and others. As Chater argued, Nyafaru Farm was declared a "no-go area" during the war and re-opened in 1980 because it continued to threaten the existence and work of the pro-government whites in the area.[52]

Besides closing Nyafaru Farm, the RSF also arrested many of its members. SaMuomba recalled that:

> Nyafaru Farm was declared a no-go area in 1976 and we went to our sister farm in Ruwa. Phineas Hazangwi, Richard Jangano, Wilson Matimbira, Tinaani Muomba, and Pearson Kasu were arrested. One of our members had established another Farm at Chiendambuya and we were now connected. The boys came through Chiendambuya, and we assisted them. I stayed at Ruwa still doing

political activities until independence. I only came back to Nyafaru, in June 1980, and became a teacher.[53]

Because of the RFS's brutal methods of burning homes, killing people, and making arrests, most of the families who worked at Nyafaru Farm and others from the Tangwena villages fled and crossed the border to Mozambique. In Mozambique, Chief Tangwena already had a second home where his followers began to conduct community farming at Gonakudzingwa called *Mashamba de povo*—a Mozambican term meaning chief's farm or garden.[54] The farm belonged to Chief Tangwena, and people grew their crops and worked together as a displaced community. It was from Gonakudzingwa that the Tangwena people continued to resist colonial oppression and assist guerrilla fighters until the attainment of Zimbabwe's self-rule in 1980.

CONCLUSION

The quest for self-rule among the Tangwena people and the Nyafaru Farm community reveals the limits of colonial state sovereignty as local ideas of indigenous sovereignty (*kuzvitonga kuzere*) contradicted the Rhodesian and Portuguese versions of state sovereignty. By utilizing indigenous leadership and their location in the borderlands, as well as local knowledge of the terrain, the Nyafaru Farm and Tangwena people defied the colonial state's mechanisms of control and oppression in their quest for self-rule. In addition, not only was Nyafaru Farm a transit zone but a recruitment base, a place from where people fought to attain self-rule against Rhodesian state forces. Because the area shared a porous border with Mozambique, the government of which, after independence, was supporting the Zimbabwean liberation movements, the Tangwena area became a fiercely contested warzone between the Rhodesians and the Tangwena people. Even prior to the recruitment of guerrillas from the area and the local community's role in guiding liberation fighters across the border, there was already a local struggle for self-determination and to defend *nyika* from the pro-government white farmers, the Hanmers, in the Gairezi homelands. As such, this chapter argues that the Tangwena and Nyafaru war predated the so-called mass-nationalist movements in Zimbabwe. This "local war" was deeply entrenched in and revolved around indigenous ideas of sovereignty, as well as the related issues of ownership of land, its boundaries, and resources.

NOTES

1. There is a significant amount of scholarship on the Zimbabwe war of liberation, and it is impossible to cite them in a footnote. For discussion on everyday life

during the war and gendered wartime experiences, see Enocent Msindo and Nicholas Nyachega, "Zimbabwe's Liberation War and the Everyday in Honde Valley, 1975 to 1979," *South African Historical Journal,* 71, no. 1 (2019): 70–93; Josephine Nhongo-Simbanegavi, *For Better or Worse? Women and ZANLA in Zimbabwe's Liberation Struggle* (Harare: Weaver Press, 2000). For the Tangwena people, see Donald S. Moore, *Suffering for Territory: Race, Place and Power in Zimbabwe* (London: Duke University Press, 2005); Henry Moyana, *The Victory of Chief Rekayi Tangwena* (Harare: Longman, 1987); Didymus Mutasa, *Black Behind Bars: Rhodesia 1959–1974* (Harare: Longman Zimbabwe, 1983).

2. Ngwabi Bhebe and Terrence. O. Ranger, *Soldiers in Zimbabwe's Liberation War* (Harare: University of Zimbabwe Publications, 1995), 2.

3. Bhebe and Terrence, *Soldiers in Zimbabwe's Liberation War*, 2.

4. Moore, *Suffering for Territory*. See also Moyana, *The Victory of Chief Rekayi Tangwena*.

5. Terrence O. Ranger, *Peasant Consciousness and Guerrilla War in Zimbabwe: A Comparative Study* (London: Currey, 1985). See also Anna Weinrich, *African Farmers in Rhodesia: Old and New Peasant Communities in Karangaland* (London: Oxford University Press, 1975).

6. Ranger, *Peasant Consciousness,* 340.

7. Ranger, *Peasant consciousness*, 340.

8. Elena Dell 'Agnese, E., and Anne-Laure Amilhat Szary, "Borderscapes: From Border Landscapes to Border Aesthetics," *Geopolitics,* 20, no. 1 (2015): 1–10.

9. Arjan Harbers, "Borderscapes, The Influence of National Borders on European Spatial Planning," in *Euroscapes* R. Broesi, P. Jannink, W. Veldhuis, and I. Nio (eds.), *Euroscapes* (Amsterdam: Must Publishers/Architectura et Amicitia, 2003). See also Dina Krichker, "Making Sense of Borderscapes: Space, Imagination and Experience," *Geopolitics* 26, no. 4: 1224–1242.

10. "Terrorist Wage Indiscriminate War on the Border," *Rhodesia Herald* (Salisbury), 1 March 1975.

11. See one of the earliest reports by the Native Commissioner of Inyanga District, National Archives of Zimbabwe (hereafter NAZ), L2/2/2/6/8, Native Commissioner (hereafter NC) Inyanga D. H. Moodie to Chief Native Commissioner (hereafter CNC), Salisbury, 1906.

12. The people with whom I co-created oral histories are identified pseudonymously throughout this chapter.

13. NAZ, MS 335/10/1 Clutton-Brock, G. Nyafaru, 1962–1971. Some Chi-Manyika words have 'a' and 'o' variations for the same word. For example, *muramu* or *muramo* are both words for sister-in-law. The meaning of the word does not change due to the onomastic variations.

14. NAZ, MS 335/10/1 Clutton-Brock, G. Nyafaru, 1962–1971, interview, Cephas Muropa, by Guy-Clutton Brock.

15. NAZ, MS 335/10/1 Clutton-Brock, G.

16. The Newsletter was written by Guy Clutton-Brock and Didymus Mutasa, in their capacities as directors. See Guy Clutton-Brock and Didymus Mutasa, *Nyafaru Development Company Newsletter* (Rusape: Southern Rhodesia, November 1969).

17. Interview with SaMuomba, 7 July 2015, re-interviewed 20 August 2019.

18. Mugabe's guidance and rescue by the Nyafaru Farm leaders and Tangwena people also influenced his decisions when he became Zimbabwe's president. In recognition of their war efforts, Chief Tangwena and Clutton-Brock were declared national heroes when they died in 1984 and 1995, respectively.

19. Gonakudzingwa is a mountainous place on the Mozambican side of the border where Chief Tangwena hosted them after the Nyafaru escape in 1975. Translated, Gonakudzingwa means "you could be chased away." For the Tangwena people, it was a squatting place temporarily lived in across the Mozambican border following eviction from the Gairezi area. They named it Gonakudzingwa because it was a place of uncertainty, where they could be chased away anytime. Interview with SaMare, 9 May 2022.

20. Edgar Z. Tekere, *Tekere: A Lifetime of Struggle* (Harare: Sapes, 2007).

21. While the responses of Africans across Rhodesia were similar in many aspects, such as protests and armed resistance, they were also shaped by different historical experiences and geopolitics. In the Tangwena area, when the colonial government heightened its land invasions and displacement projects, especially in the 1950s and 1960s, the Tangwena area, particularly the Gairezi region, became the center of anti-colonial resistance.

22. Robert Mugabe, *Our War of Liberation: Speeches, Articles, Interviews, 1976–1979* (Gweru: Mambo Press, 1983), 60.

23. NAZ, MS 325/33, Guy Clutton-Brock, G. Nyafaru:1962–1971.

24. International Defense and Aid Fund, *Rhodesia: The Ousting of the Tangwena* (London: Christian Action Ltd, 1972).

25. NAZ, NUC 2/1/2 NC Inyanga to Chief NC Salisbury, 26 March 1907.

26. NAZ, MS 335/10/6 Guy Clutton-Brock, G.Nyafaru, 1962–1971. See also International Defense Aid, *Rhodesia.*

27. NAZ, MS 335/10/6 Guy Clutton-Brock, G.See also International Defense Aid, *Rhodesia.*

28. Interview with SaIbwe, 7 July 2015.

29. During the late 1950s and early 1960s, the colonial government audited and redefined the acreages of African Land, proposing the "cutting of boundaries" and redefining the boundaries that were not yet ascertainable. NAZ, National Records Center, Box 62328, Provincial Native Commissioner (PNC), Progress Report, 1960. For more on Chief Tangwena's 1967 court narrative while he challenged the colonial state's boundaries, see his interview with Guy Clutton-Brock, NAZ, MS 335/10/6 Guy Clutton-Brock, G.Nyafaru:1962–1971.

30. NAZ, MS 335/10/6 Guy Clutton-Brock, G.See also International Defense Aid, *Rhodesia.*

31. NAZ, MS 335/10/6 Guy Clutton-Brock, G.See also International Defense Aid, *Rhodesia.*

32. Interview with SaMuomba, 7 July 2015.

33. Interview with SaIbwe, 7 July 2015. See also interview with Cephas Muropa. NAZ, MS335/10/7, Guy Clutton-Brock, G.Nyafaru:1962–1971.

34. Interview with Elvis Muomba, 7 July 2015. See also Patricia Chater, *The Hidden Treasure: A Memoir* (Harare: Weaver Press, 2012).

35. Interview with SaMuomba, 20 August 2019.

36. Interview with SaChazanawako, 15 September 2019 and 21 October 2021.

37. Interview with SaChazanawako, 21 October 2021.

38. Moyana, *Chief Rekayi Tangwena*, 20.

39. Moyana, *Chief Rekayi Tangwena.*

40. Interview with SaMuomba, 7 July 2015.

41. Interview with SaMuomba and Amai Muomba, 29 June 2015. At Nyafaru Farm, different activities were held including weaving, husbandry, etc. One visitor, in 1974, commented that Nyafaru was a model of order. Per the visitor, Nyafaru, by 1974, had 25 acres of maize, 10 acres of potatoes, 120 Corriedale Sheep, New Hampshire Chickens, and a variety of Rabbits, fish hatcheries with about 5,000 Trout-fish, and many other things. See "Nyafaru: A model of order-visitor," *Moto Reporter,* 19 January 1974.

42. Interview with SaMuomba, 29 June 2015.

43. Interview with Amai Muomba, 29 June 2015.

44. Interview with SaMuomba, 29 June 2015.

45. Interview with SaMuomba, 10 July 2016. SaMuomba and SaIbwe showed me the tunnel. I cannot share a picture of the tunnel in this chapter because of the limited space.

46. Interview with Amai Muomba, 29 June 2015.

47. NAZ MS 335/10/7 Clutton-Brock G, Nyafaru:1962–1971 Nyafaru and Tangwena Court Documentary. Interview with Rekayi Tangwena on how he helped Robert Mugabe to cross the border into Mozambique by Tony Ryder.

48. Martin Meredith, *Mugabe: Power, Plunder, and the Struggle for Zimbabwe* (New York: Public Affairs. 2007), 19.

49. Interview with SaMuomba, 7 July 2015.

50. See Henrik, Ellert, *The Rhodesian Front War: Counterinsurgency and Guerrilla War in Rhodesia 1962 to 1980* (Gweru: Mambo Press, 1989).

51. Interview with SaMuomba, 7 July 2015. See also, Chater, *Hidden Treasure*, 19.

52. Chater, *Hidden Treasure,* 19.

53. Interview with SaMuomba, 7 July 2015.

54. Separate interviews with SaMuomba on 20 August 2019, and SaChazanawako on 15 September 2019. See also Carole Collins, "Mozambique: Dynamizing the People," *Issue: A Journal of Opinion* 8, no. 1 (1978): 12–16.

BIBLIOGRAPHY

Chater, Patricia. *The Hidden Treasure: A Memoir*. Harare: Weaver Press, 2012.

Clutton-Brock, Guy, and Didymus Mutasa. *Nyafaru Development Company Newsletter*. Rusape: Southern Rhodesia, November 1969.Collins, Carole "Mozambique: Dynamizing the People." *Issue: A Journal of Opinion* 8, no. 1 (1978): 12–16.

Dell'Agnese, Elena, and Anne-Laure Amilhat Szary. "Borderscapes: From Border Landscapes to Border Aesthetics." *Geopolitics* 20, no. 1 (2015): 1–10.

Ellert, Henrik. *The Rhodesian Front War: Counterinsurgency and Guerrilla War in Rhodesia 1962 to 1980*. Gweru: Mambo Press, 1989.

Harbers, Arjan. "Borderscapes, The Influence of National Borders on European Spatial Planning." In *Euroscapes*, edited by R. Broesi, P. Jannink, W. Veldhuis, and I. Nio, 143–166. Amsterdam: Must Publishers/Architectura et Amicitia, 2003.

International Defense and Aid Fund. *Rhodesia: The Ousting of the Tangwena*. London: Christian Action Publications Ltd., 1972.

Krichker, Dina. "Making Sense of Borderscapes: Space, Imagination, and Experience." *Geopolitics* 26, no. 4 (2021): 1224–1242.

Meredith, Martin M. *Mugabe: Power, Plunder, and the Struggle for Zimbabwe*. New York: Public Affairs, 2007.

Moore, Donald S. *Suffering for Territory: Race, Place and Power in Zimbabwe*. London: Duke University Press, 2005.

Moore, Donald S. "Subaltern Struggles and the Politics of Place: Remapping Resistance in Zimbabwe's Eastern Highlands." *Cultural Anthropology* 13, no. 3 (1998): 344–381.

Moyana, Henry. *The Victory of Chief Rekayi Tangwena*. Harare: Longman, 1987.

Msindo, Enocent, E., and Nicholas Nyachega. "Zimbabwe's Liberation War and the Everyday in Honde Valley, 1975 to 1979." *South African Historical Journal* 71, no. 1 (2019): 70–93.

Mugabe, Robert. *Our War of Liberation: Speeches, Articles, Interviews, 1976–1979*. Gweru: Mambo Press, 1983.

Mutasa, Didymus. *Black Behind Bars: Rhodesia 1959–1974*. Harare: Longman Zimbabwe, 1983.

Ngwabi, Bhebe, and Terrence O. Ranger. *Soldiers in Zimbabwe's Liberation War*. Harare: University of Zimbabwe Publications, 1995.

Nhongo-Simbanegavi, Josephine. *For Better or Worse? Women and ZANLA in Zimbabwe's Liberation Struggle*. Harare: Weaver Press, 2000.

Paasi, Anssi, 1998. "Boundaries as Social Processes: Territoriality in the World of Flows." *Geopolitics* 3, no. 1 (1998): 69–88.

Rajaram, Prem Kumar, and Carl Grundy-Warr. *Borderscapes: Hidden Geographies and Politics at Territory's Edge*. Minneapolis: University of Minnesota Press, 2007.

Ranger, Terrence O. *Peasant Consciousness and Guerrilla War in Zimbabwe: A Comparative Study*. London: Currey, 1985.

Tekere, Edgar Z. *Tekere: A Lifetime of Struggle*. Harare: Sapes, 2007.

Weinrich, Anna. *African Farmers in Rhodesia: Old and New Peasant Communities in Karangaland*. London: Oxford University Press, 1975.

Part II

(IM)MOBILITIES, TRANSNATIONAL COMMUNITIES, AND SETTLEMENT

Chapter 5

"The River Is a Natural Resource, Not a Border?"

Understanding Tonga Borderland Community Responses to State Border Security Policy in Binga District of Zimbabwe, c. 1957 to 2017

Teverayi Muguti

This chapter examines how the Binga Tonga community has responded to state border security policy by different government administrations between 1957 and 2017.[1] The period between the establishment of Lake Kariba by the Federation of Rhodesia and Nyasaland government and the fall of the Mugabe regime in 2017 was characterized by diverse border management strategies that negatively affected the Binga Tonga borderlands community in different ways, which in turn largely resulted in negative responses to the border security mechanisms. Existing literature on the Tonga livelihoods mainly concentrates on cultural heritage in the Tonga society,[2] displacements during the construction of Lake Kariba between 1957 and the early 1960s,[3] the reconstruction of Tonga peoples' identity,[4] and human-animal relations.[5] Scholars have also widely discussed marginalization of the community in various aspects of life, including the political, economic, social, and ethnic spheres.[6] JoAnn McGregor has delineated the different ways in which the shifting role of the Zambezi river (which forms a border between Zimbabwe and Zambia) as a link and a barrier has shaped the relationship between political leaders, the environment, and the borderlands communities in areas along the Zambezi from Victoria Falls to the Kariba Dam wall.[7]

Riding on the shoulders of existing literature on the Zambezi communities' livelihoods, therefore, this chapter uses Binga District of Zimbabwe as a lens to specifically understand the complexity of Tonga borderlands community responses to the border policies that have been implemented by different government administrations in managing the Zimbabwean borders in pursuit of variegated national interests from 1957 to 2017. The chapter argues that while the state has maintained the Zambezi River borderline to protect its territorial integrity and diverse national interests, the Binga community has subtly and expressively defied the border security mechanisms through utilizing the river as a natural resource for the provision of the residents' cultural and socio-economic needs. The discord in the implementation of state border security policy and the Binga Tonga border community responses can be explained by the lack of a common interpretation of the Zambezi River between the state from above and the community from below. For the state, the Zambezi River mainly forms a territorial marker between Zimbabwe and Zambia, which should be monitored and maintained to protect Zimbabwean territory, prevent pilfering of resources out of the country, and help in the conservation of national resources such as wildlife.[8] For the Tonga borderlands community in Binga District, however, the Zambezi River is a natural resource which should be utilized for everyday household livelihoods without restrictive measures, either framed in state border security policy or any other governmental policy. Thus, the interpretation of the Zambezi River by the Tonga community informs the many ways in which they have responded to state border security policy.

While state borders have been widely studied in global border studies, they have mainly been enumerated as far as they shape state-to-state relations in various parts of the world.[9] This chapter adopts a microstudy of borderlands communities drawing from borderlands theory, as propounded by Gloria Anzaldua in her study of the Mexico border community's negotiation of the hard border security initiatives coming mainly from the United States of America.[10] In the case of Africa, Donna Flynn's challenge to the state-centric border conceptualization, together with like-minded border scholars such as Anthony Asiwaju, Mahmood Mamdani, Albert Adu Boahen, and Jeffery Herbst, is useful in grounding this study in the field of African border studies.[11] The latter group of African border scholars have emphasized the artificiality of borders, showing how the Berlin conference borders have cut across ethnicities and inherently created problems in post-colonial Africa.[12] Flynn argues that while state-to-state border interactions are important in understanding contemporary border challenges such as conflicts, terrorism, and marginalization, pragmatic solutions to the occurrences along the African borders can be generated by understanding the lived experiences of the communities surrounding the borders, rather than only concentrating on the metropolitan state interests.[13]

Admittedly, there has been persuasive interest in historicizing borderland communities in Africa in the twenty-first century, marking a shift from the macro-state examination of borders in the context of state-to-state relations. Scholars such as Paul Nugent, Wolfgang Zeller, and David Coplan have put primacy in understanding micro-histories of people living in the margins of different African states, based on experiences of the borderlands citizens themselves.[14] In the case of Zimbabwe, scholars including Anusa Diamon, Nedson Pophiwa, Francis Dube, Wesley Mwatwara, Nicholas Nyachega, and Vongai Sagonda have historicized the experiences of ordinary people in Zimbabwe-Mozambique borderlands communities, showing their agency in the context of the state border security initiatives.[15] This chapter is informed by the need to interpret the meanings attached to the border by the Binga district Tonga people in the Zimbabwe-Zambia borderlands to understand the dynamism of border security policy in Zimbabwe over time. By historicizing community responses to state border security policy in Binga, therefore, the chapter broadens the understanding of the quotidian lived experiences of borderlands communities in the context of macro-state policy administration in Zimbabwe, Africa, and the world in general.

This chapter re-examines the Binga District borderlands community's lived experiences, delineated by Muguti in his analysis of the intermeshing dynamics between border security and economic development since 2000.[16] The chapter further historicizes the years before 2000, particularly giving more space to the voices of the Binga Tonga people in explaining the varied reasons for their activities in responding to state border policy in Zimbabwe since the construction of the Kariba Dam in the late 1950s.

The following sections explain the Binga District's geographical settings, the research methods, and then chronological subsections followed by a conclusion. Broadly, the historical discussion on the Tonga people's attachment to the Zambezi River and their responses to state border security policy is done chronologically, punctuated by landmark events from the construction of the Kariba Dam in 1957 to the end of the Robert Mugabe regime in 2017.

BINGA DISTRICT GEOGRAPHICAL SETTING AND RESEARCH METHODS

Binga District is located along the Zimbabwe-Zambia maritime borderline, in north-western Zimbabwe. It is mainly inhabited by Tonga people, although Nambya, Ndebele, and Shona people also form part of the population. There are twenty-five administrative wards under the Binga Rural District Council (BRDC). The district had an official population of 159,982 people in 2022.[17] Much of the Zambezi valley is semi-arid, with a tropical savannah climate, covered mostly by mopane woodlands and poor soils.[18] With such climatic conditions, the district is drought prone and characterized by food aid from both the state and Non-Governmental Organisations (NGOs) throughout the year. Nationally, Tonga is the third largest ethnic group in Zimbabwe after Shona and Ndebele. Up to the present moment, social service infrastructure is still a challenge, despite relative improvement from the colonial period.[19] According to S. B. Manyena, "Limited access to resources such as fishing and wildlife, coupled with the Zimbabwe's socio-economic decline has caused the Zambezi Valley to become a chronic disaster area, requiring humanitarian food every year."[20]

This chapter is informed by qualitative data analysis, with data drawn from semi-structured interviews, archival data, newspaper articles, and other diverse secondary literature sources. The data was mainly collected between July 2020 and June 2022 as part of my PhD project titled, *A History of Border Security Policy in Zimbabwe: The Case of the Zimbabwe-Zambia Border, c. 1963–2017*. I have utilized archival sources at the National Archives of Zimbabwe and the National Archives of Zambia as well as newspaper articles from the Herald Library in Harare and the Chronicle Library in Bulawayo to gather data for the purpose of this study. I also collected oral data from forty interviews with community individuals, including politicians, traditional leaders, government officials, and ordinary Binga community residents. Pseudonyms have been used in referencing the interviewees in the chapter to maintain their confidentiality in line with ethical research considerations, but some interviewees had no problems in having their real names used for the publication. Ethnographic data gathered through informal conversations, observations, and real-life experiences in Binga District during my stay in the area for almost a decade have also helped in grasping various community experiences regarding state border security policy. I have also used netnography to gather online data about the everyday lives of the borderlands communities along the Zimbabwe-Zambia border, and different other border communities in Africa and the world in general for comparative purposes. The data collected from various sources was then processed through thematic and content analysis for an informed discussion on the complex Binga Tonga borderlands community's responses to state border security policy in Zimbabwe.

THE TONGA PEOPLE'S HISTORICAL ATTACHMENT TO THE ZAMBEZI RIVER AND IMPLICATIONS FOR BINGA COMMUNITY RESPONSES TO STATE BORDER SECURITY POLICY

Historically, the river was central to all areas of Tonga life, as shown in various secondary literature. The river was a source of identity and an important spiritual asset. Writing on the Tonga community in southern Zambia, Colson reveals that local people called themselves *bamulwizi,* "the river people," with a long history of interacting with the river, thereby distinguishing themselves from the people of the plateau.[21] In Binga, the Zambezi River is traditionally called *kasambabezi* which means: "Only those who know about the river can bathe in it."[22] This naming of the river suggests a special harmonious relationship between the Tonga people and the Zambezi river. Religiously, the Zambezi has played an important role in Tonga lives by being home to various spiritual sites dotted along the river before the construction of the Kariba Dam in the 1950s.[23] The river has also gained spiritual prominence through the Nyaminyami spirit god, which is believed to have resided in the river since time immemorial. According to Chikozho, "As a matter of fact, for most societies lining along the Zambezi, the river had an indomitable spiritual significance which is epitomized in the Tonga river-god Nyaminyami also known as the Zambezi River God or Zambezi Snake Spirit."[24] Matanzima, however, argues that the Tonga of Mola and Musampakaruma (Zimbabwe), as well as those of Sikongo and Simamba (Zambia) were the only communities that believed in the Nyaminyami river god.[25] Notwithstanding this contention, oral histories collected during research for this study made reference to the Binga Tonga people's varied beliefs in Nyaminyami as a provider in times of drought and different calamities.[26] From the historical origins of the Tonga, therefore, their identity, religious, as well as various other important aspects of life, were linked to the Zambezi River. This linkage to the river and their "ownership of the Zambezi River" has caused the Binga Tonga borderlands people to be reluctant to abide with any kind of instructions from government on how they should navigate and utilize the river in their everyday lives.

With respect to the functioning of the Zambezi River as a border, during the pre-colonial period, crossing the river from one side to the other had no restrictions. The Zambezi River was not considered as a frontier and several Tonga rulers, like Saba and Mola, had polities whose domains lay on either side of the river.[27] The Tonga went back and forth across the river whenever it suited them.[28] The situation changed with the establishment of colonial borders between Northern and Southern Rhodesia in the late nineteenth century when the border was marked along the river. McGregor, however, argues that although the Zambezi River had long acted as a state border between Northern and Southern Rhodesia, it had remained a central focus of life for the "river people" living along it until the 1957 Lake Kariba-induced dam displacements.[29] Since the Zimbabwe-Zambia borderline falls within the Zambezi river, therefore, state regulations and restrictions (in both Zimbabwe and Zambia) on movement within or across the river have not been warmly welcomed by the Tonga borderlands community, the "people of the river."

THE CONSTRUCTION OF THE KARIBA DAM, DISPLACEMENT, AND THE REALIGNMENT OF THE TONGA BORDERLAND COMMUNITY

The construction of the Kariba Dam and the formation of the lake brought reality to the idea of separation of the Tonga community on both sides of the Zambezi River in Northern and Southern Rhodesia respectively. In Binga, about 23,000 Tonga people were displaced between 1956 and 1957 to pave way for the construction of Lake Kariba.[30] The British relocated most people to the Northern Rhodesia side of the border and as a result many families were separated.[31] On the Zambian side of the river, an estimated 34,000 people were relocated from their ancestral land, where they had stayed for more than two hundred years, and settled, in some cases, hundreds of miles away from the river bank.[32] Thus, the establishment of the artificial lake entrenched the border in a way that broadened the separation of one people, inherently sowing seeds of disaffection in a community that highly valued family unity in its everyday lived experiences.

The effects of the dam construction to the Tonga borderlands area in terms of agricultural production, social contact, and religious practices, among other issues, have been explicated by various scholars.[33] This chapter reiterates that the creation of Lake Kariba in the aftermath of the dam construction effectively expanded the waterscape frontier zone along the Zambezi River, as the distance to cross from one territory to another was made longer. This required adjustment of the modes of transportation used to cross the Zambezi borderline between Northern and Southern Rhodesia. According to Tremmel and Roos, when the Tonga were displaced to pave the way for the construction of the Kariba Dam, many had to leave behind their source of livelihood, as well as their contact with relatives across the Zambezi river.[34] Therefore, the Tonga community resented the colonial administration not only for disrupting their economic, agricultural, and spiritual activities in the river, but also for making it much harder for them to access their relatives on the other side of the river. Thus, the barrier effects of the border in the Tonga borderlands were acutely felt in the aftermath of the Kariba dam construction, fostering a historical dislike of the maritime border along the Zambezi River among community members.

The loss of lives by resisting communities still lingers in the minds of the Tonga community in Binga District, making them bitter and inclined to resist, especially any state policies that reiterate their division from fellow Tonga communities across the river. These sentiments echo in the Binga District song, "*Cigambiyo Cipati,*"[35] which emphasizes the Tonga people's attachment to the Zambezi River. An interview with Biggy Mudenda, a Binga Tonga resident, highlighted that some families resisted government relocation and had their assets destroyed by water pushing back upstream from the Kariba Dam wall.[36] On the Zambian side of the river, there was armed resistance to government authorities by some villagers residing along the riverbank in Sinazongwe District, which shares a border with Binga District in Zimbabwe. The violent tussle with the Northern Rhodesia police resulted in the death of about six villagers.[37] The fact that some of the Tonga people sacrificed their lives in resistance to displacement from the Zambezi River during and after the Kariba Dam construction indicates how pivotal it was to the lives of the Tonga people. The horrendous tales of such loss of life partly contributes to the continued resistance toward government policy in the district by some members of the Tonga borderlands community, including efforts by state border security forces to police the border in Zimbabwe.

The construction of the Kariba Dam also disturbed the Tonga religious beliefs by creating a "spiritual border" between the Zimbabwean and Zambian waters in the dam. While the Tonga people reacted negatively to the destruction of their spiritual ritual sites along the river, they also believed that their river god, Nyaminyami, would fight against the imposition of the dam. According to Ncube, Tonga believed that Nyaminyami controlled life in the Zambezi River, so that anyone hampering with the natural flow of the river would be punished.[38] Ncube added that in the days when the Tonga were being forcibly removed from the Zambezi valley and resettled in the uplands, the name of Nyaminyami was invoked in a spirit of resistance.[39] He further highlighted that the people widely believed the river spirit disapproved of the construction of the dam and would destroy it.[40] Meanwhile, Joshua Chikozho, the Batonga Museum Curator, revealed that extreme floods that happened in 1957 and 1958, which destroyed the dam wall, were interpreted by the Tonga community as the expression of anger by the river god.[41] However, there is yet another belief about Nyaminyami that is associated with the spiritual resentment of the border between Zimbabwean and Zambian waters. According to Collen Munenge, stories told from older generations of the Tonga have it that when the dam was constructed, Nyaminyami was separated to the north from his wife, who remained on the southern side of the Zambezi water flow.[42] He noted that the periodic tremors experienced in Binga are believed to be movements of Nyaminyami trying to reunite with his wife.[43] This spiritual belief is used to justify the sentiment that traditionally the border concept has never been good for the Tonga people, not only from social, economic, and political perspectives, but also in the spiritual realms of the Binga borderlands community. On this basis, some Tonga people in Binga justify their defiance to state border policy on traditional religious grounds.

The increase of the white population during the early 1960s in the Binga borderlands community in the aftermath of the Kariba Dam construction saw a package of acts that dispossessed the Tonga people from their traditional modes of production around the river, deepening the broad unfavorable relationship between the colonial state and the community. The border was part of such an unpopular package. McGregor highlighted that in the wake of the dam construction, there was a huge increase in the state's presence as roads, missions, and a new district administrative center were constructed.[44] White private investors began to invest in commercial fishing, safari operations, and the general tourism industry around Lake Kariba, further taking control of resources from the local Tonga community.[45] While the state's presence increased dramatically in the 1960s, provision of water, schools, clinics, and other services proceeded very slowly and was soon interrupted by the war.[46] These rapid changes that limited Tonga access to their erstwhile livelihoods around the river were deleterious to the borderlands community in the immediate aftermath of the establishment of Lake Kariba. As this was also a time that the function of the river as a territorial marker between Zambia and colonial Zimbabwe became more pronounced, everything associated with the state—which brought cataclysmic changes to Tonga lives—also became unpopular in the community. The further unpopularity of the state in terms of maintaining its border with Zambia became more drastic with the outbreak of the African war of liberation that began after the Rhodesia Unilateral Declaration of Independence (UDI) in 1965.

ZAMBIAN INDEPENDENCE, THE ZIMBABWE WAR OF LIBERATION, AND THE UDI, 1964–1979

The Tonga people living along the Zimbabwe-Zambia border were negatively affected by the border relations between Zambia and Rhodesia between 1964, when Zambia officially achieved independence, and the end of the liberation war in Rhodesia in 1979. The relations between the two territories shifted in the mid-1960s away from the relatively harmonious affairs enabled by the ten-year Federation of Rhodesia and Nyasaland (1953–1963). The state-to-state relations involved initial relative soft-handedness by the Rhodesian state in relation to Zambia because it sought to maintain its economic hold on the Zambian market. However, this was not the case for the Rhodesian state's treatment of the Tonga borderland community, as the Rhodesians sought to secure the border against infiltration by the Zimbabwe People's Revolutionary Army (ZIPRA) from Zambia, from where it was launching the liberation war. The state border management between the 1960s and 1979 was a low-point for the Tonga borderland community in Binga, as it was characterized by harassment from state security services, included a ban on Tonga crossing the river to Zambia, and the laying of anti-personnel mines along parts of the Zambezi riverbank. This time period created bad memories that further evoke the unpopularity of the border function of the Zambezi River in the present-day Tonga community, but in different ways.

The onset of the armed liberation war in 1966 resulted in restrictive border policy by the Rhodesia Front (RF)-led government, which effectively closed the border in 1973 and stifled interaction between Tonga people across the Zambezi. The separation of the Tonga people in Zambia and Zimbabwe that emerged during the 1950s dam construction displacements was entrenched by the war from the mid-1960s to 1979. McGregor reveals that as the liberation war intensified, state controls over the Zambezi River crossing were increasingly harsh.[47] In 1972, the Rhodesian security forces moved along the riverbanks destroying canoes and preventing access to fishing activities for local community members.[48] In an interview with the author, Van Sinampande indicated that he was able to visit his relatives in Zambia only after Zimbabwe's independence, as movement across the river during the war years was virtually impossible.[49] Most of the interviewees consulted during research for this study broadly talked of the war years as a period where the border was totally shut, except for a few rare incidents where some Tonga people evaded the security forces to visit their relatives across the Zambezi River. The Rhodesian security forces even crossed to the opposite side of the border to intimidate borderlands communities in an effort to keep them from cooperating with the Zimbabwean combatants moving from Zambian training camps to Rhodesia.[50] Thus, state border security operations during the liberation war years created a hated barrier for the Tonga borderlands people, not only because they struggled to access water resources but also because they were unable to cross the borderline to Zambia.

The planting of landmines by the Rhodesia state along its Mozambican and Zambian borders made the borderlines deadly hotspots during and after the war period. According to a Parliamentary report on the status of Zimbabwean borders in 2014, the country had six minefields along borders with Zambia and Mozambique which covered 2,700 km, with the Victoria Falls-Mlibizi minefield covering 220 km of the river border.[51] These landmines have left borderlands communities to deal with the negative border policies of colonial Zimbabwe as they prevented movement of people across the borderline where they were laid. The minefields have continued to pose a danger to human and environmental life even after demining activities in the area by the post-independence government. The fact that the landmines further made visiting virtually impossible for the Tonga communities separated in Zimbabwe and Zambia across the Zambezi River increased disaffection against state border security policy in colonial Zimbabwe. It is because of such historical disaffection that the Binga Tonga borderlands community views most state border management strategies with skepticism, thereby diminishing cooperation over state border security policy over time.

ZIMBABWEAN INDEPENDENCE AND BORDER LIFE IN BINGA DISTRICT, 1980–1999

The end of colonial rule in Zimbabwe brought enthusiasm for change among the previously segregated African communities.[52] In terms of the Tonga borderlands community in Binga, the community expected redress with respect to the loss of economic resources, plus the social and cultural disruption that characterized the colonial era. There were various changes with respect to the border administration in the district, but the absence of a fully-fledged border post in Binga by 1999 partly shaped the continued diverging views of the utility of the Zambezi River in the district. This absence of a fully-fledged border post has over the years caused most ordinary Binga residents to disregard any other border security initiatives, as the lack of a border post was understood to mean that there "is no border" in the district. This can be understood in light of the conceptualization of the border as synonymous to a border post.[53] From the early 1980s, there were plans to establish a border post in Binga. While the state eventually heeded the community's appeal for easier movement of people across the Zambezi during the mid-1990s, many restrictions still inhibited the contact of Tonga groups on both sides of the border. The immediate concern of the Binga community with the coming of Zimbabwean independence was to address the ills of the colonial government, including the administration of the Zimbabwe-Zambia border in the district. McGregor highlights that through the 1981 BRDC Lusumpuko Plan, the district administrators advocated radical major developments in education, health, agricultural, transport, and fishing industries.[54] The plans included establishment of a border post and a scheduled waterway transport system combining passengers and cargo that was to ply across the Zambezi River.[55]

After the attainment of independence, the Tonga people's movement across the river was relatively improved simply by the end of the militaristic border security policy that had characterized the RF era. However, the Tonga people in Binga district mostly had to use the official border posts in Victoria Falls and Kariba, both more than 300 km from the district. The Binga Police Station Officer-in-Charge in 1989, Handscall Mashanda, revealed that before 1985 there was a special provision that allowed Tonga people to use the Mlibizi, an informal border crossing point along the Zambezi River, 95 kilometers from Binga Center, as an entry and exit point.[56] Mashanda added that the arrangement was discontinued because some people were abusing the privilege by smuggling cannabis and fish from Zambia, prompting the government to close all the exit points in Binga District.[57] While for the state the main objective was policing the border to prevent smuggling of drugs and a variety of other goods into the country, the closure of the border negatively impacted the Tonga people. The

Tonga had hoped that the change from the Ian Smith-led government would lead to easy access to their relatives on the Zambian side of the border. Thus, the border continued to be a barrier in the multidimensional interaction of the Tonga borderlands communities in both Binga and Sinazongwe, on the Zimbabwean and Zambian sides of the border respectively.

The Tonga people in Binga responded to the closing of the borders by the state by renewing their calls for opening of border posts that would allow them regular social contacts with their Zambian kith and kin. The need for easier access to the Zambian side was one of the major topical concerns for the Tonga borderlands community in the 1980s and the early 1990s. The Tonga people used advocacy and subtle acts of resistance to the shutting of the border crossing points by the state. In 1989, for instance, BRDC councilors appealed to the Ministry of Home Affairs, which was responsible for the state management of border posts, to establish three border posts at Mlibizi in the Saba area, Binga Center, and Mujele near the Sengwa and Zambezi River confluence.[58] In 1994, the BRDC Senior Executive Officer Isaac Zhou also revealed that local Tonga people had appealed for the establishment of a border post, arguing that they were being forced to forego some essential family engagements just a few kilometers across the river because they had no passports and money to travel through the distant border posts in Victoria Falls and Kariba.[59] Thus, in this instance, the Binga community used engagement with government officials to address their concerns relating to facilitating better social contacts with their relatives on the northern side of the Zambezi River.

The other way in which the community responded to state border policy in Binga during the 1980s and the 1990s was through evading the border security enforcement mechanisms along the river. In 1992, the then-Member of Parliament for Binga, Paul Mpande Siachimbo, highlighted that local Tonga people were resorting to illegal border jumping whenever they wanted to visit relatives in Zambia, even with the police always on the lookout for border jumpers.[60] He added that such activities were rampant in Mlibizi, Simatelele, and Zambezi Mission areas where Lake Kariba is narrow and the people could use canoes and rowing boats to cross during the night.[61] The community, therefore, disregarded the state border controls to visit their relatives on the Zambian side. In addition to just visiting relatives, Siachimbo revealed, other people in the community capitalized on the situation to engage in poaching and smuggling activities in the same manner, which, in turn, intensified the desire of the state to enforce restrictive measures.[62] In a related case in the Hwange district of Zimbabwe, villagers in the Makwa and Deka communal areas were constantly arrested by the Zimbabwe Republic Police (ZRP) for smuggling goods across the Zambezi border in 1992.[63]

The villagers justified these activities, saying they had not produced enough food in their fields, thereby forcing them to look to the river for survival.[64] However, the same villagers also revealed that the dwindling water levels in the Zambezi led to fish scarcity, so they resorted to cross-border trade with the Zambian communities on the other side of the Zambezi river.[65] To the borderlands communities, therefore, the river provided an alternative for survival in times of need through fishing, cross-border trade, and related cross-border activities, defined by the state as crimes such as poaching. On the other hand, the state, in this case through the police, sought to prevent the loss of state revenues and resources through border leakages by keeping the borderlands communities from illegally crossing the Zambezi border. As such, the everyday basic needs of the community caused many individuals to break state border regulations for survival.

In 1994, the Zimbabwean state responded to the plight of the Binga Tonga people by allowing for easier travel to and from Zambia for social reasons. Social reasons encapsulated in the approved visits included funerals, sickness, and a variety of traditional ceremonies. The Zimbabwean government negotiated with the Zambian authorities to allow borderlands communities in the two countries to move from one country to another using special permits instead of passports.[66] According to the then-Zimbabwean Acting Chief Immigration Officer, Spencer Nhari, residents of border communities were required to go to the nearest police station where they would be given permits to cross the border to enable them to travel to the neighboring country.[67] He added that the permits cost between ZW$10 and ZW$20 and could be used repeatedly for three months.[68] This move by the government resulted in the borderlands community partly embracing that change in policy. In 1995, Jericho Ndiweni, a Binga Police Station Officer-in-Charge, revealed that about sixty people utilized these permits per month in Binga district.[69] He, however, bemoaned that despite efforts by the police to centralize the crossing point at the Binga Front Harbor, the security services faced difficulties in monitoring the movement of people because they could cross at any point along the river using dugout canoes.[70] Thus, while the state introduced the permit system in an attempt to make it easier for the borderlands community to see their relatives across the border, the border was still porous, which meant that some undocumented travelers still moved across the border at any given time. As such, sections of the Binga community still disregarded the state border measures and crossed the Zambezi River without permits, showing how, to them, the border was insignificant in controlling their access to their kith and kin across the river.

To some Binga Tonga people, the passes were not an ideal solution for reinstating the social contact that existed in the Zambezi Valley before the construction of the Kariba Dam in the 1950s. A resident in Simatelele area of Binga, Bigboy Munsaka, highlighted that while the passes allowed people to cross the Zambezi without passports from the 1990s, it was the state that stipulated the number of days that one was allowed to stay on the other side of the border.[71] In a separate interview, Beauty Nyoni, another Binga resident, said that because the state did not allow travelers to carry goods such as groceries across the Zambezi in Binga, cross-border business was still not viable despite the state's gesture of passes in an effort to re-unite the Tonga people on their respective sides of the border.[72] Thus, the introduction of cross-border passes in Binga did not go a long way toward solving the plight of the community, leading to continued disregard of state border controls even with the new government's border policies.

As the state introduced the pass system in borderlands communities, it also embarked on the establishment of small, formal border posts along its borderline. In the case of Binga District, plans for establishing a formal border were mooted as early as 1994. BRDC Senior Executive Officer Zhou revealed in the same year that after state-to-state negotiations between Zimbabwe and Zambia, both agreed to establish border posts at Binga and Sinazongwe respectively.[73] He added that the purpose of the establishment of the posts was to facilitate movement of people and trade between the local borderlands communities on both sides.[74] Other small border posts which were being established by the Zimbabwean government in the 1990s include Kanyemba, linking Zimbabwe, Zambia, and Mozambique, as well as Maitengwe and Mphoeng, linking Zimbabwe and Botswana. In the case of the Kanyemba border post in Guruve District, the three governments aimed at building a bridge to boost tourism, investment, and general interaction among the borderlands communities.[75] The state, therefore, deliberately engaged in the establishment of smaller border posts along the Zimbabwean border in the 1990s, with the main objective being to improve revenue inflow into its coffers. For the Binga borderlands community, however, residents hoped that the establishment of formal border posts would allow their own local economy to benefit from cross-border business adventures, infrastructural development, and a drop in cross-border crime that would make private property safer. By the turn of the twentieth century, the formal border crossing point had not yet been established, necessitating further calls for the transformation of the Zimbabwe-Zambia border into an economic asset via a formal border crossing, rather than just a point of social interaction between the divided Tonga community on both sides of the Zambezi River. On the other hand, the state continued to try to curtail rising cross-border crime that characterized the Binga District from 2000 onward.

THE NEXUS RE-EXAMINED: BORDER SECURITY, ECONOMIC DEVELOPMENT, AND TONGA SOCIAL LIFE IN BINGA DISTRICT, 2000–2017

Muguti has examined the interlinkages between border security and economic development in Binga District for the period between 2000 and 2018.[76] In the study, he focused on the linkage between border security and development primarily as to how they affect the larger nation-state, rather than specifically the Tonga borderlands community. While the previous study revealed the need for improvement of border security mechanisms on the Zimbabwe-Zambia border in Binga District, state actors hoped the improvement would improve state revenue collection, stop leakages of wildlife, and broadly enhance infrastructural development in Binga District as a whole.[77] The current chapter revisits the discussion on the border security-economic development nexus in Binga District, while adding a third variable—Tonga everyday social life. Understanding the historical socio-cultural attachment to the river, social relations between the Tonga people on both sides, as well as the Tonga community's justifications for resisting the barrier functions of the Zambezi River border helps us better understand complexities in the Tonga borderlands community.

The period after 2000 has been characterized by advocacy by the Binga Tonga borderlands community for the relaxation of border enforcement, not only for the social reconnection of the Tonga people in Zambia and Zimbabwe, but also for the facilitation of community economic benefits. Growing calls for redressing political marginalization, identity reconstruction, and ownership of wildlife also characterized the turn of the century in Binga District.[78] Belmont Mugande argued that allowing Tonga to cross the border with only a pass aided the Tonga people only in terms of social contact, which meant that the government had not addressed the economic plight of the Tonga people in terms of benefiting from cross-border trade activities.[79] He added that while the state was protecting its economic priorities by reducing poaching and smuggling, ordinary Tonga in the Zambezi Valley had no direct economic benefit from the state effecting this border security policy.[80] Thus, the efforts by the state to facilitate the movement of the Tonga communities for social reasons through passes in the 1990s faced even stiffer resistance from the Binga people in the twenty-first century in the context of worsening economic hardships.

The long-held belief that the river is a resource for the Tonga people was further fueled by the Land Reform Program. This fight for ownership of land by the peasant community, and the government's response with a land redistribution program elsewhere in the country seem to have cemented sentiments of entitlement to the Zambezi River by the Tonga people. Speaking at World

Tourism Day celebrations at Kulizwe Lodge on October 4, 2013, Chief Pashu, a traditional leader, reiterated that the Tonga people in Binga should benefit from the river in all ways possible because they did not benefit from the land distribution program which transpired across the more agrarian districts of Zimbabwe.[81] Essentially, the chief was emphasizing that the Zambezi is a resource meant to first benefit the Tonga people in all aspects of life, even before those benefits accrue to the state and other stakeholders. This sense of entitlement has led residents of the Tonga borderlands community to be able to justify those who partake in acts ranging from smuggling and complicity in poaching syndicates and cattle rustling, among other cross-border crimes. While to the state, these acts are a contravention of assorted border security legislation, to some Tonga people partaking in the activities, they are entitled to any benefit from the Zambezi River, including defying state border security policies, because the Zambezi is "their natural resource."

Despite the narrative pushed from below by the Tonga borderlands community that the Zambezi River is a natural resource and not a border, there are sections of the community that now subsist on the existence of the border. Activities along the border, particularly informal cross-border trade, have created a "border within a border"[82] where there are two borders within the borderlands community. These are the physical borderline with Zambia and the "imagined" border between the Binga Tonga people and non-Tongas in Zimbabwe. With the tightening of border policies, especially restricting importation of various second-hand clothes bales, skin lightening creams, and sexual enhancers, borderlands communities, including Binga, have increasingly become the place for the movement of such goods from one country to another. In 2009, for instance, in Victoria Falls, there were rising cases of women charged with smuggling of prohibited pharmaceuticals. The women mainly smuggled cosmetics such as Movate, Epidem, and Extra Clair creams, regarded as hazardous to users by the Zimbabwean pharmaceutical authorities.[83]

In the 2000s, Zimbabwean cross-border traders have increasingly stopped using formal border posts to better evade state border authorities, with those who diverted from the Victoria Falls, Kariba, and Chirundu border posts using the Binga route.[84] There has been growing interest in unpacking the complexity of smuggling in different parts of the world in recent literature.[85] In the case of Binga, cross-border traders based in areas such as Bulawayo, Kwekwe, and Harare capitalize on the social relations between the Zimbabwean and Zambian Tonga borderlands communities, as members of the communities can facilitate the evasion of state border security agencies in the Zambezi River stretch. Informal conversations with cross-border traders in Binga indicated that there are people in Binga, both Tonga and non-Tonga, and Sinazongwe who facilitate their movement across the Zambezi River on their way from Harare to Lusaka and vice versa.[86] Through a complex network involving informal cross-border traders, poachers, cattle rustlers, assorted cross-border criminals, and corrupt security personnel, the function of the Zambezi as a state border has actually been used as a "resource" by some individuals in the Tonga borderland community. This experience validates the argument propounded by borderland theorists such as Flynn and Coplan, among others, who posit that although African borders were "artificially constructed," some communities in the contemporary lives cannot imagine their existence without the same borders because of the material benefits they get from legal and illegal cross-border activities.[87] Therefore, while the Binga Tonga community broadly subscribes to the notion that the Zambezi River is a resource rather than a border, leading to many nostalgic sentiments of the pre-Kariba Dam Tonga community, there are other sections of the same community who are subsisting and thriving because of the opportunities brought by the porous border, thereby acknowledging that the state border can also be a lucrative resource.

CONCLUSION

The Tonga people in Zimbabwe's Binga District have negotiated the state border security policy in a wide variety of ways from the colonial period to the present. The basis for challenging the state border security policy has been grounded in their historical social, cultural, spiritual, and economic attachment to the Zambezi River. The Zimbabwean and Zambian Tonga people reminisce about the ease with which they interacted across the Zambezi River before the Kariba Dam-induced displacements that forced them further apart. This chapter has focused specifically on how the Tonga borderlands community in Binga District has responded to various state border security policies from 1963 to 2017. While the Zimbabwean and Zambian governments see the Zambezi River as a point of territorial demarcation/border between the two countries, to the Tonga people in Binga District, the Zambezi is more prominent as a natural resource rather than a border, hence fueling activities that disregard the formal state boundaries.

The history of the Tonga people in the Binga borderlands community since 1957, therefore, is characterized by local people challenging the state to maintain the Zambezi River/Lake Kariba as a natural resource that continues to benefit ordinary people rather than merely a government-administered border meant to serve national interests. Notwithstanding the resentment over state border security policy, there are sections of the community that benefit economically from cross-border activities that the authorities have deemed illegal, like the unlawful movement of people and goods across the Zambezi River.

NOTES

1. This publication was made possible by support from the Social Science Research Council's Next Generation Social Sciences in Africa Fellowship, with funds provided by the Carnegie Corporation of New York. I am grateful to Professor Sandra Swart (my PhD Supervisor), whose invaluable guidance enabled me to come up with this publication.

2. Joshua Chikozho, Tapuwa Raymond Mubaya, and Munyaradzi Mawere, "Nyaminyami, 'The Tonga River-God': The Place and Role of the Nyaminyami in the Tonga People's Cosmology and Environment Conservation Practices," in *Harnessing Cultural Capital for Sustainability: Pan-Africanist Perspective,* eds. Munyaradzi Mawere and Samuel Awuah-Nyamekye (Bamenda: Langaa Research and Publishing Common Initiative Group, 2015), 243–264; Joshua Matanzima, "Stereotyping, Exploitation, and Appropriation of African Traditional Beliefs: The Case of Nyaminyami Water Spirit among the Batonga People of Northwestern Zimbabwe, 1860s to 1960s," *Journal of Africana* 10, no. 1 (2022): 72–99.

3. For example, Micheal Tremmel and Loes Roos, *The People of the Great River: The Tonga Hoped that the Water Would Follow Them* (Gweru: Mambo Press, 1994); Terrence M. Mashingaidze, "Beyond the Kariba Dam Induced Displacements: The Zimbabwean Tonga Struggles for Restitution, 1900s-2000s," *International Journal on Minority and Group Rights* 20 (2013): 381–404; Cecilia Govha Dhodho, "Displacement and Livelihood Vulnerability among the Tonga Women of Binga, 1958–1980," in *Tonga Livelihoods in Rural Zimbabwe*, eds. Kirk Helliker and Joshua Matanzima (New York: Routledge, 2023), 115–130; Joshua Matanzima, "We have been Displaced Several Times since 1956: The Tonga-Goba Involuntary Resettlement Experiences at Kariba Dam," *Water International* 47, no. 8 (2022): 1249–1266.

4. Siambabala Bernard Manyena, "Ethnic Identity, Agency and Development: The Case of the Zimbabwean Tonga," in *Tonga Timeline: Appraising Sixty Years of Multi-Disciplinary Research in Zambia and Zimbabwe*, eds. Lisa Cliggett and Virginia Bond (Lusaka: Lembani Trust, 2013), 45–65; Joshua Matanzima and Umali Saidi, "Landscape, Belonging and Identity in North-west Zimbabwe: A Semiotic Analysis," *African Identities* 18, no. 1–2 (2020): 233–251; Umali Saidi and Joshua Matanzima, "Negotiating Territoriality in North-Western Zimbabwe: Locating the Multiple Identities of Batonga, Shangwe and Karanga in History," *African Journal of Inter/Multidisciplinary Studies* 3 (2022): 61–74.

5. See, for example, JoAnn McGregor, "Crocodile Crimes: People versus Wildlife and the Politics of Postcolonial Conservation on Lake Kariba, Zimbabwe," *Geoforum* 36, no. 3 (2005): 353–369; Joshua Matanzima and Ivan Marowa, "Human Conflict and Precarious Livelihoods of the Tonga-Speaking People of Northwestern Zimbabwe," in *Livelihoods of Ethnic Minorities in Rural Zimbabwe*, eds. Kirk

Helliker, Patience Chadambuka, and Joshua Matanzima (Cham: Springer Geography, 2022), 107–122.

6. See, among others, JoAnn McGregor, "Living with the River: Landscape and Memory in the Zambezi Valley," in *Social History and African Environments,* eds. William Beinart and JoAnn McGregor (Oxford: James Currey, 2003); Siambabala Bernard Manyena, Andrew E. Collins, Frank Mudimba, and Danisa Mudimba, "Reducing Marginalisation of Fishermen Through Participatory Action Research in the Zambezi Valley, Zimbabwe," *International Journal of African Development* 3, no. 2 (2013): 5–22; Cecilia Govha Dhodho, "Letting them Starve: The 2008 Food Crisis and Marginalisation of the Tonga of Binga," in *Livelihoods of Ethnic Minorities in Rural Zimbabwe*, eds. Kirk Helliker, Patience Chadambuka, and Joshua Matanzima (Cham: Springer Geography, 2022), 160; Kirk Helliker and Joshua Matanzima, *Tonga Livelihoods in Rural Zimbabwe* (New York: Routledge, 2023).

7. JoAnn McGregor, *Crossing the Zambezi: The Politics of Landscape on a Central African Frontier* (Woodbridge: James Currey, 2009).

8. Teverayi Muguti, "Nexus between Border (In)Security and Economic Development in Binga District since 2000," in *Tonga Livelihoods in Rural Zimbabwe*, eds. Kirk Helliker and Joshua Matanzima (New York: Routledge, 2023), 178.

9. See, for example, Sergej V. Sevastianov, Ju Lajne and Anton, A. Kireev eds., *Introduction to Border Studies* (Vladivostok: Far Eastern Federal University, 2015).

10. Gloria Anzaldua, *Borderlands/La Frontera: The New Mestiza* (San Francisco: Aunt Lute Book Company, 1987).

11. Donna K. Flynn, "We are the Border: Identity, Exchange and the State along the Benin-Nigerian Border," *American Ethnologist* 24, no. 2 (1997): 311–330.

12. For example, Anthony Ijaola Asiwaju, *Artificial Boundaries* (Lagos: Lagos University Press, 1984); Mahmood Mamdani, "Beyond Settler and Native as Political Identities: Overcoming the Political Legacy of Colonialism," *Comparative Studies of Society and History* 43, no. 4 (2001): 651–664; Adu A. Boahen, *Perspectives on Colonialism* (Baltimore: Johns Hopkins University Press, 1987); Jeffrey Herbst, "The Creation and Maintenance of National Boundaries in Africa," *International Organisation* 43, no. 4 (1989): 673–692.

13. Flynn, "We are the Border."

14. See, Paul Nugent, "Borderland Identities in Comparative Perspective: Chieftaincy, Religion and Belonging along Ghana-Togo and Senegal-Gambia Borders," in *The Role of Tradition and Modernity in African Political Cultures and Urban Conflicts: The Case of Ghana in Comparative Perspective,* edited by Per O. Hernaes (Trondheim: Norwegian University of Science and Technology, 2005); Paul Nugent, *Boundaries, Communities and State Making in West Africa: The Centrality of the Margins*, (Cambridge: Cambridge University Press, 2019); W. Zeller, *What Makes Borders Real in the Namibian-Zambia and Uganda-South Sudan Borderlands* (Helsinki: Department of Political and Economic Studies, 2015); David Coplan, "First Meets Third: Analysing Inequality along the US-Mexico and South Africa-Lesotho Borders," *Journal of Borderland Studies* 25, no. 2 (2010): 53–64.

15. Anusa Daimon, "Commuter Migration Across Artificial Frontiers: The Case of Partitioned Communities along Zimbabwe-Mozambique Border," *Journal of*

Borderland Studies 31, no. 4 (2016): 463–479; Nedson Pophiwa, "Mobile Livelihoods-The Players Involved in Smuggling of Commodities across the Zimbabwe-Mozambique Border," *Journal of Borderlands Studies* 25, no. 2 (2010): 65–76; Francis Dube, *Public Health at Border of Zimbabwe and Mozambique, 1890–1940: African Experiences in a Contested Space* (Cham: Springer Nature, 2020); Nicholas Nyachega and Wesley Mwatwara, "On Renamo 'War': Entrepreneurial Synergies and Everyday Life in the Honde Valley Borderlands, c. 1980s–2020," *Journal of Southern African Studies* 47, no. 6, (2021): 973–991.

16. Muguti, "Border (In)Security."

17. Zimbabwe National Statistics Agency, *Population and Housing Census: Preliminary Report on Population Figures*, 2022: 56.

18. https://www.humanitarianresponse.info/en/operations/zimbabwe/assessment/zimvac-2019-rural-livelihoods-assessment-report, accessed on 23 September 2021.

19. A Binga Rural District Councilor revealed in an interview with the author that the average longest walking distances to schools and health service centers range between 10 km to 20 km, making it difficult for the ordinary citizen in the district to access these critical services.

20. Manyena, "Ethnic Identity, Agency, and Development," 35.

21. Elizabeth Colson, *Tonga Religious Life in the 20th Century* (Lusaka: Book World Publishers, 2006), 69.

22. Manyena, "Ethnic Identity, Agency, and Development," 35. My interview with Joshua Chikozho (Batonga Museum Curator). Informal conversations with the Tonga people during my stay in Binga reiterated the significance of this name in the day-to-day interactions of the people with the Zambezi River.

23. Chikozho, et al., "Nyaminyami," 248.

24. Ibid, 252.

25. Matanzima, "Stereotyping, Exploitation, and Appropriation."

26. The Nyaminyami sculpture is one of the Batonga museum artifacts that is utilized to share the religious history of the Tonga people in Binga district and beyond.

27. Godfrey Tabona Ncube, *A History of Northwestern Zimbabwe* (Kadoma: Mond Books, 2004), 5.

28. Ibid.

29. JoAnn McGregor, "Patrolling Kariba's Waters: State Authorities, Fishing and the Border Economy," *Journal of Southern African Studies* 34, no. 4 (2008): 862.

30. Pathisa Nyathi, *Zimbabwe Cultural Heritage* (Bulawayo: Ama books, 2005), 63–64.

31. Ibid.

32. National Archives of Zambia, SP4/2/49, Gwembe Tour Reports, Letter by N.J. Suckling to the Chief Editor of the *Central African Post*, 6 July 1960.

33. See, for instance, McGregor, "Living with the River".

34. Tremmel and Roos, *The People of the Great River*, 32.

35. For an analysis and interpretation of the song's significance to retelling Tonga sad memories regarding the Kariba Dam construction-induced displacements, see Itai Muwati, "Negotiating Space, Voice and Recognition: An Analysis of the 'District

Song' of the Tonga People of Binga, Zimbabwe," *Muziki, Journal of Music Research in Africa* 12, no. 2 (2015): 22–36.

36. Interview with Biggy Mudenda, Binga Centre, 13 November 2021.

37. National Archives of Zambia, SP4/2/49, Gwembe Tour Reports, Letter by N.J. Suckling to the Chief Editor of the *Central African Post*, 6 July 1960.

38. Ncube, *History of Northwestern Zimbabwe*, 24.

39. Ibid.

40. Ibid.

41. Interview with Joshua Chikozho, Batonga Museum Curator, Binga Centre, 30 September 2021.

42. Interview with Collen Munenge, Village Head in Bulawayo Kraal, Manjolo Ward, Binga, 17 September 2021.

43. Ibid.

44. McGregor, "Living with the River," 98.

45. Ibid.

46. Ibid, 99.

47. McGregor, "Living with the River," 103.

48. Ibid.

49. Interview with Van Sinampande, Retired civil servant, Binga Centre, 12 December 2021.

50. National Archives of Zambia, FA/1/172, Zambia-Rhodesia. This file has various details of boundary incursions that show a lot of incidents where Rhodesian soldiers confronted Zambian citizens either in the river or on Zambian land with the overall objective to get information on the whereabouts of guerillas and the presence of Zambian security forces in the vicinity. A document titled, "Incursions by Rhodesian Security Forces into Zambia," documents about fifty-three cases of varying border confrontations between the Zambian Police and various borderlands citizens and the Rhodesian soldiers. This heavy presence on the Zimbabwe-Zambia border affected the movement of borderlands communities across the borders.

51. Parliament of Zimbabwe, *First Report of the Thematic Committee on Peace and Security: The Status of the Country's Border, Human Trafficking and Smuggling*, July 2014, 6.

52. James Muzondidya, "From Buoyancy to Crisis, 1980—1997," in Brian Raftopoulos and Alouis S. Mlambo, eds., *Becoming Zimbabwe* (Harare: Weaver Press, 2009), 167.

53. See Muguti, "Border (In)Security" for more on how the Binga community conceptualizes border security, 179–182.

54. McGregor, *Crossing the Zambezi,* 157.

55. Ibid.

56. "Binga Call for Three New Border Posts," *Chronicle*, 2 July 1989.

57. Ibid.

58. Ibid.

59. "Zambia, Zimbabwe on plans to Open Border Post in Binga," *Herald,* 22 April 1994.

60. "Government Urged to Set up Border Post in Binga," *Chronicle*, 2 April 1992.

61. Ibid.

62. Ibid.

63. "Illegal Cross-Border Deals Worsen," *Chronicle*, 12 December 1992.

64. Ibid.

65. Ibid.

66. "Border Folks Can Now Cross to Zambia Without Passports," *Herald*, 21 December 1994.

67. Ibid.

68. Ibid.

69. "Border Crossed at Binga with no Passports," *Chronicle*, 23 April 1995.

70. Ibid.

71. Interview with Bigboy Munsaka, Simatelele Business Centre, 17 September 2021.

72. Interview with Beauty Nyoni, Mlibizi Business Centre, 18 February 2022.

73. "Border Folks Can Now Cross to Zambia Without Passports," *Herald*, 21 December 1994.

74. Ibid.

75. "Border Post to get a Bridge," *Chronicle*, 03 November 1998.

76. Muguti, "Border (In)Security."

77. Ibid.

78. See, for example, Siamambala Bernard Manyena, Andrew E. Collins, Frank Mudimba, and Danisa Mudimba, "'Are You Serious to Ask Me About Who Owns Wildlife' Politics of Autonomy Over Wildlife Resources in the Zambezi Valley, Zimbabwe," *Forum for Development Studies* 40, no. 1 (2013): 87–109.

79. Interview with Belmont Mugande, Kaani Ward resident, Binga Centre, 28 September 2022.

80. Ibid.

81. Chief Pashu's Speech at the World Tourism Day Celebrations, Kulizwe Lodge, 4 October 2013.

82. I use this phrase to show that the fact that passes give privilege to the Tongas to cross to the Zambian side without passports creates a pseudo-entity where people with different ethnic origins such as Shona and Ndebele are regarded as "others." In fact, in Binga District, there is a well-known term "*mazwakule*" meaning non-Tonga Zimbabweans, reiterating that they conceptualize the Binga borderland as a quasi-independent entity. These sentiments are cemented by the fact that the district is the only one in Zimbabwe with a District Song (anthem) "*Cigambiyo Cipati*" (see, Muwati, "Negotiating Space, Voice and Recognition," for further analysis on the lyrics of the Binga District Song) which chronicles the catastrophic consequences of the Kariba Dam-induced displacements on the Tonga borderland community. This "border within a border" concept has placed some Tonga people in Binga at a central point of controlling cross-border trade for personal profit.

83. Ibid.

84. Muguti, "Border (In)Security."

85. Max Gallien and Florian Weigand, *The Routledge Handbook of Smuggling,* (London: Routledge, 2022).

86. Informal conversations with cross-border traders at Binga Centre, 30 December 2021.

87. Flynn, "We are the Border"; Coplan, "African Border Studies."

BIBLIOGRAPHY

Anzaldua, Gloria. *Borderlands/La Frontera: The New Mestiza*. San Francisco: Aunt Lute Book Company, 1987.

Asiwaju, Anthony Ijaola. *Artificial Boundaries*. Lagos: Lagos University Press, 1984.

Boahen, Adu A. *Perspectives on Colonialism*. Baltimore: Johns Hopkins University Press, 1987.

Chikozho, Joshua, Tapuwa Raymond Mubaya, and Munyaradzi Mawere. "Nyaminyami, 'The Tonga River-God': The Place and Role of the Nyaminyami in the Tonga People's Cosmology and Environment Conservation Practices." In *Harnessing Cultural Capital for Sustainability: Pan-Africanist Perspective,* edited by Munyaradzi Mawere and Samuel Awuah-Nyamekye, 243–264. Bamenda: Langaa Research and Publishing Common Initiative Group, 2015.

Colson, Elizabeth. *Tonga Religious Life in the 20th Century*. Lusaka: Book World Publishers, 2006.

Coplan, David. "First Meets Third: Analysing Inequality along the US-Mexico and South Africa-Lesotho Borders," *Journal of Borderland Studies* 25, no. 2 (2010): 53–64.

Daimon, Anusa, "Commuter Migration Across Artificial Frontiers: The Case of Partitioned Communities along the Zimbabwe-Mozambique Border," *Journal of Borderland Studies* 31, no. 4 (2016): 463–479.

Dhodho, Cecilia Govha. "Letting them Starve: The 2008 Food Crisis and Marginalisation of the Tonga of Binga." In *Livelihoods of Ethnic Minorities in Rural Zimbabwe*, edited by Kirk Helliker, Patience Chadambuka, and Joshua Matanzima, 157–171. Cham: Springer Geography, 2022.

Dhodho, Cecilia Govha. "Displacement and Livelihood Vulnerability among the Tonga Women of Binga, 1958–1980." In *Tonga Livelihoods in Rural Zimbabwe*, edited by Kirk Helliker and Joshua Matanzima, 115–130. New York: Routledge, 2023.

Flynn, Donna K. "We are the Border: Identity, Exchange and the State along the Benin-Nigerian Border." *American Ethnologist* 24, no. 2 (1997): 311–330.

Francis Dube. *Public Health at the Border of Zimbabwe and Mozambique, 1890–1940: African Experiences in a Contested Space*. Cham: Springer Nature, 2020.

Gallien, Max, and Florian Weigand. *The Routledge Handbook of Smuggling*. London: Routledge, 2022.

Helliker, Kirk, and Joshua Matanzima. *Tonga Livelihoods in Rural Zimbabwe*. New York: Routledge, 2023.

Herbst, Jeffrey. "The Creation and Maintenance of National Boundaries in Africa." *International Organisation* 43, no. 4 (1989): 673—692.

Mahmood Mamdani. "Beyond Settler and Native as Political Identities: Overcoming the Political Legacy of Colonialism." *Comparative Studies of Society and History* 43, no. 4 (2001): 651–664.

Manyena, Siambabala Bernard, Andrew E. Collins, Frank Mudimba, and Danisa Mudimba. "'Are You Serious to Ask Me About Who Owns Wildlife?' Politics of Autonomy Over Wildlife Resources in the Zambezi Valley, Zimbabwe." *Forum for Development Studies* 40, no. 1 (2013): 87–109.

Manyena, Siambabala Bernard. "Ethnic Identity, Agency and Development: The Case of the Zimbabwean Tonga." In *Tonga Timeline: Appraising Sixty Years of Multi-Disciplinary Research in Zambia and Zimbabwe*, edited by Lisa Cliggett and Virginia Bond, 45–65. Lusaka: Lembani Trust, 2013.

Manyena, Siambabala Bernard, Andrew E. Collins, Frank Mudimba, and Danisa Mudimba. "Reducing Marginalisation of Fishermen Through Participatory Action Research in the Zambezi Valley, Zimbabwe." *International Journal of African Development* 3, no. 2 (2013): 5–22.

Mashingaidze, Terrence M. "Beyond the Kariba Dam Induced Displacements: The Zimbabwean Tonga Struggles for Restitution, 1900s-2000s." *International Journal on Minority and Group Rights* 20 (2013): 381–404.

Matanzima, Joshua, and Ivan Marowa. "Human Conflict and Precarious Livelihoods of the Tonga-Speaking People of Northwestern Zimbabwe." In *Livelihoods of Ethnic Minorities in Rural Zimbabwe*, edited by Kirk Helliker, Patience Chadambuka, and Joshua Matanzima, 107–122. Cham: Springer Geography, 2022.

Matanzima, Joshua, and Umali Saidi. "Landscape, Belonging and Identity in Northwest Zimbabwe: A Semiotic Analysis." *African Identities* 18, no. 1–2 (2020): 233–251.

Matanzima, Joshua. "Stereotyping, Exploitation, and Appropriation of African Traditional Beliefs: The Case of Nyaminyami Water Spirit among the Batonga People of Northwestern Zimbabwe, 1860s to 1960s." *Journal of Africana* 10, no. 1 (2022): 72–99.

Matanzima, Joshua. "We have been Displaced Several Times since 1956: The Tonga-Goba Involuntary Resettlement Experiences at Kariba Dam." *Water International* 47, no. 8 (2022): 1249–1266.

McGregor, JoAnn. "Crocodile Crimes: People versus Wildlife and the Politics of Postcolonial Conservation on Lake Kariba, Zimbabwe." *Geoforum* 36, no. 3 (2005): 353–369.

McGregor, JoAnn. *Crossing the Zambezi: The Politics of Landscape on a Central African Frontier*. Woodbridge: James Currey, 2009.

McGregor, JoAnn. "Living with the River: Landscape and Memory in the Zambezi Valley." In *Social History and African Environments,* edited by William Beinart and JoAnne McGregor, 353–369. Oxford: James Currey, 2003.

McGregor, JoAnn. "Patrolling Kariba's Waters: State Authorities, Fishing and the Border Economy." *Journal of Southern African Studies* 34, no. 4 (2008): 861–879.

Muguti, Teverayi. "Nexus between Border (In)Security and Economic Development in Binga District since 2000." In *Tonga Livelihoods in Rural Zimbabwe*, edited by Kirk Helliker and Joshua Matanzima, 177–192. New York: Routledge, 2023.

Muwati, Itai. "Negotiating Space, Voice, and Recognition: An Analysis of the 'District Song' of the Tonga People of Binga, Zimbabwe." *Muziki, Journal of Music Research in Africa* 12, no. 2 (2015): 22–36.

Muzondidya, James. "From Buoyancy to Crisis, 1980–1997." In *Becoming Zimbabwe, edited by* Brian Raftopoulos and Alouis S. Mlambo, 167–200. Harare: Weaver Press, 2009.

Ncube, Godfrey Tabona. *A History of Northwestern Zimbabwe*. Kadoma: Mond Books, 2004.

Nugent, Paul. *Boundaries, Communities and State Making in West Africa: The Centrality of the Margins*. Cambridge: Cambridge University Press, 2019.

Nugent, Paul. "Borderland Identities in Comparative Perspective: Chieftaincy, Religion and Belonging along Ghana-Togo and Senegal-Gambia Borders." In *The Role of Tradition and Modernity in African Political Cultures and Urban Conflicts: The Case of Ghana in Comparative Perspective,* edited by Per O. Hernaes, 9–34. Trondheim: Norwegian University of Science and Technology, 2005.

Nyachega, Nicholas, and Wesley Mwatwara. "On Renamo 'War': Entrepreneurial Synergies and Everyday Life in the Honde Valley Borderlands, c. 1980s–2020." *Journal of Southern African Studies* 47, no. 6 (2021): 973–991.

Nyathi, Pathisa. *Zimbabwe's Cultural Heritage*. Bulawayo: amaBooks, 2005.

Parliament of Zimbabwe. *First Report of the Thematic Committee on Peace and Security: The Status of the Country's Border, Human Trafficking and Smuggling*. July 2014.

Pophiwa, Nedson. "Mobile Livelihoods-The Players Involved in Smuggling of Commodities across the Zimbabwe-Mozambique Border." *Journal of Borderlands Studies* 25, no. 2 (2010): 65–76.

Saidi, Umali, and Joshua Matanzima. "Negotiating Territoriality in North-Western Zimbabwe: Locating the Multiple Identities of Batonga, Shangwe and Karanga in History." *African Journal of Inter/Multidisciplinary Studies* 3 (2022): 61–74.

Sevastianov, Sergej V., Ju Lajne, and Anton A. Kireev, editors. *Introduction to Border Studies*. Vladivostok: Far Eastern Federal University, 2015.

Tremmel, Micheal, and Loes Roos. *The People of the Great River: The Tonga Hoped that the Water Would Follow Them*. Gweru: Mambo Press, 1994.

Zeller, Wolfgang. *What Makes Borders Real in the Namibian-Zambia and Uganda-South Sudan Borderlands*. Helsinki: Department of Political and Economic Studies, 2015.

Zimbabwe National Statistics Agency. *Population and Housing Census: Preliminary Report on Population Figures*. 2022.

Chapter 6

Crossing a "Fictitious" Border

Angolan Refugees' Mobility and Settling Dynamics in the Lower-Congo (1950s–1970s)

Ana Guardião

In April 1961, the Office of the United Nations High Commissioner for Refugees (UNHCR) received the first reports concerning increasing Angolan refugee influxes to the Republic of the Congo (Léopoldville), specifically to the Lower-Congo region.[1] Although mobility across the Angolan-Congolese border had been common until then, the beginning of the decolonization war in Angola, along with the ongoing conflict in the Congo, changed the contours of the situation in the region.[2]

Both migrants and refugees were now confronted with a series of new actors and contingencies on the ground. In the following months, High Commissioner Felix Schnyder and international organizations already working in the region—the League of Red Cross Societies (LRCS) and the United Nations Operation in the Congo (UNOC)—prepared the first coordinated international humanitarian response to a refugee crisis in Sub-Saharan Africa, envisioning both emergency and integration programs. The newly independent Congolese political, economic, and administrative fragilities led to a dependency on international assistance to respond to the crisis and obstructed decision-making and operational efficiency. The ongoing violent Katanga and South Kivu secessions in the Congo, which posed security and operational difficulties and created several humanitarian crises, aggravated the situation.[3] International humanitarian actors' unpreparedness to deal with the crisis and with the Angolans also contributed to the worsening situation,[4] namely when dealing with local mobility and settlement dynamics along and across the border and refugee agency.[5]

This chapter tackles Angolans' mobility dynamics during the decolonization war and previous periods, focusing on how settlement and mobility along and across the border conflicted with the application of international instruments and defied different (international and local) humanitarian practices. Contrary to Rich's approach, which focuses on the (in)capacity of UNHCR to coerce refugees to engage in defined solutions to the crisis,[6] I argue that, to better comprehend the Angolan refugees' experience during the decolonization war, it is essential to encompass the multifaceted understandings of the border by different actors and how border understandings interacted with the complexities of employing international norms and humanitarian practices in this context. Bringing the refugee experience to the fore allows historians to not repeat the mistakes made by humanitarian organizations in the time of the crisis.

Exploring the multiple significances of the border also enables a more complete, yet still limited, understanding of refugeedom in this particular context.[7] First, international borders are central to the definition of *refugee* embedded in international instruments and, consequently, the granting of refugee status to people on the move. Eligibility for refugee status, among other factors, is thus dependent on the crossing of an international border and is determined by international organizations and state authorities in negotiating international protection and assistance mechanisms. However, as in other geographies, the establishment of the Angolan-Congolese border had been devoid of considerations about local societies' geographical understandings and was, thus, in practice, *fictitious* to a great part of the local population since it separated (and erased from the map) the Kingdom of the Kongo. Therefore, mobility across the *fictitious* border was common due to the permanence of kinship communities, mainly of Bakongo origin, in what had been established as Angolan and Congolese territory. In the late colonial period, Angola was a society in flux with rampant abuse of workers, increased European settlement, and developmental incentives that caused much migration from its northern provinces in the 1950s, later reinforced by Congolese independence in June 1960. Consequently, although the border was, to a certain extent, *fictitious*, it separated different contexts before and during the war: the Angolan one associated with violence and persecution, the Congolese one with (relative) stability and protection. Angolans resistance to external (normative, political, and humanitarian) impositions regarding their freedom of movement in the border region was a lasting process, shaped by different modalities of protest; one transversal to colonial and decolonization momentums.

Based on previous and new research in Portuguese and international archives,[8] the chapter focuses on the Angolan refugee experience and on the interactions of refugees with different humanitarian, political, military, and governmental actors by exploring mobility dynamics. Although deriving from resources in colonial and international organizations archives, the material used for this research is fruitful in accounting for refugee agency. For that purpose, it is fundamental to read against the grain. The information collected from the archives of the Portuguese secret police in Angola, which used infiltrators to gather information in the Congo, the testimonies of refugees in interviews conducted by international organizations' officials and the reports and memorandums of humanitarian agents on the ground are some examples of the documents analyzed with this approach. In the first section, the chapter analyzes mobility dynamics across the border during the late colonial period and how these were assessed in debates regarding refugee eligibility determination during the first months of the conflict. The second section explores the durableness of mobility along and across the border during the decolonization war and its multifaceted usages.

THE MULTIDIMENSIONAL CHARACTER OF MOBILITY: BORDER-CROSSING DYNAMICS AND REFUGEE ELIGIBILITY

When one considers what distinguishes refugees from other people on the move, two main issues arise for that distinctiveness which are juridically established in the 1951 Convention relating to the Status of Refugees. These are thus embedded in the internationally accepted definition of a *refugee*, which, in turn, frames the rights and duties conferred to both refugees and host-states. One relates to the causes of flight which must be associated to an imminent threat to life, a category which includes a "well-founded fear of persecution for reasons of race, religion, nationality, membership of a particular social group or political opinion." The other issue is geographical, as a refugee must cross an international border in seeking protection. The refugee "is outside the country of his nationality and is unable or, owing to such fear, is unwilling to avail himself of the protection of that country; or who, not having a nationality and being outside the country of his former habitual residence as a result of such events, is unable or, owing to such fear, is unwilling to return to it."[9] The UNHCR faced limitations to expanding its scope of action beyond the temporal and spatial constraints of the 1951 Convention, especially because of unique conditions relating to various refugee crisis situations emanating from decolonization in Africa.[10] Eligibility determination was a standard process for the HighCommissioner's engagement. In the case of Angolan refugees in the Congo, the geographical nature of the criteria had a significant role in debates about eligibility determination as it was a case of the Eurocentric nature of international legal instruments not being well adapted for African realities.

It is thus essential to provide context to the situation which led Angolans to seek refuge in the Congo in 1961. The temporality is, in its essence, controversial since, in the latter months of 1960, many Angolans were crossing the border due to "persecution and cruel inhumane treatment" by Portuguese authorities. The plea was made by leaders of the União das Populações de Angola (Union of the Peoples of Angola—UPA, later Frente Nacional de Libertação de Angola—FNLA, Angolan National Liberation Front) to the International Committee of the Red Cross (ICRC).[11] The ICRC refrained from intervening at the time and suggested the matter be taken to the UNHCR. In January 1961, the violent Portuguese response to peaceful protests on cotton plantations in Baixa do Cassange aggravated the situation.[12] Nevertheless, the attacks on prisons and a police headquarters in Luanda in February, the massacres in the northern districts of Angola by autochthonous guerrillas in the following month, and the response by Portuguese authorities and civilians established the beginning of the conflict and consequent war for independence. Reports concerning Angolan refugees in the Congo were only internationalized following these events.[13] The conflict escalation marked the emergence of the refugee crisis, which was distinctive from previous colonial abuses in Angola.

However, migration dynamics from Angola to the Congo were present long before this conflict. To a certain extent, these were associated with Portuguese authorities and civilians' manifold abuses during the late colonial period, but they also came about because of the kinship bonds between local populations on both sides of the border. These had consequences for the emergence of the conflict and the refugee crisis in the Lower-Congo region.

The Angolan-Congolese border was established in consequence of disputes between the Portuguese and the British, French, and German governments as well as the International African Association (later, the Belgian government). In fact, it was the navigation in the Zaire River and commercial rights associated with it that led to the Berlin Conferences in 1884–1885;[14] but the final borders of Angola (including the Cabinda Enclave) were established only in the early twentieth century.[15] The new border separated the Kingdom of the Kongo, whose population spread from the region north of Luanda to areas of present-day Central African Republic, as far as Maiyuba, the Gabonese Republic, and Camga in the Democratic Republic of the Congo.[16]

In the following decades, Angolans and Congolese of Bakongo origin maintained mobility dynamics across the border for trading purposes, visiting kinship, or work under seasonal contracts. For them, the fictitious character of the border was evident. According to Helio Felgas, the governor of the Congo District in Angola:

> The borders between the Belgian Congo and the Portuguese Congo are purely conventional . . . the dividing line (mostly imaginary) cuts straight through without noticing that it separated members of the same family. It is only in places where the border passes through an administrative or fiscal post or follows some important natural incident that indigenous people recognize differences in their

respective nationalities. [M]any times, they have their home on one side and the farm on the other, crossing the border as many times as they please.[17]

Moreover, not only those who lived in the border, but in all the "Portuguese Congo, from Ambrizete to Uíge and Sanza, leave . . . to the Belgian Congo to visit relatives and friends without any obstacle . . . inspection or identification." The same was true for those living in the Belgian Congo who wished to go to Angola.[18] But in the 1950s, recurrent reports of Portuguese authorities in northern Angola districts noted the increase of migration fluxes to the Congo. Furthermore, mobility characteristics were changing. Besides pendular or seasonal fluxes, Angolans were by then moving to the Congo on a permanent basis.

The increase in mobility reflected both the ease of crossing an uncontrolled border and abusive labor dynamics in Northern Angola. After the abolition of slavery in 1869, forced labor was legal in Angola, embedded in the idea of work as a moral duty and part of the Portuguese "civilizing mission," which authorities associated with humanistic and, later, developmental and human rights arguments.[19] The use of coercion for production purposes was therefore legitimized, despite increasing international pressures to reform the *Native Labor Code* (*Código de Trabalho dos Indígenas,* 1928).[20] Although increasing international scrutiny in the 1950s led to a series of metropolitan-driven reforms, locally abusive dynamics prevailed.[21] Development plans, directed European settlement in the region, led to the expropriation of land from autochthonous populations. It also led to the implementation of a "contract system" characterized by forced recruitment and resettlement within Angola and to São Tomé and Príncipe, and labor conditions analogous to slavery, which contributed to the permanence of abuse and the increasing exodus to the Congo.[22]

By the late 1950s, migration dynamics to the Congo also became more complex. Increasing international condemnation of colonial rule at the United Nations and other forums, fueled by the independence of African and Asian countries and the Algerian Independence War, instigated the formation and solidification of Angolan liberation movements, primarily operating outside the country. Emergent in this period, the UPA initiated efforts to aggregate support not only among the Bakongo in the Lower-Congo region but also among those within the Portuguese colony. According to an informant of the Belgian government, not only people but also cash flowed to the Congo to support the armed struggle.[23] The Congolese independence in 1960 and the rise to power of Joseph Kasavubu—also of Bakongo origin—reinforced the international dimension of the border and the political dimension of migration. In an inspection of conditions in Northern Angola, a Portuguese official reported the above-mentioned abuse and how this led to people's discontent.

According to Ferreira Martins, they rejoiced with the idea that "blacks ruled over whites" on the other side of the border.[24] By then, the border was also associated with independence—de facto in the case of the Congo, aspired in the case of Angola. Religious links, for example the building and expansion of "tocoismo" networks, also contributed to the strengthening of kinship and identity ties and the reinstitution of the Kingdom of the Kongo was even advanced.[25] Thus, Angolans moved across the border with different motivations: to look for better living conditions, to escape abuse, for political reasons, or in everyday trading commutes. These mobility drives were cumulative in many cases, leading to mistrust among the Portuguese in Northern Angola.[26] By the beginning of the war, hundreds of thousands of Angolans had already settled in the Congo.

So, when Angolan refugee fluxes were reported, humanitarians on the ground also informed that they were integrating among their kinship.[27] Nevertheless, the exponential influx—from about 6,000 in April to about 120,000 in July 1961—made the authorities and international humanitarian organizations worry about the possibility of rapid overpopulation and resource scarcity in the Lower-Congo. Hence, after the first Congolese appeal for international assistance in May 1961, the UNHCR sought to learn about the refugees' conditions and assess their eligibility for international protection.

In his first communication with the Office, John Kelly, the UNHCR's liaison with UNOC, identified Angolans as "probably" being within the UNHCR mandate.[28] The evaluation was confirmed by UNHCR's legal adviser, Paul Weis, who indicated that "our direct responsibility is their international protection, primarily that they receive asylum and are not sent back."[29] However, when asked whether he accepted the responsibility for these refugees, High Commissioner Schnyder made any decision dependent on a report submitted by Kelly after evaluating the situation. In the meantime, negotiations between the LRCS, led by John Thelen,[30] and the Portuguese authorities were taking place regarding repatriation conditions, posing a threat to refugee protection.[31]

The secret report depicted a picture of the refugees' situation based on a four-day mission covering the Tschela-Songololo line, in which Kelly interviewed local authorities, humanitarian field officers, and "very many" refugees. These were "extremely simple people" who spoke Kikongo and saw the "Portuguese rather as just any other tribe and the one with which they are engaged in tribal warfare."[32] However, none claimed having participated in the fight, even those who presented severe wounds. In making his case, Kelly selected several refugees' testimonies. A fifty-four-year-old male refugee feared being arrested or deported, because those "deported never returned." He had also seen "aircraft bombing and setting fire to neighboring villages." Other people from his village of Kaluena "also fled and they reached the Congo after two days walking in the bush, avoiding the roads less they encountered Portuguese authorities." A mine worker refugee stated that "Portuguese civilians had all been armed and participating actively in the looting and burning of houses and villages and the killing of their inhabitants." Since he had an above average education "he was certain to be killed." A woman reported that her husband, a fisherman, had been captured on a boat with two Congolese in the Congo River. She fled fearing he had been executed.[33] These and other testimonies served as representative of Angolans' causes of flight, but the latter also shows how life in the border was shared among local Angolan and Congolese populations. These dynamics were also relevant for eligibility purposes.

In the document, Kelly extends on the question of eligibility. Two related issues emerged, pointing out the inadequacy of the 1951 Convention and the UNHCR Statute dispositions in this case.[34] While the first related to discrepancies between international instruments, according to which eligibility is to be assessed on an individual basis, and the reality on the ground where increasing dispersed mass influxes hindered any such evaluation, the second related to mobility and nationality determination. Kelly referred to Angolan refugees as having been welcomed in the Congo by their "fellow tribesman" and granted asylum by the Congolese authorities. These factors meant that Angolans might be subject to the UNHCR Statute exclusion clauses regarding eligibility. To ascertain whether the Statute fitted the situation, he compared African and European realities. In this case, he explained, "far more important to the individual than the rights and obligations which are attached to the possession of a nationality, are the rights and obligations . . . attached to membership to a tribe. Given his tribal rights, the African refugee in the simpler society in which he lives appears normally to need no further rights [because] he is on an equal footing in all respects with his hosts." The Statute had been framed within the "more complex" European society. Hence, referring to nationality regarding the granting of international protection might not be proper. Resorting to refugees' testimonies, Kelly advocated that "they are certainly not economic migrants" and "there seems to be reason to believe that they feared violence would occur to them by reasons of their race or political opinion [or] aspirations." Thus, his solution was to declare Angolans as prima facie refugees, a mechanism envisaged to respond to mass influxes when the capacity to administer their individual claims becomes highly difficult.[35] As UNHCR evaluation papers state, prima facie determination aims to "ensure admission to safety, protection from refoulement and basic humanitarian treatment to those patently in need of it."[36]

The solution had been previously advanced to respond to the Austrian appeal regarding Hungarian refugees and the Algerian refugee crises in Tunisia and Morocco, but, in any case, international dispositions must be considered.[37] Even before Kelly's report reached High Commissioner Schnyder's desk, UN Secretary-General Dag Hammarskjöld tacitly confirmed the eligibility of the Angolan refugees because, according to Portuguese domestic law—the 1951 constitutional reform and the 1959 nationality law—they were Portuguese nationals. Nevertheless, as the crisis was being politicized at the UN and the refugees had been granted asylum by the host-state,[38] Schnyder opted not to pronounce himself on eligibility for international protection under his Office.[39] He focused on assisting the refugees through his *good offices*, following the policy adopted for Algerian refugees, for integration purposes.[40] Protection was thus delegated to a failed state facing an internal conflict and multiple humanitarian crises, based on normative asylum provisions. Decision-making on refugee management often relied on local authorities, overwhelmed with overpopulation problems, and variably allied with either Portuguese or FNLA interests.

Long local mobility dynamics and kinship affinities across the border, along with the Congolese government support for the Angolan liberation struggle and the plight of refugees, all contributed to the emergence of a debate that surfaced the inadequacies of international instruments designed to respond to specific European contexts, which led to the adoption of ad hoc policies privileging assistance to the detriment of protection. As in the case of Algerians, Angolan refugees were fleeing the conditions impelled by their ties to the Portuguese colonial regime.[41] Considerations about refugee rights in this case also resounded with Western pre-conceptions of the African *other*. Ideas of "tribe" and "nation" conflicted in Kelly's appreciation for eligibility determination, and the border, if not explicitly, seemed absent from the equation. Setting up this binary between "tribe" and "nation" also allowed Kelly to claim the refugees' "simpler society" meant they might be exempted from fundamental human rights enforcement. Notions about the *African otherness*, embedded in "civilizational" arguments, were detrimental not only in relation to refugee rights and protection but also to how humanitarians grasped how assistance modalities should be offered in this particular context.

"UNSETTLING REFUGEES": MOBILITY AS AN ASSET THROUGHOUT THE WAR

With the subject of eligibility put aside in favor of assistance, humanitarians' concerns revolved around two issues. The pressure the mass influx of increasingly malnourished refugees posed upon the local population led to apprehension about resource scarcity. Also, as refugees constantly moved in search of relatives or acquaintances, mobility along and across the border propelled tensions about refugee settlement.

The first groups of refugees arriving in the Congo lived along the border of the Congo district in Angola, from Noqui to São Salvador. They settled in villages in the Songololo and Matadi areas. Others from the Soyo region next to the Atlantic Ocean moved toward Boma. From the Cabinda Enclave, they settled in the region around Tschela. Soon, however, refugees reached Léopoldville, Thysville, Kibentele, and Popakabaka, further northeast. In a few months, Angolan refugees were dispersed all around the Lower-Congo province. They settled among kin, building their shelters within the villages, or forming new ones in the areas ceded by the local population, who also shared their resources.

In the summer of 1961, as the Portuguese counterinsurgency gained momentum, refugee flows intensified in number and rhythm. Reports on resource scarcity and overpopulation followed, primarily in the Boma-Matadi-Songololo line. A major emergency relief operation was set in place in response to the crisis. The province was divided into zones, each under the responsibility of a local voluntary organization, ranging from the Congo Protestant Relief Agency (CPRA), to Caritas Congo, the Society of Culture and Agriculture of Mayombe, and the Congolese Red Cross. The latter's work was supervised by LRCS delegates, who also kept records about developments in other zones as well as the number of refugees. The UNOC also provided resources and transportation. Emergency relief was, nevertheless, a short-term plan, as the primary goal was refugee self-sufficiency. For that purpose, the UNHCR, in cooperation with voluntary organizations, promoted rural development integration projects beginning in November. The plan was framed in a wider strategy aiming at the expansion of UNHCR's action in Africa, while responding to pressures from developing host-states in the continent.[42] If the strategy was an opportunity for humanitarian organizations,[43] it also turned refugees from subjects of international law to people notable mainly for their labor value.[44] When emergency relief ended in January 1962, about 152,000 Angolan refugees had entered the Congo.

During this first phase, refugees were requested to farm in order to reduce resource scarcity and their dependence on external aid to survive. However, a considerable proportion, predominantly men, refused to do so. The situation raised significant concern among humanitarians and local authorities, who complained about overpopulation and refugees staying "passively in front of their huts, waiting for the Red Cross trucks to get their ration."[45] In fact, as governor Felgas and the Cataractes District Commissary P. Bambi assessed, Angolan men dedicated themselves to trade and craftwork, finding agricultural labor "degradating."[46] These "skeleton men" were also convinced by FNLA propaganda that the war would soon be over. Planting crops to abandon them later was, thus, in their view, pointless.[47] Refugees also used this argument to resist UNHCR and Caritas-led rural resettlement projects that would have placed them in fertile areas, but away from urban conglomerates and the border, adding that they refused to leave their kinship and feared enslavement.[48]

Refugees favored moving along and across the border to collect resources. They could find them in the forests. As Brinkman shows, even before the war broke out, Angolans used the forests to avoid contact with Portuguese authorities who moved through the main roads. There they raised crops and forged shelter hidden from external sight. As the war changed the landscape, these spaces not only became the first place of refuge but also one used for communication. As forests were impenetrable for Portuguese troops, refugees often returned to Angola to harvest the crops left behind or contact and help those who had stayed in the northern districts. The "bush" was, in fact, penetrable by a labyrinth of paths that only the guerrillas and local autochthonous populations mastered. However, as the Portuguese army advanced, using the "bush" to return became harder. Although new paths were made, Angolans on both sides of the border found it riskier to travel.[49]

Mobility dynamics across the border created a false sense among humanitarians that refugees were willing to go back. Earlier refugee testimonies mentioning a will to return when the situation improved also influenced this perception. Hence, LRCS delegates saw repatriation as a viable solution to the crisis without considering protection issues. They noted that refugees willing to return to Angola should be incentivized to do so.[50] For that purpose, LRCS delegates were in contact with Portuguese authorities, who installed nine Portuguese Red Cross reception centers along the Angolan side of the border. The plan was later put aside as insecurity lingered, but mobility remained a problem. In late December 1961, just before the termination of the LRCS emergency operation, Gösta Streijffert, the delegate assigned to supervise it, pointed out the problem. "Some thousand refugees" had "disappeared" from October to December and "where they have gone is impossible to say." "A certain number is in Léopoldville, I should guess. Others may have gone back but it is not possible to get indications from refugees of the same villages." In an area close to Cabinda, some groups had gone back, and in parts of "the Boma [and] Matadi [territories] there had been a move eastward, thus increasing the number of refugees especially in the territories of Thysville and Madimba," to which newcomers were to be added. The latter "had lived in the bush for several months and were in a rather bad shape." Streijffert also observed it would be impossible to keep a record of refugees from the end of the operation.[51] Thus, the emergency operation termination, along with mobility dynamics, created chaos the following years regarding resource distribution and refugees' census as it became harder to distinguish between "new" and "old" arrivals, and led to the further deterioration of the refugees' situation, especially in urban areas.[52]

The referred movement toward Thysville and Madimba might have been a coincidence, but by then, this was where refugees had a better chance of getting resources. The area was under the responsibility of the CPRA, whose head, Reverend David Grenfell, was a close ally of the FNLA and, particularly, its leader Holden Roberto. The CPRA also partnered with the UNHCR to increase rural production, and the project had the highest adherence rates. In 1962, an increasing number of refugees trusted the CPRA to obtain food in order to overcome insufficient crop productivity and the overpricing of essential food commodities, in part due to overpopulation and low production. At this point, famine had reached refugees and locals alike. In CPRA reception centers, refugees continued to secure basic relief—newcomers received clothes and food for one year or until they could subsist from their crops—medical care, seeds, and utensils. As the FNLA not only had free access to the area but, to a great extent, controlled the routes, refugees could also benefit from their logistics to communicate with those still in Angola. Refugees also resorted to FNLA's military arm, the Exército de Libertação Nacional de Angola (Angolan National Liberation Army—ELNA) to get free passage to the Congo. They used ELNA documents to pass checkpoints in the Angolan forests, cross the border, and obtain relief at CPRA facilities as these were the only identification documents accepted by the voluntary organization.

However, FNLA control and their cooperation with CPRA did not only come with advantages. Although many refugees enlarged the ELNA ranks and cooperated with the FNLA, others denounced the abuses perpetrated by the movement in assembly meetings. At the time, the liberation movement successfully controlled a "state within a state," and Grenfell "effectively acted to make Angolan refugees into FNLA subjects through rations and identification papers."[53] Refugees also tried to avoid such control by hiding in the forests in Angola, bypassing both the Portuguese army and the ELNA. When in the Congo, if Angolan refugees failed to provide FNLA documents, they would be subject to endless interrogations conducted by Grenfell himself. Suspicion about possible Portuguese-coopted infiltrators justified the triage. The reverend kept detailed refugee records to administer distribution and provide FNLA officials with information.

FNLA officers also used refugee records for financial purposes. Adding to the taxes refugees paid to local and provincial authorities from 1962 onward—these differed from area to area; common examples were fees for enlisting and maintaining children in local schools or contributing to local services such as road maintenance or garbage collecting—they were also obliged to pay a weekly tribute to the FNLA and school fees if their children were to attend schools operated by the movement.[54] In a situation where misery prevailed, double taxation and poor harvests fueled disputes among refugees and between refugees and the local population. The forging of documents to obtain food was also common, as was the punishment for those caught.[55] According to testimonies collected in loco by informants of the Portuguese authorities, the situation not only led to severe protests against violence and resource deviation by FNLA and ELNA officials but also propelled the return to Angola of those refugees unable to survive under the double taxation.[56]

Although recurrent until the end of the war, Portuguese Secret Police reports on refugee returns show sparseness in numbers and cadence.[57] In Angola, refugees were sent to surveilled villages built under the rural reordering program implemented by the Portuguese authorities.[58] Escape from these facilities grew difficult as the years passed.[59] Others tried to hide in the forest, subject to famine, perilous encounters with wild animals, or the many traps set by the Portuguese army. Those caught were forced to join the local population in the villages.[60]

Refugee mobility dynamics across and along the border were a permanent feature of Angolans' refugee experience. Moving from one place to another in search of resources or kinship support was common and contrasted, for example, with obtaining health treatment, as refugees refrained from walking long distances when deprived of health facilities nearby their chosen settlements.[61] Freedom of movement—their main prerogative—was thus a resource used by refugees to counter what they saw as possible abuse in assistance modalities, as in the case of the UNHCR-Caritas resettlement program, or de facto abuse in the case of CPRA and FNLA control policies. Protection by authorities or the UNHCR against these situations was absent. Refugees' knowledge of the forest allowed them to escape various forms of domination, as had happened before the war. However, although permanent, mobility dynamics across the border adjusted as control by both belligerents increased.

Directed settlement and progressive integration in the Congo then became more attractive. Prospects of Angolan independence, which had been increasingly advocated as a sine qua non condition for refugees to return since 1962,[62] seemed ever more distant. In the following years, refugee numbers also continued to rise. Although inaccurate, international organizations estimated between 300,000 and 450,000 Angolan refugees between 1964 and 1972, while the FNLA claimed around 600,000 in 1970.[63] During this period, new arrivals were immediately settled in interior fertile lands distant from the border. The purpose of the strategy was twofold. Directed refugee resettlement to the interior decreased population density in urban and border areas and allowed for the implementation of integrated rural development programs, following the above-mentioned UNHCR strategy to respond both to newly independent countries' underdevelopment and humanitarian crises. On the other hand, moving refugees away from the border decreased the probability of casualties among refugees since they were less prone to air strikes or other forms of violence. Reports of refugees dying or being severely wounded when returning to Angola to harvest crops and Portuguese bombs penetrating Congolese territory justified the resettlement policy, which had also been endorsed by the Organization for African Unity.[64] Integration also improved with the implementation of programs directed to diverse skill training; one of the most successful was sponsored by the CPRA. Government stability and new UNHCR partnerships with other UN agencies also contributed to the increasing success of integrated rural, community development, and training programs.[65]

In spite of progressive refugee stability and advancement in directed resettlement programs in the Lower-Congo, new arrivals in the late 1960s and 1970s show that mobility across the border and spontaneous settlement persisted, namely in areas where humanitarian organizations were still absent. A case in point is a group of Angolan refugees who settled in the Dilolo area in the former Katanga province, now Haut-Katanga.[66] Fleeing violence in FNLA-controlled areas in Angola, approximately 5,000 new arrivals settled among other groups of refugees discovered to have been in the area since the beginning of the decolonization war. After conducting his first mission to the region in 1968, Otto Hagenbucle, the UNHCR representative in the Congo at the time, recommended that a permanent international presence should be put in place to provide emergency, education, and health assistance to up to 10,000 refugees, as well as improvement of communication routes and transport.[67] The recently sent UNHCR delegation registered new influxes to the area in 1971 and by the end of the following year, the Zaire central government appealed to the UNHCR to maintain its assistance operation due to persistent refugee influxes and the authorities' incapacity to deal with refugee needs.[68]

The Dilolo case demonstrates that mobility and spontaneous settlement were maintained by Angolan refugees throughout the conflict, choosing routes through the forests familiar to the local population to avoid possible confrontation with belligerents. Mastering the "bush" routes, the older as well as the newer paths, during their refugee experience was an advantage sustained by these communities' long-lasting presence on both sides of the Angolan-Congolese border.

CROSSING A "FICTITIOUS" BORDER: MOBILITY, SETTLEMENT, AND REFUGEEDOM

Refugee experiences are multifaceted and build on specific but complex contexts.[69] In the case of Angolans from the northern region of the colony fleeing the decolonization war, it is essential to encompass not only the specific circumstances of the conflict, but also local dynamics intensified and aggravated by Portuguese colonialism, a system opposed by many of the refugees. At the time, international organizations' field officers showed how the Eurocentric norms regulating the refugee regime were not only unfit for this context but also unprepared to accommodate local specificities in the policies used to adapt to that context. This, in turn, impacted Angolans' refugee experience.

In this case, mobility dynamics were central to unraveling the complexities of both policy implementation and refugee adaptation to the circumstances they faced throughout the war. The character of the Angolan-Congolese border, imposed by imperial interests, was fictitious to a great part of the local population's everyday life, but determinative in the political and humanitarian sense. It thus shaped diverse "imagined communities,"[70] conflicting in debates regarding eligibility for refugee status and international protection and also, in international assistance implementation.

Mobility dynamics between the northern districts of Angola and the Lower-Congo have challenged the very idea of a border since its establishment. They changed during the late colonial period, as they gained a more permanent and political character due to persistent colonial abuse, but mobility was also a lasting feature of normal or even daily life for many Bakongo. This mutability emphasized the need to escape before the conflict escalated for cohorts of the population, but for other Angolans their first and recurring refuge was the forests within Angola.

Understanding these previous dynamics to the conflict allows for a better grasp of Angolan refugee experiences and of their usages of mobility during the war, as well as to assess why international humanitarian organizations' solutions—repatriation and directed resettlement—failed to a certain extent. If international humanitarian organizations' archival records are poor sources to uncover the multiplicity of refugees' voices, refugees' crossings, as documented by informants, show how mobility was used as a form of protest or escape. In a context where international protection was not always available, Angolan refugees used mobility in different ways to survive, communicate, and resist what they perceived as abuse or avoid de facto abusive conduct by different humanitarian and political actors. The incapacity of the Congolese state to offer them protection, although they did grant asylum and oversaw some assistance on the ground, contributed to the manyfold abuses refugees endured. Refugees favored spontaneous over directed settlement, crossing the border in both directions to escape violence and interrogations, contact relatives, and gather resources when they felt safe.

Mobility dynamics with similar characteristics were also observed in the Eastern front of the war in the Angolan-Zambian border.[71] The case of Angolan refugees in the Congo reinforces Hansen's argument that refugees sought to control their refuge experience by attempting to regain control of their social reality that had been imposed by colonial authorities. But it also demonstrates the different ways in which mobility was used by refugees as an asset, as their main strategy to endure and evade multiple and varied adversities.

NOTES

1. Research for this chapter was co-financed by F.E.D.E.R.-COMPETE 2020—POCI, and the Fundação para a Ciência e a Tecnologia (FCT), in association with the research project *The Worlds of (Under)Development: Processes and Legacies of the Portuguese Colonial Empire in a Comparative Perspective (1945–1975)* (PTDC /HAR-HIS/31906/2017|POCI-01–0145-FEDER-031906), and the research project *Humanity Internationalized: Cases, Dynamics and Comparisons (1945–1980)* (PTDC/HAR-HIS/6257/2020).

2. Congo-Léopoldville was later known as Congo-Kinshasa (1966) to distinguish the country from its neighbor after authorities adopted the twin designation of Democratic Republic of the Congo (1964) and, posteriorly, as Zaire (1971). Since 1997, the designation of Democratic Republic of the Congo has been recuperated. The author uses the different designations according to their implementation in different periods.

3. On the Katanga secession and the complexities of international intervention in this context, see Alanna O'Malley, *The Diplomacy of Decolonisation: America, Britain and the United Nations During the Congo Crisis 1960–1964* (Manchester: Manchester University Press, 2018).

4. Jeremy Rich, "Victims or Burdens?: Angolan Refugees and the Humanitarian Aid Organizations in the Democratic Republic of the Congo, 1961–1963," *The International History Review*, 43, no. 5 (2021): 1001–1017.

5. Ana Filipa dos Santos Guardião. "Desafios coloniais na construção do sistema internacional de protecção dos refugiados: os processos de descolonização do Quénia, Argélia e Angola (1950–1075)" (PhD diss., Instituto de Ciências Sociais, 2019); Ana Guardião, "A Matter of Control: Colonial and Humanitarian Population Management Strategies, Angolan Refugees' Resistance and the Politics of Difference (1961–1964)," *E-journal of Portuguese History* 19, no. 2 (2021): 51–75.

6. Rich, "Victims or burdens?"

7. I concur with the definition of refugeedom advanced by Peter Gatrell, Anindita Ghoshal, Katarzyna Nowak, and Alex Dowdall. Here, I try to encompass the multifaceted relationships of Angolans with both humanitarian and political actors while analyzing the ways in which this context and refugee agency instigated debates about the refugee regime. See, Peter Gatrell, Anindita Ghoshal, Katarzyna Nowak, and Alex Dowdall, "Reckoning with Refugeedom: Refugee Voices in Modern History." *Social History* 46, no. 1 (2021): 70–95.

8. The author started conducting research on this topic for her PhD thesis. Part of the facts here presented build on the thesis findings as well as on sources peripheral to its main arguments. Recent research on this topic has also been conducted in Portuguese and Belgian state archives.

9. Convention relating to the Status of Refugees, 1951. https://www.unhcr.org/4ca34be29.pdf. For a juridical interpretation of the matter, see James C. Hathaway, *The Rights of Refugees under International Law* (Cambridge: Cambridge University Press, 2005).

10. Gil Loescher, *The UNHCR and World Politics: A Perilous Path* (Oxford: Oxford University Press, 2001), 44–6; Guardião, "Desafios coloniais", 45–92.

11. International Committee of the Red Cross Archives [ACICR], BAG 200.013–001. Jean Pierre Bala and M. Barros Nenaca to President of the International Committee of the Red Cross, November 15, 1960. It was impossible to know the extent of the influxes at the time. Moreover, no record of significant incidents in Angola emerged when the plea was made. The first was recorded in January 1961. Nevertheless, the author feels impelled to document the plea for it might be associated with previous violent dynamics in Northern Angola and with efforts to raise awareness of violence escalation. It might also have been used to seek the ICRC's legitimization of the liberation movement as a party to the conflict.

12. Diogo R. Curto and Bernardo P. Cruz, "Terror e Saberes Coloniais: Os Incidentes na Baixa de Cassange," in *Políticas Coloniais em Tempos de Revoltas: Angola circa 1961*, dir. Diogo R. Curto (Oporto: Edições Afrontamento, 2016), 151–188.

13. Guardião, "Matter of Control," 56.

14. By then, the river was already known as the Congo River, the present-day denomination. However, the disputes leading to the Conferences were known as the "Question of Zaire." Hence, the use of Zaire instead of Congo in this case.

15. Joaquim Oliveira, *Os Caminhos Históricos das Fronteiras de Angola* (Luanda: Cefolex, 2010).

16. On the Kingdom of the Kongo, see, for example, Koen Bostoen and Inge Brinkman, *The Kongo Kingdom: The Origins, Dynamics and Cosmopolitan Culture of an African Polity* (Cambridge: Cambridge University Press, 2018).

17. Hélio Esteves Felgas, *O Congo Belga - Ameaça ou protecção para a defesa de Angola?* (Luanda: Tipografia do Mondego, 1958), 11.

18. Hélio Esteves Felgas, *O Congo Belga - Ameaça ou protecção para a defesa de Angola?* (Luanda: Tipografia do Mondego, 1958), 11.

19. Miguel B. Jerónimo and José P. Monteiro, "The Inventors of Human Rights in Africa: Portugal, Late Colonialism, and the UN Human Rights Regime," in *Decolonization, Self-Determination, and the Rise of Global Human Rights Politics*, eds. A. Dirk Moses, Marco Duranti, and Roland Burke (Cambridge: Cambridge University Press, 2020), 285–315.

20. The *Native Labor Code* would be abolished in 1962. Other societal stratification regulations were also implemented in the 1950s. One was the *Native's Status* (*Estatuto do Índigena*, 1954, abolished de jure in 1961) which regulated the rights, but primarily the duties, of the "natives" in the Portuguese colonies, distinguishing them from the "assimilados" (those autochthonous who had achieved a "higher standard of civilization") and citizens (mainly white European settlers). Jerónimo and Monteiro, "Inventors of Human Rights," 285; Miguel B. Jerónimo and José P. Monteiro, "Das 'dificuldades de levar os indígenas a trabalhar': o 'sistema' de trabalho

native no império colonial," in *O império colonial em questão (sécs. XIX–XX): poderes, saberes e instituições*, ed. Miguel B. Jerónimo (Lisboa: Edições 70, 2013), 197–221.

21. José P. Monteiro, *The Interntionalisation of the "Native Labour" Question in Portuguese Late Colonialism, 1945–1962* (London: Palgrave Macmillan, 2022).

22. Guardião, "Matter of Control," 55. On the Portuguese development plans implemented in the colonies and the policy of white settlement embedded in them, see Miguel B. Jerónimo and António C. Pinto, "A Modernizing Empire? Politics, Culture and Economy in Portuguese Late Colonialism," in *The Ends of European Colonial Empires: Cases and Comparisons*, eds. Miguel B. Jerónimo and António C. Pinto (Basingstoke: Palgrave Macmillan, 2015), 51–80; Cláudia Castelo, *Passagens para África. O Povoamento de Angola e Moçambique com Naturais da Metrópole (1920–1974)* (Oporto: Edições Afrontamento, 2007). For a comparison with other imperial endeavors, focused on the repressive nature of late colonial development ideas and projects, see Miguel B. Jerónimo, "Repressive Developmentalisms: Idioms, Repertoires, Trajectories in Late Colonialism," in *The Oxford Handbook of the Ends of Empire*, eds. Andrew Thompson and Martin Thomas (Oxford: Oxford University Press, 2017), 537–554.

23. Archives de l'État en Belguique [AEB], Archives Africaines, 14554 - Angola bis. 1960–1961. Marcel Swinnen to Pierre Wigny, February 13, 1961.

24. Arquivo Histórico Ultramarino [AHU], MU_ISAU_A2.49.002/39.00247. José Diogo Ferreira Martins, "Distrito do Congo—Relatório parcial n.º 6," 26 July 1960.

25. Alexander Keese. "Dos abusos às revoltas? Trabalho forçado, reformas portuguesas, política 'tradicional' e religião na Baixa de Cassange e no distrito do Congo (Angola), 1957–1961," *Africana Studia*, no. 7 (2004): 247–276.

26. Although unattainable, a considerable proportion of cumulative causes is highly probable. Reports from Portuguese authorities and refugees' testimonies attest to this hypothesis.

27. Reports arrived from the LRCS and UNOC. Although with different roles and aims, both organizations were operating in the Congo in response to the so-called first Congo crisis and assisted displaced groups within the country.

28. United Nations High Commissioner for Refugees Archives [UNHCRA], doc. 1, Angolan Refugees - General, vol.1, fonds 11, series 1, box 250. John Kelly to Thomas Jameson, 19 April 1961.

29. UNHCRA, doc. 3, Angolan Refugees - General, vol.1, fonds 11, series 1, box 250. Paul Weis to Tomas Jamieson, 10 May 1961.

30. John Thelen was an American delegate of the League, who, according to Portuguese authorities, was supportive of the Portuguese position. The delegate sought to assist the Portuguese with counter-narratives of the conflict and suggested the Portuguese embassy in Léopoldville to provide for arrangements in Angola for the repatriation of refugees, namely the building of reception centers at the border directed by the Portuguese Red Cross. See, Guardião, "Desafios coloniais", 234–235.

31. Guardião, "Matter of Control."

32. Refugees were mainly of Bakongo origin, and most did not speak Portuguese. John Kelly used a local interpreter for communication purposes.

33. UNHCRA, Angolan Refugees - General, vol.1, fonds 11, series 1, box 250. J.D.R. Kelly, Report on Refugees from Angola, 26 June 1961.

34. Whereas the 1951 Convention regulates signatory states' compliance with international law as to the application of refugee rights, the UNHCR Statute determines the organization's mandate dispositions.

35. UNHCRA, Angolan Refugees - General, vol.1, fonds 11, series 1, box 250. J.D.R. Kelly, Report on Refugees from Angola, 26 June 1961.

36. Bonaventure Rutinwa, "Prima Facie Status and Refugee Protection," UNHCR New Issues in Refugee Research Working Paper no. 49, UNHCR, 2002, 1. https://www.refworld.org/docid/4ff3f8812.html

37. On the Algerian refugee crises, see, among others, Jennifer Johnson, *The Battle for Algeria: Sovereignty, Health Care and Humanitarianism* (Philadelphia: University of Pennsylvania Press, 2017); Guardião, "Desafios coloniais" (2019), and, most recently, Malika Rahal and Benjamin Thomas White, "UNHCR and the Algerian War of Independence: Postcolonial Sovereignty and the Globalization of the International Refugee Regime, 1954–63," *Journal of Global History* 17, no. 2 (2022): 331–352; for different perspectives on how the Algerian decolonization war influenced Cold War and decolonization dynamics in the 1950s and following decades, see, among others, Matthew Connelly, *A Diplomatic Revolution: Algeria's Fight for Independence and the Origins of the Post-Cold War Era* (Oxford: Oxford University Press, 2002); and Jeffrey J. Byrne, *Mecca of Revolution: Algeria, Decolonization, and the Third World Order* (Oxford: Oxford University Press, 2016).

38. For instance, the crisis was integrated into debates on the condemnation of colonial rule and on self-determination as a fundamental human right. Furthermore, the Congolese government insisted on the matter being discussed at the First Committee relating to matters of international peace and security, rather than at the Third Committee where human rights matters were debated. They also delayed ratifying the 1951 Convention. See, Guardião, "Matter of Control," 58.

39. UNHCRA, Angolan Refugees - General, vol.1, fonds 11, series 1, box 250. Felix Schnyder to Dag Hammarskjöld, 27 July 1961. As the granting of asylum was attained, Congolese ratification of the 1951 Refugee Convention was was delayed until 1965. The Congo was only accountable for state protection obligations enshrined in international instruments in 1970, after ratifying the 1967 Protocol.

40. The *good offices* were an ad hoc mechanism which allowed the UNHCR to operate outside its mandate but foresaw no provisions regarding persecution. These mechanisms—the *good offices* and *prima facie* recognition—were used to speed assistance provision while circumventing political confrontation with colonial and newly independent states. See, Loescher, *UNHCR and World Politics*, 113. It had been approved by the UN General Assembly, first in responding to the Chinese refugee crisis in Hong Kong (without ever coming into effect), and then in the Algerian refugee crises in Tunisia and Morocco. The mechanism was then approved as a general solution for the UNHCR to act outside its mandate by Resolution 1388 (xiv) and reinforced by

Resolution 1499 (xv). See, respectively, United Nations General Assembly, Resolution 1388 (xiv), November 1958 and United Nations General Assembly, Resolution 1499 (xv) December 1960, Dag Hammarskjöld Library, https://digitallibrary.un.org/record/206378?ln=en and https://daccess-ods.un.org/tmp/3364387.15457916.html.

41. Guardião, "Desafios coloniais," 164.

42. Jeff Crisp, "Mind the Gap! UNHCR, Humanitarian Assistance and the Development Process," UNHCR New Issues in Refugee Research Working Paper no. 43, UNHCR, 2001. https://www.unhcr.org/research/working/3b309dd07/mind-gap-unhcr-humanitarian-assistance-development-process-jeff-crisp.html; Loescher, *UNHCR and World Politics*, 119–122.

43. Peter Gatrell, *The Making of the Modern Refugee* (Oxford: Oxford University Press, 2013), 226.

44. Joel Glasman, "Seeing like a Refugee Agency: A Short History of UNHCR Classifications in Central Africa (1961–2015)," *Journal of Refugee Studies* 30, no. 2 (2017): 337–362.

45. International Federation of the Red Cross Archives [IFRCA], Congo 22/1/2, Délégué au Congo - M. Norredam de octobre à décembre 1961, A0949, box 1. P. Bambi, *Rapport sur situation dramatique des réfugiés angolais dans le Bas-Congo*, s.d.; IFRCA, Congo 22/1/2 M. Streijffert, Délégué au Congo 1961, A1023, box 1. Sébastien Landu, *Situation des réfugiés angolais dans le territoire de Matadi*, 30 September 1961.

46. Felgas, *O Congo Belga.*

47. IFRCA, Congo 22/1/2, Délégué au Congo - M. Norredam de octobre à décembre 1961, A0949, box 1. P. Bambi, *Rapport sur situation dramatique des réfugiés angolais dans le Bas-Congo*, s.d.

48. Guardião, "Matter of Control."

49. Inge Brinkman, "Refugees on Routes. Congo/Zaire and the War in Northern Angola (1961–1974)," in *Angola on the Move: Transport Routes, Communications and History*, eds. Beatrix Heinze and Achim von Oppen (Frankfurt am Main: Verlafo Otto Lembeck, 2008), 198–219.

50. IFRCA, Congo 22/1/2 M. Streijffert, Délégué au Congo 1961, A1023, box 1. Gösta Streijffert to Ray Schaeffer, 18 July 1961.

51. IFRCA, Congo 22/1/2 M. Streijffert, Délégué au Congo 1961, A1023, box 1. Streijffert to Schaeffer, 31 December 1961.

52. Guardião, "Desafios coloniais," 238.

53. Jeremy Rich, *Protestant Missionaries and Humanitarianism in the DRC: The Politics of Aid in Cold War Africa* (New York: Boydell and Brewer, 2020).

54. Arquivo Nacional Torre do Tombo [ANTT], Serviços de Centralização e Coordenação de Informações de Angola, liv. 128. "Relatório de Situação" n. 166, 17 June 1965.

55. Ana Guardião, "Political Beneficiaries of Humanitarianism? The FNLA and the Angolan Refugee Crisis in the Congo (c. 1960–1975)," *Cold War History* (forthcomming).

56. ANTT, Serviços de Centralização e Coordenação de Informações de Angola, liv. 118 "Relatório da Situação" n. 69, 19 July 1963; ANTT, Serviços de Centralização

e Coordenação de Informações de Angola, liv. 121 "Relatório da Situação" n. 103, 1 April 1964; "Relatório da Situação" n. 107, 29 April 1964; ANTT, Serviços de Centralização e Coordenação de Informações de Angola, liv. 122 "Relatório da Situação" n. 115, 24 June 1964; ANTT, Serviços de Centralização e Coordenação de Informações de Angola, liv. 126 "Relatório da Situação" n. 126, 13 January 1965.

57. These numbers only entailed those refugees who presented themselves to the Portuguese authorities. Most Angolans who ended up in Portuguese records had previously resorted to hiding in the forests.

58. The first two surveilled villages, called "regedorias," were put in place in the Uíge district. They were framed as a rural reordering project during the counter-insurgency campaign of 1961 to aggregate the dispersed population in the forests and the refugees supposed to return from the Congo as a result of Portuguese authorities' first repatriation negotiations. Information on analogous projects is not consistent, but refugee testimonies in Zambia account for fleeing Angola in 1965 due to Portuguese authorities gathering population in "open air camps." This is consistent with the rural reordering projects in the colony's Eastern districts and the establishment of "regedorias" for that purpose. Curto and Cruz, "Good and Bad Concentration"; Ana Guardião, "Zambia, 1970: The Refugees (Control) Act: Angolan War Refugees and Zambia's 'Unorthodox' Asylum Policy," in *Online Atlas on the History of Humanitarianism and Human Rights*, eds. Fabian Klose, Marc Palen, Johannes Paulmann, and Andrew Thompson (April 2021). urn:nbn:de:0159-2021041502. These surveilled villages also figured as the destination of refugees in a 1964 plan for mass repatriation. For the mass repatriation plan, see Arquivo Histórico Diplomático, Recuperação de Refugiados, PT/AHD/3/UM-GM/GNP01-RNP/S0029/U104847. Governo Geral de Angola, Acta n.º 2, 4 November 1964. Further research is needed to discern how these facilities were framed, their location, how they operated, as well as to distinguish these from other facilities with the same nomenclature.

59. UNHCRA, Refugees from Angola in Zaire vol. 1, fonds 11, series 1, box 42. David Grenfell, *The Work Amongst the Angolan Refugees in the Lower Congo. Annual Report for 1966*, 4 January 1967.

60. ANTT Serviços de Centralização e Coordenação de Informações de Angola, liv. 123. "Relatório da Situação" n, 107, 29 April 1964; "Relatório de Situação" n. 120, 29 July 1964.

61. UNHCRA, Angolan Refugees General, vol. 4, fonds 11, series 1, box 250. *Note sur la situation sanitaire et alimentaire des réfugiés angolais et cabindais dans le District du Bas Congo*, February 1963, doc. 331C.

62. Ana Guardião, "Viragens humanitaristas para o desenvolvimento: o caso dos refugiados angolanos no Congo-Léopoldville (1961–1975)," *Ler História* (forthcoming).

63. There are no records of refugee censuses since the end of the emergency relief program termination. From that point on, the UNHCR relied on estimates and reports provided by the CPRA, which had access only to part of the refugee population. As the example of refugees in the Dilolo area and others relating to refugees from Cabinda show, the UNHCR was ill-informed about refugee groups that spontaneously settled in the Congo during the war.

64. Tristram Betts, "Rural Refugees in Africa," *International Migration Review* 15, no. 2 (1981): 214.

65. Crisp, "Mind the Gap"; Loescher, *UNHCR and World Politics*; Guardião, "Viragens humanitaristas."

66. When the Democratic Republic of the Congo was renamed Zaire in 1971, the Katanga province also changed its name to Shaba. The 2006 Constitution later instituted the present-day designation.

67. UNHCRA, Refugees from Angola in Zaire, vol. 1, fonds, 11, series 1, box 42. Otto Hagenbucle to Geneva Headquarters, 23 September 1968, doc. 80.

68. UNHCRA, Otto Hagenbucle to Geneva Headquarters, 22 January 1972, doc. 167; UNHCRA, Refugees from Angola in Zaire, vol. 1, fonds, 11, series 1, box 42. Sûreté d'État to UNHCR Delegation, 29 December 1972, doc. 194.

69. Gatrell, et al., "Reckoning with refugeedom."

70. Benedict Andersen, *Immagined Communities: Reflections on the Origin and Spread of Nationalism* (London and New York: Verso, 2016 (1983)).

71. Art Hansen, "Refugee Dynamics: Angolans in Zambia 1966 to 1972," *The International Migration Review* 15, no. 2 (1981): 175–194.

BIBLIOGRAPHY

Andersen, Benedict. *Imagined Communities: Reflections on the Origin and Spread of Nationalism*. London and New York: Verso, 2016 (1983).

Betts, Tristram. "Rural Refugees in Africa." *International Migration Review* 15, no. 2 (1981): 213–218.

Bostoen, Koen, and Inge Brinkman. *The Kongo Kingdom: The Origins, Dynamics and Cosmopolitan Culture of an African Polity*. Cambridge: Cambridge University Press, 2018.

Brinkman, Inge. "Refugees on Routes. Congo/Zaire and the War in Northern Angola (1961–1974)." In *Angola on the Move: Transport Routes, Communications and History*, edited by Beatrix Heinze and Achim von Oppen, 198–219. Frankfurt am Main: Verlafo Otto Lembeck, 2008.

Byrne, Jeffrey J. *Mecca of Revolution: Algeria, Decolonization, and the Third World Order*. Oxford: Oxford University Press, 2016.

Castelo, Cláudia. *Passagens para África. O Povoamento de Angola e Moçambique com Naturais da Metrópole (1920–1974)*. Oporto: Edições Afrontamento, 2007.

Connelly, Matthew. *A Diplomatic Revolution: Algeria's Fight for Independence and the Origins of the Post-Cold War Era*. Oxford: Oxford University Press, 2002.

Crisp, Jeff. "Mind the Gap! UNHCR, Humanitarian Assistance and the Development Process." UNHCR New Issues in Refugee Research Working Paper no. 43, UNHCR, 2001. https://www.unhcr.org/research/working/3b309dd07/mind-gap-unhcr-humanitarian-assistance-development-process-jeff-crisp.html.

Curto, Diogo R., and Bernardo P. Cruz. "Terror e Saberes Coloniais: Os Incidentes na Baixa de Cassange." In *Políticas Coloniais em Tempos de Revoltas: Angola circa 1961*, edited by Diogo R. Curto, 151–188. Oporto: Edições Afrontamento, 2016.

Curto, Diogo R., and Bernardo P. Cruz. "The Good and Bad Concentration: Regedorias in Angola." *Portuguese Studies Review* 25, no. 1 (2017): 205–231.

Felgas, Hélio Esteves. *O Congo Belga - Ameaça ou protecção para a defesa de Angola?* Luanda: Tipografia do Mondego, 1958.

Gatrell, Peter. *The Making of the Modern Refugee.* Oxford: Oxford University Press, 2013.

Gatrell, Peter, Anindita Ghoshal, Katarzyna Nowak, and Alex Dowdall. "Reckoning with Refugeedom: Refugee Voices in Modern History." *Social History* 46, no. 1 (2021): 70–95.

Glasman, Joel. "Seeing like a Refugee Agency: A Short History of UNHCR Classifications in Central Africa (1961–2015)." *Journal of Refugee Studies.* 30, no. 2 (2017): 337–362.

Guardião, Ana Filipa dos Santos. "Desafios coloniais na construção do sistema internacional de protecção dos refugiados: os processos de descolonização do Quénia, Argélia e Angola (1950–1075)." PhD diss., Instituto de Ciências Sociais, 2019.

Guardião, Ana F. "Zambia, 1970: The Refugees (Control) Act: Angolan War Refugees and Zambia's 'Unorthodox' Asylum Policy." In *Online Atlas on the History of Humanitarianism and Human Rights*, edited by Fabian Klose, Marc Palen, Johannes Paulmann, and Andrew Thompson. April 2021. urn:nbn:de:0159–2021041502.

Guardião, Ana. "A Matter of Control: Colonial and Humanitarian Population Management Strategies, Angolan Refugees' Resistance and the Politics of Difference (1961–1964)." *E-journal of Portuguese History.* 19, no. 2 (2021): 51–75.

, Ana. "Political Beneficiaries of Humanitarianism? The FNLA and the Angolan Refugee Crisis in the Congo (c. 1960–1975)." *Cold War History* (forthcoming, 2024).

Guardião, Ana. "Viragens humanitaristas para o desenvolvimento: o caso dos refugiados angolanos no Congo-Léopoldville (1961–1975)." *Ler História* (forthcoming, 2024).

Hansen, Art. "Refugee Dynamics: Angolans in Zambia 1966 to 1972." *International Migration Review.* 15, no. 2 (1981): 175–194.

Hathaway, James C. *The Rights of Refugees under International Law.* Cambridge: Cambridge University Press, 2005.

Jerónimo, Miguel B. "Repressive Developmentalisms: Idioms, Repertoires, Trajectories in Late Colonialism." In *The Oxford Handbook of the Ends of Empire*, edited by Andrew Thompson and Martin Thomas, 537–554. Oxford: Oxford University Press, 2017.

Jerónimo, Miguel B., and António C. Pinto. "A Modernizing Empire? Politics, Culture and Economy in Portuguese Late Colonialism." In *The Ends of European Colonial Empires: Cases and Comparisons*, edited by Miguel B. Jerónimo and António C. Pinto, 51–80. Basingstoke: Palgrave Macmillan, 2015.

Jerónimo, Miguel B. and José P. Monteiro. "Das 'dificuldades de levar os indígenas a trabalhar': o 'sistema' de trabalho nativo no império colonial." In *O império colonial em questão (sécs. XIX-XX): poderes, saberes e instituições*, edited by Miguel B. Jerónimo, 197–221. Lisbon: Edições 70, 2013.

Jerónimo, Miguel B., and José P. Monteiro. "The Inventors of Human Rights in Africa: Portugal, Late Colonialism, and the UN Human Rights Regime." In

Decolonization, Self-Determination, and the Rise of Global Human Rights Politics, edited by A. Dirk Moses, Marco Duranti, and Roland Burke, 285–315. Cambridge: Cambridge University Press, 2020.

Johnson, Jennifer. *The Battle for Algeria: Sovereignty, Health Care and Humanitarianism*. Philadelphia: University of Pennsylvania Press, 2017.

Keese, Alexander. "Dos abusos às revoltas? Trabalho forçado, reformas portuguesas, política 'tradicional' e religião na Baixa de Cassange e no distrito do Congo (Angola), 1957–1961." *Africana Studia*, no. 7 (2004): 247–276.

Loescher, Gil. *The UNHCR and World Politics: A Perilous Path*. Oxford: Oxford University Press, 2001.

Monteiro, José Pedro. *The Interntionalisation of the "Native Labour" Question in Portuguese Late Colonialism, 1945–1962*. London: Palgrave Macmillan, 2022.

Oliveira, Joaquim. *Os Caminhos Históricos das Fronteiras de Angola*. Luanda: Cefolex, 2010.

O'Malley, Alanna. *The Diplomacy of Decolonisation: America, Britain and the United Nations During the Congo Crisis 1960–1964*. Manchester: Manchester University Press, 2018.

Rahal, Malika, and Benjamin T. White. "UNHCR and the Algerian War of Independence: Postcolonial Sovereignty and the Globalization of the International Refugee Regime, 1954–63." *Journal of Global History* 17, no. 2 (2022): 331–352.

Rich, Jeremy. "Victims or Burdens?: Angolan Refugees and the Humanitarian Aid Organizations in the Democratic Republic of the Congo, 1961–1963." *The International History Review*. 43, no. 5 (2021): 1001–1017.

Rich, Jeremy. *Protestant Missionaries and Humanitarianism in the DRC: The Politics of Aid in Cold War Africa*. New York: Boydell and Brewer, 2020.

Rutinwa, Bonaventure. "Prima Facie Status and Refugee Protection." UNHCR New Issues in Refugee Research Working Paper no. 49, UNHCR, 2002. https://www.refworld.org/docid/4ff3f8812.html

Chapter 7

Angolan and Mozambican Border Towns

Interconnecting and Consolidating Southern African Mobilities

Cristina Udelsmann Rodrigues

Mobility and circulation of people and goods have characterized the African continent since early history. More significant in scale than the international movements, intra-African migration is a pillar of social and economic dynamics in all regions of the continent, namely in southern Africa. While internal and international migration in the continent coexist and interrelate, extra-continental migration from sub-Saharan regions is less pronounced: more than 50 percent of African nationals in the OECD countries are from the north of the continent, while almost 75 percent of migrants from sub-Saharan Africa remain within the continent.[1]

The intra-African mobilities actively and intensively involve regional circulations and border crossings, a variety of temporary and prolonged types of settlement within the routes, and a network of urban populated hubs that support the circulations, namely those located at border regions or related to them. Urban centers within circulation routes provide housing, livelihoods, and serve as key transportation hubs for mobile populations. These urban structures combine with particular infrastructures that facilitate these movements in regions—road, railway and transportation networks, social linkages and brokerage, commercial services and transportation, and economic activity.[2] Settlement in urban and proto-urban locations within migration/movement routes is simultaneously an important asset for the continued mobility and a result of such movements. For the continent as a whole, there are no updated comprehensive mappings and descriptions of the structures (spaces and flows)—established routes and settlement patterns, hubs and sites of migration—and of the relevant infrastructures (means and resources) that facilitate these movements in specific locations, transportation networks, social networks, economies, and so forth. This is mostly due to the fact that they are adaptive and constantly changing, and research tends to focus on particular aspects, locations, or routes. Getting the "big picture" of the dynamics in place then means looking at mobility and settlement as dependent on each other: migration flows produce new settlement spaces and continually change those that already exist; the physical structures of migration support the movements and are simultaneously shaped by them.

On the other hand, international borders within the mobility and circulation networks are sensitive to changes in limitations to circulation imposed by bordering countries. Border managements and their contingencies, such as border closures and controls, have a clear impact not only on the movements and mobility but also, consequently, on settlement and urbanization. Conversely, local urban investments and the implantation of infrastructure or commerce, for example, encourages in-migration and settlement.

This chapter will demonstrate this interconnectedness between cross-border circulations and settlement using Angolan and Mozambican borderland dynamics—of closure, restrictions, or openings—as case-studies. The argument is grounded on literature exploring conceptualizations of migration and mobility, border towns and borderland dynamics, and migration-steered urbanization processes. Accounts from local residents and other urban stakeholders help sustain the argument, complementing the scarce data on population movements and on settlement. While focusing on broader aspects of the relation of intra-African migration/urbanization, the chapter will briefly refer to research conducted in Cunene, Huíla and Soyo in Angola and in Ressano Garcia in Mozambique, on lively border urban centers supporting cross-border trade, labor mobility and displacement, fostering migration and settlement (Figure 7.1).

The chapter starts by framing the argument on scholarly discussions on mobility, urbanization, and border-crossings. It then describes periods in Angola and Mozambique that markedly have been characterized by a predominant policy and practice imposed by conflicts or by the government authorities regarding border circulation and mobility in general. Both Angola and Mozambique became independent from Portuguese colonization in 1975 and in both, civil conflicts started after that. In Angola, the conflict lasted until 2002, while in Mozambique, peace was established earlier, in 1992. These changing conditions for border crossing and for movement have produced effects on settlement and urbanization over time, contributing to their expansion and growth or their loss of urban population and/or urban economic dynamism: the colonial establishment of the borders, the civil war periods and the blockages to circulation of people and merchandise, the post-war

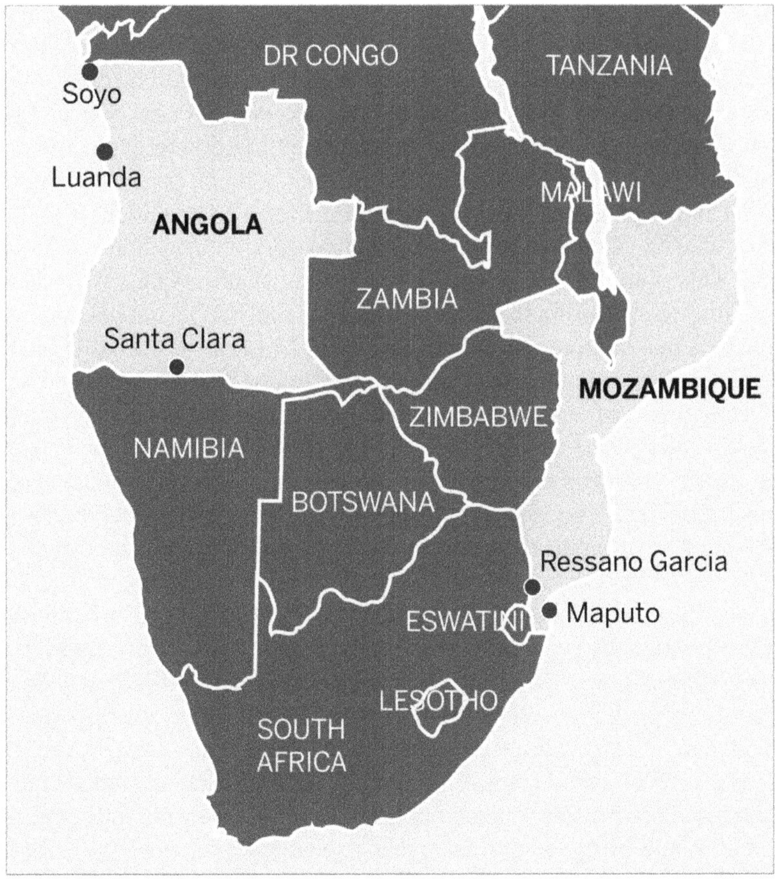

Figure 7.1 Border Posts and Border Towns Studied. *Source*: Created by the author.

freer circulations of civilians, and the recent context of restrictions to circulation imposed by the COVID-19 pandemic.

METHODS

The methodology followed for the analysis encompasses not only the literature review but also the use of case-studies in Angolan and Mozambican border towns, and others related to them, to illustrate the argument. The material collected on several occasions as part of research projects spans from the early 2000s to today, directly in the border regions at the crossing-points Santa Clara/Oshikango; Soyo, linked to the circulation between Angola/the DRC and Congo on the coast; and in Ressano Garcia/Komatipoort; and indirectly in the Huíla province,[3] linked to the Santa Clara border. The border towns and border posts were selected not only for their importance in terms of traffic flows in the respective countries but also because of the variety of cases they represent: Soyo's mining/LNG exploration site characteristics; Santa Clara, an active commercial hub adjacent to also commercially active Oshikango on the Namibian side; and Ressano Garcia, because of its commercial importance on the main route connecting Mozambique and South Africa, as well as its proximity and rail connection to the capital of Mozambique. This combination of data sources aims at providing evidence from mixed origins, exploring the qualitative and quantitative materials obtained at different research moments in both countries. Most of the data collected and used is from interviews with a variety of actors of different ages and sexes: residents, administrators, planners, traditional authorities, border management officials, businesspeople from the formal and informal economies, from shop owners and workers to peddlers, domestic workers, and other types of service providers. The interviews were accompanied by direct ethnographic observation at different moments in recent history when border towns were vibrant hubs for commerce and settlement and when they had lost this vibrancy. Soyo was, between 2008 when the LNG plant construction began and 2014, when the economic crisis hit the country's economy significantly, a very vibrant town, attracting both government and private investments, including migration and settlement of population looking for opportunities. Santa Clara, in turn, witnessed a population boom right after the end of the civil war in 2002, which was reinforced by the investments made locally by the state and private actors alike, but that was hindered by the economic crisis as well. While being an old and much-used border-crossing post, Ressano Garcia followed the same boomtown pattern of Santa Clara but only after infrastructural state-led investments such as a gas-to-power plant and a truck park were built.[4] The analysis was also complemented with research from news and other public accounts—and remote calls and contacts—during the closures imposed by the COVID-19 pandemic.

MIGRATION, MOBILITIES, BORDERS, AND URBAN SETTLEMENT

Both forced and voluntary migrations and displacements within Africa often involve border crossings. Cross-border mobility—permanent or seasonal border crossings, commuter circulations and so on—is at the heart of intra-African migration, mobilizing and affecting large numbers of individuals and households.[5] Migration and mobility lead to temporary and prolonged fixations of populations in certain locations both internally, in the same country, and internationally. Urban growth in the continent is mostly associated with rural-urban migration but it also includes more complex movements between rural and urban areas and natural population growth.[6] Mobility such as that seen in Africa and migration, which has always been an important aspect of urbanization patterns and conditions[7] continues to play a key role in urban processes taking place all over the world, and particularly in developing countries. African migrations are closely interlinked with shifting patterns of settlement and city-building.[8] Migration and varied forms of human mobility within Africa and worldwide are continually "redefining the meanings of home, community and belonging."[9] But temporary or transit settlement also explains the emergence and expansion of many towns and cities on the African continent, most particularly in border regions or within their related routes where intense transit contributes to the emergence and growth of urban hubs that support migration with lodging, services, facilities, and economies.

The numerous migratory hubs, connected to both regular and irregular circulations, are often urban locations or rapidly urbanizing if the fluxes and settlement remain significant.[10] Transit hubs within migration and mobility routes may also become destinations for migration over time, and small towns and villages along the migration routes can expand to accommodate significant numbers of people. Urban platforms for transportation and circulation, such as border towns, stand out throughout the continent, as do urban spaces connected to other transportation nodes, such as ports and towns within road and railway systems.[11] Other cities and towns inserted in transportation networks are themselves frequently not just passage locations, but also often end up being destinations for mobile populations within Africa. The close relation of towns with circulation and transportation routes is evident. Border towns, in particular, rely on the circulation of people and goods and on the opportunities created by this transit. As Storeygard indicates, "transport costs, have played a critical role in determining the growth of cities."[12] "Transport corridors" are also particularly key in fostering urban growth[13] and transport corridors in southern Africa, such as those originating in Maputo, Walvis Bay, Beira, and the trans-Cunene corridor, are expected to stimulate the growth of more border towns.[14]

Circulation in border regions as well as through border cities and towns is particularly significant and it is mostly sustained by cross-border trade. The economies involving border crossings use "green" bush paths and villages, "grey" roads, railways and border towns, or "blue" transport corridors to oceans and airports.[15] Border towns are formed, expand, and consolidate in most cases according to the levels of circulation and trade associated with them.[16]

Mobility in all its variety and local specificity critically supports multi-local households and diversified livelihoods and lives. Colonial administrations used it as the basis for labor recruitments.[17] The demarcation of African borders was part of the colonial management of mobility. Independence left the vast majority of political borders unchanged and has opened up new possibilities for intra-African migration and its associated commerce, with the first steps being made toward regional collaboration and integration, as well as new opportunities at individual levels.[18]

Most significantly, informal cross-border trade constitutes an important economic base in border regions in general[19] and in southern Africa in particular,[20] where it "provides support, income, and direct investment in development to a significant number of people in the region. It also forms an integral part of the regional economy."[21] In a number of sub-Saharan African countries, "informal cross-border trading activities . . . have succeeded in effecting extensive market integration where state-led initiatives have failed."[22] The dynamic cross-border economies, in turn, attract both urban dwellers and rural migrants to new forms of settlement in rapidly urbanizing smaller towns and cities,[23] including those within the border-crossing routes. Migration and mobility influence processes of urban growth, namely in secondary cities, with hometowns in several locations experiencing notorious consolidation, like for example in Tanzania,[24] but also elsewhere.[25]

BORDER AND BORDER-RELATED TOWNS IN ANGOLA AND MOZAMBIQUE

Both the establishment and the consolidation of towns and cities within the routes of intra-African migration are dependent on a combination of political, administrative, infrastructural, and/or economic conditions. Border towns function as hubs and structures interconnecting neighboring countries, borderland regions, and border economies. The examples of southern Angolan interconnected towns—Castanheira de Pêra (Matala, Huíla), Ondjiva/Santa Clara (Cunene province), and Oshikango (Namibia); of northern Angola Soyo and its linkages to the circulation of the Congos and references to Ressano Garcia and Komatipoort in Mozambique, provide substance to this argument. All of them have grown in size and population over the years (Table 7.1) but have experienced moments of faster growth or of stagnation within this time period.[26]

At their establishment, the administration of the colonial territories was more concentrated in the control of mobility and movements of people and economies, particularly with the neighboring countries. This concern culminated, in the late nineteenth century, with the establishment of African international borders, within a process denominated the Scramble for Africa, which began with the Berlin Conference (1884–1885). In southern Angola,

Table 7.1 Case-study Border/Border-related Towns in Angola and Mozambique

Town	*Built up area*	*Closest metropole*	*Distance to closest metropole*	*Population 1990*	*Population 2000*	*Population 2010*	*Population 2015*
Santo Antonio do Zaire	25.33 km²	Pointe Noire	160 km	14,600	39,600	130,008	205,943
Matala	21.20 km²	Luanda	672 km	20,100	50,326	71,750	Vila de Ressano Garcia Sede
5.83 km²	Cidade de Maputo	69 km	–	-	–	10,539	Namacunde / Santa Clara
15.25 km²	Windhoek	590 km	–	–	10,933	25,625	

Source: OECD/SWAC (2020), Africapolis, Agglomeration data.

colonial penetration was slow and weak and the "forgotten" southern regions of the country, if compared to others, remained as such for a long period.[27] The disputes between the Portuguese and the Germans for the territory were more intensive in 1914–1915, with the last battle to conquer Pereira D'Eça—the capital of Cunene Province, today called Ondjiva—taking place in 1915. After this, the final drawing of the border divided the Ovambo population[28] and made Pereira D'Eça an administrative strategic hub as the administrative capital from the 1960s to today and associated with the border town of Santa Clara. The South African border war related to the independence of Namibia and the Angolan civil war that followed the independence of Angola have had an enormous impact in the region, with Ondjiva and other localities totally destroyed. The population started to flee the region in the late 1970s, including the provincial government staff, most of whom took refuge in neighboring Huíla Province, in the small village of Castanheira de Pêra. By then, Castanheira de Pêra hosted the majority of those leaving Cunene, becoming a crowded active urban hub in the region. A very slow return of the population to the southern borderlands started in the 1990s, after Namibian independence, but still within a civil war context, and in this period the border town of Santa Clara started to attract people and businesses involved with cross-border trading with Oshikango on the Namibian side of the border.[29] The import of cars from Namibia to Angola was particularly significant in the first decade of the 2000s, after the end of the Angolan civil war, and fuel trafficking, from Angola to Namibia, has continued to increase since then. The population in Namacunde, also on this border, in 2002 at the end of the civil war was 112,000. Around 2010, Santa Clara alone had reached more than 20,000 while the province capital Ondjiva had about 91,000 inhabitants, according to the Government of the Province figures.

Soyo, former Santo António do Zaire, in the north of Angola, did not grow significantly until the end of the civil war. In the 1990s, the population was 14,600 inhabitants, but after 2010 it grew to 130,008 and then 227,175 at the census of 2014 in the entire municipality (estimated 201,000 for the city). Africapolis data indicated 205,943 inhabitants for the city in 2015.[30] This explosive growth occurred because the border village became a mining town of the province of Zaire, based on the large-scale oil and gas-related activities of the Angola Liquefied Natural Gas (LNG) project at the Kwanda Base that started to be built in 2008, commencing operations in 2013. Before this, Soyo was a small fishing village. The town has additionally grown because of its location on the fluvial/sea border with the Democratic Republic of Congo (DRC). It is situated on intensive migratory and trading routes, a combination of conditions favorable to settlement. But all these population flows over the years only catalyzed urban growth after the establishment of the natural gas plant, and associated urban infrastructure such as the airport, which was also built in 2008. The maritime police patrol the circulations of populations across the Congo River, which separates Soyo from the DRC, in close association with Angola LNG. The border post, located inside the Angola LNG compound, even controls the trading and transportation activities of the Soyo municipality. Towns such as Soyo have not witnessed significant improvements in connectivity in the last years, except for those brought by the LNG project: natural gas is transported by sea through the Kwanda Base port of the Angola LNG, and the airport was built to support the extractive activity. This and the combination of other attractions mean that the town has started to host a larger number of workers coming to the large-scale venture, and it also receives an influx of other populations seeking opportunities related to the town's economic growth. The capital of Zaire Province, Mbanza Congo, has lost economic and even administrative prominence to Soyo in the last years. The provincial administration staff is most of the time based not in Mbanza Congo but in Soyo, where there are better infrastructure and services.

In Mozambique, the traffic-intensive town of Ressano Garcia is located at the border post of the same name, between the capital Maputo and commercially vibrant interconnected South African towns like Komatipoort and Nelspruit. It is one example of informal growth accompanied by formal interventions. The town had existed since colonial times, but its expansion and the attraction of larger numbers of people only started after the end of the civil war in Mozambique in 1992. Since then, trade in the region has increased between Mozambique and South Africa and through this border pass many goods supplying the Mozambican market: food products, clothing, liquor, or construction materials.[31] On average, cross-border traders spent 1.52 days in South Africa on each of their trips and a majority (54 percent) would travel to Johannesburg, Nelspruit, Malelane, or Komatipoort at least once a week in 2016.[32] They would then bring the products back to Mozambique to sell, mostly in Maputo but also in the urban centers of Xai-Xai and Beira. This commerce has actively continued since the 1990s, together with other cross-border mobilities linked to labor in South Africa and tourism in Mozambique.

Following increased circulation and migration to the town, state intervention and investments, aiming at better controlling the cross-border flows and settlements, have materialized not only in a reformed border post area, but also in a traffic park and in urban planning. The population has grown from nearly 9,000 inhabitants in 2015[33] to more than 20,000 in 2016. According to the data of the University Eduardo Mondlane's Faculty of Architecture and Physical Planning, between 1952 and 2015 the built area of Ressano Garcia increased by 30.5 percent, although during the civil war period the town was destroyed and practically empty. In 2014 the Ressano Garcia Thermal power station was inaugurated, which together with the Terminal Internacional Rodoviário built in 2015 at "Km 4," attracted workers and their families to the jobs created, both in the construction and operational phases. The town is also linked by railway and by the EN4 national road to Maputo, which has contributed to increased commuting.

BORDER CONTROL AND BLOCKAGES TO MOBILITY

All border regions and networks under analysis have suffered the impact of wars and conflicts at different moments. More recently, all have been affected by restrictions to circulation imposed by the COVID-19 pandemic since 2020.

The southern Angolan/Namibian border town network was, among the cases analyzed, the most impacted by conflict for a longer time. The above-mentioned early twentieth century conquest of the region by Portuguese forces led to the establishment of Pereira D'Eça, marking the instituting of an "imperial border" between the German and Portuguese empires.[34] Later, in 1927, the international border was finally settled between Portugal and South Africa, as well as a veterinary border (or Red Line) that had a particularly significant symbolic and practical importance,[35] conditioning the local cross-border economies related to cattle.

But the harder and longer limitations for circulation and settlement in the region took place within the context of the "Border War"[36] between SWAPO forces fighting for Namibian independence and the South African army. Martial rule dominated the region until the end of the war in Namibia in 1989.[37] The South African border crossings involved military incursions into Angolan territory and were related to the independence fighting; to the protection of South Africa's investment in the Ruacana hydro-electric scheme on the Cunene River and its dam in Calueque, bordering Namibia and serving Namibia's Ovamboland through a pipeline;[38] and Cold War allegiances such as UNITA guerrilla support of South Africa by fighting SWAPO forces in eastern Angola. The establishment of the so-called *kaplyn* (cutline), a thin strip of land cleared of any growth, marked the border[39] while the erection by South Africa of a 450-kilometer-long, 2-meter-high barbed-wire fence symbolized the border control, militarization, and imposed restrictions to circulation. However, for more than twenty-three years the border was never a total barrier—like most borders, porosity means conduits and opportunities[40]—despite South Africa's efforts to limit and control movement across it. However, movement was necessarily reduced during the most intense periods of war and fighting.[41] Within the intra-Angolan circulation, the South African invasion of Ondjiva until 1989 emptied the city for a long period and the local political/military structures retreated to Castanheira de Pêra/Matala in Huíla Province,[42] one of the most notorious displacements in the country.

After the independence of Namibia, the militarized conditions for circulation across the region did not change significantly. The Angolan civil war continued until 2002, and so movement between Angola and Namibia, especially through the official posts at Namacunde and Santa Clara, was hard. UNITA guerrillas controlled several parts of the border and attacks were frequent, especially on the Ondjiva-Namibia route, where only a few traders would risk crossing the border. Accounts from a forty-five-year-old Santa Clara male resident show how war affected settlement and migration: "Between 1992 and 2002, our family ran five times to Namibia, jumping over the fence."[43] This account also shows how the porousness of the border was always a possibility, despite the physical barriers and the dangers of the conflict throughout the war. Traders would settle instead on the Namibian side of the border[44] and cross-border trade continued, despite the restrictions imposed by the conflict, as did cross-border family and ethnic ties, and refugee movement from Angola to Namibia.[45] The border remained unstable until 2002, as Namibian authorities allowed the Angolan army to operate in the region and even on Namibian soil to fight UNITA.[46]

War and conflict also affected the northern part of Angola. As a local businessman mentioned, "In 1975, oil meant nothing. The prospections in the 1980s did not even pay salaries to the local workers, just gave them food. In 1992, everything stopped. Only again in the 2000s workers from outside Soyo started to come."[47] These accounts show very clearly the phases when the populations did and did not find Soyo attractive. The town waxed and waned through weak colonial rule, a post-independence period of growth fueled by the development of the oil economy in the region, then the suspension of all economic activity and mobilities in the region during the civil war, and finally a post-war recovery and further attraction of population with the implementation of the gas project.

But despite the tighter policing of the region that led to restrictions on circulation, some cross-border businesses were maintained during the civil war period and afterward. As a resident described, "The fuel [illegal] trade to the Congo is what facilitates our lives, to get dollars. Traffickers transport fuel drums in canoes, along the river, escaping the government and the LNG control. Soyo has more than 100 small islands where they can hide the drums."[48] The local accounts of covert cross-border trade and the strategies of traders and their networks to continue border-crossings are numerous.

The halting of LNG activities in 2016 produced immediate impacts locally, not only to the economy but also to settlement and the growth of the city. While the border remained open, the circulation within the region and across the border suffered the impact of reduced economic dynamism caused by the suspension of the LNG exploration, while the fuel trafficking continued.

War and conflict in Mozambique also affected the border region at Ressano Garcia/Boane. Accounts from local residents mention not only destruction but also forced escapes of the population to safer areas. Ressano Garcia is the more used southwestern Mozambican border, more so than the Namaacha border with Eswatini, because of the trade that circulates through it. The local residents, as one put it, "dominate the border crossings. The *mukheristas* (informal traders) with trader card charge 250 Rands per person and crossing. The border services removed the traders that were literally leaning against the border and moved them to Km 4. But they still spend most of the time at the border gates and trade continues as usual."[49] Again, strategies to deal with the restrictions and permissions at the borders adapt to the conditions set by authorities, the economic and the political settings. While in Angola the 2014/15 crisis deeply impacted the economy—and border trade especially—in Mozambique the Ressano Garcia border area continued to grow during the 'hidden debt' crisis in 2016, notably between Maputo and the border, most critically supported by the metropolitan growth of the capital Maputo and Matola, and the improvements of the railway circulation.

The intensive traffic between Maputo and South Africa, however, was abruptly interrupted by the COVID-19-related border restrictions. The new restrictions also added to the already declining cross-border trade and circulation in southern Angola, while in the north, the thriving legal and illegal cross-border trade to the DRC became more controlled. COVID-19 has affected global African mobility with various travel disruptions and restrictions, as an IOM report of June 2020 attests[50] through its Displacement Tracking Matrix.[51] The continent recorded a 39 percent decrease in migration flows in early 2020 at key transit points, which only later started to rise again. The restrictions left migrants stranded throughout the continent and displaced people experienced worsening living conditions.[52] Border restrictions and closures may have had, however, a limited impact on informal trading and migration. For instance, in the southern African region, people developed new strategies for circulation through the already porous border regions.[53] The northern borders in Angola with the DRC were only officially reopened in July 2022, two years after their closure, and in southern Angola, they had opened in May of the same year. In Mozambique, while border-crossings were suspended starting in mid-2020, with some openings and closures thereafter, it has always been possible to circulate between Mozambique and South Africa despite the tighter controls. However, in all regions, the two years of "official" closure represented a huge setback for local economies, for the regional and national economies in terms of volume, although this can only be estimated given the poor records in this regard.

Controls and even blockages to cross-border circulation then have a clear impact on all types of actors, but affect differently those using the border to trade, to access services, or to access work. Laborers, forced migrants, smugglers, or traders have to regularly adapt to the crossing conditions, and in the case of these border towns, different strategies had to be mobilized to deal with changing situations.

ENCOURAGED CROSS-BORDER CIRCULATION

In all studied border regions/towns, the lifting of restrictions on circulation imposed by conflicts had consequently accelerated return and/or settlement in border regions. The local economic developments, especially after the end of the civil wars, have catalyzed urban growth, which shows the direct relation between the possibilities of circulation and urban evolution. At the same time, particularly in Angola, border control after the end of the civil war became a necessity for the Angolan government, which saw tax revenues as an important outcome of its investment in border control.[54]

The few border posts in Angola and Mozambique connected to high-traffic national or international roads and routes regained importance after the end of the civil conflicts, and the increased circulation that followed contributed to further expanded interconnected regional linkages between cities and towns and their respective markets. Santa Clara's strategic location grew in importance with the reactivation of the Namibe and Lobito ports, and the reconstruction of railways linking them to Zambia: It "facilitated the reestablishment of commercial links between urban and rural areas and between inland and coastal areas" and also helped develop a series of "intermediate trade centres."[55] The same is the case in another southern border region around Rundu (Namibia)-Calai (Angola) where "the establishment of a well-maintained network of highways, major and minor roads" that serve the populations in the region have fostered mobility, connectivity and the growth of both towns.[56] The mentioned importance of the Maputo-border railway is also to be acknowledged. Both in Angola and in Mozambique, the existence and improvement of intra-African migration infrastructures, most crucially transportation, and of circulation networks is then an important catalyst of economic dynamism and settlement, particularly in border towns.

In the southern parts of Angola, the end of the wars, combined with a major investment in a truck park and customs' facilities attracted businesses and settlement. The former cross-border relations, namely those based on trade that was already growing on the Namibian side and the access to services such as health and education in Namibia by border populations, became more intensive.[57] The growing settlement of Chinese warehouses in Oshikango on the Namibian side[58] is the most evident among the new trade-related settlements. With more than 20,000 inhabitants, it is a town created "from below, through economic opportunity."[59] Even before the end of the civil war, in the late 1990s, Angola and Namibia had agreed on a border pass allowing residents in the southern provinces to cross to Namibia up to 30 km from the border (this distance increased to 60 km in 2005). Tax exemption on cross-border trade of commodities not exceeding a certain amount also contributed to a renewed increase of small-scale trading activities, and consequently of population moving to the region. The re-activation of the cross-border trade then combined in the early 2000s with local state investments in reconstruction and infrastructure, like a truck/commercial park built to support the cross-border trade and the associated project for a business and industrial center, the Centro Empresarial do Cunene (Cunene Business Centre).

In the north of Angola, the development of the Angola LNG, made possible by the cessation of the civil conflicts, associated with infrastructure investments like the port and airport, also attracted population from other areas in the region and from other parts of the country. Many Soyo residents today have experienced intensive mobility, not only caused by the war but also fostered by changing opportunities. As one twenty-nine-year-old man, a worker at the LNG described: "I have circulated a lot. I was born in Benguela, came to Soyo to study, then I went to Cabinda and after to Luanda; and then, because of the work in the gas company, I stayed in Canada and in Indonesia for some periods."[60] This account, as with many similar local stories, shows that mobility is at the core of life trajectories, and that adaptation to the conditions and opportunities dictates settlement and movement. Another individual, also twenty-nine, mentioned regular and frequent commuting between Soyo and Congo since an early age: "I was born in the Congo and ended up working at the LNG, but I have been coming back and forth since I was born and still do."[61] A local businessman, in turn, described his life mobility from Angola to Pretoria, Luanda, and India before "settling back here and dedicating to car rentals and lodging for oil companies."[62]

The consolidation and growth of the border mining and gas town of Soyo also happened due to its location on the fluvial/sea border with the Democratic Republic of Congo (DRC) and the Congo region, in a route of intensive migration and mobility and of trade. The population flows catalyzed urban growth after the establishment of the natural gas plant and its associated urban infrastructure. For the workers at the exploration, the 28/28 system—staying 28 days in a row in the base and 28 others where they want—allows not only for prolonged stays in Soyo but also continued relations with other provinces either from where they originated or the capital Luanda. As a twenty-nine-year-old said: "We can study with this system; I am studying in Luanda currently."[63] These other types and modalities of mobility and settlement also show how adapting and seizing the best combinations for family and individual purposes shape towns, circulations, and social and economic lives in different regional contexts. On the other hand, the implantation of the LNG project and the prolonged stays of workers also made Soyo change in the view of older residents, with more and more people staying for longer. As one worker/resident referred to the change: "This was the brush before, LNG had the residential areas deforested before the construction started. In 2004, we could count the number of cars on the street. We played football on the road; and there was only one minimarket, the Estrela Branca, the rest were small grocery shops (*cantinas*)."[64] With the gas project, residents recognize that clear changes were happening in terms of urban life, namely in aspects related to traffic or commercial facilities.

On the Mozambican border, the continued trade with South Africa, developed by both small-scale *mukheristas* and large-scale traders, has been intensifying over the years. Increased trade combined with a new truck park, railroad commuting, and the implantation of an electricity project have made Ressano Garcia and Komatipoort both grow and continuously attract more residents. The traffic-intensive Ressano Garcia, which already existed in colonial times, expanded and attracted a larger number of people only after the end of the civil war in Mozambique.[65] The "cross-border micro-region" within the Maputo Corridor and the state-led program of the Maputo Development Corridor (MDC) is not only propelled by the cross-border relations but also by the "millions of migrants" that have moved into it over the years.[66] It has maintained itself as a migration corridor, an informal trade corridor, and even a criminal corridor.[67] Komatipoort and Ressano Garcia are twin towns straddling the border and "with the considerable increase in the volumes of people and traffic crossing the border, new investment opportunities have emerged for retailing and tourism developments."[68] Associated with this dynamism, state investments aiming at better controlling the cross-border flows have materialized, for instance, into a reformed border post area and a traffic park/road terminal. On the other side of the border, agglomeration and urbanization is also visible. As an owner of a lodge in Komatipoort put it, "Komatipoort exists because of the Mozambique trade."[69] The growth of Ressano Garcia compared to the district capital, Boane, is also changing due to the intensification of the trade and circulation: "Moamba may be losing population to Ressano Garcia recently."[70] A resident also mentioned that "three years ago [2014], there was one hotel in Ressano Garcia. Today there are five,"[71] emphasizing the urbanization.

The examples in this chapter then highlight the importance of less restricted mobility to a variety of residents in the border-related towns for the emergence of new dynamic urban hubs, increasingly transforming into larger towns. Santa Clara and Ressano Garcia emerged as informal agglomerations of a varied range of traders, businesspeople, and their employees. In Soyo, in turn, the infrastructural improvements fostered by the LNG terminal attracted a significant number of people and businesses to the linked activities—transportation, lodging, trade—and redirected settlement and migration to the region.

CONCLUSION

General conclusions from the analysis then emphasize the importance and vibrancy of intra-African migration and mobilities and the urban (and proto-urban) structures and hubs that support them. Among these, border towns are key loci that sustain circulation, where the tendency for agglomeration and fixation of a variety of actors is seen in many examples. Direct urbanization at border towns and indirect urban growth in towns associated with intra-African mobility and border crossing is seen throughout the continent and constitutes an important feature of the mobility and circulation.

Migration and mobility have been established as key elements configuring urban settlement, and in border regions, they are particularly affected by both short- and long-term border closures and openings. Interruptions of the circulation of people and goods, blockages, and added requirements for border-crossings drive people away and, consequently, lead to discontinued urban growth and settlement. Among the main conditions for deterred settlement, civil conflicts and war in Angola and Mozambique have been the ones causing the most impacts in recent history. Military occupations and attacks have forced, in some cases, large numbers of residents to leave and have heavily conditioned circulation and border-crossing patterns. On the other hand, temporary restrictions to circulation, such as the ones imposed by the global COVID-19 pandemic between 2020 and 2022, have had an effect on local mobility and, therefore, on the interest of some individuals to remain in border towns, where the commercial basis of the local economies has drastically decreased.

Further, state and private investments in local economies or infrastructure contribute to urbanization as they attract populations to border towns and other urban places within circulation routes. Local stimulation of circulation of people and goods has encouraged settlement and consolidation of urban spaces in Angola and Mozambique over the years. Having these correlations in mind is key to addressing urban development in border regions and their related urban spaces, where mobile populations often seek economic opportunities. More knowledge on the dynamics of migration and settlement, beyond the limited population censuses, is also key to predict and promote local urban development. The potentials of intra-African migration have been at the core of the African Union perspectives on migration as they provide economic opportunities for a large number of Africans. The ambitions of the free-trade area in the continent are then interlinked to both effective and migration-conducive border management and to the migration/mobility-steered urbanization processes that can serve mobile populations with economic and residential opportunities and development.

NOTES

1. Robert E. B. Lucas, "African Migration," in *Handbook of the Economics of International Migration*, eds. Barry R. Chiswick, Paul W. Miller (Amsterdam: North-Holland, 2015), 1445–1596.
2. Cristina Udelsmann Rodrigues and Jesper Bjarnesen, *Intra-African Migration* (Brussels: European Parliament's Committee on Development, 2020).
3. Also comprises data from a survey conducted in Matala in 2021. This research was funded by the Riksbankens Jubileumsfond, grant number P19–0271:1, for the tri-country (Angola, Democratic Republic of Congo, and Zambia) research project Changing Urban Residency. https://changingurban.se/.
4. Cristina Udelsmann Rodrigues, "Built on Expectations: Angolan and Mozambican Emergent and Stagnant Rural Towns," *African Study Monographs* 42 (2022): 187–204.
5. Paul Nugent and Anthony I. Asiwaju, eds., *African Boundaries: Borders, Conduits and Opportunities* (London: Pinter, 1996).
6. Cecilia Tacoli, Gordon McGranahan and David Satterthwaite, *Urbanization, Rural–Urban Migration, and Urban Poverty* (IOM: World Migration Report, 2015).
7. Deborah Potts, "Urban Economies, Urban Livelihoods and Natural Resource-Based Economic Growth in Sub-Saharan Africa: The Constraints of a Liberalized World Economy," *Local Economy* 28, no. 2 (2013), 170–187; AbdouMaliq Simone, "A Town on Its Knees?" *Theory, Culture & Society* 27, no. 7–8 (2011): 130–154.
8. Marie-Laurence Flahaux and Hein De Haas, "African Migration: Trends, Patterns, Drivers," *CMS* 4, 1 (2016).
9. Loren B. Landau and Oliver Bakewell, "Introduction: Forging a Study of Mobility, Integration and Belonging in Africa," in *Forging African Communities: Mobility, Integration and Belonging*, eds. Oliver Bakewell and Loren B. Landau, (London: Palgrave Macmillan, 2018): 1.
10. Cristina Udelsmann Rodrigues and Jesper Bjarnesen, *Intra-African Migration*, 2020.
11. Hugh Lamarque and Paul Nugent, *Transport Corridors in Africa* (Suffolk: James Currey, 2022).
12. Adam Storeygard, "Farther on Down the Road: Transport Costs, Trade and Urban Growth in Sub-Saharan Africa," *The Review of Economic Studies* 83, no. 3 (2016): 1263.
13. Wolfgang Zeller, "'Now We Are a Town': Chiefs, Investors, and the State in Zambia's Western Province," in *State Recognition and Democratization in Sub-Saharan Africa: A New Dawn for Traditional Authorities?,* eds. Lars Buur and Helene Maria Kyed (New York: Palgrave Macmillan, 2007): 209–231; Wolfgang

Zeller, "Danger and Opportunity in Katima Mulilo: A Namibian Border Boomtown at Transnational Crossroads," *Journal of Southern African Studies* 35, no. 1 (2009): 133–154.

14. Ana Duarte, Fernando Pacheco, Regina Santos, and Elling N. Tjønneland, *Lobito Corridor: Diversification and Development or White Elephants* (CMI and Catholic University of Angola, April 2015); Paul Nugent, "Border Towns and Cities in Comparative Perspective," in *A Companion to Border Studies*, eds. Thomas M. Wilson and Hastings Donnan (Chichester: John Wiley & Sons, 2012), 557–572.

15. Gregor Dobler, "The Green, the Grey and the Blue: A Typology of Cross-Border Trade in Africa." *The Journal of Modern African Studies* 54, no. 1 (2016): 145–169.

16. Wolfgang Zeller, "'Now we are a Town'; Wolfgang Zeller, "Danger and Opportunity in Katima Mulilo"; Paul Nugent, "Border Towns and Cities in Comparative Perspective."

17. Anthony I. Asiwaju, "Migrations as Revolt: The Example of the Ivory Coast and the Upper Volta before 1945." *Journal of African History* 17, no. 4 (1976): 577–594; Frederik Cooper, *Decolonization and African Society: The Labor Question in French and British Africa* (London: Cambridge University Press, 1996); Hannah Cross, *Migrants, Borders and Global Capitalism: West African Labour Mobility and EU Borders* (London: Routledge, 2013).

18. Jonathan Crush, Vincent Williams, and Sally Peberdy, *Migration in Southern Africa.* (Policy Analysis and Research Programme of the Global Commission on International Migration, 2005).

19. Kate Meagher, "Smuggling Ideologies: From Criminalization to Hybrid Governance in African Clandestine Economies." *African Affairs* 113, no. 453 (2014): 497–517.

20. Cristina Udelsmann Rodrigues, "Angola's Southern Border: Entrepreneurship Opportunities and the State in Cunene." *The Journal of Modern African Studies* 48, no. 3 (2010): 461–484.

21. Sally Peberdy, "Mobile Entrepreneurship: Informal Sector Cross-Border Trade and Street Trade in South Africa." *Development Southern Africa* 17, no. 2 (2000): 217.

22. Yahaya Hashim and Kate Meagher, "Cross-border Trade and the Parallel Currency Market: Trade and Finance in the Context of Structural Adjustment: A Case Study from Kano, Nigeria," *Research Report 13* (Uppsala: Nordiska Afrikainstitutet, 1999).

23. Jytte Agergaard, Niels Fold and Kate Gough, *Rural-Urban Dynamics: Livelihoods, Mobility and Markets in African and Asian Frontiers* (Taylor & Francis, 2009); Deborah Fahy Bryceson, "Birth of a Market Town in Tanzania: Towards Narrative Studies of Urban Africa." *Journal of Eastern African Studies* 5, no. 2 (2011): 274–293; Deborah Bryceson and Danny MacKinnon, "Eureka and Beyond: Mining's Impact on African Urbanisation." *Journal of Contemporary African Studies* 30, no. 4 (2012): 513–537; Gregor Dobler, "Oshikango: The Dynamics of Growth and Regulation in a Namibian Boom Town." *Journal of Southern African Studies* 35, no. 1 (2009): 115–131; Wolfgang Zeller, "Danger and Opportunity in Katima Mulilo."

24. Manja H. Andreasen, Jytte Agergaard, Robert Kiunsi, and Ally H. Namangaya, "Urban Transformations, Migration and Residential Mobility Patterns in African Secondary Cities," *Geografisk Tidsskrift-Danish Journal of Geography* 117, no. 2 (2017): 93–104.

25. Claire W. Herbert and Martin J. Murray, "Building from Scratch: New Cities, Privatized Urbanism and the Spatial Restructuring of Johannesburg after Apartheid," *International Journal of Urban and Regional Research* 39, no. 3 (2015): 471–494; Femke van Noorloos, "New Master-Planned Cities in Africa: Translocal Flows 'Touching Ground'?" in *Handbook of Translocal Development and Global Mobilities*, eds. Annelies Zoomers, Maggi Leung, Kei Otsuki, and Guus Van Westen (Northampton: Edward Elger: 2021), 204–215.

26. Cristina Udelsmann Rodrigues, "Built on Expectations."

27. William Gervase Clarence-Smith, *Slaves, Peasants and Capitalists in Southern Angola (1840–1926)* (London: Cambridge University Press, 1979).

28. Carlos Estermann, *Etnografia do Sudoeste de Angola* (Lisboa: Junta de Investigação do Ultramar, 1961); Maria Helena de F. Lima, *Nação Ovambo* (Lisboa: Aster, 1977); Cristina Udelsmann Rodrigues, "The Kwanhama Partitioned by the Border and the Angolan Perspective of Cross-Border Identity," *African Studies* 76, no. 3 (2017): 423–443.

29. Gregor Dobler, "Oshikango."

30. Data from https://africapolis.org/download/Africapolis_agglomeration_2020.xlsx.

31. António Júnior, Yasser A. Dadá, and Momade Ibraimo, "Relações Transfronteiriças de Moçambique," *Observador Rural*, Documento de Trabalho 27 (Maputo: Observatório do Meio Rural, 2015).

32. Inês Raimundo and Abel Chikanda, "Informal Entrepreneurship and Cross-Border Trade in Maputo, Mozambique," *SAMP Migration Policy Series* 73 (Cape Town: SAMP, 2016).

33. According to Júnior et al. (2015), the administrative post Ressano Garcia had 8,997 inhabitants that year.

34. Giorgio Miescher, *Namibia's Red Line: The History of a Veterinary and Settlement Border* (New York: Palgrave Macmillan Publishing, 2012).

35. Giorgio Miescher, *Namibia's Red Line.*

36. Ian van der Waag and Albert Grundlingh, *In Different Times: The War for Southern Africa 1966–1989* (Stellenbosch: African Sun Media, 2019).

37. Ana Leão and Martin Rupiya, "A Military History of the Angolan Armed Forces from the 1960s Onwards—As Told by Formers Combatants," in *Evolutions & Revolutions: A Contemporary History of Militaries in Southern Africa*, ed. Martin Rupiya (Pretoria: Institute for the Security Studies, 2005), 7–41; Piero Gleijeses, "Cuba and the Independence of Namibia," *Cold War History* 7, no. 2 (2007): 285–303; Chris Saunders, "The Namibian/Angolan Border in the Namibian War for Independence," in *In Different Times: The War for Southern Africa 1966–1989*, eds. Ian Van der Waag and Albert Grundlingh (Stellenbosch: African Sun Media, 2019), 15–27.

38. van der Waag and Grundlingh, *In Different Times.*

39. Miescher, *Namibia's Red Line*.
40. Nugent and Asiwaju, *African Boundaries*.
41. Saunders, "The Namibian/Angolan Border."
42. Cristina Udelsmann Rodrigues, "Survival and Social Reproduction Strategies in Angolan Cities," *Africa Today* 54, no. 1 (2007): 91–105.
43. All interviews in this chapter have been anonymized. Interview with DKM, Santa Clara, May 2016.
44. Dobler, "Oshikango."
45. Selma M.W Nangulah, Ndeyapo M. Nickanor, and Jonathan Crush, *Northern Gateway: Cross-Border Migration Between Namibia and Angola*, (Cape Town: Idasa, 2005).
46. Saunders, "The Namibian/Angolan Border."
47. Interview with DN, forty-one-year-old businessman, Soyo, 2016.
48. Interview with DN, a forty-one-year-old businessman, Soyo, 2016.
49. Interview with SN, thirty-year-old, Ressano Garcia, April 2017.
50. International Organization for Migration, DTM (Covid 19)—Global Mobility Restriction Overview, 8 June 2020; International Organization for Migration, West and Central Africa—Covid-19—Impact on Mobility Report, May 2020.
51. Data can be found at: https://dtm.iom.int/.
52. Udelsmann Rodrigues and Bjarnesen, *Intra-African Migration*.
53. Inocent Moyo, "Covid-19, Dissensus and De Facto Transformation at the South Africa–Zimbabwe Border at Beitbridge," *Journal of Borderlands Studies* 37, no. 4 (2022): 781–804.
54. Dobler, "Oshikango"; Udelsmann Rodrigues, "Angola's Southern Border."
55. Duarte, Pacheco, Santos and Tjønneland, *Lobito Corridor*, 21.
56. Achim Röder, Michael Pröpper, Marion Stellmes, Anne Schneibel, and Joachim Hill, "Assessing Urban Growth and Rural Land Use Transformations in a Cross-Border Situation in Northern Namibia and Southern Angola," *Land Use Policy* 42 (2015): 351.
57. Udelsmann Rodrigues, "Angola's Southern Border."
58. Dobler, "Oshikango."
59. Dobler, "Oshikango," 129.
60. Interview with EZ, Soyo, 2016.
61. Interview with JN, Soyo, 2016. 2016.
62. Interview with DN, a forty-one-year-old businessman, Soyo, 2016.
63. Interview with JN, Soyo, 2016.
64. Interview with EZ, a twenty-nine-year-old male, Soyo, 2016.
65. Udelsmann Rodrigues and Bjarnesen, *Intra-Africa Migration*.
66. Fredrik Söderbaum and Ian Taylor, *Afro-Regions: The Dynamics of Cross-Border Micro-Regionalism in Africa* (Uppsala: Nordiska Afrikainstitutet, 2008): 35.
67. Söderbaum and Taylor, *Afro-Regions*, 37.
68. Christian M. Rogerson, "Spatial Development Initiatives in Southern Africa: The Maputo Development Corridor," *Tijdschrift voor Economische en Sociale Geografie* 92, no. 3 (2001): 340.
69. Interview with JD, a sixty-two-year-old businessman, Komatipoort, 2017.

70. Interview with MA, sixty-eight-year-old academic, Maputo, 2017.

71. Interview with JB, a forty-five-year-old male road terminal worker, Ressano Garcia, 2017.

BIBLIOGRAPHY

Agergaard, Jytte, Niels Fold, and Kate Gough. *Rural-Urban Dynamics: Livelihoods, Mobility and Markets in African and Asian Frontiers*. Taylor & Francis, 2009.

Andreasen, Manja H., Jytte Agergaard, Robert Kiunsi, and Ally H. Namangaya. "Urban Transformations, Migration and Residential Mobility Patterns in African Secondary Cities." *Geografisk Tidsskrift-Danish Journal of Geography* 117, no. 2 (2017): 93–104.

Asiwaju, Anthony I. "Migrations as Revolt: The Example of the Ivory Coast and the Upper Volta before 1945." *Journal of African History* 17 no. 4 (1976): 577–594.

Bryceson, Deborah, and Danny MacKinnon. "Eureka and Beyond: Mining's Impact on African Urbanisation." *Journal of Contemporary African Studies* 30, no. 4 (2012): 513–537.

Bryceson, Deborah Fahy. "Birth of a Market Town in Tanzania: Towards Narrative Studies of Urban Africa." *Journal of Eastern African Studies* 5, no. 2 (2011): 274–293.

Clarence-Smith, William Gervase. *Slaves, Peasants and Capitalists in Southern Angola (1840–1926)*. London: Cambridge University Press, 1979.Cooper, Frederik. *Decolonization and African Society: The Labor Question in French and British Africa*. London: Cambridge University Press, 1996.

Cross, Hannah. *Migrants, Borders and Global Capitalism: West African Labour Mobility and EU Borders*. London: Routledge, 2013.

Crush, Jonathan, Vincent Williams, and Sally Peberdy. *Migration in Southern Africa*. Policy Analysis and Research Programme of the Global Commission on International Migration, 2005.

Dobler, Gregor. "Oshikango: The Dynamics of Growth and Regulation in a Namibian Boom Town." *Journal of Southern African Studies* 35, no. 1 (2009): 115–131.

Dobler, Gregor. "The Green, the Grey and the Blue: A Typology of Cross-Border Trade in Africa." *The Journal of Modern African Studies* 54, no. 1 (2016): 145–169.

Duarte, Ana, Fernando Pacheco, Regina Santos, and Elling N. Tjønneland. *Lobito Corridor: Diversification and Development or White Elephants*. CMI and Catholic University of Angola, April 2015.

Estermann, Carlos. *Etnografia do Sudoeste de Angola*. Lisboa: Junta de Investigação do Ultramar, 1961.

Flahaux, Marie-Laurence, and Hein De Haas. "African Migration: Trends, Patterns, Drivers." *CMS* 4 no. 1 (2016).

Gleijeses, Piero. "Cuba and the Independence of Namibia." *Cold War History* 7, no. 2 (2007): 285–303.

Hashim, Yahaya, and Kate Meagher. "Cross-border Trade and the Parallel Currency Market: Trade and Finance in the Context of Structural Adjustment: A Case Study from Kano, Nigeria." *Research Report 13*. Uppsala: Nordiska Afrikainstitutet, 1999.

Herbert, Claire W., and Martin J. Murray. "Building from Scratch: New Cities, Privatized Urbanism and the Spatial Restructuring of Johannesburg after Apartheid." *International Journal of Urban and Regional Research* 39, no. 3 (2015): 471–494.

International Organization for Migration, DTM (Covid 19)—Global Mobility Restriction Overview, 8 June 2020.

International Organization for Migration, West and Central Africa—Covid-19—Impact on Mobility Report, May 2020.

Júnior, António, Yasser A. Dadá, and Momade Ibraimo. "Relações Transfronteiriças de Moçambique." *Observador Rural*, Documento de Trabalho 27. Maputo: Observatório do Meio Rural, 2015.

Lamarque, Hugh, and Paul Nugent. *Transport Corridors in Africa*. Suffolk: James Currey, 2022.

Landau, Loren B., and Oliver Bakewell. "Introduction: Forging a Study of Mobility, Integration, and Belonging in Africa," in *Forging African Communities: Mobility, Integration and Belonging*, edited by Oliver Bakewell and Loren B. Landau, 1–24. London: Palgrave Macmillan, 2018.

Leão, Ana, and Martin Rupiya. "A Military History of the Angolan Armed Forces from the 1960s Onwards—As Told by Formers Combatants." In *Evolutions & Revolutions: A Contemporary History of Militaries in Southern Africa*, edited by Martin Rupiya, 7–41. Pretoria: Institute for the Security Studies, 2005.

Lima, Maria Helena de F. *Nação Ovambo*. Lisboa: Aster, 1977.

Lucas, Robert E. B. "African Migration." In *Handbook of the Economics of International Migration*, edited by Barry R. Chiswick and Paul W. Miller, 1445–1596. Amsterdam: North-Holland, 2015.

Meagher, Kate. "Smuggling Ideologies: From Criminalization to Hybrid Governance in African Clandestine Economies." *African Affairs* 113, no. 453 (2014): 497–517.

Miescher, Giorgio. *Namibia's Red Line: The History of a Veterinary and Settlement Border*. New York: Palgrave Macmillan Publishing, 2012.

Moyo, Inocent. "Covid-19, Dissensus and De Facto Transformation at the South Africa–Zimbabwe Border at Beitbridge." *Journal of Borderlands Studies* 37, no. 4 (2022): 781–804.

Nangulah, Selma M.W., Ndeyapo M. Nickanor, and Jonathan Crush. *Northern Gateway: Cross-Border Migration Between Namibia and Angola*. Cape Town: Idasa, 2005.

Noorloos, Femke van. "New Master-Planned Cities in Africa: Translocal Flows 'Touching Ground'?" In *Handbook of Translocal Development and Global Mobilities*, edited by Annelies Zoomers, Maggi Leung, Kei Otsuki, and Guus Van Westen, 204–215. Northampton: Edward Elgar, 2021.

Nugent, Paul, and Anthony I. Asiwaju, eds. *African Boundaries: Borders, Conduits and Opportunities*. London: Pinter, 1996.

Nugent, Paul. "Border Towns and Cities in Comparative Perspective." In *A Companion to Border Studies*, edited by Thomas M. Wilson and Hastings Donnan, 557–572. Chichester: John Wiley & Sons, 2012.

Peberdy, Sally. "Mobile Entrepreneurship: Informal Sector Cross-Border Trade and Street Trade in South Africa." *Development Southern Africa* 17, no. 2 (2000): 201–19.

Potts, Deborah. "Urban Economies, Urban Livelihoods and Natural Resource-Based Economic Growth in Sub-Saharan Africa: The Constraints of a Liberalized World Economy." *Local Economy* 28, no. 2 (2013): 170–87.

Raimundo, Inês, and Abel Chikanda. "Informal Entrepreneurship and Cross-Border Trade in Maputo, Mozambique." *SAMP Migration Policy Series* 73. Cape Town: SAMP, 2016.

Röder, Achim, Michael Pröpper, Marion Stellmes, Anne Schneibel, and Joachim Hill. "Assessing Urban Growth and Rural Land Use Transformations in a Cross-Border Situation in Northern Namibia and Southern Angola." *Land Use Policy* 42 (2015): 340–354.

Rogerson, Christian M. "Spatial Development Initiatives in Southern Africa: The Maputo Development Corridor." *Tijdschrift voor Economische en Sociale Geografie* 92, no. 3 (2001): 324–346.

Saunders, Chris. "The Namibian/Angolan Border in the Namibian War for Independence." In *In Different Times: The War for Southern Africa 1966–1989*, edited by Ian Van der Waag and Albert Grundlingh, 15–27. Stellenbosch: African Sun Media, 2019.

Simone, AbdouMaliq. "A Town on Its Knees?" *Theory, Culture & Society* 27, no. 7–8 (2011): 130–54.

Söderbaum, Fredrik, and Ian Taylor. *Afro-Regions: The Dynamics of Cross-Border Micro-Regionalism in Africa*. Uppsala: Nordiska Afrikainstitutet, 2008.

Storeygard, Adam. "Farther on Down the Road: Transport Costs, Trade and Urban Growth in Sub-Saharan Africa." *The Review of Economic Studies* 83, no. 3 (2016): 1263–1295.

Tacoli, Cecilia, Gordon McGranahan, and David Satterthwaite. *Urbanization, Rural–Urban Migration, and Urban Poverty*. IOM: World Migration Report, 2015.

Udelsmann Rodrigues, Cristina, and Jesper Bjarnesen. *Intra-African Migration*. Brussels: European Parliament's Committee on Development, 2020.

Udelsmann Rodrigues, Cristina. "Angola's Southern Border: Entrepreneurship Opportunities and the State in Cunene." *The Journal of Modern African Studies* 48, no. 3 (2010): 461–484.

Udelsmann Rodrigues, Cristina. "Built on Expectations: Angolan and Mozambican Emergent and Stagnant Rural Towns." *African Study Monographs* 42 (2022): 187–204.

Udelsmann Rodrigues, Cristina. "Survival and Social Reproduction Strategies in Angolan Cities." *Africa Today* 54, no. 1 (2007): 91–105.

Udelsmann Rodrigues, Cristina. "The Kwanhama Partitioned by the Border and the Angolan Perspective of Cross-Border Identity." *African Studies* 76, no. 3 (2017): 423–443.

Waag, Ian van der, and Albert Grundlingh. *In Different Times: The War for Southern Africa 1966–1989*. Stellenbosch: African Sun Media, 2019.

Zeller, Wolfgang. "'Now We Are a Town': Chiefs, Investors, and the State in Zambia's Western Province." In *State Recognition and Democratization in Sub-Saharan Africa: A New Dawn for Traditional Authorities?* Edited by Lars Buur and Helene Maria Kyed, 209–231. New York: Palgrave Macmillan, 2007.

Zeller, Wolfgang. "Danger and Opportunity in Katima Mulilo: a Namibian Border Boomtown at Transnational Crossroads." *Journal of Southern African Studies* 35, no. 1 (2009): 133–154.

Chapter 8

Cross-Border Mobility of Mozambicans to South Africa and the Growth of Informal Trade in the City of Xai-Xai 2005–2022

Victor Simões Henrique

This study describes the contribution of the informal cross-border trading from Mozambique to South Africa, using the Ressano Garcia border and the growth of informal trade in the city of Xai-Xai in Gaza Province in Mozambique. It also describes the opportunities offered by South Africa for the Mozambican informal traders, including family survival. This chapter narrates this story in the changing context where the main attraction of going to South Africa is no longer the gold mines, as it was for many since the beginning of the twentieth century. Rather, the new attraction pulling Mozambicans to South Africa is the practice of informal trade.

While this chapter does not trace the history of migration fully, it starts in the last quarter of the nineteenth century, after the discovery of diamonds and gold in Kimberley and the Witwatersrand, respectively. The migration of Mozambicans to the mines ebbed and flowed, but by the end of the twentieth century, it eventually declined. Consequently, fewer Mozambicans were working in formal employment, but, on the other hand, the flow of Mozambicans to South Africa continues. These migrants differ in that they focus on the exploitation of commercial opportunities. Thus, drawing on oral histories, this chapter recounts the daily life of those involved in informal trade migration through interviews conducted in Xai-Xai from 2021 to 2022. While many changes have been noted because of this changing dynamic, one of the biggest is that more women than men are now involved in migration.

BRIEF NOTES ON THE CITY OF XAI-XAI

The city of Xai-Xai is the capital of the Gaza province in the south of Mozambique, with an estimated population of around 160,000 inhabitants, mostly belonging to the Tsonga ethnic group.[1] The resident population in Xai-Xai comes from almost all districts of the province of Gaza, with a considerable influx of migrants from the rural areas.

Its main economic activities are agriculture, based on the cultivation of cereals, with emphasis on corn and rice, which are produced on the banks of the Limpopo River. The river runs through the city of Xai-Xai. Livestock, with an emphasis on cattle, constitute one of the oldest economic activities practiced in the area. Being the provincial capital, the city also has a sizeable number of civil servants, who are divided into various sectors such as education, health, agriculture, and more.

In the last two decades, there has been an emergence and development of other economic activities, most of which are not linked to the public sector. The largest of these is the practice of informal cross-border trade in South Africa, with women predominating in the trade.

A BRIEF HISTORY OF BORDER CROSSING OF MOZAMBICANS TO SOUTH AFRICA

Many Mozambicans today move back and forth to and from South Africa, especially using the Ressano Garcia border crossing. The inhabitants of the city of Xai-Xai predominantly use this crossing, along with residents from other surrounding districts like Chongoene, Chibuto, Chokwe, Limpopo, and Bilene, as well as residents of Maputo. These residents all consider the Ressano Garcia border crossing as the gateway to *el dourado* (the place of gold), and the main gateway through which they might change their social status. This is due to the numerous opportunities that South Africa potentially offers, and so utilizing the Ressano Garcia crossing for increased economic opportunity has become the main goal for many young people and adults in the region.

The concept of crossing the border in search of better opportunities in South Africa has a long history and has involved different actors over time, but it has always had a common objective—the search for better living conditions. Southern Mozambique has a long history of sending labor migrants to South Africa. The first period of intensified crossing started with the late nineteenth century discovery of the Kimberley diamonds and Witwatersrand gold deposits. In the twentieth century, the recruitment of southern Mozambicans largely happened through the efforts of the Witwatersrand Native

Labour Association (WNLA), the monopoly arm of the South African mines. While the mines paid Mozambican miners low wages, like all migratory workers in the racially discriminatory system, the wages did allow many in southern Mozambique to accumulate money to satisfy social and economic imperatives. These included paying for traditional marriages (*lobola*) and buying cattle and other agricultural inputs, like plows and hoes, which were used to promote agriculture in their home villages. These migrant miners were also able to invest the income they acquired in the purchase of goods and in construction, such as fine clothing, the construction of sturdy masonry houses, and building cisterns to retain water, especially in areas with irregular rainfall.

The second period of migrant labor began after the independence of Mozambique in 1975.[2] During this period, the mines reduced their hiring, and many Mozambicans emigrated illegally, many still using the border at Ressano Garcia. They, too, like their earlier predecessors, were seeking better job opportunities, this time with a greater focus on the agricultural sector, especially on large South African plantations, and on informal trade activities, like street vending. Because their work was not as well paid as the miners had been, on their return they did not have the same ability to spend as broadly or widely.

In the second period, a new aspect began to emerge, which marked and continues to mark the process of crossing the border for Mozambicans in search of economic opportunity in South Africa. That aspect is the rise and intensification of informal cross-border trade, which has been developing over time. A key moment happened in 2015 when the governments of Mozambique and South Africa reached an agreement for the abolition of entry visas between the two states, which allowed for an ever-greater circulation of people and goods. The abolition of entry visas created conditions for a greater development of informal trade activity, an activity that is part of the economic reforms suggested when Mozambique joined the Bretton Woods institutions.[3] Thus, this chapter will focus on the second phase of border crossing, particularly at the Ressano Garcia border post, the main route used by Mozambicans in search of goods for commercialization.

The main differences between the two periods of migration are the sex of those who cross the border, their destinations in South Africa, and, in some cases, their country of origin. The first period was dominated by men crossing the border destined for the mining sector, as well as for work on plantations and other formal employment. The second period has been dominated by women crossing the border and going to supermarkets and stores, from where they buy various goods and bring them back to market them in Mozambique. It has also been dominated by traders originally from other countries.

THE EMERGENCE AND DEVELOPMENT OF CROSS-BORDER TRADE IN THE STUDY AREA

The beginning of informal commercial activity in Gaza Province was influenced by multiple factors, especially human and natural ones. One of the biggest factors, however, was the reduction in the hiring of labor for the mining sector in South Africa since 1975. In 1975, around 118,000 Mozambican workers were recruited to mines in South Africa. In 1976, after Mozambican independence, the number dropped to around 41,000 hired workers, and it continued to decline, with only 39,731 being hired in 1983.[4] Thus, there were more unemployed people in the rural regions from which most of the male migrants had come. Therefore, many families had to look for new sources of income. Many tried to develop small rural commercial operations or commercialize agricultural products produced on local farms in urban areas. In many cases, this cultivation benefited from work tools such as plows and cattle they had accumulated during the time period when they had been working on contract at the mines.

Corroborating the arguments above, Gaspar showed that the reduction in hiring for the South African mining sector was due to multiple factors, like the growing mechanization of the mining sector, the internalization of the workforce (the hiring of more South Africans and fewer labor migrations from other regional countries), and the tense relations between the South African apartheid regime and the new government of the People's Republic of Mozambique. The socialist policy of the Mozambican government from its independence in 1975 discouraged the hiring of Mozambican labor, calling it a continuation of the exploitation of workers in the service of the South African capitalist economy.[5]

Without many other options, many Mozambicans resorted to informal cross-border trade activities, which allowed them to provide, however modestly, for their families as small-time goods sellers. Others migrated to urban areas in search of jobs as night guards, salespeople, and counter assistants in shops, many of which were owned by Asians, and in independent small stalls in Xai-Xai. Many used informal trade as a steppingstone to try to advance economically. Some interviewees in the city of Xai-Xai stated that when they emigrated to urban areas, they often started as street vendors. Some graduated to owning their own small establishments, which usually first consisted of mobile stalls, where they sold basic products such as batteries, small light bulbs, cigarettes, matches, needles, safety pins, and sweets, among other things.

Further making life difficult for many Mozambicans from Gaza Province in the wake of mass retrenchments in South Africa's mining sector was the Civil War that broke out in 1976, lasting until 1992, between the government and the Resistência Nacional Moçambicana (Mozambican National Resistance or RENAMO). The RENAMO attacks carried out during the civil wWar destroyed the basis for the development of rural areas throughout Gaza, affected agricultural production, and displaced thousands of Mozambicans, both to urban areas, considered safe, and to neighboring countries. RENAMO was initially founded in and with support from the former southern Rhodesia (Zimbabwe) soon after Mozambique's independence declaration. The Central Intelligence of Rhodesia initially supported RENAMO as a way of making Mozambican territory off-limits to Zimbabwean guerrilla groups, but after Zimbabwe's 1980 independence, it was also supported by the apartheid regime in South Africa. The civil war was highly disruptive to daily life and was a very important element for the emergence and development of informal cross-border trade for many residents in Gaza Province. The war caused a massive rural exodus, as populations abandoned their homes and places of production, from which they had previously obtained resources for their survival, because of the threat of violence. According to Chingono, the war caused the collapse of the rural economy and also hurt employment opportunities in urban areas due to the disruption. It also led to an increase in displaced persons, most of whom were farmers in the war-affected areas.[6] These former farmers were forced to turn into street vendors, selling mainly secondhand clothing and foodstuffs.

Nhambi also argued that the civil war was a factor that contributed to the great rise in informal commerce in urban areas.[7] He posited that in the 1980s, the spread of the war in southern Mozambique and, particularly important for this chapter, in Gaza Province, disrupted agricultural production and created massive displacements in the countryside. This disruption crushed the peasant economy in many areas and created hundreds of thousands of internally displaced people who moved as refugees to neighboring countries.

Mosca also argues that in rural areas, informal commerce originated in the rupture of the commercial network as the result of the civil war.[8] The main argument is largely similar to Nhambi's, that the destruction of rural livelihoods from 1976 to 1992 led to an exodus to urban areas. He goes further, however, by arguing that those fleeing rural areas who had financial resources began to direct them to economic activities in urban areas such as semi-collective transport, commonly known as *Chapa Cem*, and informal commerce. These economic activities had to replace the residential space in rural areas that had always been the economically productive space supporting the needs of the family group. Thus, the rural exodus during the civil war came with not just a search for better security conditions, but also a fundamental economic reorientation for many rural Mozambicans in Gaza Province.

Other authors who have studied the origins of informal cross-border trade have also noted that this activity derives not just from the rural exodus and the fall in agricultural production, but also from structural adjustment programs, unemployment, the porosity of borders, and a lack of employment opportunities, especially for youth.[9] Further, natural factors have also played a role, including the severe drought that occurred in almost the entire southern region of Mozambique between 1983 and 1986, which intensified the economic crisis that had been going on since the proclamation of national independence in 1975 and contributed to the collapse of subsistence agriculture. Women, who were the main practitioners of agriculture, out of necessity searched for other survival strategies in the cities. There they found work as domestic servants and carried out small commercial activities, such as selling wild fruits and distilling and marketing alcoholic beverages based on locally available products like sweet cane, cashews, and oranges.

Informal traders have, for a long time, also used other income-generating activities that aimed, initially, to help compensate for the bad agricultural years. These included the production and sale of ceramic items like pots for water conservation and food preparation, and the collection and sale of wood for use as a cooking fuel. In the study areas, house construction materials were also exploited, especially the stakes, ropes, grass, and *macuti* (the palm leaves from coconut trees that are generally used in the coastal regions for the construction of precarious housing). The increased need for such products as urban areas saw an influx of population led to their commercialization, a trend which contributed greatly to the increase in informal commerce in urban areas. These small-scale traders have also now applied the knowledge gained from domestic trade to the evolving cross-border trade with South Africa.

The liberalization of the economy started when Mozambique, in the throes of an economic crisis, signed the accession agreements to the Breton Woods institutions on September 24, 1984, following a decision taken at the Frelimo Congress of April 1983. Frelimo, Frente de Libertação de Moçambique or the Liberation Front of Mozambique, was the party in power starting at independence in 1975. The 1983 Party Congress saw a turn away from socialism toward a liberalization of the economy through a loosening of controls on prices, retail trade, transport, and agriculture, as well as the decentralization of planning to the districts. This Congress represented a significant departure from the socialist policies the Frelimo government had followed since 1977. These changes led the Frelimo government to sign a deal with the International Monetary Fund in May 1987. The Economic Rehabilitation Program, initiated in 1987, established a structural adjustment plan that was implemented during the period from 1987 to 1989. This period of austerity exacerbated an economic situation that had been tough for many residents from 1981 onward. The war and long-standing drought had adversely affected the production and livelihoods of the population, leading to widespread deprivation and famine along with the immense costs in terms of human suffering and material losses resulting from the massive brutality of the civil war.[10]

These changes and the precarity they forced on many in southern Mozambique led to a significant increase in the informal economy in rural areas in Mozambique. While the poverty and deprivation were real, the structural changes did allow for the opening of the economy to market forces, as this period saw the abandoning of a centrally planned economy that marked the first years after independence. Abreu noted that the informal economy appeared and grew after the end of the planned economy, as state control over prices, interest rates, and exchange rates had previously limited private initiative and the full functioning of markets.[11] He further noted that in Mozambique, the informal sector emerged and thrived as a counterweight to the process of liberalization and opening of the economy to foreign investment. While acting as an antidote to unemployment, the informal economy also generally operates outside the tax system and official statistical record keeping. While Abreu praises the informal sector for representing a qualitative leap in the subsistence economy, there are some drawbacks for the state and the public coffers as well.

At the same time that economic reforms were starting, political negotiations began that were aimed at putting an end to the civil war. This process led to the negotiated settlement that ended the war as well as a new Constitution for the Republic that was adopted in 1990. This solidified the change to a multiparty system and a market economy. The key passages in the new Republic of Mozambique Constitution were:

> ARTICLE 31. 1. The parties express political pluralism, contribute to the formation and manifestation of the popular will and are a fundamental instrument for the democratic participation of citizens in the governance of the country.

> ARTICLE 41. 2. The national economy comprises the following types of property that complement each other: a) State property; b), cooperative ownership; c) mixed ownership; d) private property.[12]

These parts of the constitution were the institutional framework that opened space for the practice of the informal economy on the one hand, and, on the other, the recognition of political pluralism. It meant the end of the one-party rule that had prevailed in Mozambique after independence, and also brought about the conditions necessary for the signing of the General Peace Agreement between the government and RENAMO on 4 October 1992. The end of the war and the ensuring peace stimulated the free movement of people and goods and allowed a greater openness to the exercise of informal trade activity.

In the context of the liberalization of the economy, many of the women who started to engage in informal cross-border trade justified their motivations for entering this activity by pointing to factors like the low purchase prices of products from South Africa, especially when compared to the prices in the markets in Maputo. This allowed them to have a profit margin, even after including travel and transport costs. The informal economy and cross-border trading, thus, represented an economic lifeline for individuals and their families, as informal trading is the main source of livelihood for many families. The informal traders interviewed in Xai-Xai noted that a lack of formal employment meant they were unable to support their dependents, like children and other family members, in any other way. While some of the informal traders were women and other new entrants to the realm of migration, others had previously worked in the mines of South Africa. With the end of their employment contracts, these ex-miners had to return to Mozambique, where they invested part of their remittances in informal commercial activity. These entrants had advantages from their time working previously in South Africa, like a mastery of commercial products supply points, experiences with travel processes, and the knowledge of cities, like Johannesburg, where many informally traded products are found. They also often had knowledge of some useful local languages like English and Zulu.

THE CATEGORIES OF INFORMAL TRADERS IN XAI-XAI

From the interviews with informal traders in Xai-Xai, this chapter divides them into several categories, which correspond to similar categories found by Chikanda and Raimundo in their study of informal traders.[13] The first category consists of those who cross the borders to South Africa, destined for market cities of Komatipoort and Johannesburg, where they purchase goods to sell in informal markets in Mozambique. This category consists primarily of individual entrepreneurs, meaning that the same individuals who travel sell the products they purchase in establishments, whether small stands or stalls that they own. They might also employ other individuals who help them run the establishments, especially when they are gone buying more product. They often retail clothing, beauty items, household appliances, and other household goods.

The second category consists of traders who cross the border destined for South African cities to buy products that they largely sell wholesale to other informal traders, though they might sell small quantities of these goods themselves, too. The main places visited by these cross-border traders are Johannesburg, where they buy furniture, clothing and footwear, jewelry, vehicle accessories, building materials, and hardware; Durban, where they purchase various clothing and vehicle accessories; and Komatipoort, where food products are often purchased, with an emphasis on meat and meat products. These traders ensure a wide variety of products are available for sale in Gaza Province, ranging from footwear, clothing, food products—in particular, meat, eggs, chicken and their derivatives, corn flour, cooking oil, onions, potatoes, and carrots—household appliances, and plastic items, especially chairs, buckets, and miscellaneous crockery.

There is a third and final category of informing traders, described later in the chapter, who do not travel across the border. Rather, they make their purchases in Mozambique, especially in Maputo, buying secondhand clothes for later commercialization. This group, while physically staying in the country, often relies on good imported to Maputo by other informal traders who have crossed the South African border to procure their goods.

Many of the main buyers in this second category of wholesale informal traders are of foreign origin, especially residents of Burundian descent, whose goods tend to be diversified. There are also traders of Indian origin in this category who are often the owners of formal commercial establishments in Xai-Xai, including shops that sell products such as clothing, footwear, crockery, electrical appliances, furniture, and sometimes foodstuffs such as onions and potatoes. The Burundian traders tend to only sell food products such as flour, onions, potatoes, crackers, sardines, chicken and their derivatives, and various meats, especially beef and steak, most of which is imported from Komatipoort. One of these informal traders noted that the entire enterprise of informal trading was based on building levels of trust, and the wholesalers were quite good at this:

> Whenever they need the goods, we supply ourselves and the money pays in phases, but they always comply with the dates agreed in the scope of supply, I supply pork in packages of 5 kg each, as well as *rachel*, *palone* [varieties of sausage], cooking oil and sometimes onion, but I think it's better to work with foreigners because they're honest in their pay.[14]

The mostly foreign wholesale traders develop a very high level of trust with their customers, which they need because sales are not always made promptly. They sell on a form of credit whereby they deliver the goods to the establishments and agree on the dates for the collection of the outstanding bill. This amounts to an informal banking system for the informal traders, though again it all takes place out of sight from the formal banking system, the tax system, and any government oversight.

These wholesalers and the individual traders who also cross the border often face more scrutiny at the border because they are not Mozambican. On account of this, many of the foreign traders use Mozambican intermediaries to actually cross the border, leading to more local employment.

> In [the] Ressano [Garcia Border Post], when the police authorities discover that you are not Mozambican, the process of searching the goods has been very intense. The taxi takes a long time because of the searches and folders, because they think that we transport other things than normal goods, which brings with it several constraints, not only for me but especially for other passengers traveling in the same car. So, it is more practical to order from the Mozambican *mukheristas* [cross-border middlemen and women], which are not complicated during the trip.[15]

Thus, the foreign traders operating in Xai-Xai often send their Mozambican friends and employees to purchase wholesale products that they then re-sell to local informal traders because it is safer and more convenient. In this way, they eliminate the need to cross the border themselves, as they have been the target of a lot of extortion by the police and border authorities, especially at the Ressano Garcia crossing. This wholesale purchasing procedure with informal traders has been giving rise to a new phenomenon in commercial activity that has not yet been deeply studied, which is the formalization of the informal. Imported products are bought informally by importing agents and are sold in establishments without the payment of duty rights. Though the goods entered the country informally, they then enter the formal value chain through merchants who own the stores without having ever been "formalized" in official import/export statistics. An informal trader expounded on how this process worked:

> I have been guaranteeing the supply of plastic goods, namely chairs and tables, as well as basins to the Indian [traders] of Chokwe, Chibuto Macia and Xai-Xai. Upon payment of part of the value of the goods, and after a week or two, I come to pick up the remaining value. Normally the [traders] purchased these products in Maputo, in Chinese stores, but due to the [higher] quality of our product they prefer to work with merchandise from South Africa.[16]

All formal traders, including retailers and wholesalers, work with the *mukheristas* (a southern Mozambican word for cross border traders) to supply merchandise in their stores. They supply products like juices, chickens, eggs, *palones*, mayonnaise, corn flour, sardines, and other foodstuffs with which they equip their establishments.[17] The informal traders who supply these shops note that they are taking a financial risk when they come back with goods and then have to find others to sell the goods. One trader noted this, saying:

> For the best performance in this activity, we count on those who have stalls and stores for our merchandise to leave [to be sold] quickly. So, [the sellers] pay a

> part of the value [up front] and we leave our products and after some time we return to collect the remaining money. The profit is not much large under these conditions, but there is always a guarantee that the goods will leave [be sold].[18]

Informal cross-border traders are also responsible for the supply of goods in some formal commercial establishments. In order to get the goods into the formal commercial sector, they often use negotiation mechanisms which can include bribing governmental authorities so that they do not have to declare the origin of the goods that they commercialize. Thus, the formal commercial sector is also, perhaps somewhat ironically, contributing to the growth of informal commercial activity in Xai-Xai and Gaza Province.

In addition to the Indians and Burundians, Nigerian traders living in Xai-Xai are also part of similar types of commercial activity. They have a slightly different niche, however, largely as importers of vehicle parts. They also work slightly differently. Rather than crossing the border themselves or hiring Mozambican intermediaries, they hire drivers who are already crossing the border. These drivers take a list of products to be purchased, usually in the city of Johannesburg, and bring them back.

> I won't talk much about this activity, but some products that you have here in the store, are bought in South Africa. I pay money to these drivers to bring me some products, such as engine oils, filters, rims, and sometimes tires, as well. I can gain trust with my customers who think that all Nigerian pieces are fake. When [the drivers] bring in [the parts], I pay the transport and a bribe to pay at the border.[19]

Here we see that not all cross-border traders even need to cross the border. What distinguishes them, however, is that they are paying for goods to cross the border, again without being officially declared. The cross-border traders, especially those of Nigerian origin, understand that crossing the border themselves can be a risky proposition because of the attitude of border officials. Another trader noted:

> To be honest, we buy some items in South Africa. I don't always like to go there because of the complications at the border. Even within South Africa, when they find out there's a Nigerian in the car, they make a big search and think we're dealing drugs. That's why I entrust the drivers to bring my goods. They know the stores where to buy them, which I explained to them. On their way back I pay the agreed amount and nothing else.[20]

The reports related to this practice once again show the depth of the trust necessary for those who are involved in informal trade. They also highlight the complicated dynamics of nationality and citizenship that drive the system.

Informal traders who do not have a Mozambican passport allege that they face higher scrutiny and thus are subjected to high rates of illicit payment at the borders. A local Mozambican woman noted:

> I always transport car accessories for two Nigerians, one from Macia, the other from Xai-Xai. They give me the price and the list of accessories they need for me to buy. Then on their way back, they pay the cost of transporting their goods. They find this procedure safer than traveling to Johannesburg, because the level of distrust and consequently insecurity to which they are subject is very high.[21]

The third category of traders are those who profit from cross-border trade, but who do not undertake or even pay for the act of crossing borders themselves. Rather, they go to larger urban centers—Maputo is the most common destination for those from Gaza Province—to purchase items from wholesalers there who have procured items from across the border. One trader recounted how this system, like the others detailed above, has been rationalized to allow all participants to make a profit from the trade. However, it takes specialized knowledge of the local market in Xai-Xai, as margins are much thinner.

> My friends and I stayed in Maputo, in the warehouses downtown, where the bales of second-hand clothes are reasonably priced, even including transport. They always have profit margins left. An important aspect when buying bales of second-hand clothes is always good to buy considering the season of the year. For example, there is a high demand for sweaters and blankets [in the] winter period, while sheets, skirts, and other things like that, have more high demand in summers. Some products we buy from *mukheristas* who bring [goods] mainly from Komati[poort]. They sell to us at prices that allow us to have some profit margin. They bring eggs, chickens, detergents, and cooking oil to me. Sometimes I send them to bring onions and potatoes, but it doesn't make much profit, because some customers prefer to buy the potato, onion, and carrot of national production.[22]

In all these interviews, which were conducted in the informal markets in Xai-Xai, it was evident that there was a wide variety of imported products for sale. Some of the market traders, most of whom were women, specialized in their stalls with particular products, but most shops contained a wide range of products, many of which obviously came from cross-border trade. The women traders who engaged in these sorts of commercial transactions, to succeed, had to have a broad range of skills. Depending on which form of cross-border trade they used, the women had to have extraordinary negotiating skills to profitably deal with store managers in South Africa and the cross-border drivers who transported the goods, customs officials in Mozambique, and they had to have a knowledge of border procedures. Additionally, some of them had to develop and use their bribing skills to not just import goods, but also to bring goods from the informal sector into the formal sector. This allowed them to avoid paying taxes related to import duties, renting places to run their businesses, and avoiding business taxes. This was all important to the informal traders, who often were eking out a precarious existence and supporting their families on the margins of the new economic order in Mozambique.

CONCLUSION

Throughout this chapter, the mobility of a variety of categories of Mozambican traders to South Africa was outlined, and this highlighted the growth of informal commerce in the growing city of Xai-Xai. It is important to note that this explosive growth in informal traders was only able to take place because of the implementation of economic reforms in Mozambique, initiated in the late 1990s, through the country's acquiesce to the structural adjustment conditions demanded by the Bretton Woods institutions. These forced Mozambique to embark on a process of profound economic transformation that culminated in the introduction of the market economy and the abandonment of the centrally planned economy that had been in force since national independence in 1975.

It was in the context of the liberalization of the national economy that the practice of informal commerce emerged. Residents of rural communities and of smaller cities like Xai-Xai suddenly had to figure out alternatives for economic survival while the country was under great transformation and economic difficulties. The natural droughts that had devastated the south of Mozambique in the 1980s combined with the violence of the civil war that lasted from 1976 to 1992 caused large displacements of rural populations and a disruption of subsistence agriculture. These factors caused a rural exodus that led to explosive growth in regional and national urban centers that were ill-prepared to receive them.

Another factor that pushed many southern Mozambicans from Gaza Province to alter their economic activities was the reduction in the hiring of migrant mine workers in South Africa, which increased the number of unemployed residents in the region at the same time as the other crises were hitting. It was the confluence of these factors that forced many in Xai-Xai and Gaza into informal commerce as one of the only alternatives that allowed individuals to obtain resources necessary for survival. This, naturally, took different forms for different people, with much of the early informal trade being local, while the cross-border trade, especially with South Africa, came later with a relaxation of the visa policies.

Knowing and understanding the various categories of informal traders who import goods to be subsequently sold in Xai-Xai helps explain the various ways through which informal traders obtain goods, and the ways in which this trade allows people to make some money if they know and understand the local markets and border procedures. These networks are comprised not just of Mozambican informal traders, but also include other traders of foreign origin, especially those of Burundian, Indian, and Nigerian origin. These traders illustrate how there is not simply one "border policy" to understand, but rather different border regimes for different individuals. All these trade networks are, too, facilitated by other "support" industries like, in this case, transport drivers who facilitate this trade. Finally, the chapter noted that the informal trade has not just changed commercial networks but has contributed greatly to the elevation of the social status of women, who are some of the main practitioners of this activity, though they often are still existing on the margins in very precarious positions.

NOTES

1. Instituto Nacional de Estatística, *IV Recenseamento Geral da População e Habitação,* 2017.
2. Ramos Cardoso Muanamoha, "The Dynamics of Undocumented Mozambican Labour Migration to South Africa" (PhD Diss., University of KwaZulu Natal, 2008), 31–32.
3. Victor Simões Henrique, *"A contribuição comércio informal e transformações sociais e económicas no meio rural na província de Inhambane (1990–2014),"* *Africa[s]* 18, no. 5 (2021): 210.
4. Manuel G. Araújo, "O Sistema de Aldeias Comunais em Moçambique, Transformações na Organização do Espaço Residencial e Produtivo" (PhD Diss., Universidade de Lisboa, 1988).
5. Napoleão Gaspar, The Reduction of Mozambican Workers in South African Mines, 1975–1992: A Case Study of the Consequences for Gaza Province—District of Chibuto (MA Thesis, University of the Witwatersrand, 2006).
6. Mark Chingono, *The State, Violence and Development*: *The Political Economy of War in Mozambique* (Cambridge: Cambridge University Press, 1998), 114.
7. Simão Nhambi and Jeremy Grest. *Mobility, Migration and Trade: Interactive Flows Between Durban and Southern Mozambique* (IESE: 2007), 117.
8. João Mosca, *Economicando*, (Maputo: Alcance Editores, 2009).
9. Daniel Ndlela, *Informal Cross Border Trade: The Case of Zimbabwe* (Johannesburg: Institute of Global Dialogue, Occasional Paper 52:59, 2006); Elton Muzvidziva, *The Nature of Informal Cross Border Trade and its Implications for Regional Integration: The Case of Forbes and Machipanda Border Posts of Zimbabwe and Mozambique* (Harare: Netherlands Development Organization, 2006).

10. Marc Wuyts, "Economia política do colonialismo português Moçambique," *Estudos Moçambicanos* 1 (1980): 9–22.
11. António Pinto de Abreu, *O sector Informal em Moçambique Uma abordagem monetária* (Maputo: Staff Pape, 2008).
12. *Constituição da República de Moçambique de 1990* (Maputo: Imprensa Nacional, 1990).
13. Abel Chikanda, and Inês Raimundo, "Informal Entrepreneurship and Cross-Border Trade Between Mozambique and South Africa," *African Human Mobility Review* 3, no. 2 (2017): 968.
14. Interview with Trader A, Xai-Xai, interviewed by Victor Simões, 20 May 2021.
15. Interview with Trader B, Xai-Xai, interviewed by Victor Simões, 22 May 2022.
16. Interview with Trader C, Xai-Xai, interviewed by Victor Simões, 15 April 2021.
17. Interview with Trader D, Xai-Xai, interviewed by Victor Simões, 15 April 2022.
18. Interview with Trader C.
19. Interview with Trader D.
20. Interview with Trader E, Xai-Xai, interviewed by Victor Simões, 20 May 2022.
21. Interview with Trader F, Xai-Xai, interviewed by Victor Simões, 28 June 2021.
22. Interview with Trader G, Xai-Xai, interviewed by Victor Simões, 25 May 2022.

BIBLIOGRAPHY

Abreu, António Pinto de. *O sector Informal em Moçambique Uma abordagem monetária.* Maputo: Staff Paper, 2008.

Araújo, Manuel G. "O Sistema de Aldeias Comunais em Moçambique, Transformações na Organização do Espaço Residencial e Produtivo." PhD diss., Universidade de Lisboa, 1988.

Blumberg, Rae Lesser, Joyce Malaba, and Lis Meyers. *Women Cross-Border Traders in Southern Africa: Contributions, Constraints and Opportunities in Malawi and Botswana.* USAID, 2016.

Casimiro, Isabel Maria. *Mulheres em actividades geradoras de rendimentos experiencias de Moçambique.* Salvador da Bahia: IX Congresso Luso Brasileiro, 2011.

Chikanda, Abel, and Inês Raimundo. "Informal Entrepreneurship and Cross-Border Trade Between Mozambique and South Africa." *African Human Mobility Review* 3, no. 2 (2017): 943–974.

Chingono, Mark. *The State, Violence and Development: The Political Economy of War in Mozambique, 1975–1992.* Cambridge: Cambridge University Press, 1998.

Constituição da República de Moçambique de 1990. Maputo: Imprensa Nacional, 1990.

Crush, Jonathan, Sally Peberdy, and Vincent Williams. *International Migration and Good Governance in the Southern Africa Region.* Cape Town: South African Migration Project, 2006.

Crush, Jonathan, Vincent Williams, and Sally Peberdy. *Migration in Southern Africa.* Global Commission on International Migration, 2005.

Dodson, Belinda, et al. *Gender Migration and Remittances in Southern Africa.* Johannesburg: SAMP, 2008.

Döpcke, Wolfgang. "Uma política exterior depois do apartheid? Reflexões sobre relações regionais da África do Sul, 1974–1998." *Revista Brasileira de Política Internacional* 41, no. 1 (1998): 133–161.

Gaspar, Napoleão. "The Reduction of Mozambican Workers in South African Mines, 1975–1992: A Case Study of the Consequences for Gaza Province—District of Chibuto." MA Thesis, University of the Witwatersrand, 2006.

Koroma, Suffyon, et al. *Formalization of Informal Trade in Africa: Trends, Experiences and Socio-Economic Impact.* Accra: Food and Agricultural Organization, 2017.

Harries, Patrick. *Work, Culture and Identity: Migrant Laborers in Mozambique and South Africa, 1860–1910.* Johannesburg: Witwatersrand University Press, 1994.

Henrique, Victor Simões. "A contribuição comércio informal e transformações sociais e económicas no meio rural na província de Inhambane (1990–2014)." *Africa[s]* 18, no. 5 (2021): 179–193.

Instituto Nacional de Estatística. *IV Recenseamento Geral da População e Habitação,* 2017.

Jairoce, Jorge Fernando. "A mulher e o comércio informal transfronteiriço, vulgo "mukhero" no sul de Moçambique: Casos das fronteiras de Namahacha e de Ressano Garcia, 1984–2016." PhD diss., Universidade Federal do Rio Grande do Sul, 2016.

Junior, António. *A contribuição do comércio transfronteiriço no desenvolvimento local: o caso do distrito de Muidumbe.* Maputo: Publifix Edições, 2014.

Kachere, Wadzanai. "Informal Cross Border Trading and Poverty Reduction in the Southern Africa Development Community (SAD): The Case of Zimbabwe." PhD Diss., University of Fort Hare, 2011.

Mosca, João. *Economicando.* Maputo: Alcance Editores, 2009.

Muanamoha, Ramos Cardoso. "The Dynamics of Undocumented Mozambican Labour Migration to South Africa." PhD Diss., University of KwaZulu Natal, 2008.

Mudyazvivi, Elton. *The Nature of Informal Cross Border Trade and its Implications for Regional Integration: The Case of Forbes and Machipanda Border Posts of Zimbabwe and Mozambique.* Harare: Netherlands Development Organization, 2006.

Mungoi, Dulce Maria Domingos Chale João. "Identidades viajeiras: Família e transnacionalismo no contexto da experiência migratória de moçambicanos para as minas da terra do rand, África do Sul." PhD diss., Universidade Federal do Rio Grande do Sul, 2010.

Ndlela. Daniel. *Informal Cross Border Trade: The Case of Zimbabwe.* Johannesburg: Institute of Global Dialogue, Occasional Paper 52:59, 2006.

Nhambi, Simão, and Jeremy Grest. *Mobility, Migration and Trade: Interactive Flows Between Durban and Southern Mozambique.* IESE, 2007.

Nshimbi, Christopher Changwe, and Inocent Moyo. *Migration, Cross-Border Trade and Development in Africa: Exploring the Role of Non-State Actors in the SADC Region.* Cham: Palgrave Macmillan, 2017.

Wuyts, Marc. "Economia política do colonialismo português Moçambique." *Estudos Moçambicanos* 1 (1980): 9–22.

Chapter 9

Cultural Capital, Virtual Borderlands, and the Making of the Southern African Communities in Two Zambian Novels

Mwaka Siluonde

This study explores the relationship between cultural capital on-the-move and its creation of what we shall in this chapter refer to as "virtual borderlands." We posit that the borders and borderland spaces in which Southern African Communities are created should be viewed as non-physical spaces where culture evolves, is exchanged, and is birthed as people (and cultural capital) move from one place to another. Deleuze and Guattari's ideas of territorialization and deterritorialization are used to explore how Zambian fiction,[1] specifically Banda-Aaku's *Patchwork*[2] and Saidi's *Day of the Baboons* imagine ways in which cultural capital interacts,[3] is influenced, and influences other cultures along its path and in the places where new communities are created. This is because a close look at the cities (Lusaka in *Patchwork* and Ndola in *Day of the Baboons*) in which the novels are set defines them as spaces where migrant communities are created despite them being located hundreds of kilometers from any physical border.

As is demonstrated, such cities generally accommodate and create safety havens for migrants who have left their home countries for various reasons.[4] Our aim is to discuss whether the cities were sites of cultural negotiation which led to new communities being built along ethnic lines, or any experience or common links that tie people together. We are further interested in interrogating whether the resultant new communities are ever stable entities or communities that are constantly evolving. Communities that we suggest are changing as members sometimes move in and out and others are disrupted as new communities are formed. Hence, the chapter examines whether these cities and other spaces away from physical borders could be considered stable or liminal spaces (both physical and virtual) where Southern African Communities are always being made/remade while evolving.

We firstly hypothesize that borderlands cannot be restricted to a physical place where the nation begins or ends because people (and cultural capital with them) are always on the move, always settling and resettling. It is for this reason that our discussion is mainly anchored on Deleuze and Guattari's idea of territorialization and deterritorialization.[5] At the center of their proposition is that whenever people are uprooted, deterritorialized, from one place there is always a sense in which they seek to make another place their home. As Deleuze and Guatarri point out, the desire to reterritorialize or own new territory is often strong when people or assemblages, whether individuals or communities, move from one place to another.[6]

Put succinctly, territorialization and deterritorialization are always opposite forces working together in any community where, as Hillier and Abrahams note, "stabilisation, or territorialisation, acts to sharpen borders, homogenise components and so on. Deterritorialization, or destabilisation, acts to free up fixed relations."[7] This means, regardless of location, there is always a chance that as a new community is being created, there is a prior community that is breaking down at the same time. This is important to our present discussion because it reveals a vicious cycle that is constantly triggered by something that stimulates movement from one place to another but does not preclude the movement from one community to another in the same location or as a result of a community evolving. We imagine that this is what is happening when migrants in the two fictional works under discussion cross from one national border to another. Particularly, the above is what we aim to examine in the discussion of the *coloreds* (the apartheid classification for mixed-race people who did not fit into the black-white binary) from South Africa in *Day of the Baboons* and the ZAPU Rhodesian freedom fighters from Southern Rhodesia in *Patchwork* when they migrate to Ndola and Lusaka past physical borders respectively.[8] We suggest that if the territorialization/deterritorialization exchange can happen anywhere, then wherever it happens becomes a border, albeit a virtual one if it is far from the physical border.

It must further be highlighted that as people, migrants in this case, move from one place to another, they carry with them a stock of culture—language, food, dressing from their home country or community. Depending on how the stock of culture interacts—how it is influenced and/or influences other cultures along the way—determines whether a new community will be formed or not. It is for this reason that the term "cultural capital-on-the-move" is introduced, borrowing from Bourdieu's idea of cultural capital.[9] The term, however, is not used as Bourdieu does in Sociology of Education.[10] Bourdieu envisioned cultural capital as certain prior competencies, knowledge, and resources that children from privileged families entered the school system with. This cultural capital gave them an advantage in school and guaranteed their success in comparison to children from other backgrounds.

Instead, we use the sociological term loosely to refer to knowledge, behavior, and so on, that someone may have gotten from past interactions. This best describes the likelihood of migrants being able to create new communities by applying the culture they already carry, or as influenced by the cultural capital they find along their path. As such, culture-carrying migrants who are capable of influencing and being influenced by other communities with ease advance the idea of unstable elements that cannot be relied on to create anything stable. Thus, new Southern African Communities, created by individuals and the non-static cultural capital they carry, are likely in some cases to create virtual boundaries away from the physical border spaces.

It must, however, be noted that what we imagine as cultural capital or stock culture on the move does not suggest that migrants originate from homogenous communities with a fixed cultural capital that they carry with them. Rather, the stock culture based on their past experiences is itself based on varied and ever-changing relations and activities. This challenges the existence of a homogenous community to which they belong prior to migration. As Guattari and Deleuze[11] opine, an assemblage, even as an individual entity, is inherently a bricolage or heterogenous entity, in this case comprising of diverse cultural aspects from prior experience.[12] I use the term assemblage on one hand to refer to an individual as an embodiment of diverse, inherent cultural capital. On the other hand, an assemblage can be viewed as a collective assembly comprising of individual assemblages, with each bringing along their inherent cultural capital. This means that the community from which a migrant originates must be viewed as comprising of individuals that are different from each other. Individuals, whose differences, relations, and influences—both internal and external—already comprise the stability or fixity one would expect from the traditional idea of a community.

That is why it will be illustrated using the communities referred to in the selected novels that what leads to the creation of new communities is a response to particular stimuli—the crossing of virtual borders such as common ethnicity or race, shared histories, shared experiences, and so on. Such thoughts are akin to Anderson's view of a nation and, by extension any community as an imagined community—born out of a deliberate move to create kinship ties or communal ties anchored on certain aspects such as some of the ones suggested here.[13] Hence, because these are bound to change due to contact with different stimuli—the crossing of virtual borders—the imagined community is possibly found to be an infinite, viscous, never homogenous, dynamic, ever-changing entity.

The above views controvert the idea of static entities, individuals and communities that move from one border to another and settle at physical borders simply because these spaces symbolize entry or crossing over into a new country of choice. In fact, as Erel notes, migrant research has often treated migrants' cultural capital as "reified and ethnically bounded, assuming they bring a set of cultural resources from the country of origin to the country of migration that either fit or do not fit."[14] On the contrary, our argument is that when migrants cross physical borders into new countries, they are exposed to many cultural and other aspects that can sometimes result in transformation. This is especially true if they trigger the same restlessness that made migrants leave their home country in the first place.

In cases such as the above, someone may cross a border physically but at the same time still be in need of crossing a "virtual border" which may result in a change of location, cultural orientation, or anything else. The thesis advanced here is one of the reasons Bourdieu's cultural capital theory is criticized in sociology of education. As Goldthorpe observes "Bourdieu would reject any attempt to differentiate between those aspects of culture in the teaching of which class or other socially conditioned influences might readily be present."[15] Yet it is these "socially conditioned influences" that could influence a pupil's success more than the prior privileges and social position. In the same way, it is those spaces and influences that, if eclipsed, would be denied the light of day when borderlands and cultural capital continue to be viewed as static. As such, the idea that we can create or arrive at a destination called new Southern African Communities, with physical borders characterized by static, stable and fixed culture, is not tenable. These communities cannot and do not exist. Instead, as will be discussed using the two works of fiction, borderlands, the creation of new Southern African Communities in relation to migrant cultural capital, can best be described as individuals and communities which move about like nomads, leaving or/and picking up traces of other cultures.[16] Through this process, they either break up or create new communities, while leaving others untouched as need may be.

This is because in the first place, the lives of individuals making up Southern African Communities, even before they move from one place to another, and in cities such as the ones discussed here from *Day of the Baboons* and *Patchwork,* are, according to Manase, always characterized by "dislocation and restlessness. Most of the urban dwellers' lives have been disrupted socially or economically. In most cases the characters are portrayed as feeling estranged from their families and homes as well as showing elements of anxiety. Various factors contribute to the assumption of these dislocated and restless identities."[17] Of interest are the instabilities, restlessnesses, and vulnerabilities that lead to the creation of virtual borders, and not the expected physical borders, as the only destinations where new communities can be created. It is because of all these possible triggers in many possible physical and non-physical spaces that lead us to our suggestion that it is impossible to keep insisting that borderlands are fixed spaces where Southern African Communities can be built.

METHODOLOGY

The research used communities from two selected Zambian novels, Saidi's *Day of the Baboons* and Banda-Aaku's *Patchwork,* as case studies to establish the role of virtual borderlands in creating Southern African Communities. The qualitative research purposefully sampled the two novels by virtue of them being set in communities comprised of migrants from around Southern Africa. Such communities were viewed as more likely to facilitate our investigation of the role of virtual borderlands in creating Southern African Communities because the people making up these communities had not only crossed physical borders but also settled in cities distant from the border itself. It is such settlement that raises the question of whether there could be other border crossings, besides physical ones, that warrant examination. If so, what constitutes such borders, in this case virtual borders, and do the migrants crossing them enter or create homogenous communities once such borders are crossed?

Reading these novels together is justified by the fact that they, though fictitious, include historical fact in relation to the communities of interest. It is the case that *Day of the Baboons* evolves, in part, around the slaying of Miss Burton by Africans in colonial Northern Rhodesia. The Ndola communities might be referred to using fictional names, but Ndola is the actual, historical setting.[18] In *Patchwork,* the attack on a Zimbabwean African People's Union (ZAPU) camp might be fiction, but similar attacks actually took place. The best-known case is the massacre of people and fighters staying at the ZAPU camp in Chikumbi, in the farming area north of Lusaka. The place was heavily bombed, using napalm, as revenge for the downing of a civilian plane inside Rhodesia, by members of the Zimbabwe People's Revolutionary Army (ZIPRA), the military wing of ZAPU.[19]

A thematic approach was used to identify salient themes or examples of virtual borders that are crossed in the communities referred to by the novels. Some of the themes that emerged were virtual borders relating to race, ethnicity, dialogic confrontations, shared experiences, homogeneity in relation to created communities, and so on. These themes assisted in answering the question of whether Southern African Communities created in the two novels are created in *virtual borderlands,* non-physical spaces where culture evolves, is exchanged, and is birthed as people and cultural capital move from one place to another. Put succinctly and conceptually, the key question addressed was: How do *virtual borderlands* create Southern African Communities in the novels selected?

VIRTUAL BORDERLANDS AND "CULTURAL CAPITAL-ON-THE-MOVE" IN SAIDI'S *DAY OF THE BABOONS* AND BANDA-AAKU'S *PATCHWORK*

Fiction re-imagines ways in which cultural capital interacts in complex ways that reconfigure our understanding of borderlands as physical spaces in which new Southern African Communities are born. This is because there is a need for reorientation toward the idea that fixation on spatial and physical borders as spaces where new Southern African Communities are born often eclipses the role that social structures and relations play in creating new communities. This is because migrants do not always settle in physical border spaces. As such, our suggestion in this chapter is that places where such cultural exchanges and interaction take place, as we observe in *Day of the Baboons* and *Patchwork,* be considered in the light of Bakhtin's idea of place as a metaphorical road on which "spatial and temporal paths of the most varied people–representatives of all social classes, estates, religions, nationalities, ages—intersect at one spatial and temporal point."[20] In *Day of the Baboons,* different cultures, both white and black, come into Zambian urban areas during the colonial federation of Rhodesia and Nyasaland, contending for both political and social space. As the protagonist's, Absolom or Abednego, stepfather observes about the whites, "[s]ome of them are not Boers, you know, sonny. Some of them come from England, Scotland, Wales and Ireland, some even from Germany."[21] As such, whether they migrate as individual or collective assemblages, to borrow Deleuze and Guattari's term, whichever space they interact in, the inherent cultural capital and consequent inherent instability and fluidity, due in part to their being heterogenous entities that carry with them previous experiences, becomes the repertoire and platform that determines whether a new community will be formed or not.[22]

It is important to note that communities meeting at such cross-roads, the "virtual borders" mentioned above, are not homogenous in nature. This is because, whether individual or group, these assemblages already have internal heterogeneity. That is why when we purport that the *colored* community in *Day of the Baboons* and the ZAPU camp in *Patchwork* are characterized by a "common" cultural capital, it is likely that our imagination is based on Anderson's "imagined community," varied but held together by certain aspects and certainly never homogenous.[23] Although the ZAPU camp was likely dominated by Ndebeles, it still had dwellers from other ethnic groups of what is now Zimbabwe. What holds the group together is the relation to the ZAPU freedom fighters/party. Similarly, when one speaks of the cultural capital that Misheck and Ma Dhlamini carry as they interact at the *shebeen* in *Day of the Baboons,* it is in full cognizance that it is not necessarily homogenous Zambian and *colored* communities they represent respectively. For instance, Misheck carries traces of all the cultural capital, the stock of culture from his previous experiences before he ever interacts with the proprietor and other *coloreds* at the *shebeen*. Misheck carries his father's ethnicity from Southern province, cultural capital from Subuchi compound where he lives, and the cultural influence from the European education he has received, together with the content he teaches as a schoolteacher.[24] Akin to the ZAPU camp community, he is interacting with and exchanging cultural content in all the interactions he has with people, material, and so on. As such, it may be suggested that indeed cultural capital is always on the move crossing virtual borders.

As a result of the diverse nature of cultural capital coming together in these borders, now designated "virtual borders," there is always a form of negotiation among the different assemblages. The negotiation and subsequent choices have to do particularly with which boundaries will be crossed, negotiated, merged, or introduced to create, reshape, or establish new communities altogether. In the two novels studied, we witness how through deterritorialization and reterritorialization, or uprooting and rooting of characters and culture in the novels, new cultural relations and communities are born.[25] The textual public places, such as the *shebeen* in *Day of the Baboons*, which bring together different characters from different places, offer a possibility for the birth of intercultural relationships. This is noted in the relationship that develops between Misheck, the indigenous black teacher and one of the protagonists, and Ma Dhlamini, the *colored* proprietor of the *shebeen*, on one hand, and the *coloreds* and Ma Dhlamini on the other hand. This is facilitated by Ma Dhlamini's ability to negotiate and make the relationships possible. Such negotiation is common among migrants and, in the study of Turkish and Kurdish migrants in Britain and Germany, Erel observes that, as migrants move from one place to another, they "create mechanisms of validation for their cultural capital, negotiating both ethnic majority and migrant institutions and networks."[26] Noting that migrants move with cultural capital, it still needs validation for it to be accepted. In order for that to happen, the migrants must negotiate with the ethnic majority and other migrants and institutions that may already exist.

The above is what we witness with Ma Dhlamini, who has been deterritorialized in both South Africa and Nyasaland for reasons not mentioned in the novel, but now manages to finally settle and get validated in Ndola, Zambia. This is only after successfully negotiating her way into the ethnic majority through Misheck, an indigenous Zambian, and migrant institutions and networks through other *coloreds* from South Africa. For Misheck, Ma Dhlamini uses the fact that both their fathers were gangsters in Johannesburg to negotiate and validate their relationship. We are told that Misheck "thought of her as a big sister. He had told her about his father being gangster in Johannesburg. Her response had been that 'then we must be related,' she had announced joyously. 'My father is a gangster too!'"[27] It is not strange after this to find Misheck playing the keyboard for the *colored* patrons at the *shebeen* in exchange for free alcohol. With regards to the *coloreds,* all Ma Dhlamini does is establish an exclusively *colored shebeen* which facilitates the group's interaction on racial terms. Hence, it is clear to see how only through negotiation does Ma Dhlamini manage to create new communities using common history with Misheck and the race factor with the *coloreds*' *shebeen* community. Therefore, it is here, far from the physical South African and Zambian borders, that the gap, the "virtual border," between Ma Dhalmini and Misheck and the *coloreds* is symbolically crossed.

In some cases, new communities are created by dialogic confrontation between old and new cultural capital. It is not always as smooth, and a result of a migrant's input, such as Ma Dhlamini's case above. Rather, as we observe in the confrontation between Misheck and the visiting *coloreds,* it is the indigenous person, using an inherent stock of cultural capital, that affects the incoming migrants and causes a change in the complexion of the migrant community. The visiting *coloreds* approach Misheck with the apartheid mentalities they are used to from South Africa where blacks are considered inferior to *coloreds*, at least according to the racial hierarchy of the apartheid era in which the novel is set. So while they come to Zambia to get away from white supremacy in that country, the desire to gain territory (territorialization) or create a new community leads to conflict when the *coloreds* try to exercise racial superiority over Misheck, whom they insist is inferior because he is black:

> "For a black sem you play good piano jong (friend)."
> "You too are a black sem?" Misheck asked softly.
> "What? Me? Voet-sek man. Look here, man. I am *coloured,* see? Born in Cape Town. I don't live with all them black sems."
> "Your father, was he Welsh?" Misheck asked, in a needing voice
> "No man. My mother was Welsh. Voet-sek, man. Why you ask me all them stupid bloody questions, man?"
> "So," Misheck said, "your father was an African, a black sem . . . "
> "So your father was a black sem, like me eh," Misheck said . . . The room was quiet, except for the insane giggling of the woman with the European laugh.
> "You know Sisi," Misheck said deliberately, not taking his eyes off the eye patch. "I hate these half-Europeans. Even in our country they want to ape the white man. They think they are Europeans."[28]

Misheck feels undermined when one of the *coloreds*, Mr. Hughes, makes a condescending comment about him and so he retaliates by pulling Mr. Hughes down. There is clear miscommunication between the two because

Mr. Hughes expects Misheck to accept *colored* superiority based on the South African apartheid cultural code. Yet Misheck responds in a different cultural code and challenges Mr. Hughes, because in Zamiba apartheid, with its racial hierachy, does not exist. What is pertinent about this confrontation is that the *colored* community cannot insist on the South African cultural code but must now be transformed and adjust to a new cultural code in the new country where they have settled. This means a new *colored* community may be said to have been formed through an element of reshaping of the *colored* community as a result of Misheck's influence based on his cultural capital. This does not include apartheid or the experience of *colored* superiority/inferiority.

In addition, the above situation with the *coloreds* in *Day of the Baboons* suggests that new communities of migrants are sometimes formed along ethnic and racial lines. This is because the pursuit for ethnic kindred or ethnic acceptance may facilitate the creation of virtual borders in spaces apart from physical borders. For many ethnicities and races, crossing a border in such cases is synonymous with crossing ethnic lines and not necessarily the physical border. In *Day of the Baboons,* Ma Dhlamini crosses a physical border when she enters Zambia but can be said to have crossed a racial border when she locates and decides to settle with other *coloreds* in an area called Tipiwa in Ndola, where other *coloreds* are said to have settled. As such, one way in which new communities are created is through the alignment of migrants along ethnic lines in the countries they migrate to.

In fact, there is evidence to suggest that one of the causes of segregation in countries such as the United States of America is that: "Foreign-born individuals are isolated within enclaves composed of persons of their nationality."[29] Naturally, everyone else follows suit, and that is why when other *coloreds* visit from South Africa they stay in the *colored* area and only patronize the *colored shebeen* despite there being other drinking places in other compounds in Zambia and the city of Ndola. Thus, we can observe how in *Day of the Baboons*, Ndola is divided along ethnic/racial lines with Subuchi reserved for blacks, Tipiwa for people like Ma Dhlamini, and other places only for Europeans. That is why on his first visit to Subuchi, one of the black passengers on the bus tells Mwansa, Shadreck, who has just moved to the city from the village that: "Before long, you are going to discover that this place, Subuchi, is where we belong. Not in town, not with the Europeans and their big vicious dogs."[30] Anyone else coming into the country simply aligns themselves to these enclaves and we suggest that entering the enclaves is entering a new border space, which has nothing to do with a physical border. Migrants only feel they have truly crossed this "virtual border" when they cross over from non-familiar racial and ethnic space into familiar territory, which often takes place in spaces removed from the physical border.

What our discussion suggests so far is that cultural exchange, negotiation, and new communities can be born anywhere as long as there is an appropriate stimulus. The stimulus not only may range from the need for ethnic or racial association, negotiation, as already discussed, but also the common experiences among migrants and citizens of a host country/space whether they warrant it or not. This is what one observes in Banda-Aaku's *Patchwork* where the feeling of community between the Southern Rhodesians at the Sakavungo farm and the Sakavungo family is based on shared experiences related to ZAPU activities. The freedom fighters have set up a camp right next to the farm, and the curfews, displacement, fear, and regular attacks which affect everyone, regardless of whether they are Southern Rhodesian or Zambian, create a new community at the farm. The community is created by uniting residents and erasing any national, ethnic, or employer/employee distinctions between them.

What makes the community is no longer affiliation to known groups and nationalities but rather the unity of purpose that comes from shared experiences when such lines are crossed. This is Soja's inference concerning modern-day Los Angeles where what one finds is not the expected division of physical spaces along particular social groups and classes. Rather, it is "the seemingly paradoxical but functionally interdependent juxtapositions [that] are the epitomising features of contemporary Los Angeles."[31] It is not the physical locations and borders as we know them that define places, but more so the social interaction and cultural capital shifting, evolving, and building new communities stemming from common experiences. Such social interaction is noted between members of the ZAPU camp and the Sakavungu farm occupants when the guerrilla fighters frequent the Sakavungu camp for eggs and vegetables. Such interactions become sites for the exchange of cultural capital and the means through which cultural capital moves in and out of the ZAPU camp. This makes it difficult to imagine that the ZAPU camp is homogenous. We further note the communal integration during and in the aftermath of the Rhodesian regime's attack on the ZAPU camp where the Sakavungo farm residents are seen trekking to the farmhouse kitchen seeking solace and food. At this stage, no one is thinking about rank, nationality, or employer/employee status, but rather simple survival. This is clear when Mr. Sakavungo orders Sissy, the Southern Rhodesian housekeeper, to give food and access to baths to ZAPU soldiers.[32] It is this creation of community based on shared experience and crisis that clearly facilitates the unconscious and unwarranted crossing of virtual borders and the creation of new communities.

In some cases, not even the subjects involved realize that they have crossed into a new community, and this is probably what Zu, the Southern Rhodesian servant, is trying to explain to Black, an indigenous servant. Black is of the view that Zambian soldiers should not get involved in the Zimbabwean liberation war between Ian Smith's regime and ZAPU because it is a Southern Rhodesian war. On the contrary, Zu uses an analogy to demonstrate how the lines of nationality have been erased and a new community created by the shared experiences related to ZAPU activities in Zambia: "My friend, if I am a guest in your house and an intruder breaks in, would you sit back and watch him because it's me he is after?"[33] As such, by virtue of the ZAPU activities being on the farm in Lusaka, Zambia, one cannot separate themselves from the effects of resultant attacks and curfews, which affect people of both Zambian and Southern Rhodesian nationality alike. As Soja envisions, sometimes, and in places far away from physical borders and without changing locations, new communities are born in urban spaces as "some things fall apart, dissipate, new nodalities form and old ones are reinforced."[34] Hence, as observed in the novel from the after-effects of the attack on the Sakavungo farm and Zu's analogy, the new is capable of creeping in on a community, stripping it of other things as national boundaries are crossed. All that is left is a new or transformed community built on common experiences, whether the subjects realize it or not.

However, Southern African Communities must be considered as highly malleable, ever-evolving entities. This is because of the potential and ease with which communities change when a different stimulus is introduced, or the uniting factor—in this case the presence and activities of ZAPU—is removed. This challenges the idea of reified communities that simply cross borders as they are and settle in new physical bordering societies without influencing or being influenced by other cultures they find. This means that a community, such as the one created at the Sakavungo farm, comprising of older (the family) and newer (the Southern African servants) communities, is susceptible to change as some aspects are introduced, while still others are removed. The result is an infinite cycle of construction/deconstruction and stability/instability. That is why in *Patchwork*, Sissy the Zimbabwean housekeeper at the Sakavungo farm warns Pumpkin not to take her presence for granted. It is also for this reason that Hillier and Abrahams, in discussing assemblages, note that the elements that make up a community or "relational assemblages of elements are inherently unstable and fluid. Assemblage boundaries are indeterminate and frequently challenged, transgressed, and/or extended as new connections occur and old ones rupture."[35] This supports our earlier assertion that prior to any interactions, individuals, including migrants such as Misheck in *Day of the Baboon,* are already unstable entities because of their previous experiences, and the cultural capital they carry.

It is this inherent instability, based on the cultural capital migrants carry, that makes movement from one country to another a twofold affair: the crossing of a physical boundary but also the crossing of a virtual boundary. This is because whether at the physical boundary or further inland, the boundaries of cultural capital are constantly threatened and sometimes broken as migrants influence and are influenced by other social spaces and cultural capital. An example is Sissy, who came from Southern Rhodesia, settled at the Sakavungu farm, joined the community there, and married her fourth husband, Zu, while at the farm. However, she cautions that she "only married Zu because her second one, the one she says loved her very much, walked over the [physical] border into Zaire to look for emeralds. He promised he would be back for her and she's still waiting. She often says, 'the day he comes back for me is the day my days of washing clothes, polishing floors and refereeing fights in Tata's house will be over.'"[36] We observe many possibilities after this knowledge, which supports the assertion of the malleability and temporality of Southern African Communities. It is possible for the community in relation to Sissy's situation to remain stable as long as her husband is in Zaire. Yet, this stability is threatened by the possibility of her husband's return, which could lead to the disruption of the farm community should she decide to leave and follow her husband. What would break the community is not Sissy's actual movement across a physical border, but the virtual boundary created by his absence, which is the only thing standing between her and a new community with him.

The rate at which new communities are created and destroyed includes situations where individuals alternate between different communities on a needs basis. As such, individuals may alternate among a number of communities each time creating and destroying communities, as well as re-creating alternatives when they move back to their original community with new cultural capital added to their stock. This is what we witness with individuals such as the *ciNyanja*-speaking Mr. Prakesh, the cameraman in *Patchwork*, who has to code switch and temporarily join a new speech community depending on the people with whom he is working. His behavior is reminiscent of how assemblages, individual or collective, behave differently depending on what material, image, or group they need to identify with at a particular time. To further illustrate assemblage specificity in relation to context, one can further borrow Roffe's use of the analogy of a tree in autumn: "'A flash of red, a movement, a gust of wind, these elements must be externally related to each other to create the sensation of a tree in autumn.' Here we can see that there is no predetermined model of a tree; only an immanent and contingent world of relations."[37] What creates the autumn tree with its autumn characteristics is the tree exhibiting only those characteristics that make it fit into the image of autumn. Likewise, a tree in winter would not have the same image but would have to use inherent characteristics specifically related to winter-ness.

The same can be said about the *ciNyanja*-speaking Mr. Prakash in *Patchwork* who switches to *ciNyanja* when he goes to take pictures of the Sakavungo family, shocking the children when he greets them:

> Perched on a chair in the living room, a camera hanging around his neck, he greets Amos, Job and me as we troop in: "Muli bwanji. Muli bwanji . . . "
> " . . . An Indian speaking Nyanja." Amos elbows me and jerks his head at Mr Prakash as we settle in the sofa.[38]

We realize Mr. Prakash has temporarily crossed a language community boundary and that this is not his normal linguistic space because of the childrens' reaction. In addition, we are told that, "from his smile he's obviously pleased with himself for having mastered a few Nyanja words."[39] Such switches, despite their temporariness, cannot be precluded from signifying the crossing of borders, even if only temporarily. In addition, this highlights why borderspaces cannot be restricted to physical spaces or the creation of Southern African Communities as something reified and static.

Therefore, we note that there will always be things that enter any physical space or community causing individuals to physically migrate or causing a shift and disruption in a community that may exist in any location in a mother country or along paths of movement. This could be the reason people decide to migrate from one country to another in the first place, but may also be the same reason they fail to settle in the border towns or physical borders of the new country they enter. This challenges a continued insistence on border spaces as physical, because people will always settle in spaces where they do not feel threatened. Instead, they will move from any place where they feel threatened, insecure, restless, or anxious and break boundaries or borders—sometimes physical and sometimes virtual—that they may have built around themselves. It is how the South African *coloreds* and the ZAPU freedom fighters both found themselves in Zambian cities far from their home countries and any border towns. In his article on mapping the urban space, Manase affirms that people do not simply decide to move from one place to another for no reason.[40] Rather, urban spaces have triggers that "include pressures impacting on their life experiences in their different urban spaces as well as vulnerabilities, which are associated in one way or another, to colonialism, apartheid and the shifting global economy."[41] The main causes of migration in the novels are threats and vulnerabilities related to the colonial Ian Smith government in Southern Rhodesia and the apartheid government in South Africa.

Yet one can further argue that ZAPU fighters do not settle in a physical border town simply because they have entered Zambia, but rather in Lusaka. They are made to settle hundreds of kilometers from any physical border because close proximity to Zimbabwe would make them more vulnerable to their enemy in Southern Rhodesia. Still, when the ZAPU camp is attacked by forces of the Ian Smith regime, there is no indication that the threat to their security will result in their further movement. One would very well conclude that, despite the attack, they still feel secure because it might very well be, as Sissy observes, that the Smith regime will not strike the same camp twice. The decisions related to when and where the ZAPU fighters might move support the assertions of this chapter that the creation of new communities can happen anywhere. The creation of these "virtual borders" has little to do with physical borders, but more to do with the influence of vulnerabilities, insecurities, and threats that make migrants move from one place to another.

CONCLUSION

In conclusion, we aimed at demonstrating that the concept of borderlands and borders should not be limited to physical spaces. This is particularly because Southern African Communities were born in many places in the novels discussed. A border should instead be considered as any virtual space or whatever repertoire/liminal space, whether ethnic, racial, political, and so on, where different cultural capital negotiation takes place to enable the creation of new communities. We supported this assertion with an exploration of the interaction of cultural capital and the process by which new communities in Southern Africa were created in Lusaka and Ndola in Saidi's *Day of the Baboons* and Banda-Aaku's *Patchwork*. This is because cultural exchanges and the establishment of new Southern African Communities in the novels take place in cities and spaces that are hundreds of kilometers away from physical borders. This discussion has reoriented thinking of borders to include those spaces far from physical borders where new communities are formed. These spaces might otherwise remain in the shadows if our focus is limited to physical spaces as the only places where diverse cultures interact and form new Southern African Communities.

We argued that kilometers away from physical borders, "virtual borders" become spaces where cultural capital is negotiated, leading to the formation of new cultural communities. This is what one witnesses in the discussion of how Ma Dhlamini, the *colored shebeen* proprietor from South Africa, in *Day of the Baboons* negotiates her way into a friendship with Misheck, an indigenous black Zambian man, and how she manages to penetrate and unite the *colored* community by establishing the exclusively *colored shebeen*. It was further noted how sometimes the creation of communities happens far from the physical borders because what is guiding the choice of location is the intention to settle along ethnic lines. This is clear in how the city of Ndola is divided along ethnic lines with Europeans, *coloreds*, and blacks all having their own designated areas. Therefore, it does not come as a surprise that when the visiting *coloreds* in the novel cross the physical border into Zambia from South Africa, they settle in Ndola and not in any border town. The natural drift toward familiar ethnic/cultural/racial communion suggests a more complex relationship between migration and the creation of new communities which dispels the fixation on physical borders and border spaces.

A further study of how relationships and communities are formed in *Patchwork* led to the conclusion that borderlands and the creation of Southern African Communities must not be restricted to anything static. This is because migrants carry with them "cultural-capital-on-the move," which influences where and how new communities would be created. As such, because people and the cultural capital they carry with them are always on the move, always settling and resettling, borderlands cannot be restricted to a space near the physical boundaries of the state. In fact, as migrants move from one place to another, there is always a common link and reason based on common experiences, which causes some communities to build up and exist while others break down. And these do not always have anything to do with common borders.

The common link for the Sakavungu family and their Southern Rhodesian servants is the common experience they have as a result of the violent conflict in neighboring Southern Rhodesia. This includes the ZAPU freedom fighters whose camp is right next door to the farm. Furthermore, one learns from the ZAPU freedom fighters' situation that urban citizens will not always move or settle simply because of a physical border, but will go places as long as they feel vulnerable or challenged by political, colonial, or economic reasons. That is enough for them to move from one place to another, and that is why we suggest that the point at which they cross over into safe space, virtual or physical, is what should be considered a border space. It is for this reason that borders, and the communities formed, must not be considered as reified communities, but rather temporal spaces that are ever evolving and, in some cases with individuals that, like the *ciNyanja*-speaking Indian cameraman, are always moving in and out of speech communities depending on context. Hence, borders and border spaces must be considered liminal spaces, both physically and virtually, where Southern African Communities are always being made and remade while evolving.

NOTES

1. Gilles Deleuze and Felix Guattari, *A Thousand Plateaus* (Minneapolis: University of Minnesota Press, 1987).
2. Ellen Banda-Aaku, *Patchwork* (Johannesburg: Penguin, 2011).
3. William Saidi, *Day of the Baboons* (Lusaka: Zambia Educational Publishing House, 1991).

4. Irikidzayi Manase, "Mapping the City Space in Current Zimbabwean and South African Fiction," *Transformation: Critical Perspectives on Southern Africa* 57 (2005): 88–104.

5. Deleuze and Guattari, *A Thousand Plateaus.*

6. Deleuze and Guattari, *A Thousand Plateaus.*

7. Jean Hillier and Gareth Abrahams, *Deleuze and Guattari: Jean Hillier in Conversation with Gareth Abrahams* (Melbourne: Melbourne University, 2013), 17.

8. Saidi, *Day of the Baboons*; Banda-Aaku, *Patchwork.*

9. Pierre Bourdieu, *Cultural Reproduction and Social Reproduction in Knowledge, Education and Cultural Change* (London: Tavistock, 1973).

10. Bourdieu, *Cultural Reproduction.*

11. Deleuze and Guattari, *A Thousand Plateaus.*

12. Ben Anderson and Colin McFarlane, "Assemblage and Geography," *Area* 43, no. 2 (2011): 124–127.

13. Benedict Anderson, *Imagined Communities: Origin and Spread of Nationalism* (London: Verso, 1991).

14. Umut Erel, "Migrating Cultural Capital: Bourdieu in Migration Studies," *Sociology* 44, no. 4 (2010): 642.

15. John Goldthorpe, "Cultural Capital: Some Critical Observations," *Sociologica* 2 (2007): 6".

16. Mwaka Siluonde, "Oral Narrative Mnemonic Devices and the Framing of the Zambian Novel in English: A Study of Selected Novels" (PhD diss., University of the Free State, 2020), 101–102.

17. Manase, "Mapping the City," 93–94.

18. Walima T. Kalusa, "The Killing of Lilian Margaret Burton and Black and White Nationalisms in Northern Rhodesia (Zambia) in the 1960s," *Journal of Southern African Studies* 37, no. 1 (2011): 63–77

19. Preller Geldenhuys, *Rhodesian Air Force Operations with Air Strike Log* (Durban: Just Done Productions Publishing, 2007).

20. Mikhail Bakhtin, *Rabelais and His World* (Bloomington: Indiana University Press, 1984), 243.

21. Saidi, *Day of the Baboons*, 175.

22. Deleuze and Guattari, *A Thousand Plateaus.*

23. Anderson, *Imagined Communities.*

24. Saidi, Day of the Baboons.

25. Deleuze and Guattari, *A Thousand Plateaus.*

26. Erel, "Migrating Cultural Capital," 642.

27. Saidi, *Day of the Baboons*, 107.

28. Saidi, *Day of the Baboons*, 104–105.

29. David Cutler, *Ghettos and the Transmission of Ethnic Capital* (Cambridge: Harvard University Press, 2002), 2.

30. Saidi, *Day of the Baboons*, 39.

31. Edward Soja, *Post Modern Geographies: The Reassertion of Space in Social Theory* (London: Verso, 1989), 191.

32. Banda-Aaku, *Patchwork*, 107.
33. Banda-Aaku, *Patchwork*, 105.
34. Soja, *Post Modern Geographies*, 235.
35. Hillier and Abrahams, *Deleuze and Guattari,* 20.
36. Banda-Aaku, *Patchwork*, 63.
37. "Gilles Deleuze," Roffe, accessed on 10 July 2022, http://www.iep.utm.edu/d/deleuze.htm.
38. Banda-Aaku, *Patchwork*, 76.
39. Banda-Aaku, Patchwork, 76.
40. Manase, "Mapping the City," 94.
41. Manase, "Mapping the City," 94.

BIBLIOGRAPHY

Anderson, Benedict. *Imagined Communities: Origin and Spread of Nationalism.* London: Verso, 1991.

Anderson, Ben, and McFarlane, Colin. "Assemblage and Geography." *Area* 43, no. 2 (2011): 124–127.

Bakhtin, Mikhail. *Rabelais and His World.* Bloomington: Indiana University Press, 1984.

Banda-Aaku, Ellen. *Patchwork.* Johannesburg: Penguin, 2011.

Bourdieu, Pierre. *Cultural Reproduction and Social Reproduction in Knowledge, Education and Cultural Change.* London: Tavistock, 1973.

Cutler, David. *Ghettos and the Transmission of Ethnic Capital.* Cambridge: Harvard University Press, 2005.

Deleuze, Gilles, and Guattari, Felix. *A Thousand Plateaus.* Minneapolis: University of Minnesota Press, 1987.

Erel, Umut. "Migrating Cultural Capital: Bourdieu in Migration Studies. " *Sociology* 44, no. 4 (2010): 642–660.

Geldenhuys, Preller. *Rhodesian Air Force Operations with Air Strike Log.* Durban: Just Done Productions Publishing, 2007.

Goldthorpe, John. "Cultural Capital: Some Critical Observations." *Sociologica* 2 (2007): 1–24.

Gunn, Simon. "Translating Bourdieu: Cultural Capital and the English Middle Class in Historical Perspective." *British Journal of Sociology* 56, no. 1 (2005): 49–64.

Hillier, Jean, and Gareth Abrahams. *Deleuze and Guattari: Jean Hillier in Conversation with Gareth Abrahams.* Melbourne: Melbourne University, 2013.

Kalusa, Walima T. "The Killing of Lilian Margaret Burton and Black and White Nationalisms in Northern Rhodesia (Zambia) in the 1960s." *Journal of Southern African Studies* 37, no. 1 (2011): 63–77.

Manase, Irikidzayi." Mapping the City Space in Current Zimbabwean and South African Space." *Transformation Critical Perspectives in Southern Africa* 55 (2005): 88–104.

Saidi, William. *Day of the Baboons*. Lusaka: Zambia Educational Publishing House, 1991.

Siluonde, Mwaka. "Oral Narrative Mnemonic Devices and the Framing of the Zambian Novel in English: A Study of Selected Zambian Novels." PhD diss., University of the Free State, 2020.

Soja, Edward. *Post Modern Geographies: The Reassertion of Space in Social Theory*. London: Verso, 1989.

Part III

GENDER AND THE POLITICS OF (IL)LEGAL BORDER CROSSING

Chapter 10

"You Have to Pay with Your Body"

The Precarity of Subaltern Basotho Migrant Women within the Lesotho-South Africa Border(land)s

Munyaradzi Mushonga and Stephanie Cawood

> *[She was] told not to shout as that noise would call for more boys to come and have fun [rape her]. As they were raping her, they told her that was what they do to all women who thought were smart enough to cross the river for free.*[1]
>
> (Matsepi, interview, January 10, 2022)

This chapter's major scholarly intervention(s) pivot(s) around the gendered dynamics of African migration in Southern Africa in the twenty-first century. It does so by bringing into sharper focus the subjectivities of Basotho migrant women within liminal[2] spaces such as border(land)s, spaces that are on the one hand dangerous, and on the other, full of promise, thus enriching and bringing into conversation borderlands and gender studies.[3] These dynamics operate at the intersections of state sovereignty and gendered re-(b)ordering practices along the Lesotho-South Africa border. While we acknowledge that the gendering of the border has implications for all people residing in or passing through this liminal space, we situate our arguments within feminist political geography and border studies. The chapter draws on both practical and conceptual implications for subaltern Basotho migrant women as they negotiate border-dwelling and legal and extra-legal border-crossings in and out of South Africa due to the difficult economic conditions within enclaved Lesotho. During the COVID-19 pandemic, women's experiences and intersectional vulnerabilities living and traversing these borderlands became particularly complex and treacherous, and many of the indignities documented in this research relate to this period.

We demonstrate, through a combination of narrative[4] and analytical styles, the traumatic sexual harassment, assault, rape, extortion, and robbery these women endure at the hands of the marauding *paqama* scouts/touts within the Lesotho-South Africa border(land)s, a mosaic of gendered liminal spaces that are inhospitable not only to the sexed subaltern subject but also to all in its space.[5] Within the Lesotho-South Africa border(land)s, these notorious border intermediaries or "human smugglers" are sometimes referred to as "young boys"[6] or *(li/di)rururbele,* meaning butterflies.[7] Cross-border human smuggling is not unique to the Lesotho-South Africa border(land)s, but is found anywhere borders need crossing. The focus of this research was on the dynamics of the Lesotho-South African border(land)s. For each official Lesotho-South Africa border post, there are two or more extra-legal crossing points, most of which are manned by paqama scouts.

Conventional mobility studies have not given women's mobilities much attention.[8] This chapter, while highlighting the precarity of subaltern Basotho migrant women within the liminal Lesotho-South Africa border(land)s, also aims to correct fallacies about the immobility of women by foregrounding their increased mobility, especially in this context.[9] Ulicki and Crush contend that "contemporary women's cross-border movement is unprecedented in its scope, scale, and complexity [and that] the specificity and gender distinctiveness of this movement have yet to be adequately analyzed and understood," hence this contribution.[10]

Two detailed narratives of sexual harassment, rape, attempted rape, extortion, and robbery are used in this chapter to demonstrate the agency of subaltern Basotho migrant women, in the same way Marouan posits that the "illegal" migration of African women in North Africa to Europe is an indicator of agency, "an articulation of an embodied consciousness and the belief in one's human right to choose where and how to live."[11] These two life (her) stories reveal the complex, contradictory, and gendered nature of border(land)s in Africa and beyond. Thus, the act of voluntarily crossing the border "illegally," notwithstanding the obvious dangers, demands that these women be seen not only as victims but also as agents of their situation. There is nuance in seeing victims as agents and agents-as-victims (victagents), what Rothberg likes to call "the implicated subject" in which "interlocking systems of oppression produce implicated subjects as well as victims and perpetrators."[12] According to Marouan, there is a need to re-examine traditional narratives about women migrants as victims, and instead "present their experiences as complex and dialectical: women's migratory journeys reinforce gender inequalities while simultaneously disrupting them."[13] This understanding thus disrupts the victim-perpetrator binary. However, women's exploitation at the hands of cross-border intermediaries speaks to the long, historical, systemic violence and dehumanization of black women's bodies in particular, and women's bodies in general.

Located in the Global South, the chapter contributes to research on migration, gender, and border(land)s. Largely based on oral testimonies, the chapter highlights how Basotho migrant women who are "assisted" by borderlands touts or scouts to cross the Lesotho-South Africa border "illegally" end up being demeaned, sexually harassed, raped, and otherwise harmed by their "helpers." Ulicki and Crush further posit that some of these women, of whom the majority are seasonal employees on farms along the Lesotho-South Africa border in the Free State Province, also end up falling victim to "sexual violence and rape by supervisors, male workers, and soldiers from neighbouring barracks,"[14] including being demonized and violently excluded through acts of xenophobia, oppression, and persecution amplifying their intersectional vulnerabilities.[15]

METHODOLOGY

Methodologically, this chapter relied predominantly on oral interviews carried out by the researchers from October to November 2021 during the adjusted alert level 1 of the COVID-19 pandemic in South Africa. The interviews were carried out by two research teams (RT), one in Lesotho, and another in South Africa, to ensure that voices from both sides of the border were represented. Ethical clearance was obtained from the UFS General Humanities Research Ethics Committee (GHREC).[16] Participants were drawn from transnational communities within the Lesotho-South Africa borderlands, namely Matatiele/Qacha's Nek; Sterkspruit/Quthing; Zastron/Mohale's Hoek; Wepener/Mafeteng; Ladybrand/Maseru; Ficksburg/Maputsoe; Qwaqwa/Phuthaditjhaba/Butha-Buthe and their hinterlands, and from the main official and unofficial crossing points between the two countries. They included borderlands residents, (wo)men travelers, traders/hawkers, border scouts, port officials, school pupils, teachers, and farmers along the Lesotho-South Africa border.

More than fifty people were interviewed. Interview methods included using face-to-face conversations, focus group discussions (FGDs), open-ended questionnaires, hand-written testimonies, WhatsApp platform messages, and the draw-and-write method. For interviews, open-ended questions were posed to individual informants or groups of informants (focus groups), and their responses were recorded, if they consented, on a digital voice recorder or cellphone. Desktop research complemented the interviews. These multiple methods of data collection were combined in a triangulated approach in order to guard against unreliable or invalid results.[17] The use of multiple methodological strategies is based on the understanding that individually, research methods may fall short, but that in combination, methodological weaknesses are counterbalanced.[18]

The majority of participants preferred to provide verbal informed consent prior to interviewing, with only a few willing to sign the consent form. The majority of interviews were conducted in the Sesotho language, the dominant language used by borderlands residents, scouts, and traders. A number of interviews with school pupils, teachers, immigration officials, farmers, and security personnel were conducted in English. Interviews were transcribed and translated into English, where necessary, by some members of the research team shortly after taking place, with full cognizance that translation may be subject to the challenges of translator bias. These can include distortions arising from differences in the meaning of words, syntactical and cultural contexts, the lack of equivalent words in the target language, and ambiguity in the original language.[19] While the original interview transcripts may contain the real names of interviewees, the names used in this chapter are pseudonyms to protect the privacy of informants.

GENDERED "BORDERS AND ORDERS," PUSH-PULL FACTORS, AND THE (IM)MOBILITY OF WOMEN

Newman[20] and Krishna[21] remind us that the notion of the Westphalian[22] nation-state is conventionally associated with the idea of enclosed territories with absolute and complete territorial integrity, the sovereignty of the state as demarcated by its boundary lines, and connected systems for and agencies of inclusion and exclusion. In the public imagination, borders are associated with material barriers or natural manifestations such as mountain ranges or water bodies.[23] Newman transforms the idea of boundaries as immovable and obdurate barriers, into spaces with "their own internal dynamics, creating new realities and affecting the lives of people and groups who reside within close proximity to the boundary or are obliged to transverse the boundary at one stage or another in their lives."[24] In this sense, borders are physically and socially constructed, but are also simultaneously tangible and symbolic.

Borders became places where identities are checked and verified, where some people are fenced in (interiority) while others are fenced out (exteriority), and where de-individuation takes place through regulated inspection, judgment, (biometric) surveillance, and crimigration.[25] It is a space of fragmentation, homogeneity, multiple identities,[26] citizenship, differences, and similarities where identities are constantly defined and redefined on a daily and changing basis.[27] This nation-centric and state-centric solidification and securitization of border(land)s has led to the further marginalization of subaltern populations.[28]

Borders and borderlands are gendered in multiple ways. Borders are gendered in relation to how women and men interact with them, and their embodied experiences within this liminal space. In fact, the body is a crucial site for examining how bodies and borders intersect.[29] The gendering of borders is also reflected in the reproduction of the gendered public/private binary of legal and extra-legal or undocumented border crossings, as well as in the phenomenon of dwelling in the borderlands as border residents. Borders can be major sites of bodily danger, conflict, and violence, and borderlands as liminal spaces represent danger that compounds pre-existing vulnerabilities, especially exposing women living in borderlands and those crossing borders to exploitation and abuse.[30] The border(land)s along the 909 kilometer, permeable borderline between Lesotho and South Africa are viewed as crime-prone areas with high levels of prostitution, violent crime, abuse, victimization, property-related crimes, gun running, drug smuggling, and livestock rustling that coincide with extra-legal border crossing networks collectively compromising human security.[31]

The study of boundaries and borders is an important theme in political geography and is often predicated on exploring the tensions between the permeability of borders and border identities and what Sharpe calls "the inescapable materiality" of both.[32] While national borders are barriers to movement and seem static, the geopolitical order imposed by national boundaries has never been fixed but dependent on history. In political geography, "borders and orders" are studied in relation to power and resistance as part of the border dynamics. In the politics of scale, borders can be global or international barriers, but they can also be regional and local, or a combination of both, as is the case with the Lesotho-South Africa border.[33]

In many instances, the borders of post-colonial nation-states have been superimposed on the boundaries of colonial territories.[34] The Lesotho-South Africa border traces the colonial boundaries of what used to be called Basutoland, and is simultaneously an international border and a contested and permeable regional boundary.[35] The border is contested, like many other colonial borders, because it was imposed on the Basotho as part of a colonial boundary settlement that gave large tracts of Basotho land to the Orange Free State (now the Free State Province of South Africa), and split the Basotho people between separate political territories. This has led to the notion of the Basotho as one nation, but two countries.[36]

While the idea of a world without borders was proposed by some proponents of globalization after the end of the Cold War, as part of an effort to facilitate the free flow of capital and commodities across international boundaries, the last decades have seen many nation-states making efforts to "secure" their borders, increasing the criminalization of extra-legal border-crossing in the name of curbing cross-border criminal activity. Mize attributes these actions to the rise of neoliberal nativism as a by-product of a contradictory process of globalization.[37] Such discourses of exclusion are often framed as "territorial security" rather than "human security" or the militarization of the border. Cross-border activities like drug trafficking, money laundering, smuggling of goods, human trafficking, and unlawful migration are all identified as threats to state security and used as justification for the militarization of the border, which is another crucial aspect of gendered (b)ordering.[38] (Figure 10.1)

The urge to migrate is a human trait and can be attributed to multiple factors. To understand the phenomenon, scholars developed a "push-pull" model. Within this model, generic push factors that induce people to leave their homes include economic hardship, poverty, unemployment, political persecution, conflict, war, discrimination (racial/religious), natural disasters, and a lack of access to basic social services. Generic pull factors inducing people to come to a new place include better economic opportunities and social services, political stability and safety, and family reunification.[39] The Lesotho-South Africa border has seen a constant flow of multidirectional, cross-border movements since the late 1800s. The reasons for this ongoing cycle have varied over time, but include visiting family, seeking livelihoods in the South African agricultural or mining industries, and accessing

Figure 10.1 "Paqama Gate" Called "At 60" Manned by "Paqama boys". *Source*: Photograph taken by authors.

amenities in South Africa such as retail, banking, clinical services, and educational opportunities.[40]

Historically, many Basotho men crossed the border to seek work in South African gold and diamond mines, but Basotho women also routinely crossed the border to work on farms, as domestic workers, laundry women, petty traders, brewers, smugglers, or in commercial sex work, with Bloemfontein becoming a powerful magnet for these women.[41] For Basotho women, the mass retrenchment of male mine workers from South African mines that started in the late 1980s and accelerated in the twenty-first century devastated the income base for many rural communities in Lesotho, and meant that even more women migrated.[42] By 2001, Coplan concluded that female migrants outnumbered male migrants despite many efforts to restrict female mobility.[43] Despite high unemployment in South Africa, many commercial farmers of seasonal crops in the eastern Free State Province prefer recruiting female laborers from Lesotho, sometimes clandestinely. One migrant told researchers: "Farmers come to villages in Lesotho with lorries and collect those who would like to work. They cover the people in the lorries with tarp when crossing the border. The lorries are rarely checked at the border; perhaps there is collusion with border officials."[44]

When gainful employment proved unavailable, women had to turn to alternative methods to raise money, including being coerced into sex work by criminal organizations such as the Marashea Gangs.[45] These gangs were dominated by Basotho male migrants in South African mining towns and are well known for their violent domination of women and girls.[46] In the late nineteenth and twentieth centuries, Basotho women also trekked to the mining towns of South Africa for "illicit brewing and sexual services" and were reputed to be among the more common purveyors of sexual services in Southern Africa.[47] While none of our interviewees mentioned sex work as a reason for Basotho women crossing the border, this may be due to the sensitivity of the subject.

Human trafficking from Lesotho increased significantly in the 1990s due to the somewhat looser border controls in post-apartheid South Africa, but the bureaucracy to legally cross the border to engage in various day-to-day activities remained cumbersome and time-consuming.[48] Crossing the border with proper papers was always quite expensive, but during the recent pandemic, required COVID-testing made the crossing even more prohibitive. Stringent border controls, however, did not make people less mobile; it merely pushed people into using extra-legal avenues (Figure 10.2).

Where migrants cannot or will not cross borders legally, they often subvert official bordering practices by engaging in extra-legal border crossing, whether through bribery of receptive border officials or by using illegal crossing points and cross-border networks controlled by paqama scouts in

Figure 10.2 The Informal "taxi rank" at Qacha's Nek "Paqama gate" on the Lesotho Side. *Source*: Photographs taken by authors.

the Lesotho-South Africa border(land)s. These networks often also engage in the smuggling of people, drugs, cars, guns, and livestock. For a fee, paqama scouts assist travelers to cross the border at points outside of the formal border posts. Even travelers with valid passports may choose extra-legal border crossing for pragmatic purposes. This echoes Coplan's observation that "the border itself has been, from the time it was demarcated, less a regulatory boundary than a business."[49]

Therefore, a border is more than a boundary. It creates a liminal and dynamic space—the borderland—or frontier that affects people's lives, behavior, and identity construction.[50] Routledge explains how the enactment of geopolitical policies to exercise power and dominance in determining who gets to cross a border and who does not, is met with contestation and resistance in a "geopolitics of below" derived from the position of the marginalized and excluded.[51] In this sense, the borderland becomes not only a hegemonic space, but also a subversive space, and this is certainly evident in how people engaged with the Lesotho-South Africa border during the pandemic.

SUBALTERN STRUGGLES AND THE PRECARITY OF SUBALTERN BASOTHO MIGRANT WOMEN IN THE LESOTHO-SOUTH AFRICA BORDER(LAND)S

As already highlighted, the (im)mobility of subaltern Basotho women is driven by multiple factors, and when they cannot cross the border legally, they find ways to cross "illegally," which exposes them to various forms of risk, including sexual harassment and rape. Women use paqama "gates" for many reasons, including the lack of official passports and permits and the time and distance it would require to travel to the nearest official crossing point.[52]

The need for extra-legal border crossing became particularly pressing during the COVID-19 pandemic. Starting in March 2020, South Africa closed all of its land borders. While some reopened temporarily in October 2020, a new wave of the virus closed them again in early 2021. Even when they were open, border controls were even stricter and required an expensive COVID-19 PCR test that pushed legal border crossing beyond the means of many people.[53] During this time, the deployment of the South African military to help curb human traffic left the border(land)s even more militarized.

As reflected in numerous testimonies, many people with valid travel documents chose to use paqama routes to avoid the hyper-strict border controls involving scrutiny, de-individuation, inspection, cost, and judgment.[54] Many were fearful of the COVID test, a fear capitalized on by some paqama scouts who, like the Marashea Gangs of old, exploited the precarity of women travelers to sexually harass, rape, kill, and rob, perpetuating the exploitation and dehumanization of the subaltern black female body. Some migrants were forced to cross extra-legally because South African employers confiscated their travel documents and passports in order to restrict the movement of labor for the duration of the contract, as had been reported on some farms.[55]

Yet, the act of crossing "illegally" comes with its own risks. Some of the risks include being arrested, physically arduous hikes through farmland, thick bush, rocky mountains, or flooded rivers, broken bottles that paqama scouts deliberately scatter at particular "illegal" river crossing points,[56] crossing fees charged by paqama scouts, theft of belongings, extortion, and robbery, and sexual harassment, rape, and even murder.[57] With the border regulations making legal crossing prohibitively difficult, these women and men do not cross under conditions of their own choosing, but under those dictated by both state and non-state actors. The de facto regulators in this liminal border(land)s are the paqama scouts, a group most travelers thought colluded with the police, soldiers, and immigration officials.[58]

The paqama scouts use a variety of means to ferry their clients across the rivers, or across the land borders. Some paqama scouts ferry clients on inflatable tubes across the Mohokare/Caledon River when the water is high. Another popular method is to ferry as many as four to five passengers on an inflatable mattress across the river.[59] In other places, scouts use salvaged car bonnets to cross their clients; sometimes they carry their clients on their backs or on their shoulders.[60] Such crossings are treacherous when river levels are high, but passing through borderlands for many women can be a traumatizing and dehumanizing experience, regardless of water levels.[61] Most of these clients of the paqama scouts are subaltern Basotho women and girls, who do display agency in facilitating their own mobility despite state and non-state barriers to border crossing, but they are also exposed to bodily harm when they place the security of their possessions and lives wholly in the hands of the paqama scouts. It was during one such perilous journey crossing the Mohokare River that both Matsepi and Mampho survived different forms of sexual assault, as detailed later in this chapter.

Describing how perilous the "illegal" journey across the Mohokare is, a newspaper article from Lesotho noted: "The trip across the *Mohokare* River that divides Lesotho and South Africa is not for the faint-hearted. There have been several incidents when some people have been swept away by the raging waters. Some women were helped to cross only to be raped after when they were on the other side of the river."[62] However, crossing non-riverine borders can also be dangerous, and was described by one of our interviewees: "Sometimes the [*paqama* scouts] who assist you can rob you of everything. There was a case of two girls who were allegedly raped and killed there."[63]

Women are particularly affected by sexual violence during the "illegal" journey across the border because of the liminality of crossing. But this can also be true for legal crossing. At best, official international ports of entry are sites where ordinary people encounter the full force of the bureaucratic state in its systems of inclusion, exclusion, paperwork, harassment, and corruption. In this sphere, women are already vulnerable as they have to navigate a system that is masculinized and patriarchal, but women engaging in extra-legal border crossing using illicit cross-border networks are even more vulnerable. This vulnerability does not necessarily end after crossing the border, and women often continue to face risks of smuggling, human trafficking, prostitution, abuse, and violence, with very little protection from the law.[64]

Human rights abuses such as illegal detention, forced labor, and sexual violence are not only confined to the Lesotho-South Africa border(land)s, but have been documented on many other perilous migrant journeys, including the migrants traversing the Sahara Desert in order to reach Europe via Libya.[65] Violence against extra-legal female migrants, refugees, and border residents often goes under-reported or gets ignored. Criminalizing border crossing makes these women very vulnerable as predators know that any crime committed against them is less likely to be reported out of fear that survivors may be arrested as illegal immigrants.[66] Where unaccompanied women and girls rely on human smugglers for clandestine border crossings such as *paqama*, sometimes the only currency they have to pay with may be their sexuality.[67] Ultimately, many women are trafficked in this way and end up in the commercial sex industry in the country where they had hoped to obtain a better future.

The precarity of women during illegal border-crossings was revealed by the testimonies of many of our research participants. In Sterkspruit, near the Telle Bridge crossing, one male broke down in tears as he narrated, in graphic detail, the story of a young girl who was sexually harassed by paqama scouts, or "*likepe*" as they are called in this area. The girl told him how one of these scouts touched her inappropriately and whispered sexual remarks. Another male participant added that some women were helped to cross the river, only to be raped when, on completion of the crossing, once they were (illegally) in South Africa.[68] These incidents highlight how precarious this liminal space can be for women migrants, whose intersectional vulnerabilities become amplified in this context. In the informal and "illegal" dimensions of this space, women's bodies become the battlegrounds—territories to conquer—for male phallic power.[69] This is part of a larger trend where, in post-apartheid South Africa, sexual violence has become a "socially endorsed punitive project for maintaining patriarchal order."[70] (Figure 10.3)

When paqama scouts carry their female clients on their shoulders or backs, they are presented with a rare opportunity to fondle their bodies, which in some cases, culminate in rape. Mamajone, a survivor of sexual harassment, told us that when the river is full, the paqama scouts offer to carry you on their backs and "that is when they will touch you all over your body."[71] In a focus group, one elderly woman lamented the closure of the Telle Bridge border post due to COVID-19 and recounted her own dehumanizing experience at the hands of the paqama scouts:

> I do not know how to cross in the river. Then this child says, "madam I will carry you." Now, they carry us, they touch us, they touch you everywhere because they are carrying you. They say, "hey grandma, do not fall." They touch you inappropriately and this makes you uncomfortable.[72]

Another informant described the paqama scouts as fraudsters who "threaten to leave you in the middle of the river if you refuse to adhere to their sudden price increases."[73] Thus, although it is extremely dangerous for both men and women to cross at the illegal crossing sites, girls and women are more vulnerable than men, as they are also at risk of sexual violence.

Figure 10.3 The "Paqama gate" Near Telle Bridge Border Post within Eyeshot of Officials. *Source*: Photograph taken by authors.

This vulnerability is well known, even to most men who use the crossing points. One man near Telle Bridge described the sexual exploitation of women during the "illegal" crossings:

> Sir, it was last year that one teacher from Lesotho died, and we had to go and pay our last respects. Some of us did not have passports. And now we had to cross at these illegal crossing points. [We] had to rely on those boys who assist with crossing in there. What I saw there! The way these boys handled women in there was so uncomfortable. You would not be happy if it was your wife who was carried across the river. He touched them in a very suggestive way; in a way that made them uncomfortable. He took the first one, and the third one. When he got to the last one, who was younger and rather beautiful, she was touched excessively. He was touching her in a very repulsive way. When they were in the middle of the river, you could tell that she was at his mercy—it was very embarrassing. These are situations that we come across there. I had never seen

> something as repulsive as that. It was as though I could help, but there was no way I could carry them because I fear the water. Some of the women get raped because these people have seen them naked. They end up taking an opportunity and rape them. Sometimes they rape and kill them. So, these are the things that exist at illegal crossings. These people have now seen these women, they have seen their naked bodies, and some of them end up being raped.[74]

This testimony sums up the traumatic experiences women endure at the hands of paqama scouts. Despite all these adversities, women have not been passive bystanders, but rather have devised a number of risk mitigation strategies. These include soliciting the company of adult children, relatives, friends, and even husbands to accompany them on this journey, hiring chauffeurs who are connected to corrupt immigration officials, police, and soldiers, directly bribing immigration officials, and sometimes directly challenging the advances of paqama scouts.

These strategies are part of a larger trend whereby "illegal" crossers have created a sense of community due to the dangers, and this has helped many find courage in the face of adversity, as the following stories of Matsepi and Mampho show.

"YOU HAVE TO PAY WITH YOUR BODY": SEXUAL ASSAULT AND RAPE IN THE LESOTHO-SOUTH AFRICA BORDER(LAND)S

In the first part of this section, the focus is Matsepi's narrative of her ordeal and acts of bravery. The second part of the section offers the story of Mampho's gang rape by four paqama scouts sometime in November 2020 as narrated by Matsepi, who views her own ordeal through Mampho's traumatic experience. These narratives highlight the precarity of subaltern Basotho migrant women and the dangers in liminal spaces of the border(land)s. These narratives are not only stories of resilience and bravery in the political economy of the everyday, but also indicators of agency as survivors rather than victims.

Matsepi's Sexual Harassment and Attempted Rape

Matsepi narrowly escaped being raped or thrown into the flooded Mohokare River in August 2021. She is one of the few *victagents* of sexual harassment and robbery who had the courage to share her experience. First contact was made with Matsepi during a research visit to Maseru Bridge in November 2021, where researchers randomly approached people who were crossing into South Africa. After hearing about the research project, Matsepi agreed to participate and anonymously share her experiences. She was reticent to share any of her experience at that moment, but shared her cell number to facilitate an interview at a later stage. When a telephonic interview was arranged, she prevaricated and suggested that she would rather share her story in writing, either via WhatsApp or email. She finally shared her traumatic experience via text. In a subsequent telephone conversation to thank her for her brave candor, she explained her reticence and said, "I didn't want to talk about it. It felt so new every time I talk about it."[75] After a few follow-up WhatsApp exchanges, Matsepi requested that correspondence cease and her number be deleted.

According to Matsepi's written account, sometime in August 2021, she needed to cross from Lesotho into South Africa to go to Bloemfontein for a routine business trip. Matsepi says she did not have a valid permit because of COVID-19 regulations. While figuring out how to cross Maseru Bridge undetected, Matsepi was approached by paqama scouts who offered to assist her to cross extra-legally via one of the paqama "gates" for a fee of R400, which she paid on the spot. She says she "entered the river fully dressed" in the company of one scout and when she arrived on the opposite bank, two other scouts appeared. The three demanded a further R300, and when she said she didn't have it, they told her that if they searched her bag and found money, they would take all of it. At that point, another scout took her to the banks of the Mohokare River and told her "that is where strong-headed people ended."[76] In a thicket of trees very close to the formal Maseru Bridge border post (see Figure 10.4), the scouts "teased me and told me to change my [wet] jeans [so that] they could sit down and admire my sexy body, and maybe I could pay them in kind because I said I no longer had money."[77] (Figure 10.4)

Rape and the threat of rape are tools used by paqama scouts to terrorize women who refuse to comply with their demands. After Matsepi refused to take off her jeans, the scouts threatened to kill her, at which point she gave them a further R300. After walking a short distance out of the forest, "those three boys demanded a further R150 which they said was for the patrolling soldiers for my final passage."[78] When she flatly refused, one of the scouts threatened her with a knife and said "I should give them the money to pay those police."[79] After refusing to give them the R150, "the two boys held me and the one I crossed with searched all my jeans' pockets and took the rest of what's left and ran back to the river."[80] Matsepi said she was lucky to be left with R220 which was hidden away. Her story illustrates the extreme vulnerability of extra-legal migrants in the marginal spaces of crossing, where scouts hold the power, sometimes even over life and death. Moyo argues that if people could be smuggled across the border, they could equally be kidnapped and coerced into the sex or undocumented labor trade, or for illegal

Figure 10.4 The "Paqama gate" Near Maseru Bridge Border Post within Eyeshot of Officials. This is where Matsepi and Mampho were assaulted behind the thicket. *Source*: Photograph taken by authors.

organ harvesting, which are all forms of human trafficking that have been documented in South Africa.[81] Matsepi's story illustrates how these processes work, at some times, in the informal crossings between Lesotho and South Africa.

After surviving her ordeal, Matsepi found her way to the taxi rank and boarded a taxi to Bloemfontein. Inside the vehicle, her thoughts strayed to "all the drama and how I escaped fate as even rape."[82] Another passenger, whom we will call Mampho, who saw her coming from the river, observing her deep contemplation, asked if she was alright, to which she responded in the affirmative. But Mampho persisted in questioning Matsepi and recounted her own traumatic rape by four paqama scouts at the same crossing point.

Mampho's Gang Rape by Four Paqama Scouts/Touts

Matsepi shared what transpired during her meeting with Mampho on the taxi to Bloemfontein:

> When I thought about my incident and what that girl told us in a full passenger vehicle to Bloemfontein from Maseru Bridge, saying she feels ashamed because she could not talk about it to anyone. . . . She said you may think I am lying,

> but this is real. Because she saw us coming from the river, and I remained quiet until we reached Ladybrand. When we were about to leave Ladybrand she said, "Sister, are you ok?" I said hmmmm. She said I know experiences down there; you would not look this frustrated if nothing wrong happened. That is when she started narrating her story [of being raped by four scouts], but still I didn't tell them what happened. That is when I wanted to cry. But I said, "how can I cry for money when people are telling stories like this."[83]

Mampho's ordeal, as told by Matsepi, took place sometime in November 2020, when Mampho paid paqama scouts to bring her across the Mohokare River, which culminated in her rape.

> She was accompanied alone just like me. With high levels of [water], she was going to be carried on the shoulders by one of the boys. Her pair of jeans was tight, she had to remove them. Her "helper" also had to remove clothes; they were fully nude. They successfully crossed and met two other boys on the other side of the river. Just a few meters from the river, they met another fourth boy.[84]

Mampho was taken to a sparse forest near the bridge and the taxi rank under the pretext that they needed to hide "from the police so that she could get dressed," and as she tried to pull on her pair of jeans, Mampho was hit from behind, fell to the ground, and was then gang-raped.[85] As she was being raped, she was told "not to shout as that noise would call more boys to come and have fun, [telling her] that was what they do to all women who thought were smart enough to cross the river for free."[86]

After surviving being raped by the four scouts, Mampho was left helplessly lying in the dirt. Out of fear of further assault, she forced herself to get up and walk "slowly in the wilderness to the [taxi] rank."[87] In the taxis first to Ladybrand and then onward to Bloemfontein, Mampho paid for three seats. One of the taxi drivers asked her why she was paying for three seats to which she replied that she wanted to lie down because she was not feeling well. At that point the driver is said to have turned around and sarcastically commented, "Who knows, she might have paid with her pussy as that was what Basotho deserved for illegal crossing."[88]

Matsepi's narrative was similar to stories the research team heard elsewhere in the border(land)s. At Telle Bridge, one informant insisted that the "*dikepes*" (the local term for paqama scouts) should never be trusted because they unilaterally change the passage fees mid-crossing and any attempt to negotiate the ever-changing price could prove fatal: "When you get to the other side, they pull a gun on you, and you end losing all your things."[89]

Despite her terrible ordeal at the hands of paqama scouts, Mampho continued using paqama "gates" and scouts.[90] We argue that this reflects the agency of women and other subalterns beyond the realm of victimhood, where they become *victagents*. After probing Matsepi as to why Mampho was continuing to risk her life, Matsepi reported that, according to Mampho, "it was a matter of life or death" to be able to continue to cross the border.[91] Coplan posits that, while for Basotho men South Africa could be seen as the land of wage slavery, "for women, it represents relative choice, opportunity, and independence."[92] This may partly explain why Mampho described the act of crossing the border "illegally" as a matter of "life and death." Despite the "restrictions inherent in border policies that curtail movement and mobility on one hand, [crossing the border 'illegally' underscores] migrant women's human right to mobility through border crossing."[93]

Matsepi and Mampho are among the few women *victagents* with the courage to talk about their traumatic experiences. As mentioned before, crimes committed against extra-legal migrants, refugees, and borderlands residents are often not reported or under-reported because so many fear being arrested for breaking the law by crossing "illegally." Therefore, the full scale of sexual assaults and other crimes committed against women crossing through the paqama "gates" will never be known. While narratives of sexual exploitation of migrant women were few in the many oral testimonies we collected, the narratives of Matsepi and Mampho, and the fact that so many men and women talked about sexual violence, suggest that these experiences are, unfortunately, far from uncommon.

While we have illuminated criminal and violent behavior by some paqama scouts and corruption by state officials, we also caution against viewing all, or even most, paqama scouts as rapists and all, or even most, border and security officials as corrupt. Some paqama scouts are honest people who work hard to support their families and serve their clients with care as is reflected by the glowing "references" some "illegal" crossers gave those who assisted them. One woman interviewed near Butha-Buthe said: "The honesty and professional service I always get from them [paqama scouts] makes me to use them all the time. . . . I have heard of horrible stories of rape and theft, but not in this area."[94] Other informants affirmed that paqama scouts were hardworking and honest people who "save lives, create possibilities and redress global inequalities."[95] Moreover, a deeper analysis into their activities reveals that the paqama scouts are part of a well-organized and thriving border ecosystem that keeps many people economically afloat, as noted in the chapter by Twala and Magaiza in this volume.

CONCLUSION: STRATEGIES TO ENHANCE HUMAN SECURITY AND DE-BORDERIZATION

This chapter illustrates the potential danger lurking in the Lesotho-South Africa border(land)s, especially for women. We have argued that women's everyday intersectional vulnerabilities are compounded by the precarity they face in this gendered space. Gendered (b)ordering can impact women's lives in various ways. Women dwelling in border(land)s are exposed to a volatile domain, where the violation of human security is normalized. In this liminal space, violence can be state-driven and linked to the militarization of the border, but it can also come from non-state actors, such as human smuggling networks. The Lesotho-South Africa border, like the South Africa-Zimbabwe border, is also a high-crime area with high levels of prostitution, abuse, violent crime, crime against property, gun running, drug smuggling, and livestock rustling that compromise human security in the borderlands.[96]

In the twenty-first century, states have increasingly militarized and fortified their borders as a symbol of state-centric hypermasculinity, and this tendency was amplified during the COVID-19 pandemic. Across southern Africa, the closures of international and even state or provincial borders, and the deployment of the military to protect these borders were heightened during the pandemic. Even with a renewed state commitment to border "security," states have had limited success curbing cross-border mobility and criminal activity around borders. If anything, the securitization has led to increasing levels of "illegal" transboundary movement. The Lesotho-South Africa border is highly permeable because of the natural terrain featuring rugged mountains, shallow rivers, and heavily populated borderlands regions, which makes it nearly impossible to control. This has allowed the extra-legal cross-border trafficking of humans, livestock, weapons, and other goods to flourish.[97]

Rigid colonial borders have changed the landscape of mobility in Africa, but post-independence African governments have also, if anything, exacerbated the problem of borders, leaving subaltern migrant women more exposed to all forms of danger when they choose extra-legal avenues for migration. So, we raise the question of what this case study from the Lesotho-South Africa border(land)s can suggest for plans to enhance human security in border(land)s. We first need to put the so-called "migrant crisis" into perspective. Lesotho is completely encircled by South Africa and, due to colonial border arrangements, Basotho people and even families are found on both sides: "Sesotho transcends Lesotho, the Basotho are a borderland and cross-border people."[98]

For many, crossing the border is a daily necessity. When following formal procedures becomes too cumbersome, they find alternative ways. It is for these historical reasons, as well as the failure of recent increased militarization of the borderlands, that stricter border controls have utterly failed to curb illegal cross-border movements of people, livestock, and goods. In 2020, *News24* reported that the South African National Defense Force spends R88 million annually to patrol the border, with limited success at interdicting "illegal" crossers.[99] With Lesotho's population of roughly 2.2 million people and given the permeability of the border, and the historical and contemporary reasons for many to cross, it suggests that securitization and militarization are not the answers. We would suggest that the real problem is the cross-border criminal syndicates involved in various forms of trafficking. Restricting the movement of ordinary people or forcefully repatriating undocumented migrants will not curb extra-legal mobilities. Extra-legal cross-border networks facilitate the movement of rustled livestock, illicit goods, weapons, and humans in ways that threaten human security in this space, in particular, women's security in the borderlands.

In order to enhance human security along the Lesotho-South Africa border, we would argue that the idea of de-borderization be seriously considered. By removing artificial boundaries to the free movement of people and making it easier for ordinary citizens to move around, these illicit networks may be starved of an important source of income. Ordinary people, especially Basotho migrant women, would not have to risk life and body to cross the border just to live their daily lives. At the same time, this would allow security forces to redirect their resources to rooting out criminal networks, instead of spending time criminalizing ordinary citizens for crossing the border "illegally" when the border actually "crossed" them in the first place.

NOTES

1. Matsepi, interview by Munyaradzi Mushonga, January 10, 2022. Matsepi (not real name) is a thirty-nine-year-old woman from Lesotho. She shared her experiences of sexual assault and near-rape through a hand-written script and via a telephonic (WhatsApp) follow-up conversation on 18 January 2022.

2. The concept of liminality is derived from the liminal stage in rites of passage coined by folklorist Arnold van Gennep to describe the transitional phase from one life stage to the next and later expanded by anthropologist Victor Turner, as the concept of liminality to describe the space "betwixt and between" two states that is removed from ordinary life. See Victor Turner, "Process, System, and Symbol: A New Anthropological Synthesis," *Daedalus* 106, no. 3 (1977): 61–90. In this sense, border(land)s are viewed as liminal spaces, which are separate from ordinary life, societal rules, and governance where the normal expectations of human security, common decency, and the rule of law are suspended and replaced by alternate norms and forms of control.

3. All interviews in this chapter were carried out by two research teams (RT), one based in Lesotho and another in South Africa, both of which were coordinated by the first author as the principal investigator. These interviews were made possible courtesy of generous funding received from the National Institute for the Humanities and Social Sciences (NIHSS) and the University of the Free State (UFS) Humanities Interdisciplinary Research Project housed in the Dean's Office.

4. Narrative essays bring out more informants' experiences, thoughts, and feelings, thus connecting with readers on an emotional level. In the process, they communicate key messages in a direct way, and the subjectivity of the stories shared is their strength.

5. *Paqama* is the act of crossing a point by bending or crawling under a fence/barrier. Paqama "gates" are the illegal crossing points/routes between Lesotho and South Africa. Paqama scouts are intermediaries that facilitate illegal border crossing between Lesotho and South Africa, and depending on locality, they are known by many different names—*"lirurubele"*/*"gungubele"* (butterflies) at Maseru Bridge; *"lirutle"* at Butha-Buthe; *"likepe"* (boats) at Quthing, Telle Bridge, and Maputsoe; *"litsiroane"* (birds) at Mafeteng/Van Rooyen's Border Gate; *"amaPhara"* or *"bo nkukise"* (those who help carry the load) at Qacha's Nek. It is these paqama scouts who are accused of sexual harassment and rape of women and girls. See also the chapter by Twala and Magaiza in this volume for a further discussion of these places and people.

6. We discovered that in all localities along the Lesotho-South Africa border, the paqama scouts are also called "boys." A majority of these are aged between fifteen and twenty years, some of whom have dropped out of school. Some informants even labeled them "children" who rape and rob those they assist to cross the river. In the text, we refer to them as "paqama scouts" or just "scouts" due to the ways that the term "boy" was used as a pejorative during the apartheid and colonial periods.

7. "Crossing 'River Jordan'," *The Post* (Maseru), 17 November 2020. https://www.thepost.co.ls/crossing-river-jordan/.

8. Theresa Ulicki and Jonathan Crush, "Gender, Farmwork, and Women's Migration from Lesotho to the New South Africa," *Canadian Journal of African Studies* 34, no. 1 (2000): 76.

9. In critical theory, subaltern is a term used to denote people who are marginalized and subordinated through prisms of race, gender, class, ethnicity, etc. The term is borrowed from Gayatri Spivak, "Can the Subaltern Speak?" in *Marxism and the Interpretation of Culture*, eds. Cary Nelson and Lawrence Grossberg (London: Macmillan, 1988). In this chapter, it refers to women, mainly black, African women.

10. Ulicki and Crush, "Gender, Farmwork, and Women's Migration," 77.

11. Maha Marouan, "At the Border, on the Margins," https://africasacountry.com/2022/10/at-the-border-on-the-margins. Accessed 5 February 2023.

12. Michael Rothberg, *The Implicated Subject: Beyond Victims and Perpetrators* (Palo Alto: Stanford University Press, 2019), 202.

13. Marouan, "At the Border."

14. Ulicki and Crush, "Gender, Farmwork, and Women's Migration," 76.

15. Franzisca Zanker, "African Perspectives on Migration: Re-centring Southern Africa," *Migration Studies* 10, no. 2 (2022): 284.

16. Ethical clearance number UFS-HSD2020/2195/21.

17. Scott F. Turner, Laura B. Cardinal, and Richard M. Burton, "Research Design for Mixed Methods: A Triangulation-Based Framework and Roadmap," *Organizational Research Methods* 20, no. 2 (2017): 243–267; Amy L. Hall, and Ray C. Rist,

"Integrating Multiple Qualitative Research Methods (Or Avoiding the Precariousness of a One-Legged Stool)," *Psychology & Marketing* 16, no. 4 (1999): 291–304.

18. Turner, Cardinal, and Burton, "Research Design," 244.

19. Martin Müller, "What's in a Word? Problematizing Translation Between Languages," *Area* 39, no. 2 (2007): 206–213; Susan Ervin and Robert T. Bower, "Translation Problems in International Surveys," *Public Opinion Quarterly* 16, no. 4 (1952): 595–604.

20. David Newman, "Boundaries," in *A Companion to Political Geography*, eds. John Agnew, Katharyne Mitchell, and Gerard Toal (Malden: Blackwell, 2003), 133.

21. Sankaran Krishna, "Boundaries in Question," in *A Companion to Political Geography*, eds. John Agnew, Katharyne Mitchell, and Gerard Toal (Malden: Blackwell, 2003), 303.

22. The principle of state sovereignty emerged at the Treaty of Westphalia (1648). The treaty was the signature that ended the Holy Roman Empire and served as the basis for the modern system of nation-states. The Westphalian doctrine assumed that legitimate states had to correspond to nations, i.e., groups of people united by language and culture. While this doctrine was applied in Europe, the Berlin Colonial Conference (1884–1885) inaugurated the exclusion and dismemberment of Africa from sovereignty, only for it to be imposed on Africa after World War II.

23. Newman, "Boundaries," 125–126.

24. Newman, "Boundaries," 123.

25. Mark B. Salter, "To Make Move and Let Stop: Mobility and the Assemblage of Circulation," *Mobilities* 8, no. 1 (2013): 7–19; Daromir Rudnyckyj, "Technologies of Servitude: Governmentality and Indonesian Transnational Labor Migration," *Anthropological Quarterly* (2004): 407–434; Matthew Longo, *The Politics of Borders: Sovereignty, Security, and the Citizen after 9/11* (Cambridge: Cambridge University Press, 2017).

26. For example, in Telle and Sterkspruit, on either side of the border, there are different ethnic groups living together (Basotho, Xhosa, Hlubi, etc.) and there is mutual respect of various cultural practices.

27. Roelof J. Kloppers, "Border Crossings: Life in the Mozambique/South Africa Borderland since 1975" (DPhil Diss., University of Pretoria, 2005), iii.

28. The term border(land)s is used in certain places to highlight the existence of, first, a border or borders as both officially designated crossing points and natural barriers to something, and second, to emphasize the fact that beyond a border or borders as crossings points or barriers, there is a borderland(s) which is inhabited by transnational communities. 'Illegal' crossing takes place in both zones.

29. Jennifer L. Fluri, "Feminist Political Geography" in *The Wiley Blackwell Companion to Political Geography*, eds. John Agnew, Virginie Mamadouh, Anna J. Secor, and Joanne Sharp (Malden: Blackwell, 2015), 236, 239.

30. Seema Shekhawat, Debidatta Aurobinda Mahapatra, and Emanuela C. Del Re, "Introduction: Borders, Violence and Gender" in *Women and Borders: Refugees, Migrants and Communities*, eds. Seema Shekhawat and Emanuela C. Del Re (London: I.B. Tauris, 2018), 6.

31. Sabrina Dean, "Tackling Crime Along the South Africa-Lesotho Border," *Farmer's Weekly,* 1 August 2020. https://www.farmersweekly.co.za/opinion/by-invitation/tackling-crime-along-the-south-africa-lesotho-border/.

32. Joanne P. Sharp, "Feminist and Postcolonial Engagements" in *A Companion to Political Geography*, eds. John Agnew, Katharyne Mitchell, and Gerard Toal (Malden: Blackwell, 2003), 59.

33. Richard Howitt, "Scale" in *A Companion to Political Geography*, eds. John Agnew, Katharyne Mitchell, and Gerard Toal (Malden: Blackwell, 2003), 138–39.

34. Krishna, "Boundaries in Question," 302.

35. Newman, "Boundaries," 129.

36. Newman, "Boundaries," 130; David B. Coplan, "A River Runs Through It: The Meaning of the Lesotho-Free State Border," *African Affairs* 100, no. 98 (2001): 83, 85, 87. See also the chapter by Aerni-Flessner in this volume.

37. Ronald L. Mize, "Interrogating Race, Class, Gender and Capitalism Along the U.S.-Mexico Border: Neoliberal Nativism and Maquila Modes of Production," *Race, Gender & Class* 15, no. 1/2 (2008): 134.

38. Shekhawat, Mahapatra, and Del Re, "Introduction," 4.

39. Donna S. Kline, "Push and Pull Factors in International Nurse Migration," *Journal of Nursing Scholarship* 35, no. 2 (2003): 107–111; Mulugeta Dinbabo and Themba Nyasulu, "Macroeconomic Immigration Determinants: An Analysis of 'Pull' Factors of International Migration to South Africa," *African Human Mobility Review* 1, no. 1 (2015): 27–52; Aimée-Noël Mbiyozo, "Gender and Migration in South Africa: Talking to Women Migrants," *ISS Southern Africa Report* 2018, no. 16 (2018): 1–36.

40. Coplan, "A River Runs Through It," 89–90; Ulicki and Crush, "Gender, Farmwork, and Women's Migration," 65, 68; David B. Coplan, "You Have Left Me Wandering About: Basotho Women and the Culture of Mobility," in *"Wicked" Women and the Reconfiguration of Gender in Africa,* eds. Dorothy L. Hodgson and Sheryl A. McCurdy (Oxford: James Currey, 2001), Migrant Labour and the Discomforts of Home. See also Coplan, "A River Runs through It." The majority of these women migrants are either older or married, divorced, or widowed.

41. Coplan, "You Have Left Me Wandering About," Migrant Labour and the Discomforts of Home.

42. Ulicki and Crush, "Gender, Farmwork, and Women's Migration," 72. They posit that as many as 70% of married female farmworkers from Lesotho have an unemployed spouse in the household.

43. Coplan, "You Have Left Me Wandering About," Migrant Labour and the Discomforts of Home. See also Coplan, "A River Runs Through It," 102.

44. Ulicki and Crush, "Gender, Farmwork, and Women's Migration," 65.

45. Marashea is a collective of mainly Basotho gang members who operated mainly in South African mining towns in the twentieth century. They have been in existence since the late 1940s. The gang takes its name after the victorious Russians, who defeated Hitler's Germany during World War II.

46. Gary Kynoch, "'A Man among Men': Gender, Identity and Power in South Africa's Marashea Gangs," *Gender and History* 13, no. 2 (2001): 250. Ulicki and Crush, "Gender, Farmwork, and Women's Migration," 65.

47. Coplan, "You Have Left Me Wandering About," Migrant Labour and the Discomforts of Home.

48. France Maphosa, "Lesotho and Botswana: Small Countries, Porous Borders," *South Africa's Migration Policies: A Regional Perspective*, CDE Workshop No. 8, 2011: 16–17.

49. Coplan, "A River Runs Through It," 90.

50. Newman, "Boundaries," 128.

51. Paul Routledge, "Anti-Geopolitics," in *A Companion to Political Geography*, eds. John Agnew, Katharyne Mitchell, and Gerard Toal (Malden: Blackwell, 2003), 236.

52. A Telle village resident in Quthing, Lesotho stated, "Some of us have passports, but it is because the border is closed; so, we cannot go to Van Rooyen's Gate, yet we are going to Sterk[spruit] it will be far." It is only about 39 kilometers from Telle Bridge to Sterkspruit one way as the "crow flies," and about 239 kilometers from Telle Bridge to Sterkspruit via Van Rooyen's Gate one way. Residents of Qacha's Nek in Lesotho indicated that it was nearer and cheaper to travel to Matatiele, which is only about 40 kilometers away one way as the "crow flies," than to Maseru, which is about 230 kilometers away one way. The closure of several border-gates due to COVID-19 led to the proliferation of paqama "gates." One interviewee simply stated that due to the border closure on account of COVID-19, people were crossing "anywhere along the river." (Simo, interview by RT, 31 October 2021, Sankatane village resident).

53. During the COVID-19 pandemic, the cost of PCR tests was anywhere between R300 and R1300, and this was beyond the reach of many people, particularly the poor.

54. One female informant from Sankatane village, Mohale's Hoek, says that people cross through the river even if they have documents because it sometimes takes longer to use the official point. (Interview with forty-five-year-old woman, 10 November 2021, Sankatane Village, Mohale's Hoek).

55. Ulicki and Crush, "Gender, Farmwork, and Women's Migration," 76.

56. Paqama scouts are known to deliberately scatter broken bottles in the depths of "illegal" river crossing points in order to force travelers to either hire their gum boots, opt to be carried at the back or on the shoulders, or to be ferried in the home-made/improvised "boats".

57. Interview with Matsepi, 18 January 2022, Ha Hoohlo; Interview with fifty-six-year-old woman, 8 October 2021, Maseru; Interview with Mamajone, 13 November 2021, Telle Bridge, South Africa. A number of women have complained about how these scouts steal from them.

58. Describing her experience of crossing "illegally," this is how one informant described what she thinks is an elaborate network involving state and non-state actors: "I think these boys work together with the police. If you try to take that route alone, you will find the police. If you are with [informal guides], nothing."

59. There are heartbreaking images and videos that have been widely circulated on social media and the Internet showing risky extra-legal river crossings of the Mohokare River. For a video showing how passengers are transported on an inflatable

mattress, see https://www.youtube.com/watch?v=QZ-EbvCCrKk. See also https://migrants-refugees.va/2021/02/24/my-heart-bleeds-for-my-people/.

60. At Telle Bridge, paqama scouts use car bonnets. For this, they are sometimes referred to as "*likepe*" (boats).

61. Shekhawat, Mahapatra, and Del Re, "Introduction," 13.

62. "Crossing 'River Jordan,'" *MENAFN-The Post,* 17 November 2020, https://menafn.com/1101141011/Crossing-River-Jordan, accessed 27 February 2022. See also "Diving Squad Recovers 50 Bodies," *The Post* (Maseru), 9 March 2021, https://www.thepost.co.ls/news/diving-squad-recovers-50-bodies/.

63. Interview with DM, 22 October 2021, Nkululekong, Matatiele. Two residents of Nkululekong also mentioned that one woman was allegedly raped and killed in Qacha's Nek's paqama "gates." Interview with MM1 and MM2, 22 October 2021, Nkululekong, Matatiele.

64. Shekhawat, Mahapatra, and Del Re, "Introduction," 13.

65. Erhabor Idemudia and Klaus Boehnke, *Psychosocial Experiences of African Migrants in Six European Countries: A Mixed Method Study* (Bremen: Springer, 2020), 119.

66. Shekhawat, Mahapatra, and Del Re, "Introduction," 13.

67. Shekhawat, Mahapatra, and Del Re, "Introduction," 14.

68. Interview with 12 Makalakaleng men, 13 November 2021, Telle Bridge, South Africa.

69. Naomi Nkealah, "Commodifying the Female Body: Xenophobic Violence in South Africa," *Africa Development* 36, no. 2 (2011): 132.

70. Helen Moffett, "Sexual Violence, Civil Society and the New Constitution," in *Women's Activism in South Africa: Working Across Divides,* eds. Hannah E. Britton, Jennifer N. Fish, and Sheila Meintjes (KwaZulu-Natal: University of KwaZulu-Natal Press, 2008), 129.

71. Mamajone, Interview.

72. Interview with 8 Makalakaleng women, 13 November 2021, Telle Bridge, South Africa.

73. Interview with Mamajone.

74. This group of men was composed of farmers, caretakers, contractors, pensioners, self-employed people, and a pastor. They were aged between 40 and 70. Interview with 12 Makalakaleng men.

75. Interview with Matsepi, 18 November 2021.

76. Interview with Matsepi, 10 January 2022.

77. Interview with Matsepi, 10 January 2022.

78. Interview with Matsepi, 10 January 2022.

79. Interview with Matsepi, 10 January 2022.

80. Interview with Matsepi, 10 January 2022.

81. Inocent Moyo, "On Borders and the Liminality of Undocumented Zimbabwean Migrants in South Africa," *Journal of Immigrant & Refugee Studies* 18, no.1 (2020): 61; Thozama Mandisa Lutya, "Human Trafficking of Young Women and Girls for Sexual Exploitation in South Africa," in *Child Abuse and Neglect: A Multidimensional Approach*, ed. Alexander Muela Aparicio (Rijeka: InTech, 2012); Lanre

Olusegun Ikuteyijo, "Between Prosecutors and Counsellors: State and Non-State Actors in the Rehabilitation of Victims of Human Trafficking in Nigeria," in *Gender and Mobility in Africa: Borders, Bodies and Boundaries,* eds. Kalpana Hiralal and Zaheera Jinnah (Cham: Palgrave, 2018): 139–157.

82. Interview with Matsepi, 10 January 2022.

83. Interview with Matsepi, 10 January 2022.

84. Interview with Matsepi, 10 January 2022.

85. Interview with Matsepi, 10 January 2022.

86. Interview with Matsepi, 10 January 2022.

87. Interview with Matsepi, 10 January 2022.

88. Interview with Matsepi, 10 January 2022.

89. Interview with 12 Makalakaleng men, 13 November 2021, Telle Bridge, South Africa.

90. Interview with Matsepi, 10 January 2022.

91. Interview with Matsepi, 18 January 2022.

92. Coplan, "You Have Left Me Wandering About," Russianism, Rhythm, and Rebellion.

93. Marouan, "At the Border."

94. Interview with a female resident of Butha-Buthe, 15 November 2021.

95. Interview with a female resident of Leribe, 14 November 2021.

96. See the works of Francis Musoni and Inocent Moyo on the South Africa-Zimbabwe border, mainly Beitbridge, the busiest border post in Africa. For more on this area, see also the chapters by Musoni and Tshabalala in this volume.

97. Dean, "Tackling crime."

98. Coplan, "You Have Left Me Wandering About," Traveling Women.

99. Jason Felix, "SANDF Spends R88m Annually to Protect Border with Lesotho," *News24*, 2 October 2020, https://www.news24.com/news24/southafrica/news/sandf-spends-r88m-annually-to-protect-border-with-lesotho-20201002.

BIBLIOGRAPHY

Coplan, David B. "You Have Left Me Wandering About: Basotho Women and the Culture of Mobility." In *"Wicked" Women and the Reconfiguration of Gender in Africa,* edited by Dorothy L. Hodgson and Sheryl A. McCurdy. Oxford: James Currey, 2001. https://hdl.handle.net/2027/heb99037.0001.001.

Coplan, David B. "A River Runs Through It: The Meaning of the Lesotho-Free State Border." *African Affairs* 100, no. 98 (2001): 81–116.

Dean, Sabrina. "Tackling Crime along the South Africa-Lesotho Border." *Farmer's Weekly*, 1 August 2020. https://www.farmersweekly.co.za/opinion/by-invitation/tackling-crime-along-the-south-africa-lesotho-border/.

Dinbabo, Mulugeta, and Themba Nyasulu. "Macroeconomic Immigration Determinants: An Analysis of 'Pull' Factors of International Migration to South Africa." *African Human Mobility Review* 1, no. 1 (2015): 27–52.

Ervin, Susan, and Robert T. Bower. "Translation Problems in International Surveys." *Public Opinion Quarterly* 16, no. 4 (1952): 595–604.

Felix, Jason. "SANDF Spends R88m Annually to Protect Border with Lesotho." *News24*, 2 October 2020. https://www.news24.com/news24/southafrica/news/sandf-spends-r88m-annually-to-protect-border-with-lesotho-20201002.

Fluri, Jennifer L. "Feminist Political Geography." In *The Wiley Blackwell Companion to Political Geography*, edited by John Agnew, Virginie Mamadouh, Anna J. Secor, and Joanne Sharp, 235–247. Malden: Blackwell, 2015.

Hall, Amy L., and Ray C. Rist. "Integrating Multiple Qualitative Research Methods (Or Avoiding the Precariousness of a One-Legged Stool)." *Psychology & Marketing* 16, no. 4 (1999): 291–304.

Howitt, Richard. "Scale" In *A Companion to Political Geography*, edited by John Agnew, Katharyne Mitchell, and Gerard Toal, 138–157. Malden: Blackwell, 2003.

Idemudia, Erhabor, and Klaus Boehnke. *Psychosocial Experiences of African Migrants in Six European Countries: A Mixed Method Study*. Bremen: Springer, 2020.

Ikuteyijo, Lanre Olusegun. "Between Prosecutors and Counsellors: State and Non-State Actors in the Rehabilitation of Victims of Human Trafficking in Nigeria." In *Gender and Mobility in Africa: Borders, Bodies and Boundaries*, edited by Kalpana Hiralal and Zaheera Jinnah, 139–157. Cham: Palgrave, 2018.

Kline, Donna S. "Push and Pull Factors in International Nurse Migration." *Journal of Nursing Scholarship* 35, no. 2 (2003): 107–111.

Kloppers, Roelof J. "Border Crossings: Life in the Mozambique/South Africa Borderland Since 1975." DPhil Diss., University of Pretoria, 2005.

Krishna, Sankaran. "Boundaries in Question." In *A Companion to Political Geography*, edited by John Agnew, Katharyne Mitchell, and Gerard Toal, 302–314. Malden: Blackwell, 2003.

Kynoch, Gary. "'A Man among Men': Gender, Identity and Power in South Africa's Marashea Gangs." *Gender and History* 13, no. 2 (2001): 249–272.

Longo, Matthew. *The Politics of Borders: Sovereignty, Security, and the Citizen After 9/11*. Cambridge: Cambridge University Press, 2017.

Lutya, Thozama Mandisa. "Human Trafficking of Young Women and Girls for Sexual Exploitation in South Africa." In *Child Abuse and Neglect: A Multidimensional Approach*, edited by Alexander Muela Aparicio, 87–115. Rijeka: InTech, 2012.

Maphosa, France. "Lesotho and Botswana: Small Countries, Porous Borders." In *South Africa's Migration Policies: A Regional Perspective* (CDE Workshop No. 8), edited by Ann Bernstein, 15–18. Johannesburg: The Centre for Development and Enterprise, 2011.

Marouan, Maha. "At the Border, on the Margins." *https://africasacountry.com/2022/10/at-the-border-on-the-margins.* Accessed 5 February 2023.

Mbiyozo, Aimée-Noël. "Gender and Migration in South Africa: Talking to Women Migrants." *ISS Southern Africa Report,* no. 16 (2018): 1–36.

Mize, Ronald L. "Interrogating Race, Class, Gender and Capitalism Along the U.S.-Mexico Border: Neoliberal Nativism and Maquila Modes of Production." *Race, Gender & Class* 15, no. 1/2 (2008): 134–155.

Moffett, Helen. "Sexual Violence, Civil Society and the New Constitution." In *Women's Activism in South Africa: Working Across Divides,* edited by Hannah E. Britton, Jennifer N. Fish, and Sheila Meintjes, 155–184. KwaZulu-Natal: University of KwaZulu-Natal Press, 2008.

Moyo, Inocent. "Zimbabwean Dispensation, Special and Exemption Permits in South Africa: On Humanitarian Logic, Depoliticisation and Invisibilisation of Migrants." *Journal of Asian and African Studies* 53, no. 8 (2018): 1141–1157.

Moyo, Inocent. "On Borders and the Liminality of Undocumented Zimbabwean Migrants in South Africa." *Journal of Immigrant & Refugee Studies* 18, no.1 (2020): 60–74.

Moyo, Inocent. "COVID-19, Dissensus and de facto Transformation at the South Africa–Zimbabwe Border at Beitbridge." *Journal of Borderlands Studies* 37, no. 4 (2022): 781–804.

Müller, Martin. "What's in a Word? Problematizing Translation Between Languages." *Area* 39, no. 2 (2007): 206–213.

Musoni, Francis. "Cross-Border Mobility, Violence and Spiritual Healing in Beitbridge District, Zimbabwe." *Journal of Southern African Studies* 42, no. 2 (2016): 317–331.

Musoni, Francis. *Border Jumping and Migration Control in Southern Africa.* Bloomington: Indiana University Press, 2020.

Newman, David. "Boundaries." In *A Companion to Political Geography*, edited by John Agnew, Katharyne Mitchell, and Gerard Toal, 123–137. Malden: Blackwell, 2003.

Nkealah, Naomi. "Commodifying the Female Body: Xenophobic Violence in South Africa." *Africa Development* 36, no. 2 (2011): 123–136.

Plambech, Sine. "Sex Work on the Other Side of the Sea." *https://africasacountry.com/2018/03/sex-work-on-the-other-side-of-the-sea.* Accessed 19 February 2023.

Rothberg, Michael. *The Implicated Subject: Beyond Victims and Perpetrators.* Palo Alto: Stanford University Press, 2019.

Routledge, Paul. "Anti-Geopolitics," In *A Companion to Political Geography*, edited by John Agnew, Katharyne Mitchell, and Gerard Toal, 236–248. Malden: Blackwell, 2003.

Rudnyckyj, Daromir. "Technologies of Servitude: Governmentality and Indonesian Transnational Labor Migration." *Anthropological Quarterly* 77, no. 3 (2004): 407–434.

Salter, Mark B. "To Make Move and Let Stop: Mobility and the Assemblage of Circulation." *Mobilities* 8, no. 1 (2013): 7–19.

Sharp, Joanne P. "Feminist and Postcolonial Engagements" In *A Companion to Political Geography*, edited by John Agnew, Katharyne Mitchell, and Gerard Toal, 59–74. Malden: Blackwell, 2003.

Shekhawat, Seema, Debidatta Aurobinda Mahapatra, and Emanuela C. Del Re. "Introduction: Borders, Violence and Gender." In *Women and Borders: Refugees, Migrants and Communities*, edited by Seema Shekhawat and Emanuela C. Del Re, 1–20. London: I.B. Tauris, 2018.

Spivak, Gayatri. "Can the Subaltern Speak?" In *Marxism and the Interpretation of Culture*, edited by Cary Nelson and Lawrence Grossberg. London: Macmillan, 1988.

Turner, Scott F., Laura B. Cardinal, and Richard M. Burton. "Research Design for Mixed Methods: A Triangulation-Based Framework and Roadmap." *Organizational Research Methods* 20, no. 2 (2017): 243–267.

Turner, Victor. "Process, System, and Symbol: A New Anthropological Synthesis." *Daedalus* 106, no. 3 (1977): 61–90.

Ulicki, Theresa, and Jonathan Crush. "Gender, Farmwork, and Women's Migration from Lesotho to the New South Africa." *Canadian Journal of African Studies* 34, no. 1 (2000): 64–79.

Zanker, Franzisca. "African Perspectives on Migration: Re-Centring Southern Africa." *Migration Studies* 10, no. 2 (2022): 283–289.

Chapter 11

Women Entrepreneurs and Border Jumpers in the Zimbabwe-South Africa Border

Francis Musoni

In the mid-1980s, the South African government installed an electric fence along its border with Zimbabwe in a bid to stop uncontrolled movements from its northern neighbor.[1] Together with the fence, South African authorities deployed armed security guards to patrol the border and launched a campaign to encourage white farmers to occupy vacant farmlands along the country's borders with Botswana, Zimbabwe, and Mozambique.[2] Although it became more dangerous for people to cross the South African border at undesignated points, these measures did not eradicate the phenomenon of border jumping, which had emerged with the beginning of state-centered controls of mobility in the 1890s. Evidence of the persistence of border jumping first emerged in March 1985, when a Zimbabwean man was electrocuted "as he tried to clip the fence with wire-cutters, apparently to sneak into South Africa."[3] Many more people died before international pressure forced the South African government to reduce the fence's electric current to a non-lethal level in 1993.[4] Given that border jumpers used various strategies to evade official systems of migration control, it has not been possible to quantify the full extent of border jumping across the Zimbabwe-South Africa border during this period or at any given time. However, available records show that 28 percent of the 47,031 people that the South African border officials arrested for trying to illegally enter the country between 1994 and 1995 were Zimbabweans. Also, the number of Zimbabwean illegal migrants deported from South Africa rose from 12,931 in 1994 to 45,922 in 2000.[5]

By 2009, when I began the research that informs this chapter, the Zimbabwe-South Africa border had become a hot bed of crime and violence associated with border jumping. While some people swam across the Limpopo River—which runs between the two countries—and crawled under or jumped over the South African border fence, others enlisted the help of unregistered transport operators, locally referred to as *malayitsha* (or *omalayisha)* and human smugglers (*maguma-guma*) who removed portions of the fence and charged fees for the use of the "alternative gates" they created.[6] Various kinds of informal economic activities had also emerged in the border towns of Beitbridge (on the Zimbabwean side) and Musina (on the South African side), as well as in the rural communities adjacent to the border. For example, hotels and grocery stores existed side-by-side with makeshift lodges and street vendors, while multinational freight companies faced competition from hundreds of unlicensed moving agents. It was also evident that most of the people who regularly crossed the border through informal channels and engaged in various economic activities that thrived on border jumping were women.[7]

Given this scenario, this chapter seeks to understand the ways in which women navigated this violent and somewhat securitized space, from the mid-1990s to the early 2000s. It shows that, like their male counterparts, women who participated in border jumping and other informal activities deployed various strategies to evade state controls of mobility and trade between the two countries. The chapter, therefore, presents such women as enterprising actors who sought to obtain maximum returns from their engagements and interactions with other people in the border zone.[8] It also characterizes them as rational actors seeking to "seize control of their own lives and . . . struggle to establish their own destiny."[9] As the following discussion shows, most of the women I encountered while collecting data for the chapter understood that the activities they participated in were prohibited and generally regarded as against the border's intended master plan. By engaging in such activities, the women exhibited a deep understanding of the border's utility as a lucrative zone of opportunities, especially against the backdrop of the extended economic crisis in Zimbabwe.[10]

In pursuing this research, my study benefitted from several reports of non-governmental organizations, which provided various kinds of support to women abused by the *maguma-guma*, *malayitsha*, and other actors.[11] I also found useful other studies that emphasized the vulnerability of women who were forced into border jumping by the economic crisis in Zimbabwe.[12] However, while I strongly believe that understanding women's victimhood and vulnerability in this region helps in formulating policy interventions and other practical responses to the challenges prevailing in the Zimbabwe-South Africa border zone, focusing on these issues alone occludes other aspects which are critical to better understanding women's agency and creativity in pursuit of livelihood opportunities. In seeking to go beyond the humanitarian and human rights discourse in order to understand the experiences of women who engaged in border jumping and other informal economic activities in the Zimbabwe-South Africa border, the chapter follows Walker and

Galvin's, questioning simplistic ideas about human trafficking.[13] Vanyoro deploys a similar framing in his analysis of the experiences of Zimbabwean male migrants sheltering in the South African border town of Musina, where he argues that the use of categories of victim or victor does not adequately capture everyday experiences, lived realities, and complexities of interactions in border zones.[14] Also, while women's participation in migration and other cross-border activities is often viewed as a disruptor of gender-based restrictions and inequalities,[15] this chapter shows that the Zimbabwe-South Africa border was a highly gendered space in which women's agency was shaped by the prevailing gender norms in the region.[16]

ESAP AND THE FEMINIZATION OF MIGRATION ACROSS THE ZIMBABWE-SOUTH AFRICA BORDER

Although this chapter focuses on the period from the 1990s to the early 2000s, it is important to note that the history of border jumping in this region is much longer than that. As I argued elsewhere, this phenomenon emerged in the 1890s, as state authorities in present-day Zimbabwe (former Southern Rhodesia) and their counterparts in South Africa started controlling mobility across the Limpopo River, which had been turned into a colonial boundary.[17] However, male migrant workers from different parts of Zimbabwe, Malawi, Zambia, and northern Mozambique were the dominant participants in migration across the Zimbabwe-South Africa border during much of the twentieth century. Although most of them were recruited and transported by the South African mine-recruitment agency known as the Witwatersrand Native Labor Association (WNLA), other migrant workers crossed the border through "secret paths." Sometimes, these "secret crossings" were undertaken with the assistance of unlicensed labor recruiters who took advantage of the loopholes in the systems of migration control that the two countries put in place at various moments. Since mine owners, farmers, and other businesses in the labor-intensive economy of South Africa preferred to employ male workers, women rarely featured in official discussions of border jumping and migration controls in general. There is evidence, though, showing that women also crossed the Zimbabwe-South Africa border through unofficial channels before the period under study in this chapter.[18] However, this does not seem to have been a common practice.

It was not until the 1990s that large numbers of women became involved in formal and informal movements across the Zimbabwe-South Africa border.[19] While other scholars view this feminization of migration across the Zimbabwe-South Africa border as a product of South Africa's supposed relaxation of border controls just before the end of apartheid rule, such a shift in the dynamics of migration between the two countries should also be linked to other developments in the region.[20] One of these was the Zimbabwean government's decision to implement a five-year reform program at the behest of the International Monetary Fund and the World Bank. In line with the program, which came to be known as the Economic Structural Adjustment Program (ESAP), Zimbabwean authorities undertook to reduce public expenditure by "removing subsidies on basic foodstuffs, reducing budgetary allocations, even to essential services such as education and health care, and downsizing the public service."[21] To a large extent, ESAP failed to achieve its stated objectives. Instead of bringing macroeconomic growth and a reduction in poverty levels among the people of Zimbabwe, ESAP led to company closures, currency devaluation, and massive job losses, not to mention the gutting of state bureaucracy, the number of civil servants, and public services. Within two years of ESAP, Zimbabwe's unemployment rate rose from about 10 percent to more than 20 percent, while the value of real earnings fell from about US$1,600.00 to a paltry US$100.[22]

As the country battled rising unemployment, inflation, and increased shortages of basic commodities, the region witnessed a huge increase in the number of Zimbabwean women who regularly traveled to South Africa in search of livelihood opportunities. While some of these women took up professional jobs in various sectors of the South African economy, others became seasonal workers on South Africa's border farms. What is perhaps more interesting for our current discussion is that Zimbabwean women became major players in cross-border trading activities, which had emerged as a driver of human mobility between the two countries.[23] Such women were the primary suppliers of basic commodities such as cooking oil, sugar, and cleaning detergents, which were sold on the streets and in backyard shops, commonly referred to as tuckshops, across Zimbabwe. Given Zimbabwe's decline in industrial production from the mid-1990s onward, it was common for consumers to obtain even large items like motor vehicle parts, refrigerators, television sets, kitchenware, and other household equipment from informal cross-border traders, who were mostly women.[24] To raise money to buy items for resale, Zimbabwean women sold different types of handcrafts that were in demand in South Africa.

Some of the women who left Zimbabwe during the period this chapter explores did so to escape state-sponsored political violence, which increased after the formation of the opposition Movement for Democratic Change (MDC) in September 1999. As the ruling Zimbabwe African National Union—Popular Front (ZANU PF) sought to stop the increasingly popular MDC from taking power, political contestations such as the June 2000 general election, the March 2002 Presidential election, the March 2005 general election, and the March 2008 Presidential and Parliamentary elections, turned extremely violent.[25] One direct result of this was the forced displacement of thousands of Zimbabweans who felt targeted by the ruling party. Given the long tradition of cross-border migration, South Africa became a major destination for Zimbabweans seeking refuge from political persecution.

In addition to Zimbabweans who left the country due to political violence, some went to South Africa after the destruction of thousands of informal housing and business structures under the country's 2005 urban cleanup program, officially code-named "Operation Restore Order" or "Operation *Murambatsvina*." Given that the majority of Zimbabweans were without formal jobs, many people in the urban areas lived in makeshift housing structures and survived through the informal economy. As such, there has been intense debate over the motives behind *Murambatsvina*. The Zimbabwean government justified the cleanup as an operation meant "to deal with crime, squalor and landlessness, and rebuild and reorganize urban settlement and small and medium enterprises (SMEs) in a way that would bring dignity, order and prosperity to the stakeholders and the nation at large."[26] However, the manner in which the program was executed—without providing alternative accommodation and sources of livelihood for the victims—caused some analysts to conclude that *Murambatsvina* was a politically motivated project targeting MDC supporters. For example, the Executive Director of the United Nations Human Settlements Programme (UN-Habitat), who also served as a United Nations Special Envoy on Human Settlement Issues in Zimbabwe, castigated this exercise as "a smokescreen for motives that had little to do with addressing the problem of informal structures and restoring order within urban areas."[27] What became clear within a few days of the launch of *Murambatsvina* was that the operation pushed thousands of Zimbabweans deeper into poverty and destitution, forcing some to look for refuge in South Africa and other countries in the region.

As the Zimbabwean economy deteriorated further in post-*Murambatsvina* years, more and more Zimbabweans turned to labor migration and cross-border trade as major sources of livelihood.[28] While some of the people who traveled to South Africa as migrant workers or informal cross-border traders followed official channels, many others resorted to clandestine crossings of the border.

WHEN BORDER JUMPING SEEMS TO BE THE ONLY WAY OUT

In her seminal study of the forces that gave rise to "fiscal disobedience" in the Chad basin in Central Africa, Roitman reminds us about the importance of exploring "the reasoning that leads one to engage in illegal practices—or more distinctly, to maintain the status of illegality."[29] I see this as a call for researchers to always seek to understand the motives, desires, and long-term goals of people who engage in activities and practices that are illegalized. Roitman's advice is particularly important in our current discussion because the dominant narrative of border jumping in Southern Africa holds that conditions of insecurity, such as those discussed above, were *the* cause of "illegal" border crossings in the sub-continent.[30] While insecurity surely explains some crossings, it is equally important to distinguish factors that pushed Zimbabwean women out of their country from those that forced, encouraged, or "pulled" them to cross the South African border without following official channels. Although the declining economy, political violence, and Operation *Murambatsvina* compelled many Zimbabwean women to consider moving out of the country, these factors did not *cause* people to cross the border clandestinely. Instead, the challenges they would have faced when trying to leave their country and enter South Africa through legal channels played a huge role in fueling border jumping between the two countries.

For example, stringent visa conditions that the South African government announced in October 1996 made it difficult for Zimbabweans to cross the border legally. Although previously Zimbabweans intending to travel south of the Limpopo were only asked to show their passports and explain the reasons for their trips, the new travel policy required the production of letters of invitation from business associates, friends, or relatives legally resident in South Africa. The invitation letters had to include identity and contact information of the South Africa-based businesses or individuals inviting specific Zimbabwean travelers, such as their national identity numbers and physical addresses. To reduce cases of Zimbabweans who overstayed, South African authorities also required invitation letters to show the lengths of the intended visits. Those visiting the country without invitations had to show proof of confirmed and paid hotel accommodation before they could obtain visas. Zimbabwean travelers were also required to show that they were able to sustain themselves while in South Africa by providing bank statements or traveler's checks.[31]

Although many prospective travelers could obtain invitation letters from relatives and friends living and working in South Africa, they struggled to produce acceptable bank statements. Others could not afford visa application fees, as well as the costs of obtaining photographs and other documents that were required to apply for visas. What worsened the situation was that Zimbabwe had only two places for potential travelers to get visas for South Africa—Harare and Bulawayo.[32] This meant that inhabitants of Beitbridge district and other areas close to the border with South Africa, in particular, had to take long trips to Harare or Bulawayo to obtain visas before they could cross the border, which was a walking distance from their homes. The process of obtaining Zimbabwean passports and other identity documents had also become fraught, with corruption, long delays, and other challenges that made it harder for prospective travelers to cross the border through legal, official channels.

I had a discussion in May 2010 with a group of Zimbabwean migrants who returned from South Africa under the auspices of the International Organization for Migration's Assisted Voluntary Return and Reintegration (AVRR) program. The discussion revealed some of the factors that encouraged Zimbabwean women, along with their male counterparts, to avoid official channels for travel out of the country. For example, one woman participant said, "most of us do not want to be border-jumpers. We do that because of the situation at the passport offices in this country. The passport fees are too high for us, especially when you are not working. I would rather jump the border and use that money for other things in South Africa."[33] Apart from high passport fees, the Zimbabwean authorities were no longer accepting the A5-sized birth certificates issued by authorities in the 1970s and early 1980s as official documents. To apply for a passport in twenty-first-century Zimbabwe, potential travelers were required to attach an A4-sized birth certificate. Although the government claimed that holders of A5 birth certificates could obtain the preferred size anywhere in the country, the process presented significant challenges to prospective travelers. As the group discussion revealed, it took even more time and money to obtain the new birth certificate.

The prevalence of corruption among officials in Zimbabwe's passport offices was also identified as a cause for concern. In this respect, participants in the group discussion argued that some employees of the Registrar's office deployed all sorts of tactics to extract bribes from people applying for travel documents. For example, a woman who claimed that she jumped the border more than forty times between February 2007 and May 2010 said, "I gave up on getting a passport a long time ago. After applying for a passport in 2005, I spent six months visiting the passport office checking for my passport." Continuing, she said "every time I went there I was told that the passport was not ready. However, other people who applied after me were able to get theirs in short periods of time—some in a single a month."[34] She claimed that staff at the passport offices delayed processing her application because they wanted her to pay a bribe. She said, "I just forgot it. Nowadays, when I want to travel, I just pick up my handbag and board the bus. I do not get bothered about all these things. I have been arrested and deported many times, but I keep going back to South Africa."[35]

Similarly, another woman recounted how she tried for three days, but failed to submit her application for a passport at the main passport offices in the Makombe Building in Harare in 2008. Having arrived at the passport office at four o'clock in the morning, she was surprised to find that there was already a long queue of people waiting to be served. When the passport office opened at half past eight, one officer started giving out small papers with numbers written on them. The officer stopped giving out numbers just three people from where the woman stood, before announcing that the people who had received the numbers were the only ones who were going to be served that day. This meant she had to remain in the queue until the following day. She said, "I realized that if I left the queue, I was going to lose my position and that was going to make it difficult for me to be served the next day."[36] Despite obtaining the number the following day, she could not turn in her application. She spent half the day waiting in another queue for officers to hand out application forms. After completing the forms, she joined another queue hoping to submit her documents the same day, but the office closed before she could turn in her completed forms. She said, "I had to come back at 4 AM the following day—joining another queue. When I finally reached the service desk where they took fingerprints, I was told that my pictures were not of the correct type needed. That broke my back, and I gave up."[37]

WOMEN'S EVASION OF BORDER CONTROL MEASURES

In 1996, Griffiths wrote that, "the ruthlessness and cost of trying to create impermeable frontiers is beyond the capability of most states, and where they even partially succeed, clandestine cross-border movements are redirected away from frontal assaults to more subtle means of evasion and entry."[38] This is true in the Zimbabwean case. As pointed out in the Introduction, the South African government's decision to build an electrified fence and deploy armed security personnel along the border with Zimbabwe did not stop border jumping. Instead, what this development did was to make border jumping more sophisticated, and dangerous, as hundreds of Zimbabweans whose livelihoods depended on cross-border activities devised various strategies to circumvent the fence and other measures of border control. A major by-product of the fence's construction was the rise of gangs of young men who helped people cross the South Africa-Zimbabwe border without following official channels. Commonly referred to as *maguma-guma*, these informal border agents, or human smugglers, often used wire cutters to remove portions of South Africa's border fence or dug holes under the fence to help their clients enter through these "alternative gates." It was also common for *maguma-guma* to throw blankets and other non-conductive materials over the fence to allow their clients to jump safely over to the South African side of the border.[39]

By the end of the 1990s, it was a well-known "secret" that Zimbabwean women and men who could not afford the fees nor endure long periods of waiting for the processing of their passports engaged *maguma-guma* to help them cross the border when they did not have the required travel documents. All they had to do was to raise enough money for bus rides to the border town of Beitbridge, where they met with *maguma-guma* and negotiated the terms of the contracts while still on the Zimbabwean side of the border. Depending on the season of the year, *maguma-guma* also charged for helping border jumpers cross the Limpopo River. Given that they did not have boats or canoes, for when the river was in flood, *maguma-guma* usually instructed their clients to join hands and slowly drag their feet until they crossed. Keeping their feet down and joining hands when crossing the river was the strategy to avoid being swept away. To minimize chances of arrest, *maguma-guma* carefully studied the routine of South African border patrol units and avoided using the same crossing point, or "gate" for more than two days in a row. It was also common for them to work with corrupt border officials whom they bribed.[40]

Along with *maguma-guma*, Zimbabwean women also used the services of unlicensed cross-border transport operators, locally referred to as *omalayitsha*.[41] This is the group that helped cross-border traders bypass restrictions on imports, and to evade customs and taxation fees at the border-post. With the use of various strategies, including hiding goods in their vehicles and giving bribes to Customs and Immigration officials on both sides of the border post, *malayitsha* helped informal traders smuggle different kinds of goods that were in short supply in Zimbabwe. On their trips to South Africa, the *malayitsha* often transported "undocumented" travelers whom they either smuggled through the border-post or simply transported to undesignated crossing points—informal "gates"—along the border.

When the South African government put in place a visa-free facility for Zimbabwean government employees who needed to take short visits to the country in 2004, the border zone witnessed a spike in the use of fake government pay slips, which were sold to desperate Zimbabweans. While it is likely that some women successfully deployed this strategy as they crossed the border, others were not as fortunate. A good example is the case of a woman called Natalie Peacock who hired a former employee of the Zimbabwe Revenue Authority named Samson Murozvi to forge a government pay slip and a temporary pass, which was commonly referred to as an Emergency Travel Document (ETD), so that her husband Tristan could travel to South Africa. When Tristan presented the documents at the Beitbridge border post, the immigration officer on duty noticed that although the temporary pass had the holder's photograph and signature, it did not have some of the standard security features that legitimate ETDs had. Following some further investigations, the trio was arrested, tried, and ordered to pay fines, after being found guilty.[42]

It was also common for border jumpers to use other people's identity documents to travel between the two countries. Evidence of this abounds at the Beitbridge Magistrate's Court, where most cases of attempted border jumping are tried. For example, on February 6, 2006, Abigail Ndlovu attempted to travel from Zimbabwe to South Africa, presenting a South African passport belonging to Happiness Ndlovu as her own. Although an attendant at the Passport Control Desk stamped the passport authorizing Ndlovu to proceed, a more attentive police detective at another checkpoint in the border-post noticed an anomaly and arrested Abigail.[43] In another case, on March 17, 2010, the police arrested Lisa Dube of Lupane District in Zimbabwe when she tried to use Patricia Mazikana's passport to enter South Africa. According to the case register, Dube got the passport from Damane Mzingeli, a motorist who had provided her a ride from a rural township of Tsholotsho to Beitbridge. The attendant at the control desk who inspected the passport when Dube presented it for stamping noticed that the photograph on it did not match the holder's face and called the police, who arrested Dube.[44]

Some of the border jumpers, both men and women, made use of a strategy that came to be known as "pay as you go," or *kudhiza,* which means paying something in return for a favor. This was a very simple, but risky practice in which border jumpers without proper paperwork bribed their way through several checkpoints at the Beitbridge border-post from the Zimbabwean side to the South African end. As was the case with those who paid *maguma-guma* and *omalayitsha* to take them across the border, the popularity of this strategy rested on the fact that one did not need to make prior arrangements or know anyone at the border to try to cross in this manner. What was important was for the traveler to know the right time to get to the border—usually at night—and to have at least 100 rand in smaller bills of 10 or 20 rand. The traveler would then walk through the border-post with confidence, just like everybody else. If any of the border officials stopped and asked him/her for a passport, the strategy was to simply hand over cash to that official and proceed. As the May 2010 group discussion with Zimbabwean returnees from South Africa revealed, people with expired passports or without visas in their passports used this strategy quite often. When asked to produce their travel documents, a traveler in such a position would insert a 10- or 20-rand bill in their passport before handing it to the inspecting official.[45] Given that the two countries deployed their agents at various points in the border-post, travelers who deployed this strategy probably got away with it because such agents accepted the bribes and let them pass through the border-post.

BORDER JUMPING AS BUSINESS: WOMEN ENTREPRENEURS IN THE BORDER ZONE

In addition to the women who regularly traveled across the Zimbabwe-South Africa border as informal traders, and those who jumped the border to look for jobs in South Africa, some women made a living by providing various kinds of services to border jumpers. This section examines two groups of service providers. The first group consists of women who provided temporary accommodation to border jumpers, many of whom spent several nights in the border region trying to figure out the best way to evade police and customs officials. By 2010, numerous women in Beitbridge's high-density suburb of Dulibadzimu had turned their houses into makeshift lodges where border jumpers could stay anonymously without fearing arrests by law enforcement agents. Similar kinds of housing arrangements were also known to exist in the rural villages near the unofficial crossing points that border jumpers commonly used. Some of the women who owned such houses worked closely with *maguma-guma*, *omalayitsha,* and corrupt border officials who often directed their clients to the "safe" houses while waiting for the right time for them to cross the border. In some cases, house owners also sold food, alcohol, cigarettes, foreign currency, and other items that the travelers needed. It was also common for such houses to be used as temporary storage facilities for smuggled goods en route to their intended destinations.[46]

The second group consists of female sex workers who found the border town of Beitbridge to be very good for business, owing to the number of people who passed through it daily. Although Beitbridge sex workers met their clients in various places, including beer halls, lodges, and truck stops, they were mostly found in an informal settlement known as Mafuro Manyoro that was located about 800 meters from the Immigration and Customs Control building. Before it was destroyed by government officials in 2011, Mafuro Manyoro had become Beitbridge's hub for prostitution. As I learned from several residents of Beitbridge in 2010, some of the sex workers who lived in this informal settlement often worked in networks involving border police officers, immigration officials, truck drivers, and other transport providers who assisted "undocumented" travelers in crossing the border clandestinely. The sex workers received border jumpers from truck drivers and other motorists who illegally transported them from various departure points to Beitbridge. If such people were willing to pay higher fees to cross the border without following the formal channels, the sex workers would direct them to specific border officials who provided the travelers with fake "border passes," which they presented to anyone who asked them to show passports at various checkpoints through the border-crossing process. Travelers who were not able to pay high prices were often handed over to *maguma-guma* who helped their clients cross via the unofficial crossing points away from the border-post.[47]

Some of these activities are reminiscent of a long history of women's creative engagement with border jumping and other informal economic activities in the border region. A good example of this happening decades before the period studied in this chapter relates to a case of two women, a mother and daughter, who were involved in the "illegal" transportation of border jumpers in the 1930s. As narrated by a Rhodesian police detective deployed to Beitbridge in 1938, N. F. Nonia, otherwise known as Mary Gamble, used her vehicle to transport border jumpers from various parts of the country to Beitbridge, where she dropped them off prior to reaching the border checkpoint. From there, "the natives would be instructed to report to Nonia's daughter at Messina, whence they would be taken to employment in the Union."[48] While it is unlikely that Nonia and her daughter engaged in these activities to earn their living, it is possible they did this to make some extra money. The fact that both owned or drove cars in 1938 shows that they belonged to the small upper middle class of African women and men during the colonial period. Still, they were engaged in activities that facilitated border crossing for those whose paperwork was, likely, not in order. Their situation, with access to a vehicle, though, was different from that of most Zimbabwean women who jumped the border as job seekers or informal traders in the 1990s and early 2000s.

A 1978 interview between a researcher called Dawson Munjeri and a Zimbabwean former migrant named Amon Mlambo also reveals that women's creative use of sexuality in their engagement with border jumpers also did not start in the 1990s. While describing how migrants avoided the official channels of mobility between the two countries in the 1940s, Mlambo talked about women who intercepted male migrants in the border region and enticed them into sexual relationships. He said, "when you came from Johannesburg you would find women who were sent to welcome you. You were met by women who would cry out, 'that one is mine, and that one is mine,' and they would help you carry your luggage and take you to their homes . . . many people never made it to their homes for they would have been enticed by the women. They would actually pay *lobola* and then they would die there."[49] While migrants married in this way and settled in the border region, there were cases where villagers sent off women to intercept migrants with the view of robbing them of their belongings. Thus, we see the border as a space of social contestation and a dangerous space fraught with the potential for crossers to lose their lives or livelihoods in earlier periods as well.

WOMEN AND VIOLENCE IN THE BORDER ZONE

Before concluding this discussion, the article would be remiss to not examine the issue of women's victimhood, which was mentioned at the beginning of the chapter. Between November 2008 and March 2009, the South African office of the International Organization for Migration (IOM) conducted research on the challenges facing Zimbabwean women and children traveling illegally to South Africa. Among its major findings, the IOM noted that *maguma-guma* and *malayitsha* "took advantage of travelers' impulse towards informal channels of crossing the border as well as their lack of knowledge about South Africa's immigration laws to exact money and abuse people in desperate situations."[50] Perhaps the most common form of violence that self-styled border agents committed was raping women and girls who either sought their help or were trying to independently cross the border at undesignated points.[51] The story of Chipiwa, a fifteen-year-old girl from Harare, sheds more light on some of the abuses that female border jumpers endured. As narrated in the IOM report, Chipiwa and her sister left Harare for Johannesburg without the necessary travel documents. They arrived at the Beitbridge bus terminus at night and did not know how to proceed across the border. As they wandered at the terminus, two men who identified themselves as *malayitsha* approached them and offered to take them to Johannesburg. The two sisters paid 750 rand and boarded the *malayitsha*'s car, which took them to some rural homestead where they were made to join a group of other travelers, mostly comprised of women, who were gathered there. After spending two days at that place, where they heard stories of rape and physical assaults perpetrated by their kidnappers, Chipiwa and her sister managed to escape and walked back to the Beitbridge town.[52]

Stories such as those contained in the IOM report resonate with events narrated in the trial of two women arrested for using other people's passports, which I witnessed at the Beitbridge Magistrates' Court on April 30, 2010. After both women gave their testimonies, admitting to committing the offense and explaining why they tried to cheat the system, the judge warned them and the public in attendance about the risks of abuse travelers faced when trying to cross the border at undesignated points. He pointed out that he and other court officials had previously dealt with horrendous cases, including one in which more than ten men gang-raped a woman as she tried to enter South Africa through one of the unofficial crossing points. What the judge did not talk about was that corrupt state officials also abuse travelers, especially women, who tried to cross the border through unofficial channels. An interview with Kate Ndou, who was the Senior Irregular Migration Advisor at the IOM Reception Center in Beitbridge, revealed that the IOM helped several victims of abused by border officials. One of the cases which Ndou talked about involved a South African immigration official who took an undocumented Zimbabwean woman into the toilet so he could give her a "border pass," but ended up raping her.[53]

To mitigate the health risks that women who were sexually abused while trying to cross the border through unofficial channels faced, the IOM, Doctors without Borders (MSF), and other NGOs operating in the border region provided counseling and other forms of support to those who reported their ordeals. For example, in June 2010, the MSF clinic in Musina had more than thirty-five Zimbabwean women receiving treatment for sexually transmitted infections they contracted after *maguma-guma* abused them.[54] Similarly, the IOM's Beitbridge office, on the Zimbabwean side of the border, employed two nurses who provided different kinds of treatments, including the Post Exposure Preventative (PEP) kits given to women who it was feared might have been exposed to HIV/AIDS, who reported to the office within seventy-two hours of being sexually abused. Along with offering treatment, the IOM organized several "Migration Health Awareness" workshops in Beitbridge district. At one of the IOM workshops, which I attended, the facilitators encouraged women who planned to cross the border at undesignated points to wear female condoms before embarking on the journey through the "no-man's-land" between the two countries.[55] By encouraging female border jumpers to wear condoms on their trips to South Africa, the IOM reasoned that if such women could not prevent rape by using safer avenues to cross the border, at least they could minimize chances of contracting HIV or other Sexually Transmitted Infections. Desperate measures such as this not only show how dangerous the situation was for women who crossed the border through unofficial channels, but they also reflect the extent to which border jumping between these countries stretched the capacity of state and non-state institutions to control activities in the border zone.

CONCLUSION

One of the unintended results of the historical construction of an electrified fence on the South African side of the border with Zimbabwe is the continued prevalence of violence associated with unregulated crossings at this border today. Zimbabwean women who engaged with this border—as cross-border traders, migrant workers, or street vendors in the border towns of Beitbridge and Musina—from the 1990s to the early 2000s, endured various forms of violence perpetrated by corrupt state officials and self-styled border agents (the *malayitsha* and *maguma-guma*). While there is a growing literature on women's victimhood and vulnerability, very little has been done to understand the Zimbabwe-South Africa border as simultaneously a zone of barriers and possibilities. By presenting the women who crossed the border through unofficial channels (border jumpers), those who helped other people evade official controls of the border, and still others who sold sex in Beitbridge as entrepreneurs, this chapter sought to better understand the opportunities and risks that came with participation in these "illegalized" activities. As the foregoing discussion shows, while the border provided livelihood opportunities for Zimbabwean women struggling with the effects of the economic crisis that the country grappled from the mid-1990s to the early 2000s, their agency was still limited by the violence and gendered norms that prevailed in this region.

NOTES

1. Although the fence also covered a significant portion of South Africa's border with Mozambique, my study focused on the Zimbabwe-South Africa border.

2. "Electric Fence," *Africa Research Bulletin* Political Series, 22, no. 1 (1985). See also, "South Africa: Troops Reinforcing a Porous and Dangerous Border," *IRIN News,* 26 May 2010.

3. Hugh McCullum, "South Africa's Fence of Death," *Horizon* (Harare), 19 August 1992. See also, "Electric Fence" *Africa Research Bulletin.*

4. Ieuan Griffiths, "Permeable Boundaries in Africa," in *African Boundaries: Barriers, Conduits and Opportunities,* eds. Paul Nugent and Anthony Asiwaju (New York: Pinter, 1996); McCullum, "Fence of Death."

5. Jonathan Crush, "The Discourse and Dimensions of Irregularity in Post-apartheid South Africa," *International Migration* 37, no. 1 (1999): 125–151; Lyndith Waller, *No. 19: Irregular Migration to South Africa During the First Ten Years of Democracy* (Waterloo: SAMP Migration Policy Brief, 2006).

6. The term *maguma-guma* is a plural form of *guma-guma,* which denotes the use of crooked ways to achieve one's objectives. *Malayitsha* is a plural form of *layitsha,* which refers to the act of loading stuff into a cart or vehicle. In this case, *malayitsha* refers to people who performed the task. They were carriers of people and goods across the border. Often, the *maguma-guma* treated their "clients" with violence of extreme proportions such as rape, assault, and even murder. For further discussion on this, see Tinashe Nyamunda, "Cross-Border Couriers as Symbols of Regional Grievance? The Malayitsha Remittance System in Matabeleland, Zimbabwe," *African Diaspora* 7, no. 1 (2014): 38–62; Blair Rutherford, "The Politics of Boundaries: The Shifting Terrain of Belonging for Zimbabweans in a South African Border Zone," *African Diaspora* 4, no. 2 (2011): 207–229.

7. For further discussion of women's involvement in trade and other informal economic activities across the Zimbabwe-South Africa border, see Rekopantswe Mate, "'Looking for Money': Hustling, Youth Survival Strategies and Schizoid Subjectivities in Zimbabwe's Crisis," *African Identities* (2021): 1–20; B. Dzawanda,

M.D. Nicolau, M. Matsa, and W. Kusena, "Livelihood Outcomes of Informal Cross Border Traders Prior to the Rise of the Virtual Cash Economy in Gweru, Zimbabwe," *Journal of Borderlands Studies* 38, no. 1 (2023): 75–94.

8. For a similar analysis of migrant women as "economic agents," see Akin Fadahunsi and Peter Rosa, "Entrepreneurship and Illegality: Insights from the Nigerian Cross-border Trade," *Journal of Business Venturing* 17 (2002): 397–429; Teresa Barnes, "Virgin Territory? Travel and Migration by African Women in Twentieth-Century Southern Africa," in *Women in African Colonial Histories,* eds. Jean Allman, Susan Geiger, and Nakanyike Musisis (Bloomington: Indiana University Press, 2002).

9. David Newbury "From 'Frontier' to 'Boundary': Some Historical Roots of Peasant Strategies of Survival in Zaire," in *The Crisis in Zaire: Myths and Realities* ed. Nzongola-Ntalaja (New Jersey: Africa World Press, 1986): 96.

10. Maxim Bolt, "Waged Entrepreneurs, Policed Informality: Work, the Regulation of Space and the Economy of the Zimbabwean-South African Border," *Africa* 82, no. 1 (2012): 111–130.

11. Forced Migration Studies Program, *Zimbabwean Migration into Southern Africa: New Trends and Responses* (Johannesburg: Witwatersrand University, 2009); Forced Migration Studies Programme & Musina Legal Advice Office, *Special Report: Fact or Fiction? Examining Zimbabwean Cross-Border Migration into South Africa* (Johannesburg: Witwatersrand University, 2009); Tesfalam Araia, *Report on Human Smuggling across the South Africa/Zimbabwe Border* (Johannesburg: Forced Migration Studies Programme, 2009); Human Rights Watch, *Neighbors in Need: Zimbabweans Seeking Refuge in South Africa* (New York: Human Rights Watch, 2008); International Organization for Migration, *Migrants' Needs and Vulnerabilities in the Limpopo Province, Republic of South Africa* (Pretoria: International Organization for Migration, 2009).

12. Rudo Gaidzanwa, *Voting with Their Feet: Migrant Zimbabwean Nurses and Doctors in the Era of Structural Adjustment* (Uppsala: Nordiska Institute, 1999); David A. McDonald, et al., "Guess Who's Coming to Dinner: Migration from Lesotho, Mozambique and Zimbabwe to South Africa," *International Migration Review* 34, no. 3 (2000): 813–841; Maxim Bolt, *Zimbabwe's Migrants and South Africa's Border Farms: The Roots of Impermanence* (Cambridge: Cambridge University Press, 2015).

13. Rebecca Walker and Treasa Galvin, "Labels, Victims, and Insecurity: An Exploration of the Lived Realities of Migrant Women Who Sell Sex in South Africa," *Third World Thematics: A TWQ Journal* 3, no. 2 (2018): 277–292.

14. Kudakwashe Vanyoro, "'This Place is a Bus Stop': Temporalities of Zimbabwean Migrant Men Waiting at a Zimbabwe-South Africa Border Transit Shelter," *Incarceration* 3, no. 1 (2022): 1–17.

15. Belinda Dodson, "Women on the Move: Gender and Cross-border Migration to South Africa from Lesotho, Mozambique and Zimbabwe," in *On Borders: Perspectives on International Migration in Southern Africa,* edited by David A. McDonald (Waterloo: SAMP, 2000); Belinda Dodson, "Porous Borders: Gender and Migration in Southern Africa," *South African Geographical Journal* 82, no. 1 (2000):

40–46; Tanja Bastia, "Intersectionality, Migration and Development," *Progress in Development Studies* 14, no. 3 (2014): 237–248; Patience Mutopo, "Women Trading in Food across the Zimbabwe-South Africa Border: Experiences and Strategies," *Gender & Development* 18, no. 3 (2010): 465–477.

16. Doris Buss, et al., "Gender and Artisanal and Small-Scale Mining in Central and East Africa: Barriers and Benefits," GrOW Working Paper Series, Institute for the Study of International Development, McGill University, 2017.

17. Francis Musoni, *Border Jumping and Migration Control in Southern Africa* (Bloomington: Indiana University Press, 2020).

18. National Archives of Zimbabwe [NAZ] S1226, Statement by Austin Makawa Regarding Illegal Emigration of Natives, 21 March 1939.

19. Dodson, "Women on the Move."

20. John O. Oucho, "Cross-border Migration and Regional Initiatives in Managing Migration in Southern Africa," in *Migration in South and Southern Africa: Dynamics and Determinants,* eds. Pieter Kok, et al. (Pretoria: HSRC, 2006); Jonathan Crush, "Migrations Past: An Historical Overview of Cross-Border Movement in Southern Africa," in *On Borders: Perspectives on International Migration in Southern Africa,* ed. David A. McDonald (Waterloo: SAMP, 2000); Jonathan Klaaren and Jay Ramji, "Inside Illegality: Migration Policing in South Africa after Apartheid," *Africa Today* 48, no. 3 (2001): 35–47; Anthony Minaar and Mike Hough, *Who Goes There?: Perspectives on Clandestine Migration and Illegal Aliens in Southern Africa* (Pretoria: HSRC, 1996); Jean Pierre Misago, Loren Landau, and Tamlyn Monson, *Towards Tolerance, Law, and Dignity: Addressing Violence against Foreign Nationals in South Africa* (Arcadia: IOM, 2009).

21. Lovemore Zinyama, "Who, What, When, and Why: Cross-border Movement from Zimbabwe to South Africa," in *On Borders: Perspectives on International Migration in Southern Africa,* ed. David A. McDonald (Ontario: SAMP, 2000), 72.

22. According to Zimbabwe's Ministry of Public Service Labour and Social Welfare, the number of people retrenched increased from about 1,200 in 1991 to about 14,000 in 1993. See Central Statistical Office, *Labour Statistics* (Harare: Government of Zimbabwe, 2004).

23. Mate, "Looking for Money"; Dzawanda, "Livelihood Outcomes."

24. Dzawanda, "Livelihood Outcomes."

25. Human Rights Watch, *'Bullets for Each of You': State-Sponsored Violence Since Zimbabwe's March 29 Elections* (New York: Human Rights Watch, 2008); Human Rights Watch, *Neighbors in Need.*

26. "Response by Government of Zimbabwe to the Report by the UN Special Envoy on Operation Murambatsvina/Restore Order," *The Herald* (Harare), 17 August 2005.

27. Anna K. Tibaijuka, "Report of the Fact-Finding Mission to Zimbabwe to Assess the Scope and Impact of Operation Murambatsvina," UN-Habitat, 2005.

28. Bolt, *Roots of Impermanence*; Blair Rutherford, "The Uneasy Ties of Working and Belonging: The Changing Situation for Undocumented Zimbabwean Migrants in Northern South Africa," *Ethnic and Racial Studies* 34, no. 8 (2011): 1303–1319.

29. Janet Roitman, *Fiscal Disobedience: An Anthropology of Economic Regulation in Central Africa* (Princeton: Princeton University Press, 2005), 21.

30. Hussein Solomon, *Of Myths and Migration: Illegal Immigration into South Africa* (Pretoria: University of South Africa, 2003); Francis B. Nyamnjoh, *Insiders and Outsiders: Citizenship and Xenophobia in Contemporary Southern Africa* (Dakar: CODESRIA Books, 2006); Minaar and Hough, *Who Goes There?*

31. Zinyama, "Cross-border Movement."

32. David McDonald, et al., "Guess Who's Coming for Dinner: Migration from Lesotho, Mozambique and Zimbabwe to South Africa," *International Migration Review* 34, no. 3 (2000): 813–841.

33. All testimonials and interviews in this chapter have been anonymized. Returning Migrants' Group Discussion with author, IOM offices, Beitbridge, 17 May 2010. As of May 2010, the minimum fee for a passport application in Zimbabwe was US$143. Considering that the majority of civil servants earned US$100 per month, passport fees were unreachable for most people. This fee was revised downward to US$50 toward the end of 2010.

34. Returning Migrants' Group Discussion.

35. Ibid.

36. Ibid.

37. Ibid.

38. Griffiths, "Permeable Boundaries," 68.

39. Information obtained through an author interview with Mulamuli Mbedzi, Rukange Village, Beitbridge, 26 May 2010, as well as an informal conversation with patrons at MaSibanda's Shebeen, Beitbridge Town, on 15 May 2010. For similar observations, see International Organization for Migration, *Migrants' Needs and Vulnerabilities in the Limpopo Province, Republic of South Africa* (Pretoria: International Organization for Migration, 2009).

40. Ben Makato (pseudonym), interview with author, Nottingham Estate, Beitbridge, 27 June 2010. Although Makato was formally employed at Nottingham Estates (on the Zimbabwean side of the border), he supplemented his income by helping people to cross the border through unofficial channels.

41. France Maphosa, "Transnationalism and Undocumented Migration Between Rural Zimbabwe and South Africa," in *Zimbabwe's Exodus: Crisis, Migration, Survival,* eds. Jonathan Crush, and Daniel Tevera (Cape Town: SAMP, 2010), 346–360.

42. *State vs. Natalie Alice Fenn Peacock and Tristan John Peacock*, Bulawayo Provincial High Court, 15 May 2008.

43. *State vs. Abigail Ndlovu*, Beitbridge Magistrates' Court, 6 February 2006.

44. *State vs. Lisa Dube*, Beitbridge Magistrates' Court, 17 March 2010.

45. Returning Migrants' Group Discussion.

46. Information obtained through an informal conversation with patrons at MaSibanda's Shebeen, Beitbridge Town, on 15 May 2010.

47. Information obtained from Returning Migrants' Group Discussion with author, IOM offices, Beitbridge, 17 May 2010; author interview with Kate Ndou (pseudonym), IOM Reception Center, Beitbridge, 14 May 2010; informal conversation with patrons at MaSibanda's Shebeen, Beitbridge Town, on 15 May 2010.

48. NAZ S1226, Statement by Austin Makawa Regarding Illegal Emigration of Natives, 21 March 1939.

49. NAZ AOH/46, Amon Makufa Mlambo, interview with Dawson Munjeri, Rhodesdale, 13 December 1978.

50. International Organization for Migration, *Migrants' Needs,* 4.

51. See also the chapter by Mushonga and Cawood in this volume for a discussion of this in the context of the Lesotho-South Africa border and its informal crossers.

52. Ibid, 25–26.

53. Kate Ndou (pseudonym), interview with author, IOM Reception Center, Beitbridge, 14 May 2010.

54. Phyllis Kachere, "Raped by Omaguma-Guma: Heavy Price to Pay for Zimbabwean Women Crossing Border Illegally," *The Sunday Mail* (Harare), 6–12 June 2010.

55. Information obtained through attending a workshop on "Health and Safe Migration" organized by the International Organization for Migration's Beitbridge Office at Chikwarakwara Business Center (in Beitbridge) on 29 June 2010.

BIBLIOGRAPHY

Araia, Tesfalam. *Report on Human Smuggling across the South Africa/Zimbabwe Border*. Johannesburg: Forced Migration Studies Programme, 2009.

Barnes, Teresa. "Virgin Territory? Travel and Migration by African Women in Twentieth-Century Southern Africa." In *Women in African Colonial Histories*, edited by Jean Allman, Susan Geiger, and Nakanyike Musisis, 164–190. Bloomington: Indiana University Press, 2002.

Bastia, Tanja. "Intersectionality, Migration and Development." *Progress in Development Studies* 14, no. 3 (2014): 237–248.

Bolt, Maxim. *Zimbabwe's Migrants and South Africa's Border Farms: The Roots of Impermanence*. Cambridge: Cambridge University Press, 2015.

Bolt, Maxim. "Waged Entrepreneurs, Policed Informality: Work, the Regulation of Space and the Economy of the Zimbabwean-South African Border." *Africa* 82, no. 1 (2012): 111–130.

Buss, Doris, et al. "Gender and Artisanal and Small-Scale Mining in Central and East Africa: Barriers and Benefits." GrOW Working Paper Series. Montreal: Institute for the Study of International Development, McGill University, 2017.

Central Statistical Office. *Labour Statistics*. Harare: Government of Zimbabwe, 2004.

Crush, Jonathan. "Migrations Past: An Historical Overview of Cross-Border Movement in Southern Africa." In *On Borders: Perspectives on International Migration in Southern Africa,* edited by David A. McDonald, 12–24. Waterloo: SAMP, 2000.

Crush, Jonathan. "The Discourse and Dimensions of Irregularity in Post-apartheid South Africa." *International Migration* 37, no. 1 (1999): 125–151.

Dodson, Belinda. "Women on the Move: Gender and Cross-Border Migration to South Africa from Lesotho, Mozambique and Zimbabwe." in *On Borders:*

Perspectives on International Migration in Southern Africa, edited by David A. McDonald, 199–150. Waterloo: SAMP, 2000.

Dodson, Belinda. "Porous Borders: Gender and Migration in Southern Africa." *South African Geographical Journal* 82, no. 1 (2000): 40–46.

Dzawanda, B., M.D. Nicolau, M. Matsa, and W. Kusena. "Livelihood Outcomes of Informal Cross Border Traders Prior to the Rise of the Virtual Cash Economy in Gweru, Zimbabwe." *Journal of Borderlands Studies* 38, no. 1 (2023): 75–94.

Fadahunsi, Akin, and Peter Rosa. "Entrepreneurship and Illegality: Insights from the Nigerian Cross-border Trade." *Journal of Business Venturing* 17 (2002): 397–429.

Gaidzanwa, Rudo. *Voting with Their Feet: Migrant Zimbabwean Nurses and Doctors in the Era of Structural Adjustment.* Uppsala: Nordiska Institute, 1999.

Griffiths, Ieuan. "Permeable Boundaries in Africa," in *African Boundaries: Barriers, Conduits and Opportunities*, edited by Paul Nugent and Anthony Asiwaju, 68–83. New York: Pinter, 1996.

Fadahunsi, Akin, and Peter Rosa. "Entrepreneurship and Illegality: Insights from the Nigerian Cross-border Trade." *Journal of Business Venturing* 17 (2002): 397–429.

Forced Migration Studies Program. *Zimbabwean Migration into Southern Africa: New Trends and Responses*. Johannesburg: Witwatersrand University, 2009.

Forced Migration Studies Programme & Musina Legal Advice Office. *Special Report: Fact or Fiction? Examining Zimbabwean Cross-Border Migration into South Africa*. Johannesburg: Witwatersrand University, 2009.

Human Rights Watch. *'Bullets for Each of You': State-Sponsored Violence Since Zimbabwe's March 29 Elections.* New York: Human Rights Watch, 2008.

Human Rights Watch. *Neighbors in Need: Zimbabweans Seeking Refuge in South Africa.* New York: Human Rights Watch, 2008.

International Organization for Migration. *Migrants' Needs and Vulnerabilities in the Limpopo Province, Republic of South Africa*. Pretoria: International Organization for Migration, 2009.

Klaaren, Jonathan, and Jay Ramji. "Inside Illegality: Migration Policing in South Africa after Apartheid." *Africa Today* 48, no. 3 (2001): 35–47.

Maphosa, France. "Transnationalism and Undocumented Migration Between Rural Zimbabwe and South Africa." In *Zimbabwe's Exodus: Crisis, Migration, Survival,* edited by Jonathan Crush and Daniel Tevera, 346–360. Cape Town: SAMP, 2010.

Mate, Rekopantswe. "'Looking for Money': Hustling, Youth Survival Strategies and Schizoid Subjectivities in Zimbabwe's Crisis." *African Identities* (2021): 1–20.

McDonald, David A., et al. "Guess Who's Coming to Dinner: Migration from Lesotho, Mozambique and Zimbabwe to South Africa." *International Migration Review* 34, no. 3 (2000): 813–841.

Minaar, Anthony, and Mike Hough. *Who Goes There?: Perspectives on Clandestine Migration and Illegal Aliens in Southern Africa*. Pretoria: HSRC, 1996.

Misago, Jean Pierre, Loren Landau, and Tamlyn Monson. *Towards Tolerance, Law, and Dignity: Addressing Violence against Foreign Nationals in South Africa.* Arcadia: IOM, 2009.

Musoni, Francis. *Border Jumping and Migration Control in Southern Africa.* Bloomington: Indiana University Press, 2020.

Mutopo, Patience. "Women Trading in Food Across the Zimbabwe–South Africa Border: Experiences and Strategies." *Gender & Development* 18, no. 3 (2010): 465–477.

Newbury, David. "From 'Frontier' to 'Boundary': Some Historical Roots of Peasant Strategies of Survival in Zaire." In *The Crisis in Zaire: Myths and Realities*, edited by Nzongola-Ntalaja, 87–99. New Jersey: Africa World Press, 1986.

Nyamnjoh, Francis B. *Insiders and Outsiders: Citizenship and Xenophobia in Contemporary Southern Africa.* Dakar: CODESRIA Books, 2006.

Nyamunda, Tinashe. "Cross-Border Couriers as Symbols of Regional Grievance? The Malayitsha Remittance System in Matabeleland, Zimbabwe." *African Diaspora* 7, no. 1 (2014): 38–62.

Oucho, John O. "Cross-border Migration and Regional Initiatives in Managing Migration in Southern Africa." In *Migration in South and Southern Africa: Dynamics and Determinants,* edited by Pieter Kok, et al., 47–70. Pretoria: HSRC, 2006.

Roitman, Janet. *Fiscal Disobedience: An Anthropology of Economic Regulation in Central Africa.* Princeton: Princeton University Press, 2005.

Rutherford, Blair. "The Politics of Boundaries: The Shifting Terrain of Belonging for Zimbabweans in a South African Border Zone." *African Diaspora* 4, no. 2 (2011): 207–229.

Rutherford, Blair. "The Uneasy Ties of Working and Belonging: The Changing Situation for Undocumented Zimbabwean Migrants in Northern South Africa." *Ethnic and Racial Studies* 34, no. 8 (2011): 1303–1319.

Solomon, Hussein. *Of Myths and Migration: Illegal Immigration into South Africa.* Pretoria: University of South Africa, 2003.

Tibaijuka, Anna Kajumulo. "Report of the Fact-Finding Mission to Zimbabwe to Assess the Scope and Impact of Operation Murambatsvina." UN-Habitat, 2005.

Vanyoro, Kudakwashe. "'This Place is a Bus Stop': Temporalities of Zimbabwean Migrant Men Waiting at a Zimbabwe-South Africa Border Transit Shelter," *Incarceration* 3, no. 1 (2022): 1–17.

Walker, Rebecca, and Treasa Galvin. "Labels, Victims, and Insecurity: An Exploration of the Lived Realities of Migrant Women who Sell Sex in South Africa." *Third World Thematics: A TWQ Journal* 3, no. 2 (2018): 277–292.

Waller, Lyndith. *No. 19: Irregular Migration to South Africa During the First Ten Years of Democracy.* Waterloo: SAMP Migration Policy Brief, 2006.

Zinyama, Lovemore. "Who, What, When, and Why: Cross-border Movement from Zimbabwe to South Africa," in *On Borders: Perspectives on International Migration in Southern Africa,* edited by David A. McDonald. Ontario: SAMP, 2000.

Chapter 12

Of *Paqama Gates* and *Paqama Scouts*

The Innerworkings of Regulated Illegal and Irregular Border Crossing between Lesotho and South Africa

Chitja Twala and Grey Magaiza

Despite the existence of a well-defined border demarcation, official border crossing points, and border officials tasked with regulating migration between Lesotho and South Africa, instances of illegal and irregular border crossing remain common. This has given rise to a flourishing market for illegal border crossing facilitators, commonly known as *paqama scouts*, who operate at illegal and unregulated border crossing points between the two countries. Borders can be understood as contradictory constructions that embody a blend of continuity and discreteness. Discreteness refers to the tangible physicality of borders, while their continuity undermines their objective identification. Borders may also be viewed as zones of change, conflict, or collaboration; lawlessness, ungovernability, or ambiguity. Borderlands serve not only as everyday spaces for cross-border cooperation, trade, and cultural engagement but also as reflections of broader processes of social and identity-making transformation. This chapter examines the roles of paqama scouts to better explain, problematize, and understand illegal and irregular crossing between these two countries. The chapter focuses on the combination of their role and the use of *paqama gates* to amplify cross-border economic interests.

Furthermore, this chapter acknowledges that the functions and roles of boundaries are constantly evolving in response to the socio-political context of those who use them. To illustrate the complex and dynamic interactions of the paqama scouts in regulating illegal and irregular border crossings between Lesotho and South Africa, cross-border activities in these countries are examined. We argue that, like many of South Africa's neighbors, illegal border crossing initiatives at certain borders are and were driven by individuals who saw economic opportunities in such activities. Lesotho's economic dependence on South Africa, despite being recognized internationally as a sovereign state, contributes to this situation.

METHODOLOGICAL CONSIDERATIONS

Lessons will emerge of how activities are undertaken at the illegal crossings, also called *paqama gates*, facilitated by paqama scouts on both sides of the Lesotho-South Africa borders. These lessons will show how the engagements of paqama scouts in illegal border crossing have become normative practice with little adherence to the regulations and policies governing the crossing of the borders. This lacuna remains despite having some scholarly works on the history of illegal crossings on these borders.

Drawing upon secondary sources, individual interviews conducted with the paqama scouts, and those using their services, this chapter explores the place of the paqama gates and paqama scouts in the historiography of borderland studies. For this chapter, reference to the gates should not be construed within the formalized border gates imagery controlled by the border patrols and officials, but rather as illegal/informal cross points, hence, called the *paqama gates*.

Currently, there is a well-established literature stream on the relationship between Lesotho and South Africa's cross-border activities, with cross-border stock theft having recently received a significant amount of scholarly attention.[1] To date, there has been no academic research conducted on the specific activities carried out by the paqama scouts in the paqama gates in the Lesotho-South African borderlands. This is noteworthy because Lesotho, being a total enclave within South Africa, has only one neighboring country. In a similar vein to other countries neighboring South Africa, the process of crossing borders has undergone a significant shift since the implementation of COVID-19 restrictions. This study used oral interviews to document lived experiences and histories of border communities. The spatial enactment of the study covered border points such as Butha-Buthe/Qwaqwa in the north, along the Mohokare/Caledon River boundary, and down through Quthing/Sterkspruit all the way to Qacha's Nek/Matatiele in South Africa's Eastern Cape Province.

To pursue the arguments presented in the chapter, the two main concepts, namely, *paqama gates* and *paqama scouts*, are defined. The *paqama* phenomenon broadly connotes illegal crossings at the border between Lesotho and South Africa. Our efforts to document the origin of the term were unsuccessful, but it remains broadly used. This chapter will focus on the vernacular term *paqama* to describe the movement across the border. In this context, *paqama*, which in literal Sesotho translation means the act of going under a fence, refers to illegal crossings made by travelers, such as crawling under fences or crossing rivers. Even in areas where fence-crossing is not involved, however, such crossings are still referred to as *paqama*.[2]

The chapter considers how historical, transnational processes of "legalized" illegal border crossings have affected women who fell victim to the paqama scouts. It explores how historical, geopolitical, and economic forces have structured peoples' movement across this border, largely pulling Basotho men into South Africa in migratory systems of wage labor and pushing women to cross "illegally," thereby making them more likely to fall victim to unscrupulous paqama scouts.

Like other scholars such as Doherty and Doyle, we emphasize that political and environmental factors are key in understanding the borderlands' challenges. We also agree that a full analysis must examine how power has grown in recent years for those in charge of the borders.[3] The chapter further shows how, in a smart, opportunistic move, the paqama scouts take advantage of porous border management that leaves voids into which they step.

This chapter does four key things. Firstly, it critically examines the development of paqama scouts in the context of the "illegal" and "irregular" border crossings known as paqama gates between Lesotho and South Africa. Secondly, it briefly explores the experiences of women who have crossed the border, and the sexual and gender-based violence they have encountered from paqama scouts. Thirdly, it questions the narratives that cause people to forego crossing at official crossing points, thus promoting *paqamaring* (the act of crossing a paqama gate), including the lack of official documents/passports and affordability, as well as the associated risks. Finally, the chapter analyzes the regulation and practices of paqama scouts, as well as the varying reactions they elicit from different actors. By doing all of this, this chapter adds another important piece to our understanding of the intricate and fluid nature of illegal border crossings in the southern African region and the broader African continent.

CONTEXTUALIZING LESOTHO'S BORDERS WITH SOUTH AFRICA AND THEIR PROLIFERATION

Lucey argues that cross-border activities between Lesotho and South Africa are characterized by the proliferation of transnational crime and cross-border cooperation between police agencies. She further explains: "In southern

Africa, such cooperation is of a relatively recent vintage and has developed in the context of a fraught political background."[4] Understanding a contemporary border or border region demands some theoretical and historical contextualization of borders in general. In justifying this, Anderson and O'Dowd note: "Territorial borders both shape and are shaped by what they contain, and what crosses or is prevented from crossing them. . . . Ultimately the significance of borders derives from the importance of territoriality as an organizing principle of political and social life. The functions and meanings of borders have always been inherently ambiguous and contradictory."[5] This statement highlights the complex nature of the border situation between Lesotho and South Africa. As the largest sovereign state enclave in the world, Lesotho's borders with South Africa have contributed to ambiguity and contradictions in both foreign relations and in the obstacles they present for people trying to cross them. The enclave status and current borders of Lesotho are the direct result of a complicated process of nineteenth-century diplomatic negotiations, land dispossessions, and disputes. The borders of today are largely like those of 1868 when Basutoland became a British colony, but there have been ongoing debates over the border demarcation between the two countries in the twentieth and twenty-first centuries.[6]

According to Coplan and Quinlan, the late nineteenth and early twentieth centuries in Lesotho were marked by "competing but overlapping notions of nationalisms" with agreement across chief/commoner, Protestant/Catholic, educated/initiated divides in Basotho society only on the need to defend the borders of the realm.[7] Monyane gets to the core of the economic problems that Lesotho faced, writing: "Lesotho is a small mountainous country which is surrounded by and economically dependent on South Africa. It has an area of 30,355 square kilometres. As its name implies, it is the land of Basotho . . . the unstable and problematic nature of the economic situation in Lesotho has made sustainable development difficult."[8]

Interrogating the enclave status of Lesotho, Pheko also asks a rather rhetoric question: "How did you become a country within a country?"[9] He notes that Lesotho's existence as an enclave within the borders of another country is not something that many people, either scholars or laypeople, have ever questioned: "Although a lot has been written about Lesotho, its history; political economy . . . no one has ever attempted to go beyond its existence. No one has ever attempted to state why Lesotho became a country inside another country."[10]

In large part because of Lesotho's precarious geopolitical situation, the economic dependence that most ordinary Basotho still have on South Africa has led to the exploitation of porous borders by paqama scouts on both sides for illegal cross-border activities. While the scouts, at times are exploiting the vulnerabilities of crossers, this observation also supports the notion that borders can play a significant role in development, as noted by Moyo, Nshimbi, and Laine. They contend that: "Despite attempts by the state to criminalize and illegalize non-state actors, evidence on the ground suggests that these are not only resilient and play an important development impact but are also a permanent feature of the southern Africa region borders."[11]

Theorists focusing on borders have demonstrated that since the 1990s, border controls have proliferated and expanded geographically, moving selectively beyond borderlines into the interior or exterior of national territories.[12] The notion of border "internalization" is arguably a Eurocentric conception, relevant primarily in contrast to the homogenization of national space that took place (albeit unevenly) across Europe by the mid-twentieth century. In contrast, many African states have witnessed persistent intra-state socio-spatial differentiation around ethnicity and economic organization.[13]

BORDERLANDS AND CROSS-BORDER HISTORIOGRAPHIES

Historians and researchers have often focused on managing illegal border crossings, with investigations into the lives and experiences of those crossing being more difficult to conduct. This chapter attempts to redress this imbalance by examining the inner workings and impact of cross-border networks on gender relations, economic spin-offs, and the legalization of illegal crossings. Specifically, this chapter argues for an understanding of these inner workings in the context of the proliferation of borders from the 1990s to the present day. We draw on recent literature on border proliferation and management to historicize the situation. This literature emphasizes the overdetermination of border crossings and the entanglement of state-led territorialization with local resource appropriation. Additionally, we acknowledge the substantial literature on colonialism and colonial boundaries across the continent, which presents diverse and contested viewpoints. Mukisa examines the emergence of colonial boundaries in disrupting the economic, security, political integration, and unity of the Africans. He explains how the Africans post-independence reacted to colonialism. In his publication, he traces the challenges of colonial boundaries back to the 1960s with the establishment of the Organization of African Unity (OAU). According to him, most African leaders, including Kwame Nkrumah, argued against the existence of the boundaries.[14]

While colonial boundaries continue to be problematic in many places, Nshimbi and Fioramonti also note that the African Union (AU) and other regional institutions have also failed to promote the free movement of people, as highlighted by the lack of movement on the Draft Protocol on the facilitation of Movement of Persons in the Southern African Development

Community (SADC).[15] Regional migration in southern Africa has historically been driven by labor migration, which, when regulations and policies are not enforced, leads to cross-border challenges.[16] In taking the argument further, Lipschutz argued that globalization had an impact on fostering global liberalization and economic integration. However, he contends that borderland policies and regulations ultimately impede on the sovereignty of states, thus leading to such regulations being violated.[17]

Although this chapter focuses on Lesotho and South African borders, lessons from other African countries are vital. Aghemelo and Ibhaseblor, with their focus on Cameroon, identified colonial boundaries as a major headache for contemporary African states. These authors note: "The manner in which European nations descended on Africa during the closing years of the nineteenth century in their scramble for territory, was bound to leave a heritage of artificially controlled borderlines, which now demarcate the emergent African states."[18] Rukema and Phophiwa historicize migrant workers between Southern Rhodesia and the Union of South Africa, particularly the Musina border crossing, and note that migrant labor inflows are still originating from the same proximal zones.[19]

In other work on the Zimbabwe-South Africa borderlands, Musoni questions academic theories that label cross-border movements as "illegal," "informal," and "clandestine." Tracing border crossing over a 130-year period, he argues that the various governments of these two states failed to legalize cross-border migration during those years, but instead imposed regulations limiting people's freedom to move between them.[20] The book challenges claims by some scholars that instability since the 1990s is the primary cause of illegal immigration in southern Africa. Empirical evidence shows that many who cross illegally are denied necessary documents such as passports, visas, and permits for the official route. Also, in the book he documents how the strict border control measures imposed by the South African government after 1990 have exacerbated the situation at the border. This has led to many Zimbabweans resorting to illegal border crossings and working with smugglers to evade government control, which has made the crossing more dangerous and expensive. The similarity of these findings to the activities of the paqama scouts described in this chapter is notable.

Little of the scholarship about the Lesotho-South African borderlands has focused on understanding the rationale or significance of the inner workings of the paqama scouts. This is, in part, because a lot of border scholarship has focused on aspects of international borders that target the geopolitical elite, with limited or no interest in the agency and experiences of the common people.[21] Motivated by both humanitarian and financial concerns, these innerworkings deviate from scholarship on borders and international relations. In 2014, Weisfelder wrote an article questioning whether relations between Lesotho and South Africa were "honest and cooperative." Noting that Lesotho's dependence on South Africa made the relationship like that of a "master-servant," he argued: "Regional relationships may differ in their impact upon Lesotho. They may create a mosaic of costs and benefits with differential consequences for economic, political, and social sectors. Indeed, South African leverage over Lesotho may have been augmented because of the predominant role it has gained in regional institutions."[22]

In another publication, Weisfelder points out that Lesotho was in a precarious position because it is surrounded by South Africa, which always dictated terms of subordination due to the complicated history of migrations in southern Africa.[23] This is also complicated by the many factors around identity and belonging where citizens of the neighboring states of Botswana, Lesotho, Namibia, and Swaziland (BLNS) both belong to and are othered in South Africa. This is important because "for Basotho the experience of being part of South Africa culturally and economically, but differentiated politically, has created fungible multiple identities that persist. A horde of undocumented workers and visitors from Lesotho cross the permeable frontier and blend with most Sesotho-speaking ethnic compatriots who reside in the Free State and in the urban areas of South Africa."[24] Thus, studying border crossers is critically important for fully understanding both the worlds that migrants have made in both countries, and for understanding the complications of state-to-state relations, especially on issues regarding the border.

Some studies have focused on the Lesotho-South Africa border, and on the ways in which ordinary Basotho cross. Moremoholo examined trade relations and commerce between Lesotho and KwaZulu-Natal, including the smuggling of dagga, stock theft, and illegal immigration between Lesotho and KwaZulu-Natal. The study cites mountainous terrain, harsh winters, and lack of police patrolling as factors contributing to the ease of border crossings, but the author also notes the South African government's comparative lack of attention to this border. This contrasts with the attention paid, via the construction of an electric fence, to the Zimbabwe-South Africa border.[25]

Mignolo's (de)colonial thinking on the issue of borders is also drawn upon in this chapter, highlighting the role of imaginary borders in limiting people's freedom of movement in an age of transnational power. Despite the emergence of transnational power fields, borders will not disappear, but rather take on new meanings in the age of people, finance, and communication.[26]

Many people in border towns on both the Lesotho and South African sides resort to illegal means of crossing the border. Topographies of crossing vary according to the geography of each area. Rivers, mountains, and even farmland crossed by a fence are the most common typographies that border crossers encounter. Those in dire need of crossing the border use every means available to them. Coplan notes that the flow of commodities, trade, and labor across the Mohokare/Caledon border bridges shows that the river is a political rather than an organic social boundary, and that it is the center of a cross-border way of life.[27] This is the starting point for our discussion of paqama scouts and paqama gates.

UNPACKING THE NOMENCLATURE OF *PAQAMA GATES* AND *PAQAMA SCOUTS*

We begin by presenting the etymology of the concepts *paqama gates* and *paqama scouts*, as well as providing a typology of different types of illegal cross border activities. In an interview with a woman who wished to remain anonymous, the *paqama* concept was explained like this: *"Paqama ke ho tshela nokeng kapa tshela terata, ka lebaka la ho hloka passporoto. Ho re motho a fumane passporoto, o tlameha hopatala chelate e ngata"* (*Paqama* refers to processes of crossing from Lesotho to South Africa or vice versa in a river or fence, by people without passports. For one to get a passport, one needs to pay a lot of money).[28] Illegal border crossings happened not solely because crossers lacked proper documentation, but also because there were restrictions on border gate closing times. This was true in ordinary times, but was additionally a challenge and burden for those needing to cross in recent years due to the extended closures and border restrictions imposed during the COVID-19 pandemic.

Borderlands areas with diverse populations often give rise to new terminologies that reflect the local context and dominant group. For instance, in the Sesotho-speaking Wepener area of the Free State province in South Africa, the intermediaries who facilitate illegal crossings are referred to as *ditsaise* (those who assist with illegal crossings), while those who are assisted to cross are called *ditsiroane* (those assisted with illegal crossings). Teboho Mohatle from Qalabaneng in Lesotho was one of the paqama scouts from the Van Rooyen gate and confirmed that they are called *ditsaise.* He could not, however, provide more information on the meanings or origins of these names.[29]

The etymology of *paqamaring* is embodied in the agency of the paqama scouts at each site informed by their local actions such as crossing a river, navigating border security, or traversing a mountain and understanding where the border is located. At Maseru Bridge, the paqama scouts are called *lirurubele,* which means butterflies, because they carry individuals to and from South Africa, while in Butha-Buthe they were called *lirutle* because they were likened to notorious locusts as they must illegally traverse the mountains. In the southern Lesotho district of Quthing, once you cross the Senqu/Orange River, the first major town is Sterkspruit, which has many isiXhosa speakers, but most residents are Sesotho speakers. The border between Sterkspruit and

Moyeni/Quthing town is located at the Telle River, which helps explain why the name given to the paqama scouts at Telle border gate is "boats" or *dikepe*. Here, the scouts would carry those illegally crossing using old car bonnets as *dikepe* when the water is high.

In the towns of Wepener and Sterkspruit, where Sesotho is spoken, paqama scouts are given Sesotho names. At the Qacha's Nek border gate near the South African town of Matatiele, the notion of *paqama* originates from a torn-down border fence, where historically people would either scramble under or jump over to cross the border, thus describing the original *paqama* which means to crawl under. Naming conventions for the scouts are determined by locality and dominant vernacular. All names for paqama scouts have an element of spatial transcendence, reflecting their role in facilitating mobility and relocation.

The paqama scouts are typically young males aged between 16 and 30, who belong to a social network of young people using illegal border crossing as a means of economic survival. They play a crucial role as intermediaries in the illegal crossing value chain, enabling mobility in both directions between South Africa and Lesotho. As fixers, they assist with illegal crossing at various unofficial and alternative border crossings, giving them credibility and legitimacy.

The paqama gates are the illegal crossing points used by young males to transition between Lesotho and South Africa. These sites become unofficial entry and exit points between the two countries. The term *paqama gate* is used to differentiate these sites from the official border gates used for legal mobility. The behaviors and processes at each paqama gate vary with some used more by people crossing back and forth and others used primarily for smuggling goods into Lesotho from South Africa. In Butha-Buthe, we encountered such a gate. Ironically, this "gate" in Butha-Buthe was within full view of the official border post, and we could see individuals carrying loads of products across the international boundary. When we asked one of the paqama scouts why they use that paqama gate, they stated that "it's easier to use that one when you are carrying a load, because they are protected."[30] When probed about the protection, this gate passed through a protected corridor of both the border authorities and other paqama scouts. Any paqama scout that used this corridor would not be robbed or dispossessed of their goods.

In Lesotho's Berea District, an observation was made where the paqama scouts assisted many individuals to cross the Mohokare/Caledon River to and from South Africa. They knew the crossing points where it was difficult for the cops and soldiers to reach and carefully navigated their movements. Monyane Ramphalile Tsoelipe recalls that they tried to avoid contact with the border officials. He noted that sometimes the paqama scouts did not want to engage the officials for reasons of not wanting to share their hard-earned commission with them.[31] The contested role of paqama scouts presents analytical opportunities to explore the extent to which their operations are legitimized at various border crossings. These opportunities are rooted in the dual perceptions of paqama scouts as both criminals and entrepreneurs, and how these perceptions intersect with the law and their operations.

Interestingly, many of the borders between Lesotho and South Africa are named after people in Lesotho or villages in that country. Kolisang alluded: "Here where the border is located, the village is called Sephapo but our offices are on the side of the South African border. I have noticed that in most cases these border gates are named after the villages. Other examples include Maseru border gate, which is named after the capital city of Lesotho, Maseru. The Van Rooyen's gate is named after a place called Van Rooyen. However, I am not sure as to why is that the case."[32]

Borders are a contested reality, with the flexible transnational movement of goods often easier than the movement of people. The border gates are named after Lesotho villages across the border, often because the border has, since its demarcation in the nineteenth century, been a space that Basotho from Lesotho needed to cross. Ntswaki Kolisang, a police officer at Sephapo's gate, explains that most border gates are named after Lesotho villages across the border.[33] For example, Sephapo gate is located between Zastron and Wepener in the Free State Province and serves Lesotho nationals residing across the border in a village named Ha Sephapo, after Chief Sephapo.

Oral accounts from individuals in the area and those working at the small border gate suggest that stock theft activities are prevalent a few kilometers away from it, keeping border patrols occupied. The topography of the region, with its rugged hills, means that illegal crossings through the paqama gates are commonplace, stretching border patrol resources to such an extent that crossings become "legal" if they occur out of sight of patrols. Kolisang explains:

> As the police, we don't have problems with the people crossing the borders at the border gates. Our main challenge as the police here is when people are illegally crossing through the fence. As the police working on these borders, we are the first line of defense for South Africa to be protected. It is our responsibility to ensure that people coming in and outside the country are legal and also protected. Our problem is that many people are avoiding coming to the border gates and opt for illegal crossing over the border fence. We have good relations with our counterparts in Lesotho. We constantly liaise with each other when there are problems on either side of the borders.[34]

On the challenges confronted at the borders, Kolisang added:

> To curb this challenge of illegal crossing and cutting of the fence, we sometimes do what we call the borderline patrols. If we find people crossing illegally, we make some arrests, and the courts then decide on what to do with them. Sometimes a person could be deported to Lesotho or maybe getting a fine. That is up to the courts. For us is just to make arrests. Our main challenge is that they get bail, fine or deportation but the very same day they come back for illegal crossing again. . . . They tell us that they are coming to South Africa for greener pastures this side. Most of them know that we don't have night shifts and knock-off at 16:00 and that is when they come and illegally cross over the fence. The fact that we don't have a night shift, stock and car theft is rife this side. We sometimes work closely with the soldiers patrolling the borders, however, the thieves use other spots and cut the fence to continue with their illegal activities.[35]

It must be stated from the onset that border crossing without proper documentation is an illegal act and assisting anyone to do so is also an illegal activity. The paqama scouts are very aware of this and one insisted that: "When we do this, we have to avoid the police and the army because if they catch us, we will go to jail or pay a fine or a bribe."[36] This was also confirmed by an interviewee called Cobra who stated: "When the police came, we used to hide ourselves as a means of showing respect to them and the work they were doing. . . . You see, the police and the soldiers are not people we could work with because we are using the *paqama* gates. When they arrive, we must respect them because they are also at work. That is why when they arrive, we just leave."[37]

The paqama scouts operate within an illegal framework and must therefore find ways to avoid engaging law enforcement at the borders. Despite this, they are still perceived by some as legitimate entrepreneurs, informers, or saviors; while for others, they are viewed as criminals and, potentially, a threat, especially to women travelers.

PAQAMA ACTIVITIES AT THE BORDER GATES

As already noted, the Lesotho-South Africa border is a space for many illegal crossings because of the regional political-economy and because of bureaucratic hassles that make legal crossing more difficult. Majikijela and Tati note that irregular migration is driven by a multifaceted and complex set of factors. They explored the structural changes in the participation of African migrants in the labor force of South Africa from 2002 to 2011, arguing that there was a strong increase in the deployment of African immigrants in terms of occupation, employment sector, and income groups.[38] During our research, we found that the COVID-19 pandemic and concomitant restrictions on border crossing had made legal crossings from Lesotho into South Africa difficult. This was compounded by the high cost and limited availability of COVID-19 tests, which many people could not afford or access. Boima reported that border officials demanded higher bribes from people who sought to make a legal crossing but did not or could not fulfill the COVID-19 regulations. Due to these factors, many individuals resorted to using alternative methods of crossing the border.[39]

Furthermore, South Africa closed some of its borders as part of the rationalization of its border management/control processes. This meant people residing close to certain borders could not cross, as they felt that they "can't travel all the way to Maseru Bridge to cross when the supermarkets they need are less than 45 minutes away."[40] These circumstances partially legitimized the *paqama* businesses, resulting in more orderly and regularized services. During our interviews with paqama scouts at border sites, they provided clear rates for assistance in crossing the border, ranging from R30-R150 depending on distance and amount of luggage. This pricing mechanism illustrates the formalization or legitimization of *paqama* activities, despite these actions being part of a subaltern border economy. The widespread awareness of the paqama scouts at all border points further suggests that they have become legitimate actors, albeit illegal ones, in border processes.

Another interviewee from Van Rooyen border gate, Jonas Matete, born in Mafeteng, Lesotho, stated:

> I used to cross the border in and out of the country before COVID-19 started. Since the beginning of COVID-19, things have been tough because we are to submit the COVID results especially when it comes to testing. . . . People are using the illegal gates because they are running away to pay the R300 at the borders when they come to South Africa. That is the reason they go to the 60s. There is a board there indicating the driving speed to be 60, hence, the place is called the 60s. Those operating to assist people to cross illegally are stationed there at the 60s. The locals are also taking ownership of the illegal crossing and making a fortune on that. For example, in some areas one could cross illegally without any assistance but because of these "*paqama* gates" they usually ask for "protection payments" even if their services are not utilized.[41]

The issue of "protection payments" can be seen as a form of extortion, where those involved demand money from individuals who are crossing the border illegally. This creates a market for themselves by exploiting vulnerable individuals. In some cases, "protection payments" are necessary to protect these individuals from being taken advantage of by others who pose as paqama scouts. Motete further notes:

> Another reason why people used the "paqama gates" was because of the expiry of their allocated days to South Africa. When applying for extension of the days, that sometimes takes longer than expected resulting in them using illegal means to cross the boundaries to avoid fines and possible arrests.[42]

During interviews with the paqama scouts at various border points, they perceived their role as "sacrosanct" and essential in helping people cross to South Africa. Although they were aware of the illegality of their activities, they claimed to provide a necessary service to their clients. However, their acts of mobilizing, recruiting, and assisting with illegal movement across the border create an ambiguous status for the paqama scouts. They acknowledge the socio-economic hardships in Lesotho and consider *paqamaring* as facilitating philanthropic and humanitarian actions since individuals who cross the border illegally do so to improve their socio-economic status.

One individual who was *paqamaring* at Qacha's Nek mentioned that she was rushing back to Matatiele for work after attending a funeral. She had been illegally migrating between Lesotho and South Africa for over five years and had an in-depth understanding of the rituals and processes at the paqama gate. These rituals involved following strict orders from the paqama scouts, who monitored the movements of the border control authorities and the pre-arranged vehicles transporting those who crossed illegally between Matatiele and Qacha's Nek.[43]

A resident from Van Rooyen explained that he had three years assisting people to cross the borders illegally. People requesting his services were those without passports or whose passport was invalid, and the majority of those were coming from Lesotho into South Africa. It was striking to note that some of those who crossed illegally to South Africa had proper documents which they used to access pension grants in South Africa, but they were not willing to pay for the services at the border gates, which they claimed were too expensive.[44] Minnaar and Hough also confirmed that at times South African pensions were paid to some illegal border crossers after they had disguised in various ways to appear as South African citizens.[45]

Residents of Tsupaneng, Manganeng, Ditshweneng, Ha Mpholeng, and Ha Ramohapi—all communities that are near to the Mafeteng-Wepener border crossing—frequently cross illegally next to the official Van Rooyen gate into South Africa. The paqama scouts operating at these illegal gates have a symbiotic relationship with taxi drivers in the area. Taxi drivers drop commuters off next to the paqama gate for illegal crossing and pick up those transiting the opposite way across the border. One paqama scout operating from the Van Rooyen gate noted that their "clients" come to a location called the 60s in Wepener for assistance in crossing illegally. According to the scout, the primary challenge they face is the risk of arrest, and they must always evade soldiers. This was not only due to the risk of being arrested, but also because "sometimes we assist people to cross over whom are destined in committing crime. Some of them carry weapons."[46]

The paqama scouts legitimized themselves and built trust among their clients by constantly engaging in everyday crossing practices. They loitered around at the exit points of formally recognized border gates, making themselves visible through gestures and body language, including the use of sign language to capture the attention of potential clients. At Telle Bridge, paqama scouts would nod in the direction of South Africa. If a possible client nodded in affirmation, then they would move in the direction of the client and whisper to indicate their availability and the exact spot where they could be met. One of the paqama scouts near the bridge mentioned that: "We also know our clients, and we can see them even before they formally approach us."[47] It seems like there is a reciprocal understanding between the paqama scouts and the clients that use their services. One individual who has been using the paqama scouts to shop and transact business in South Africa felt that she had a good relationship with the scouts: "The honesty and professional service I always get from them makes me to use them all the time. . . . I have heard of horrible stories of rape and theft but not in this area."[48]

Motete Ncheche affirmed the status of individuals like paqama scouts when indicating that although they might be viewed as illegal, they save lives and, to some extent, create opportunities to redress the past legacies of colonial and apartheid inequalities.[49] The honest engagement and adherence to the cross-border regulations by the paqama scouts could sound ironic, but they were not feeding off the desperation of others. They perceived their role as creating avenues of escape by enabling individuals to cross into South Africa for much-needed goods and services that they could not otherwise access through formal procedures. This was confirmed by Moeketsi Matekane: "Some of the people when they want to cross. Some they [are] using what we call *paqama*, you understand. If they don't have a passport, they are just using *paqama* to enter to that side. And even those people of Lesotho, when they came here in South Africa, some they don't go to the border gate they just doing trespasses to the mountains and come to this side."[50] Each honest encounter with a paqama scout increased their value as service providers, further embedding their formalization and building trust for this "illegal ecosystem."

The paqama scouts find it difficult to adhere to cross-border regulations, despite their attempts to work with the authorities, since they are operating in the shadows of formal procedures. They have set up informal structures to identify intruders in their business venture. Such people are quickly weeded out. One paqama scout at Butha-Buthe mentioned that, "we know each other here, we even have a book of all the people operating here and we are about 150 of us."[51] He further stated that they have a savings club for all the paqama scouts in case they are arrested and need money for bail or bribing the police officers. The ability of the paqama scouts to organize was not just at Butha-Buthe but at almost all the border sites that were researched. Another paqama scouts went further, stating that, "we don't tolerate criminal behaviour here, if you steal from our clients, we will find you. When we catch you, you will pay back the customer and pay a fine to us and of course we will beat you as well."[52]

The paqama scouts legitimize themselves as fixers through their ability to self-organize and self-regulate, increasing their social currency and forming a tight-knit community that looks out for each other and cares for the safety of those for whom they facilitate crossings. An informal intelligence system exists at each crossing site, allowing scouts to be aware of who has crossed and when. By weeding out criminal elements that may encroach on their business, they maintain a crime-free operation and attract repeat customers. This high level of networking and social capital contributes to the legitimacy of the *paqama* business.

While they work to weed out criminality among themselves, they also sometimes work with the police and intelligence services to assist with information regarding occurrences on the *paqama* routes. A police officer stated: "We actually rely on them for information regarding suspicious goods and people coming into Lesotho."[53] The same was also confirmed by the paqama scouts who stated that "we come across things on our routes, [and] we don't want criminals to take over our routes and we lose our livelihood . . . [so] we inform the police."[54] An intelligence officer at one of the border crossings mentioned that they use the paqama scouts as "informal scouts to note who comes in and out of Lesotho."[55]

The paqama scouts play multiple roles that consolidate their positionality as key allies in the fight against cross-border crime. Despite their engagement in illegal cross-border activities, they seek to establish themselves as law-abiding individuals and entities that do not tolerate other forms of criminal activities in their operational space. Many students from Lesotho cross the border daily into South Africa to attend school, especially in the Free State Province. Phepheng Phepheng, who transports these learners from Mafeteng to Wepener, explained:

> Our first challenge is that we are battling to get passports. The second one is that of COVID-19. We don't have money for tests. In Lesotho we are unemployed and don't have money. The border officials know that I am transporting school kids. I have been doing this job for the past two years. At the border gates a payment of R300 is needed. There is also a small gate called Tsupane which is the officially non-functional. The soldiers continuously harass those people and arrest them. We know that it is an offence to cross without a valid stamped passport and without a valid COVID-19 certificate.[56]

While students could cross legally with special permits given to those enrolled in South African schools, individuals like Phepheng who transported them had to go through the process of producing valid permits and stamping passports every time they crossed the border. This complicated the transportation, and some drivers even resorted to offering bribes to avoid harsh penalties.

Some users of the paqama gates previously used the formally established border gates, such as migrant laborers in South Africa who visited their families in Lesotho monthly. However, due to COVID-19 restrictions and the requirement for vaccination certificates, crossing the borders became a financial burden. The Telle Bridge border post was closed for over a year due to the COVID-19 restrictions. For people from the Telle area in Quthing District, Lesotho, their nearest border post was Van Rooyen's Gate near Mafeteng. Crossing there would not have given people from Telle access to their normal cross-border town of Sterkspruit because of the long distances involved. Therefore, people from the Telle area during COVID relied on the *dikepe* (the local name for paqama scouts) to help them cross the usually shallow Telle River so that people could continue to do business in the same places, thereby helping to economically sustain Sterkspruit in South Africa. This was only possible because the Lesotho residents were willing and able to cross illegally.

THE RISKS ASSOCIATED WITH ILLEGAL CROSSING THROUGH *PAQAMA*

Moeketsi Matekane alluded that if there was free movement between these two countries, that would put an end to the issue of *paqamering*. This could minimize the risks of people being raped, assaulted, and killed when they were in the "grey zone" of legality trying to cross between Lesotho and South Africa. He argued that people migrate to South Africa because of poverty and starvation in Lesotho, something that could be addressed by the two governments.[57]

Although the use of the paqama gates and the services of the paqama scouts tends to be an alternative for those without proper documentation, there are challenges accompanying this. Despite the efforts of paqama scouts to create an anti-crime network to protect their business, there are plenty of horror stories about crimes against those crossing illegally. In Maseru, an interviewee stated that "I was almost left in the middle of nowhere after the fare was unilaterally changed and I did not have the new fare."[58] The paqama scouts in Maseru have been known to increase their fares mid-journey for people illegally crossing the border, and reports suggest that some individuals were physically assaulted for not paying the new fees. Mushonga's chapter in this volume provides a detailed account of the sexual violence experienced by many women at the hands of the paqama scouts.

During the festive season, the risk of potential loss of life increases due to increased rainfall in the summer season when rivers like the Telle and Mohokare, which are major border crossings between Lesotho and South Africa, are overflowing with a swift current. Additionally, border authorities are more vigilant, and surveillance is heightened during this time. As a result, the paqama scouts and their clients are left with no option but to use the river as a crossing point when land crossings are inaccessible due to the presence of border security, including police and soldiers. The paqama scouts have witnessed their colleagues "drowning and some clients too . . . it's really painful because some think they can defeat the river, but the river can become angry and powerful."[59]

The scouts and their clients both, further, pointed out that they sometimes suffer physical abuse at the hands of border authorities. One paqama scout in Qacha's Nek mentioned how if they were caught by Defence Force patrols, "the soldiers would make them sit in the sun for hours and if they complain, they are beaten up."[60] The soldiers are mostly feared because they can be aggressive and may cause injuries. In Butha-Buthe, a scout described how "the soldiers made a *sjambok* from thin tree branches and asked me to lie down. They beat me up because they thought I was stealing livestock. It was so painful because I have never stolen livestock."[61] Borders are known to be zones of criminal activity, including livestock theft. Despite the efforts made by the paqama scouts to cooperate with the authorities, they still run the risk of being suspected of livestock rustling. The risks associated with illegal border crossings range from fare changes to physical and sexual violence, and even death. The fact that these crossings take place in an extra-legal setting means that for both the paqama scouts and their clients, there is a lot of risk involved. While aspects of this system have become regularized, the fact that crossings are, by definition, illegal, means that there will likely always be stories of tragedy and abuse that occur alongside the regularized aspects of the crossings.

CONCLUSION

Although limited historical inquiry has been conducted on the investigation of the paqama gates and paqama scouts, as demonstrated in this chapter, the act of illegal border crossing has a long-standing history, which has been exacerbated by the COVID-19 pandemic. Hearing and understanding the narratives surrounding the paqama scouts, and their clients at the border are crucial for understanding the mechanics of such crossings. The institutionalization of such practices is not unique to the Lesotho and South Africa border, but also occurs on the US-Mexico border with *coyotes*, and the Zimbabwe and South

Africa border with the *gumba kumba* (see chapters in this volume by Musoni and Tshabalala for more discussion of the Zimbabwe-South Africa border). Highlighting the institutionalization of paqama scouts and paqama gates on the Lesotho and South Africa border, and the lengths to which all involved in this system will go to continue facilitating crossings despite legal obstacles and security force interventions, shows how border policy must respond in a more humane manner to the scope and scale of the problems that militarization, securitization, and bureaucratization have all helped create. The illegal crossings that the poorest individuals and communities in society are forced to make are survival strategies for these people, for whom the border is simply one more impediment to surmount in their quest to live healthy, happy, and prosperous lives.

NOTES

1. John Aerni-Flessner, Chitja Twala, Munyaradzi Mushonga, and Grey Magaiza, "A Transnational History of Stock Theft on the Lesotho-South Africa Border, Nineteenth Century to 1994," *South African Historical Journal* 73, no. 4 (2021): 903–926; Gary Kynoch and Theresa Ulicki, "'It is Like the Time of Lifaqane': The Impact of Stock Theft and Violence in Southern Lesotho," *Journal of Contemporary African Studies* 18, no. 2 (2000): 179–206; Gary Kynoch, Theresa Ulicki, Tsepang Cekwane, Booi Mohapi, and Mampolokeng Mohapi, Ntsoaki Phakisi, and Palesa Seithleko, "Cross-Border Raiding and Community Conflict in the Lesotho-South Africa Border Zone," *Southern African Migration Programme* 21 (2001): i–44; Selloane Khoabane and Phillip A. Black, "The Effect of Livestock Theft on Household Poverty in Developing Countries: The Case of Lesotho," *A Working Paper of the Department of Economics and the Bureau for Economic Research at the University of Stellenbosch: Stellenbosch Economic Working Papers*, 2/09 (2009); Selloane Khoabane and Phillip Black, "On the Economic Effects of Livestock Theft in Lesotho: An Asset-Based Approach," *Journal of Development and Agricultural Economics* 4, no. 5 (2012): 142–146.
2. For more information on this, see Chitja Twala, "Differentiations and Similarities in the Nomenclature of '*Paqama* Gates' Along the Lesotho-South Africa Border," Paper presented at the University of Southern Queensland College Research Seminar Series, 29 March 2022.
3. Brian Doherty and Timothy Doyle, "Beyond Borders: Transnational Politics, Social Movements and Modern Environmentalism," *Environmental Politics* 15, no. 5 (2006): 697–712.
4. Amanda Lucey, "Cross-Border Policing: Lesotho and South Africa," in *Cooperation and Accountability in the Cross-Border Policing of Southern Africa*, eds. Sean Tait and Elrena van der Spy (Cape Town: African Policing Civilian Oversight Forum, 2010), 53–68.

5. James Anderson and Liam O'Dowd, "Borders, Border Regions and Territoriality: Contradictory Meanings, Changing Significance," *Regional Studies* 33, no. 7 (1999): 594.

6. See also the chapters in this volume by Aerni-Flessner and Mushonga and Cawood.

7. David Coplan and Timothy Quinlan, "A Chief by the People: Nation versus State in Lesotho," *Africa: Journal of the International African Institute* 67, no. 1 (1997): 32.

8. Chelete Monyane, "Lesotho's Transition to Democratic Rule: An Era of 'Fragile' Democracy" (MA thesis, University of KwaZulu-Natal, 2005), 1–2.

9. Kutloano Pheko, "The Birth and the Existence of Lesotho: A Diplomatic Lesson" (MA Thesis, University of Malta, 2017), iii.

10. Ibid, 2.

11. Inocent Moyo, Christopher C. Nshimbi, and Jussi P. Laine, "Implications of the Micro Processes of Encounter and Contest in Borders," in *Borders, Sociocultural Encounters and Contestations: Southern African Experiences in Global View*, eds. Christopher C. Nshimbi, Inocent Moyo, and Jussi P. Laine (London: Routledge, 2020), 141.

12. See Etienne Balibar, *Politics and the Other Scene* (London and New York: Verso, 2002); Corey Johnson, Reece Jones, Anssi Paasi, Louise Amoore, Alison Mountz, Mark Salter, and Chris Rumford, "Interventions on Rethinking 'The Border' in Border Studies," *Political Geography* 30, no. 1 (2011): 61–68; Matthew Longo, *The Politics of Borders: Sovereignty, Security, and the Citizen after 9/11* (Cambridge: Cambridge University Press, 2018).

13. The majority of Lesotho's households are constrained with respect to the opportunities by which they could satisfy their consumption wants. For growing numbers of households, this left only temporary or permanent migration to South Africa for employment as the least advantageous way to obtain the necessary income for survival. For more, see John Bardill and James Cobbe, *Lesotho: Dilemmas of Dependence in Southern Africa* (Boulder: Westview Press, 1985), 45.

14. Richard S. Mukisa, "Toward a Peaceful Resolution of Africa's Colonial Boundaries," *International Relations and Human Rights* 44, no. 1 (1997): 7.

15. Christopher C. Nshimbi and Lorenzo Fioramonti, *A Region Without Borders? Policy Frameworks for Regional Labour Migrations Towards South Africa* (Johannesburg: African Centre for Migration & Society, 2013), 41–43.

16. *Ibid.*

17. Ronnie D. Lipschutz, "Crossing Borders: Global Civil Society and the Reconfiguration of Transnational Political Space," *GeoJournal* 52, no. 1 (2000): 17.

18. Austin T. Aghemelo and Solomon Ibhasebhor, "Colonialism as a Source of Boundary Dispute and Conflict Among African States: The World Court Judgement on the Bakassi Peninsula and its Implications for Nigeria," *Journal of Social Sciences* 13, no. 3 (2006): 177.

19. Joseph R. Rukema and Nedson Phophiwa, "Cross Border Mobility Between Zimbabwe and South Africa: Historical and Contemporary Trajectories of Development in Musina, South Africa," *Mankind Quarterly* 61, no. 2 (2020): 273–292.

20. Francis Musoni, *Border Jumping and Migration Control in Southern Africa* (Bloomington: Indiana University Press, 2020).

21. Maano Ramutsindela, "Placing Subnational Borders in Border Studies," *South African Geographical Journal* 101, no. 3 (2019): 349–356.

22. Richard Weisfelder, "Lesotho's Interactions with South Africa and Regional Organizations in Southern Africa," *South African Journal of International Affairs* 21, no. 1 (2014): 109–110.

23. Richard Weisfelder, "Why Lesotho Needs a Distinctive Diplomatic Strategy," *Africa Insight* 27, no. 1 (1997): 32–43.

24. Weisfelder, "Lesotho's Interactions," 110.

25. Manthatisi C. Moremoholo, "The Nature of Cross Border Linkages Between Lesotho and KwaZulu-Natal and Aspects of Basotho Migrants in Pietermaritzburg" (MA thesis, University of Natal, Pietermaritzburg, 1998), 82.

26. For more, see Walter D. Mignolo, "Geopolitics of Sensing and Knowing: On (De)Coloniality, Border Thinking and Epistemic Disobedience," *Postcolonial Studies, Latin America and the Politics of Knowledge* 14, no. 3 (2011): 273–283; Walter D. Mignolo, "Introduction: Coloniality of Power and De-Colonial Thinking," *Cultural Studies* 21, no. 2/3 (2007): 155–167.

27. David Coplan, "A River Runs Through It: The Meaning of the Lesotho-Free State Border," *African Affairs* 100, no. 398 (2001): 81.

28. All interviews conducted for this research have been anonymized in the chapter. Personal collection: Interview with JN conducted by Chitja Twala, Maseru Bridge, 16 April 2022.

29. Personal collection: Interview with TM conducted by Mohau Soldaat and Munyaradzi Mushonga, Van Rooyen Gate, 12 November 2021.

30. Personal collection: Interview with one of the paqama scouts who preferred to remain anonymous, conducted by Grey Magaiza, Butha-Buthe, 30 October 2021.

31. Personal collection: Interview with MRT by Grace Masemote Molale and Tsenolo Seloma, Ha Fusi, Berea District, 2 November 2021.

32. Personal collection: Interview with NK conducted by Mohau Soldaat, Sephapo Gate, 12 November 2021.

33. Interview with NK, 12 November 2021.

34. *Ibid.*

35. *Ibid.*

36. Personal collection: Interview with MN conducted by Chitja Twala, Maseru Bridge, 16 April 2022.

37. Personal collection: Interview with Cobra, conducted by Tokoloho Lephoto and Grey Magaiza, Qacha's Nek, 23 October 2021.

38. Yamkela Majikajika & Gabriel Tati, "Structural Changes in the Participation of African Migrants in the Labour Force of South Africa," *Alternation* 24, no. 1 (2017): 336–366.

39. Interview with NB, 30 October 2021.

40. *Ibid.*

41. Personal collection: Interview with JM conducted by Mohau Soldaat, Mohlomi Masooa, and Munyaradzi Mushonga, Wepener, 12 November 2021.

42. *Ibid.*
43. Interview with anonymous paqama scouts, 3 November 2021.
44. *Ibid.*
45. Anthony de V. Minnaar and Mike Hough, *Who Goes There? Perspectives on Clandestine Migration and Illegal Aliens in Southern Africa* (Pretoria: HSRC Publishers, 1996).
46. Interview with TM, 12 November 2021.
47. Personal collection: Interview with MS conducted by Chitja Twala, Maseru Bridge, 16 April 2022.
48. Personal collection: Interview with SM conducted by Chitja Twala, Ladybrand, 17 April 2022.
49. Interview with MN, 16 April 2022.
50. Personal collection: Interview with MM conducted by Mohlomi Masooa, John Aerni-Flessner, and Tokoloho Lephoto, Matatiele, 21 October 2021.
51. Personal collection: Interview with one of the paqama scouts who preferred to remain anonymous, conducted by Grey Magaiza, Butha-Buthe, 1 November 2021.
52. Personal collection: Interview with one of the paqama scouts who preferred to remain anonymous, conducted by Grey Magaiza, Quthing, 2 November 2021.
53. Interview with NK, 12 November 2021.
54. Personal collection: Interview with ML conducted by Chitja Twala, Maseru Bridge, 16 April 2022.
55. Personal collection: Interview with an intelligence officer who preferred to remain anonymous, conducted by Grey Magaiza, Telle Bridge, 4 November 2021.
56. Personal collection: Interview with PP conducted by Mohau Soldaat, Wepener, 12 November 2021.
57. Interview with MM, 21 October 2021.
58. Interview with ML, 16 April 2022.
59. Interview with MN, 16 April 2022.
60. Personal collection: Interview with one of the paqama scouts who preferred to remain anonymous, conducted by Grey Magaiza, Qacha's Nek, 3 November 2021.
61. Interview with MN, 16 April 2022.

BIBLIOGRAPHY

Aerni-Flessner, John, Chitja Twala, Munyaradzi Mushonga, and Grey Magaiza. "A Transnational History of Stock Theft on the Lesotho–South Africa Border, Nineteenth Century to 1994." *South African Historical Journal* 73, no. 4 (2021): 903–926.

Aghemelo, Austin T., and Solomon Ibhasebhor. "Colonialism as a Source of Boundary Dispute and Conflict Among African States: The World Court Judgement on the Bakassi Peninsula and its Implications for Nigeria." *Journal of Social Sciences* 13, no. 3 (2006): 177–181.

Alden, Chris, and Mills Soko. "South Africa's Economic Relations with Africa: Hegemony and its Discontents." *The Journal of Modern African Studies* 43, no. 3 (2005): 367–392.

Anderson, James, and Liam O'Dowd. "Borders, Border Regions and Territoriality: Contradictory Meanings, Changing Significance." *Regional Studies* 33, no. 7 (1999): 593–604.

Balibar, Etienne. *Politics and the Other Scene.* London: Verso, 2002.

Bardill, John E., and James Cobbe. *Lesotho: Dilemmas of Dependence in Southern Africa.* Boulder: Westview Press, 1985.

Coplan, David, and Timothy Quinlan. "A Chief by the People: Nation versus State in Lesotho," *Africa: Journal of the International African Institute.* 67, no. 1 (1997): 27–60.

Coplan, David. "A River Runs Through It: The Meaning of the Lesotho-Free State Border." *African Affairs* 100, no. 398 (2001): 81–116.

Doherty, Brian, and Timothy Doyle. "Beyond Borders: Transnational Politics, Social Movements and Modern Environmentalism." *Environmental Politics* 15, no. 5 (2006): 697–712.

Fitzgerald, David. "Rethinking the 'Local' and 'Transnational': Cross-Border Politics and Hometown Networks in an Immigrant's Union." *Center for Comparative Immigration Studies, University of California, San Diego Working Paper 58* (2002).

Johnson, Corey, Reece Jones, Anssi Paasi, Louise Amoore, Alison Mountz, Mark Salter, and Chris Rumford. "Interventions on Rethinking 'The Border' in Border Studies." *Political Geography* 30, no. 1 (2011): 61–69.

Khoabane, Selloane, and Phillip Black. "The Effect of Livestock Theft on Household Poverty in Developing Countries: The Case of Lesotho." *A Working Paper of the Department of Economics and the Bureau for Economic Research at the University of Stellenbosch: Stellenbosch Economic Working Papers*, 2/09 (2009).

Khoabane, Selloane, and Phillip Black. "On the Economic Effects of Livestock Theft in Lesotho: An Asset-Based Approach." *Journal of Development and Agricultural Economics* 4, no. 5 (2012): 142–146.

Kynoch, Gary, Theresa Ulicki, Tsepang Cekwane, Booi Mohapi, Mampolokeng Mohapi, Ntsoaki Phakisi, and Palesa Seithleko. "Cross-Border Raiding and Community Conflict in the Lesotho-South Africa Border Zone." *Southern African Migration Programme* 21 (2001): i–44.

Kynoch, Gary and Theresa Ulicki. "'It is Like the Time of *Lifaqane*': The Impact of Stock Theft and Violence in Southern Lesotho." *Journal of Contemporary African Studies* 18, no. 2 (2000): 179–206.

Lipschutz, Ronnie D. "Crossing Borders: Global Civil Society and the Reconfiguration of Transnational Political Space." *Geo Journal* 52, no. 1 (2000): 17–23.

Longo, Matthew. *The Politics of Borders: Sovereignty, Security, and the Citizen after 9/11.* Cambridge: Cambridge University Press, 2018.

Lucey, Amanda. "Cross-border Policing: Lesotho and South Africa." In *Cooperation and Accountability in the Cross-Border Policing of Southern Africa,* edited by

Sean Tait and Elrena van der Spy, 53–68. Cape Town: African Policing Civilian Oversight Forum, 2010.

Majikajika, Yamkela, and Gabriel Tati. "Structural Changes in the Participation of African Migrants in the Labour Force of South Africa." *Alternation* 24, no. 1 (2017): 336–366.

Mignolo, Walter D. "Geopolitics of Sensing and Knowing: On (De)Coloniality, Border Thinking and Epistemic Disobedience." *Postcolonial Studies, Latin America and the Politics of Knowledge* 14, no. 3 (2011): 273–283.

Mignolo, Walter D. "Introduction: Coloniality of Power and De-Colonial Thinking." *Cultural Studies* 21, no. 2/3 (2007): 155–167.

Minnaar, Anthony de V., and Mike Hough. *Who Goes There? Perspectives on Clandestine Migration and Illegal Aliens in Southern Africa.* Pretoria: HSRC Publishers, 1996.

Monyane, Chelete. "Lesotho's Transition to Democratic Rule: An Era of 'Fragile' Democracy." MA thesis, University of KwaZulu-Natal, 2005.

Moremoholo, Manthatisi C. "The Nature of Cross Border Linkages Between Lesotho and KwaZulu-Natal and Aspects of Basotho Migrants in Pietermaritzburg." MA thesis, University of Natal, Pietermaritzburg, 1998.

Moyo, Inocent, Christopher C. Nshimbi, and Jussi P. Laine. "Implications of the Micro Processes of Encounter and Contest in Borders." In *Borders, Sociocultural Encounters and Contestations: Southern African Experiences in Global View,* edited by Christopher C. Nshimbi, Inocent Moyo, and Jussi P. Laine, 141–144. London: Routledge, 2020.

Mukisa, Richard S. "Toward a Peaceful Resolution of Africa's Colonial Boundaries." *International Relations and Human Rights* 44, no. 1 (1997): 7–32.

Musoni, Francis. *Border Jumping and Migration Control in Southern Africa.* Bloomington: Indiana University Press, 2020.

Nshimbi, Christopher C., and Lorenzo Fioramonti. *A Region Without Borders? Policy Frameworks for Regional Labour Migrations Towards South Africa.* Johannesburg: African Centre for Migration & Society, 2013.

Pheko, Kutloano. "The Birth and the Existence of Lesotho: A Diplomatic Lesson." MA Thesis, University of Malta, 2017.

Ramutsindela, Maano. "Placing Subnational Borders in Border Studies." *South African Geographical Journal* 101, no. 3 (2019): 349–356.

Rukema, Joseph R., and Nedson Phophiwa. "Cross Border Mobility Between Zimbabwe and South Africa: Historical and Contemporary Trajectories of Development in Musina, South Africa." *Mankind Quarterly* 61, no. 2 (2020): 273–292.

Twala, Chitja. "Differentiations and Similarities in the Nomenclature of '*Paqama* Gates' Along the Lesotho-South Africa Border." Paper presented at the University of Southern Queensland College Research Seminar Series, 29 March 2022.

Weisfelder, Richard. "Why Lesotho Needs a Distinctive Diplomatic Strategy." *Africa Insight* 27, no. 1 (1997): 32–43.

Weisfelder, Richard. "Lesotho's Interactions with South Africa and Regional Organizations in Southern Africa." *South African Journal of International Affairs* 21, no. 1 (2014): 109–129.

Index

Page numbers in *italics* refer to figures/tables.

About the Contributors

John Aerni-Flessner is an associate professor in the Residential College in the Arts and Humanities (RCAH) at Michigan State University, and a research fellow in the Department of History, University of the Free State. His first book *Dreams for Lesotho: Independence, Foreign Assistance, and Development* is available in Lesotho from the Morija Museum and Archives. His research has focused on histories of development, borders/borderlands, independence, and Basotho communities in both South Africa and Lesotho.

Stephanie Cawood (PhD) is the current director of the Centre for Gender and Africa Studies at the University of the Free State. As a scholar, she is interested in the interdisciplinary spaces between Africa and gender studies from a decolonial/postcolonial perspective with particular interest in matters of culture and heritage, rhetoric, orality, and memory, including indigenous knowledge systems. In 2016, she was awarded a Newton Advanced Fellowship from the British Academy in collaboration with Dr. Jonathan Fisher from the University of Birmingham to pursue research on the memorializing of struggle and the dynamics of memory, space, and power in post-liberation Africa.

Ana Guardião (PhD in History granted by the Institute of Social Sciences, University of Lisbon) is a postdoctoral researcher at the University of Florence, in the project "Humanitarianism and Mediterranean Europe: A Transnational and Comparative History (1945–1990)." She also collaborates with the project "Humanity Internationalized: Cases, Dynamics and Comparisons (1945–1980)" (University of Coimbra). Her research interests combine the historically intersecting dynamics of the internationalization of human rights, humanitarianism, and developmentalism during late colonialism and decolonization processes. She has published mainly on the assistance and protection of refugees during the wars of decolonization in Africa.

Victor Simões Henrique holds a PhD in contemporary history of Africa and a master's degree in political sciences and African studies from the Pedagogical University of Mozambique. He has taught African history and Mozambican cultural anthropology at Save University in Chongoene, Mozambique since 2008. He supervises scientific monographs and master's projects in the field of history. His areas of research interest are cross-border migrations in Southern Africa, informal trade in Southern Africa, and women and local development.

Grey Magaiza is a senior lecturer in community development and is currently deputy director for the Centre for Gender and Africa Studies (CGAS) on the Qwaqwa Campus of the University of the Free State. He has research interest in applied social research in the areas of rural development, border studies and community development—particularly social entrepreneurship, rural innovation, and youth studies. He has publications spanning social entrepreneurship, climate change, traditional leadership, rural development, and curriculum enablement.

Teverayi Muguti is completing his PhD in the History Department at Stellenbosch University, South Africa. His PhD project examines state border security policy in Zimbabwe, focusing mainly on the Zimbabwe-Zambia border. His broad research interests include African border studies, borderland community livelihoods, and animal welfare history in southern Africa. Muguti is a Lisa Maskel Fellow, 2022 Erasmus+ Fellow, and 2022/2023 Next Generation Social Sciences in Africa Research Fellow.

Munyaradzi Mushonga (PhD) is the program director for the Africa Studies program in the Centre for Gender and Africa Studies at the University of the Free State and a member of the university's Decolonisation Engagement Group of Senate. He is the global academic director (GAD) for the Decolonial International Network (DIN), a space for researchers and activists committed to the imagination and actualization of a new world civilization. Munyaradzi is an interdisciplinary scholar whose scholarship and research are underpinned by the question: *What are the things that we cannot know because of what we know?*

Francis Musoni is an associate professor of African history and director of the International Studies program at the University of Kentucky. His research focuses on migrations and cross-border mobilities, borderland communities, refugees, ethnic identities, and informal economies in Africa. In addition to articles published in various journals, Musoni is the author of *Border Jumping and the Control of Migration in Southern Africa* (2020) and co-author of *Voices of African Immigrants in Kentucky: Migration, Identity, and Transnationality* (2019).

Nicholas Nyachega is a PhD candidate in African history with a development studies and social change minor, at the University of Minnesota. His dissertation conceives borderlands as *contested spaces* and *places of contradictions*. He explores the complexities of what happens in sites where state forms of power slowly penetrate other local systems of power, or when they compete. By highlighting the quotidian experiences of *borderlanders*, he reveals how and why practical realities of daily life, and borderlanders' abilities to utilize indigenous knowledge systems, challenge technologies of state power, such as border patrols, as well as states' categories of criminality and refuge-seeking.

Michael G. Panzer is adjunct professor of history at Marist College and a full-time high school teacher at Roy C. Ketcham High School. His research focuses on Mozambican history, nationalism, refugee history, and state-formation during the 1960s in southern Africa. His work has appeared in the *Journal of Southern African Studies (*2009), *Social Dynamics* (2013), and the *Portuguese Journal of Social Science* (2015). His current book project examines how Frelimo operated as a proto-state in Tanzania and Zambia, which created opportunities for political legitimacy and tested the limits of national sovereignty in frontier regions adjacent to Mozambique.

Cristina Udelsmann Rodrigues has a PhD in interdisciplinary African studies (2004) from the University Institute of Lisbon and currently works at the Nordic Africa Institute, Sweden, as senior researcher. Her main research areas include urban anthropology and sociology, poverty and development, borders, migration, and mining. She is a member of the African Borderlands Research Network. Her research is mostly conducted in Angola and in Mozambique. She has participated as a principal investigator and researcher in several collaborative projects, including on African borders, and has published on the subject.

Mwaka Siluonde is a lecturer of English literature in the School of Education at Mulungushi University, Zambia where she has been lecturing for seven years. She holds a PhD in English (literature) from the University of the Free State in South Africa through the Humanities Merit Bursary. She is currently a postdoctoral fellow funded by the Anthropology Department at the same university under the theme: *Trans Migration and Decoloniality*. Her work and research interests revolve around Zambia, Africa, and postcoloniality in literature, culture, and the arts. Of particular interest are conversations on decolonization, identity, women, orality, transnationality, and migration.

Xolani Tshabalala (PhD) is a postdoctoral fellow at the Institute for Research on Migration, Ethnicity and Society (REMESO) at Linköping University. His research interests lie within critical border studies, particularly Southern African cross-border informality, migrant labor policy, labor migrant solidarities, and decolonial research methodologies. Dr. Tshabalala also teaches on citizenship and exclusion, labor migration, working life and identity, as well as research methods.

Chitja Twala is a professor of history at the University of Limpopo (UL) and Research Fellow in the Department of History at the University of the Free State. Before joining the UL he was an associate professor (Department of History) and vice-dean (Faculty of the Humanities) at the University of the Free State (UFS). He is the author of nine chapters (co-authored two) in a book series entitled *The Road to Democracy in South Africa (1970–1990)*. He recently published a chapter co-authored with Peter Limb entitled: "The ICU in Free State Dorps and Dorpies" in the book *Labour Struggles in Southern Africa, 1919–1949* published in 2023. He is the recipient of Andrew Mellon Foundation and the NIHSS grants. He has been awarded several visiting/research fellowships: Harvard University (USA); University of Ghana; and the University of California, Los Angeles (USA).